China's Rural Industrialization Policy

China's Rural Industrialization Policy

Growing Under Orders Since 1949

Shi Cheng

palgrave
macmillan

First published 2006 by
PALGRAVE MACMILLAN
Houndmills, Basingstoke, Hampshire RG21 6XS and
175 Fifth Avenue, New York, N. Y. 10010
Companies and representatives throughout the world

PALGRAVE MACMILLAN is the global academic imprint of the Palgrave Macmillan division of St. Martin's Press, LLC and of Palgrave Macmillan Ltd. Macmillan® is a registered trademark in the United States, United Kingdom and other countries. Palgrave is a registered trademark in the European Union and other countries.

ISBN-13: 978–1–4039–9615–2 hardback
ISBN-10: 1–4039–9615–6 hardback

This book is printed on paper suitable for recycling and made from fully managed and sustained forest sources.

A catalogue record for this book is available from the British Library.

Library of Congress Cataloging-in-Publication Data
Cheng, Shi, 1953–
China's rural industrialization policy : growing under orders since 1949 / Shi Cheng.
p. cm.
Includes bibliographical references and index.
ISBN 1–4039–9615–6
1. Industrial policy–China–History. 2. Rural industries–China–History. 3. Agriculture and state–China–History. 4. China–Economic conditions–1949- I. Title.

HD3616.C63C4765 2006
338.951009173'4–dc22 2005058543

10 9 8 7 6 5 4 3 2 1
15 14 13 12 11 10 09 08 07 06

Printed and bound in Great Britain by
Antony Rowe Ltd, Chippenham and Eastbourne

To all people interested in China and economic development

Contents

List of Tables

List of Figures

List of Abbreviations

ABC	The Agricultural Bank of China
ADBC	The Agricultural Development Bank of China
AMA	Accelerating Mechanization of Agriculture
APC	Agricultural Producer Cooperative
CDH	Common Dining Hall
CDTC	"Constructing Dazhai-Type County"
CPBOE	Commune and Production Brigade-Owned Enterprise
CPBOF	Commune and Production Brigade-Owned Fund
CPBOI	Commune and Production Brigade-Owned Industry
CPC	Communist Party of China
CPCCC	Communist Party of China, Central Committee
CSPH	China Statistical Publishing House
CSY	Chinese Statistic Yearbook
CTVEY	China's Township and Village Enterprise Yearbook, the editorial committee of China's Township and Village Enterprise Yearbook, the agricultural publishing house
DHE	Dragon Head Enterprise
EYGMC	Educated Youths Going to Mountain and Countryside
FDI	Foreign Direct Investment
FSI	Five-Small Industries
FYP	Five-Year Plan
GDP	Gross Domestic Product
GLF	Great Leap Forward
GPFM	"Grain Priority" and "Farmer Making"
HPC	Handicraft Producer Cooperative
HRS	Household Responsibility System
ILCSFN	Important Literature Collection Since the Founding of the Nation Nos 1–15, The Literature Research Department of the CPCCC, Central Literature Press, Nos. 1–3, 1992; Nos. 4–7, 1993; Nos. 8–10, 1994; Nos. 12–13, 1996; Nos. 14–15, 1997.
LR	Land Reform
LTIB	Light & Textile Industry Bases of TVEs
MEB	Machinery & Electrical Bases of TVEs
PBC	The People's Bank of China
PRCERMC	People's Republic of China Economic Reference Material Collection, industry volume, 1949–52, Chinese Academy of Social Sciences and Central Archives, China Material Press, 1996; industry volume 1953–57, China Price Press, 1998; finance volume 1949–52, China Material Press, 1996; finance

	volume 1953–57, China Price Press, 1998; commerce volume 1949–52, China Material Press, 1996; commerce volume 1953–57, China Price Press, 1998.
RCB	The Rural Cooperative Bank
RCC	The Rural Credit Cooperatives of China
SEZ	The Special Economic Zone
SMC	Supply and Marketing Cooperative
SMPS	State Monopoly for Purchase and Supply
SOE	State-Owned Enterprise
SP	Spark Program
SSB	The State Statistical Bureau
TIAEB	"Trade, Industry and Agriculture Export Base"
TTS	The "Two-Track System" for Prices of Producer Goods
TVE	Township and Village Enterprises
WTO	World Trade Organization

Preface

At present, the Chinese economy is experiencing a huge transformation. If you return to your hometown in China after only one year, you may be unable to find your home, because you may be able to not judge the direction from the old streets and houses you knew well, all of which might have been torn down; you might not even judge the direction from the original landscape, because even the hillside might now be shoveled down. All these changes could make you recall the Great Leap Forward of the 1950s. China has made a number of reforms since 1949 and experienced many transformations and undulations. However, only the reforms after 1978 made its economy rise to become an important body having a significant influence on both Asia and the world. There has been massive research on China's economy, however, it is not an easy matter to understand China's economy comprehensively and correctly.

For a long time, I have been hoping to explore China's economic development from a new and objective angle in order to understand China's economy, and economic development. This book is an attempt at it. I believe that this work could be helpful in understanding China's development, and economic development in general.

This book owes a great deal to many people over the past few years. First, I would like to express my sincere appreciation to Professors Guo Zonghai and Yuan Baomin for their valuable and strict comments, and to Professor Song Linfei who provided the necessary conditions for the study. Professors Xu Yuanming and Xu Zhiming provided this study with valuable data and materials from which I benefited a great deal. I also thank Professor Yuko Arayama, who provided me with valuable comments and an opportunity to do research at the Graduate School of Economics, Nagoya University. My appreciation goes to Professors Johzen Takeuchi and Atsushi Kitahara for their insightful comments and encouragement. I give my special thanks to Professor Cheng Yi and Ms Cheng Mei, who encouraged and helped me with many things, such as the English language and related material collection. My thanks also go to Dr Zheng Yi; I benefited from his computer assistant and others during my stay in Japan. At the same time, I would also like to express my thanks to Ms Tong Lingyun for her kind help, and to Ms Lu Yan, one of my students, for her help in collecting material I urgently needed for the research, which saved me much time. I am grateful to Dr Nobuhito Suga, Dr Fumie Owaki and Dr Du Sub Shin, who were always willing to offer me help when I had problems about studying and living in Japan. I have benefited a lot from discussions with many scholars and students during this research. And I greatly appreciate, for their diligent and effective work, the staff at the library of the Graduate School of Economics, the library of the International Economic Research Center, the library of the Graduate School of International Development, and the staff of the administrative office of the Graduate School of Economics, Nagoya University, who all provided necessary conditions for the accomplishment of this research.

Last but not least, I wish to express my gratitude to my parents for their help and encouragment, which has inspired me to work hard and to inquire into things in detail.

Shi Cheng
Nagoya
October 2005

Introduction

China, as a huge emerging economic entity, is increasingly affecting world economy, and is attracting much attention all over the world. This is not only because of its sudden rise, high-speed growth and huge population, but also because of its different, mystical, and unique nature. This is the so-called "Chinese Characteristic," which has created China's miracle.

What are China's rural industrialization, characteristics, and miracle?

The biggest characteristic of China's economy is rural industrialization and the biggest miracle is also rural industrialization. The concept of "China's rural industrialization" has itself demonstrated this characteristic of China's economy. This is not only because China, by the end of the twentieth century, had the largest rural population in the world, accounting for 69 percent of its total population, but also because there is no other country in the world with a huge rural industry that holds approximately a one-half share in national industrial output, plays a vital role in the national economy, but is owned by farmers, located in the countryside and has nearly 130 million employees and innumerable emerging rural small towns and cities. It is well known that the countryside is the most centralized population area in China, but also the poorest and most backward area. For a long time, China's rural economy developed at a very slow pace. However, since China's reform and opening up from the end of the 1970s, rural industry has become the most important and active part in China's economy. This is not only because China is an agricultural country, or because China's reform started from the countryside, but also because the rise of the rural industry is the most successful one in China's reforms and has made the largest contribution to the Chinese economy. It can be said that without the success in rural industry, there will be no Chinese economic reform and no rapid development of China's economy. The vigorous development of China's rural industry has shifted hundreds of millions of farmers from agriculture to industry locally, surmounted state-owned industry, and driven the entire Chinese economy to develop at high speed towards industrialization. Thus China's rural industry has become the engine driving China's economic development and is regarded as a miracle. Jhonson (1997) argues that when a country is transforming from low income to middle income level, the engine to impel the growth of the economy comes from the countryside, not from the city; this is a phenomenon we haven't seen in any previous economic development process. Rural industrialization is one of the most important characteristics of the modern China economy.

Although China is a large country, its economy was previously small and had little influence on the world economy. Now, on the globalization wave, China's economy has a high-speed growth and is rapidly merging into the world economic system. It is growing into an economic entity having a significant influence on the world economy, in which its rural industry is playing an important role. The share of rural industry in China's total exportation was about 43 percent in 2002 (CTVEY 2003). The influence of China on the world economy is realized mainly through its rural industry. Today the products from China's rural industry are flooding almost every corner of the world. In many products such as textile and clothing, the rural industry holds a considerable share in the world market. Low-costs and a nearly inexhaustible supply of labor cause the rural industry rapidly to grow into a strong competitor in the world market. After China's accession into WTO, the relation between the rural industry and the world economy will be closer and more active. Now, each country is facing both the opportunities and challenges brought about by China's rural industry.

Central policy and its decisive role in the rural industrialization

Looking back over the last fifty years, China's rural industry experienced a winding and complex development process in which central policy played a decisive role. It is well known that in imitating the Soviet Union, China established a centralized system, in which the state controls the national economy completely. However, China's backward industry, its manual agriculture and huge population, mainly farmers, with an illiteracy rate as high as 80% nationally, caused China to be unable to imitate the Soviet experience. Therefore, China established its special system of economic management and its special development pattern, which constituted the highly centralized, military system of "general economy".

- General-controlled economy
  First, the generals controlled the national economy. Because new China was established during a long war of nearly thirty years, the military dominated new China. Mao Zedong himself was an outstanding military strate-

gist. All leaders at all levels of governments are generals who have fought a number of battles. Most of them have a poor farmer family background and have not undergone any regular higher education; some did not even go to elementary school in their childhood. Their education level and serviceman background meant that they were lacking theoretical knowledge and experience in the economic field. On 4 April 1951,[1] Chen Yun[2] pointed out: "the majority of our cadres worked in rural areas for a long time and they have very little economic knowledge." "We are politicians, strategists, but not entrepreneurs." "Our economic cadres are still layman, compared with ordinary capitalists," He gave an example saying that when it was snowing, the cargo actually sent was a shirt, and that to choose a location for building warehouses in the same way as constructing a defence position in war, made the warehouses collapse after rain. "We depend upon the state institution to manage the economy. If according to true economic principles, we will lose money in every business." Therefore, because of lacking knowledge and experience in economic management, they managed the economy still depending upon military theory and practice which they were used to in the protracted war and which was correct and suitable for the Chinese condition and successful proved by the long-term war.

- Military economic plans "concentrating on one thing only" with high targets
  Unlike a centrally planned economy with complete economic plans such as the huge and thorough development plans in the Soviet Union, China, lacking specialized knowledge and experience, was unable to make a strict and thorough scientifically economic development plan. On the other hand, for the generals, economic development may not have needed such plans; on the contrary, a quicker economic development could be realized by military economic plans. The characteristic of the military economic plan is "concentrating on one thing only" and high targets. "Concentrating on one thing only" means determining a main development goal such as "steel" in the "Great Leap Forward" (GLF) centering on strengthening national power, regardless of other goals in an economic development, especially the goal to improve people's lives. "High targets" is about total output regardless of quality, cost, and efficiency, and even whether the targets can be achieved or not. For example, in the GLF China merely made a goal to surpass Britain's steel output. Similarly its goal was "to double GDP" in its reform. "Concentrating on one thing only" is the main characteristic of a military plan. Each military campaign has only one goal, that is, to seize a place or to eliminate a certain number of enemy. However, economic plans are more complex. The "General Economy" system only has goals and targets, but no detailed theory, and no detailed and implementation steps. On 21 March 1979, Chen Yun described this situation further:

  > During the military control time in the Great Cultural Revolution, generals managed the economy. Some people had little experience but were

courageous, like Cheng Shiqing[3] in Jiangxi province. Only 60,000–70,000 automobiles were produced nationally each year at that time, however, Cheng said that Jiangxi wanted to produce 60,000–70,000 automobiles. Where were the steel plates? He also wanted Jiangxi to deliver grain to the state for replacing the total national grain import. In the past, Jiangxi delivered only 1.5 billion catties of grain to the state each year. At that time, the national import of grain was about 10.7 billion catties each year and the total grain yields in Jiangxi was 19.7 billion catties rough rice, about 13.3 billion catties husked rice. To replace the total national import of grain means that Jiangxi has only nine billion catties of rough rice left. Will that not cause the people to revolt?! They are courageous and will do anything they said randomly.

- Mass campaign
The "General Economy" system was to achieve its strategic target and impel economic development through "Mass Campaign." The "Mass Campaign" is an application of Mao's thought of the "people's war" in the economic domain. It is to mobilize all people to achieve a goal and a way for China to use its rich labor supply to substitute for scarce funds and technology. Just like a war of one-by-one military campaigns, the development of the "General Economy" is composed of one-by-one "mass campaigns." After deciding on an economic strategic target, China initiates "mass campaigns" to achieve it. Each campaign achieves a target. For instance, the GLF campaign is to surpass Britain and catch up America in steel and iron output. The "making a great effort to develop agriculture" campaign is to solve grain famine. The "mass campaign" also manifests Mao's military thought of "concentrating superior military strength to carry out a battle of annihilation." This is a non-balanced development pattern to concentrate national resources in a specific time on a specific industry for high-speed development, which then drives the national economy to develop quickly. The partial concentration of resources is to make up the overall insufficiency of resources such as funds to achieve the goal of rapid economic development.
- Militarized management
"General Economy" is a highly centralized economy, in which the state has overall control. In order to realize state control on resources, China constructed a militarized management system to implement state overall control not only in the city through nationalization, but also in the countryside through militarized people's communes. The communes helped the state to manage thousands of millions of individual farmers centrally.

Under the "general economy" system the state formulated economic plans in the same way to make a military strategy, impelled economic development in the same way to initiate a military campaign and managed the economy in the same way as managing an army. Central policy is everything. China's unique policies enable rural industry to develop differently not only from western economies, but also from the planned socialist economies in the former Soviet Union and other Eastern European countries. For example, under the policy of "heavy industry priority," both the countryside and agriculture become a subsidiary sector, which must provide surplus to support heavy industry. Although the strategy of "heavy industry priority" imitates the Soviet Union, China implemented it in a completely different way. First, the GLF stimulated the first rural industrialization wave. Afterwards, the great famine and serious economic crisis caused China to give up its radical industrialization strategy, and forced rural industry to halt by implementing "grain priority" and "farmer making" policies to construct the dual structure pattern.[4] The rural industry fell into decline. The countryside was made a production base to provide agricultural products for the city industry. Although the rural economic reform starting from the end of the 1970s aimed at accelerating agricultural development, the abandoning of "grain priority" and the introduction of the "Household Responsibility System" (HRS) actually led to the rise of rural industry and the collapse of the people's commune system. Under the reforms, rural industry developed rapidly and evolved into "China's Miracle" though the state discriminated against it and gave it in the status of "second class citizen." The collapse of the Soviet Union at the end of 1991 impelled China to abandon the "dual structure" model and the policy discriminating against non-public economy, which removed the "second class citizen" hat of rural industry and made rural industry a part of national industry. In the late twentieth century, the campaign of "ownership reform" initiated the privatization wave of rural industry. Entering the twenty-first century, China has finally started to abandon its policies of the "countryside supporting the city" and "limiting farmer immigration to city" by launching campaigns "to increase farmer income" and "farmer reducing." These policy changes, on the one hand, impel rural industrialization; on the other hand they cause rural industry and rural industrialization to merge into national industry and national industrialization. China's rural industry and rural industrialization as a special concept are losing their characteristics of the countryside and will finally come to an end.

Focus and structure

This book studies China's central policy of rural industrialization, concentrating on the rural industry (including other non-farm industries and activities in general) policy, and related policies including policy goals, and policy measures as well as policy effects on rural industrialization. In order to understand the policies and development process of rural industry more clearly and comprehensively, policies of rural commodity circulation and finance are also analyzed.

This study aims to reveal, through analyzing the central main rural industry policy as well as related policies at different periods, why and how China used a military method to control thousands of millions of farmers and how rural industrialization functioned under state control. Second, under the state control, how China shifted to economic liberalization, impelled rural industrialization, and how these policies effected rural industrialization and the national economy; next to reveal the policy characteristics and how central policy for rural industrialization evolved. The study tries to address the following issues:

- what is the goal of central policy at different stages of rural industrialization?
- policy measures China took to realize these policy goals;
- what effect central policy had on rural industrialization and China's economy;

and to show what are the "Chinese characteristic" and "China miracle," how China promotes its economy, and why China's farmers are so poor.

This is a positive study analyzing original documents objectively such as central documents, and the central leader's reports and speeches, indicating the title and date. This study is, collecting the essential data as much as possible,

- To focus on five principal conflicts:
  1) the conflict between rural and state-owned industry
  2) the conflict between rural industry and agriculture
  3) the conflict between rural collective and private industry
  4) the conflict between rural and urban populations
  5) the conflict between the rural and urban economy.
- To analyze comprehensively China's industrialization policy covering the entire historical period of new China since 1949.
- To analyze the policy comprehensively from policy background, policy goal, policy measure and policy effect on rural industrialization to show how the pattern of development was formed, what its features were, how it operated, i.e. how China controlled millions of peasants in a military way, how the state impelled its rural industry and how rural industrialization developed under state monopoly control, as well as how the pattern evolved for a liberal one.

This study focuses on policy description and analysis primarily and does not discuss what and how the policy should change. This project is divided into two major parts according to China's economic development, and there are five chapters in Part I and six chapters in Part II. Every chapter is based on policy change during a different period and covers a policy system.

The first part deals mainly with how China established and implemented state monopoly control over both rural industry and economy, and how rural industrialization developed under the highly centralized system from 1949 to 1978.

Chapters 1 and 2 analyze how the state changed the old economic system into a new one through the Land Reform Campaign and the Co-operative Campaign, centralizing government finance and state monopoly for the purchase and supply of agricultural products, etc. so as to transform China's small-scale peasant economy, and to stabilize and recover the rural economy. They also analyze how the state strengthened its control over rural economy and put it on the track of a "heavy industry priority" strategy, and how it used rural surplus to support heavy industry, as well as how the rural industry started to develop.

Chapter 3 deals with how China impelled the GLF and People's Communization Campaign, how People's Communes controlled millions of peasants and the rural economy, how the GLF promoted rural industrialization, and how they affected rural industrialization and China's economy.

The focus of Chapter 4 is on how China handled the crisis and famine caused by the GLF and people's communalization campaign by implementing policies such as "grain priority," "farmer-making," and how the state separated the countryside from the town to form a dual development pattern, as well as how these policies affected rural industry and national economy.

Chapter 5 analyzes how China carried out the "accelerating mechanization of agriculture" campaign, the "constructing Dazhai-type county "campaign, and so on, to increase grain yield and impel the people's commune system; and why rural industry was restored under these policies.

The second part of this study analyzes how the state reformed its rural system and how it relaxed control over rural industry and economy during the period 1979–2005; how rural economy under state control was liberated, and how rural industry, which had been treated as "second class citizen," rose rapidly and evolved into "China's miracle."

Chapters 6 and 7 show how the state abandoned the policies of "grain priority," the people's commune and "the state monopoly purchase" systems, lifted the ban on private enterprises, and introduced the HRS (Household Responsibility System) to completely relax control over rural economy and industry; how rural economy was gradually liberated; how the state impelled rural industry; and why the "second-class citizen" industry could rapidly rise; and how the great expansion of rural industry affected agriculture, state-owned industries and the rural collective economy.

Chapter 8 deals with how the state tried to strengthen the dual model again as a solution to the crisis after the national economy got out of control by policies such as "state-owned enterprise priority," "making great efforts to develop agriculture" and "curbing rural industry strictly"; how it handled the conflicts caused by rural industry and why the state, instead of repeating what it had done after the GLF, did not stop rural industry development.

Chapters 9 and 10 analyze why and how China discarded "the centrally planned system," the "domination of public sector in national economy" and "the dual model"; why and how the state completely relaxed its control over rural industry in shifting its economic system to a market one to allow and impel rural industry to deliver a high-speed and healthy development; how the state dealt with the conflicts caused by rural industry under the "China Township and Village Enterprise Law," and why the "ownership reform" resulted in a privatization wave in rural industry.

In Chapter 11, the analysis centers on how China at the beginning of the twenty-first century abandoning the policies of the "countryside supporting city" and "limiting farmer immigration to the city" and implements "farmer reducing," "increasing farmer income" and anti-impact of WTO for rural moderate prosperity in all respects.

Finally, a concluding remark is made for a review and conclusion on China's rural industrialization policies in the second half of the twentieth century and a perspective on them for the twenty-first century focusing on the evolution of the "Chinese characteristic" and "China miracle."

Part I

Rural Industrialization under State Monopoly Control

1
Shifting in the Land Reform Campaign

1.1 Background

China historically was a powerful nation, which had not only a long and glorious history with a bright culture, but also a strong economy. However, in modern times, China developed very slowly and long-term wars and natural disasters such as floods and drought brought the undeveloped economy unprecedented destruction after the Opium War in 1840. By 1949, China had degenerated into one of the poorest countries in the world, with the largest population of 540 million. China was a typical agricultural country dominated by traditional agriculture, handicraft industries and a big rural population comprising 90 percent of its total population, who did basically not receive even primary education and most of whom were illiterate. They could not even eat their fill and had almost no contact with the outside world. With a modern industry of only 10 percent in the national economy, China's industry was small and extremely weak. Many industries such as organic chemicals, automobiles, tractors, precision instruments and the airplane industry were not formed at all.

In 1949, China's rural economy was a small-scale peasant one focusing on agriculture with a small share of family handicraft and agricultural and subsidiary product processing. Agricultural production was poor technologically and relied on cattle and human power. In some regions production was still the Neolithic "the slash-and-burn cultivation" type. Decades of war and civil war had nearly destroyed agriculture. The grain output in 1949 was 113 million tons, only 76 percent of the pre-liberation maximum yield in 1936. Cotton was 444,000 tons, only 52 percent of the pre-liberation maximum yield in 1936. In the closed and conservative countryside where farmers, the majority of China's population, had lived from generation to generation, there was only handicraft production and no modern industry at all. In 1949 the total output value of China's handicraft (both rural and urban handicrafts) was 23 percent of the gross value of national industry, 7 percent of gross output value of both industry and agriculture (Ma and Sun, 1981, p. 172).

China was not only poor economically, but also short on natural resources. Many of per capita indexes of natural resources were much lower than the world average level. For example, its average per capita arable land was only 0.18 hectares. China's education level was also very low with an adult illiteracy rate of as high as 80 percent! New China had to begin its economic development on this poor foundation. At the same time, serious commodity scarcity and hyperinflation, along with the western blockade and the eruption of the Korean War in 1950, threatened the economy seriously.

1.2 Policy goals

To control the rural economy

On 29 September 1949, the Chinese People's Political Consultation Common Program indicated: "the state adjusts state-owned economy, cooperative economy, the farmer and handicraftsman's individual economy, private capitalism economy and state capitalism economy and causes each part of the social economy, under the leadership of state-owned economy, to take their proper place and cooperate on the division of labor to promote the entire economy." "Anything relating to the lifelines of national economy and people's life must be run by the state. Any state owned resource or enterprise is a property owned by all people. They are the main material base and leading power for the entire social economy to develop production of the People's Republic and to promote economic prosperity." In order to realize the leadership of the state on the entire national economy, in which rural economy dominated, the state had to establish its control over rural economy.

To recover agricultural production

Facing "both a poor and blank" economy, the most important task for the new state was to restore the economy. For an agricultural country, this meant recovering agricultural production. Mao Zedong proposed the principle of "three years for preparation and ten years for construction" to develop the economy. On 22–23 December 1949, Zhou Enlai (*ILCSFN*, No. 1, p. 75) pointed out that: "Production is our new China's basic task. The center of the current production task is to restore, not expand." He argued that the annual grain yield was much less than the maximum grain output of 280 billion catties before the anti-Japanese War and generally, the current task was to restore, then develop again on this foundation. "It is a success if we can achieve or surpass the prewar level in 3–5 years. Agricultural restoration is the foundation for all sectors. We cannot do anything without food. The majority of raw materials for light industry and export now must depend upon agriculture. In the state plan, apart from military and administrative expenditure, all funds must be put into restoring production." Restoring the rural economy and promoting agricultural production became at that time the No. 1 policy target.

To recover rural handicraft production

As to rural handicrafts, the state adopted a policy to protect and restore it because "handicraft production still plays a very important role in the entire national economy." For the restrictions on handicraft production such as political struggles and levying taxes randomly in some regions, on 12 June 1950, CPCCC (*ILCSFN*, No. 1, p. 282–3) indicated: "The destruction of handicraft production has seriously harmed the basic policy of our party to restore and develop production; it is a suicidal policy and is not permitted absolutely. The party members and cadres who are responsible for the mistake should be punished by party discipline." At the same time, it pointed out that, "Our policy for handicraft production is a protective policy to assist, improve and promote it, not a destructive policy by carrying on class struggle and levying tax randomly. We must protect rural handicrafts in every region strictly, such as papermaking, oil extracting, spinning and weaving, ginning, silk reeling and so on, not harm them." It urged correct tax policy and banned levying tax randomly, which would cause handicrafts to die.

The city leading the countryside and industry leading agriculture[1]

Although state policy aimed to stabilize and restore the economy and agricultural production, it was only the first step for China's long-term development strategy goal. On the eve of founding new China, the CPCCC had set the goal "to change China with steady steps from a agricultural to industrialized country." After the founding of new China, the CPCCC explicitly determined that the goal of its development strategy was to realize industrialization and adopted the policy of "industry leading agriculture, city leading countryside". On 22 December 1949, Zhou Enlai (*ILCSFN*, No. 1, p. 79) announced: "Today we have decided the policy of the 'city leading countryside, industry leading agriculture.' Capitalist society has done so; socialist society should also do so." He gave an explicit explanation for this strategy; "in our national economy, agriculture and handicrafts account for about 90 percent with modern industry only about 10 percent. Rural share is much larger than urban one, however, we cannot, according to the share, cancel or weaken the role of the 'city leading countryside, industry leading agriculture' in the development strategy. The demand of the city for grain and industrial raw material will stimulate agricultural production, and the city will guarantee and promote rural agricultural production by consumable and producer goods supply." Although Zhou Enlai also emphasized the importance of agriculture in the national economy, the priority of both city and industry had been decided by the CPCCC, and agricultural and rural development had to serve this goal. In the restoration period, the countryside provided both the city and industry with labor, funds and other resources to guarantee stability and restoration of the entire economy.

1.3 Policy controls

To centralize government finance

Although after the new political power was established, the state controlled the important domain of the national economy gradually through immediately confiscating banks and bureaucratic capital, nationalizing industry and so on, the economic chaos made by the political change was not under effective control. Although central government was responsible for the majority of national disbursement depending on increasing currency, local regions[2] and provinces collected the majority of state revenue such as grain and tax. The separation made a financial unbalance between revenue and expenditure. In addition government staff increased very fast. Therefore, China had hyperinflation which led to a serious financial and price undulation. In March 1950, the State Administrative Council of the Central People's Government decided to centralize government finance.

The goal of centralizing government finance

This aimed to reduce the unbalance between government revenue and expenditure and restrict inflation for preventing financial and price undulation. Its solution lay in cutting disbursement, reorganizing income and unifying fiscal revenue and expenditure management. "After the 12-year war and inflation, the life of the people has become extremely difficult; it is necessary for us to stop inflation diligently. If the balance between fiscal revenue and expenditure, and institutional separation between the revenue and expenditure above could not be overcome, not only the 1950 fiscal budgetary plan would be broken, but also a serious financial and price fluctuation could occur, which would put the whole nation in great trouble" (Chen Yun, 3 March 1950, *ILCSFN*, No. 1, pp. 130–1).

The main measures to centralize government finance

- Unifying government finance and revenue and expenditure
  Focusing on fiscal revenue, the state would collect all national government revenue such as public grain and tax, except a small part of authorized public grain and tax revenue, about 5–15 percent, which was levied by local government. No one could use the revenue without the Ministry of Finance's permit. In fiscal disbursement, the state formulated unified national personnel and wage standards and no one could increase personnel, organizations or expense for economic development without an agreement from the state.
- Unifying trade
  All funds, plans, and commodity dispatches of local state-owned trade companies would be unified and managed by the Ministry of Trade. Local

governments could not interfere with them. Any army or government institution could not be engaged in trade voluntarily.

- Unifying national cash management
  The People's Bank of China was assigned as the general organization to manage the national cash dispatch and also the foreign exchange rate and foreign exchange dispatch. All cash in military, government organizations and public enterprises must be saved in state banks, except those for the near future use. They could not be put into private banks. The People's Bank of China would manage the mutual cash business between them. A balance plan for cash revenue and expenditure would also be made on time (Liu and Wu, 1985, pp. 26–7).

The land reform campaign

Under the old Chinese feudalism land ownership system, the majority of lands belonged to the minority of landlords and rich farmers and the majority of farmers did not have land. They were tenants. Before the establishment of new China, land reform had already started in the liberated regions and distributed the landlord's land to poor farmers. By 1950, the regions where a land reform was already completed or nearly completed had an agricultural population of about 145 million (total population 160 million). There was still an area with an agricultural population of 264 million (total population approximately 310 million) where land reform had not been carried out. On 28 June 1950, the Central People's Government passed the "People's Republic of China Land Reform Law" and on 30 June Mao Zedong issued an order to implement the law.

The goal of land reform

This aimed to abolish the feudalist exploitation of landlord land-ownership, and to establish land ownership under farmers in order to liberate rural productive forces, develop agricultural production and pave the way to new China's industrialization (Land Reform Law, 1950).

The main content of land reform

- "To confiscate the landlord's land, farm animals and tools, surplus grain and houses in the countryside" (The second article of the Land Reform Law, 1950).
- "All land and other producer goods to be confiscated and levied, except for a part to be turned to the state as stipulated, are apportioned completely to poor farmers who do not have, or lack land, and other producer goods" (the tenth article of the Land Reform Law, 1950).

Features of the land reform

- To protect rich farmers
  In order to restore production and protect productive forces, this land reform formulated a new policy. The "China land law Outline" made in 1947, stipulated that the old-style rich farmer's unnecessary land and property would be levied. However, the sixth article of land reform law in 1950 provided "to protect rich farmers' self-cultivated land, the land cultivated by tenants, and the property, and, not to encroach upon them." At the same time, the law also stipulated that "the land rented by small landlords, as long as it is equal to or less than two times as much as the local average per capita level, should not be levied."
- To protect rural industry and commerce
  According to the land reform law, industry and commerce run by landlords and the land and property used directly in industry and commerce should not be confiscated. It is forbidden to encroach upon industry and commerce due to the confiscation of feudalist land and property. The property and legal business of countryside industrialists and businessmen should be protected; except for their house used by farmers and land in countryside. (Land Reform Law, 28 June 1950)
- Some protection of landlords
  The old land reform aimed "to confiscate all properties of the landlord," but the new land reform aimed "to confiscate the landlord's land, farm animals and tools, surplus grain, and houses in the countryside. The landlord's other properties would not be confiscated." Thus, although the target of land reform was to confiscate the landlord's land, the new reform adopted a policy to protect the landlord to some extent.

The land reform schedule

On 14 June 1950, Liu Shaoqi[3] (*ILCSFN*, No. 1, p. 289) pointed out that "we prepare in two and one-half years or three years from this winter, to complete basic national land reform, not to finish national land reform completely. This is our general plan."

Method of promoting land reform

Implementation of land reform is a mass movement organized by government. Firstly the government dispatches work teams for land reform to the countryside, then these teams mobilize farmers and establish peasant associations. Local governments promulgate rules to punish any activity to sabotage the reform. The land reform was carried on through peasant associations. The land reform process was as follows:

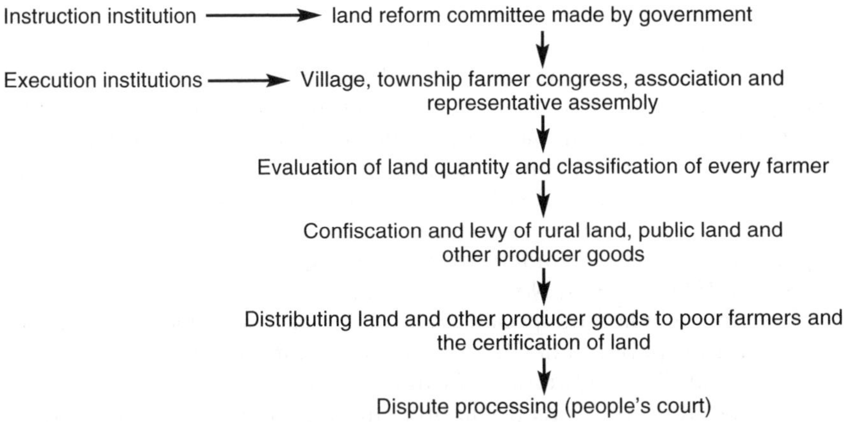

Source: The People's Republic of China Land Reform Law, 28 June 1950.

From the winter of 1949 to the spring of 1950, land reform was carried out only in the city suburbs of north China and some regions of Henan province. After the CPCCC promulgated the Land Reform Law in June 1950, the land reform campaign developed gradually in the newly liberalized regions. By the end of 1952, the land reform campaign had been basically finished, except in Xinjiang, Tibet, and a few other minority regions. About 300 million farmers, around 70 percent of the total rural population, benefited from the reform. The reform confiscated or levied 46.5 percent of total cultivated land and exempted land rent grain of 70 billion catties each year (Liu and Wu, 1985, pp. 41–2).

Establishing the state rural commercial system

In the early days of liberation, China's economy was in chaos with skyrocketing prices and hyperinflation. "Price stability is the precondition for developing production and safeguarding people's lives. We must firmly maintain the price stability which began this March" (*People's Daily* editorial, 11 June 1950). In the countryside, the state established a new commercial system to control rural commerce.

Methods of establishing the state rural commercial system

- Establishing the state companies to control markets
  On 10 March 1950, "in order to unify national state-owned trade for completing state import and export plans, leading the domestic market, adjusting national and local commodity supply and demand, and promoting rapid restoration and development of production," the

State Administrative Council of the Central People's Government decided that the Ministry of Trade of the Central People's Government was "the state leading body for all state-owned, cooperative and private trades." The Ministry of Trade set up state-owned trade companies nationwide and was responsible for managing national trade, commercial activity and instructing private commercial activity (*PRCERMC*, commercial volume 1949–52, pp. 33–4). The state-owned trade companies were to stabilize prices in the retail market, and prevent speculative traders from harassing the market (Chen Yun, 15 June 1950, *ILCSFN*, No. 1, pp. 314–5).

1) Setting up domestic specialized head companies of trade nationwide: Grain Corporation of China, Cotton Corporation of China, General Merchandise Corporation of China, Salt Corporation of China, Coal Corporation of China (including building material), Native Product Corporation of China.
2) Setting up specialized head corporations of foreign trade nationwide:
   Bristles Corporation of China, Native Product Export Corporation of China, Oil Corporation of China, Import and Export Corporation of China, Tea Corporation of China, Minerals Corporation of China.
3) Setting up grain, native product and general merchandise companies in provinces;
4) Controlling national commodity wholesale services by state-owned companies.

- Developing supply and marketing cooperatives (SMC) vigorously
  The supply and marketing cooperative is a collective organization run by individual farmers and handicraftsmen voluntarily in the commercial field. Its top organization was funded mainly by the state. Before liberation, there had been already SMCs in regions where land reform had been completed. With about 20 million members, these were mainly distributed in the Northeast, North China and East China and were only at initial stage. On 11 May 1951, the CPCCC requested to set up, as an experiment, SMCs in the newly liberalized regions. "An urgent problem in newly liberalized regions is that because of the land reform, landlords and rich farmers are incapable of local product transportation, and sales and private commerce are disrupted. At the same time, state-owned trade is incapable of solving local product transportation and sales problems completely. Therefore, farmers cannot sell their native products. At present, beside the effort to establish a state-owned commerce system and organizing private businessmen to sell local products, in the newly liberalized regions, urgent means are needed to organize farmer's co-operatives to sell local products. We should go all out to organize rural cooperatives in the newly liberalized regions broadly and generally according to the basic need to sell local products, not to be excessively careful, and not to fetter ourselves in order to solve farmers' difficulties" (ILCSFN, No. 2. p. 262).

1) Features of the SMC (supply and marketing cooperative)

A. Economic organization under state control.

SMCs assist state-owned commerce to complete state policies and plans. SMCs were economic organizations to help the state-owned economy to lead private economy and bring it under the state plan through commission and contract business. On the other hand, they promoted the sale of agricultural, subsidiary and handicraft products, supplied industrial products, and returned the profit to farmers. In the restoring time, the linking of state-owned economy with private economy in the countryside was made by the state's purchasing staple products and supplying producer goods and daily consumable which farmers' needed and the state's adjustment on private production by prices. In this commercial system, the state strengthened its control on rural economy commercially through SMCs.

B. The economic organization of the working masses on the principles that the higher-level unit serves for subordinate ones; the basic unit serves for its members. SMCs are independent operations and responsible for their own profits and losses.

C. Focusing on the sale of local products

SMC took sales of local products as its primary mission. After local product sales promotion, a SMC would buy the goods its members needed, and sell to them. It could not put its funds and labor in other business and neglect local product sale promotion. "In order to make this goal clearer, at first the cooperative's name may be the local product sale promotion cooperative, not the SMC" (CPCCC, 11 May 1951, *ILCSFN*, No. 2, pp. 262–3).

2) Methods to develop SMCs

A. Paying shares of the SMC voluntarily

The shares of a SMC would be paid by the farmers who wanted to sell their local products voluntarily and also could be paid for by native products. The more native products a person wanted to sell through the SMC, the more he would pay. The person who has no local product to sell and only purchases goods from the SMC would pay less. The shares could be paid throughout several years. The quota for each share would be decided by the members of the SMC democratically.

B. Principles for establishing an SMC

a) Establishing SMC at county and province levels

b) Establishing basic a SMC based on the market or town and its branch in the far villages.

C. Earnings distribution

The earnings would be divided into two parts temporarily, namely the common reserve fund and payment for shares bonus.

D. More sales on orders, credit or a commission basis, less on the spot and the state first for a sale.

E. SMCs could run processing factories, but not the credit operation concurrently

F. Government favorable policies for SMCs
   a) Favorable trade policy
      State commerce wholesale cargo to SMCs at a discount price according to local price generally.
   b) Favorable loan policy of the People's Bank of China for SMCs with an interest rate lower than for state-owned commerce.
   c) Favorable tax policy such as a 20 percent cut in operation tax and a one-year exemption of income tax for new SMCs.
   d) Other favorable policies such as cheaper transport fees for SMC cargo (CPCCC, 11 May 1951, *ILCSFN*, No. 2, pp. 262–3)

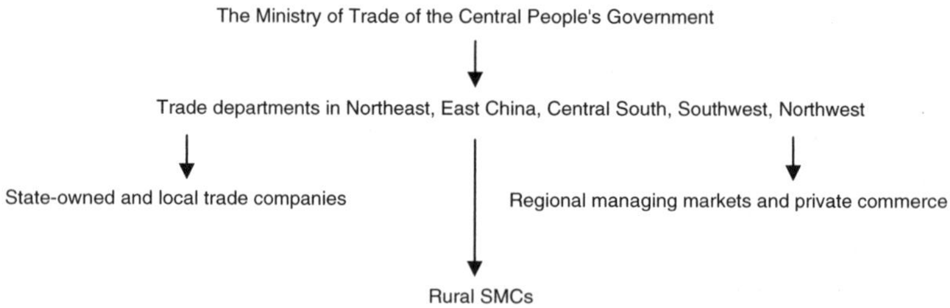

Figure 1.1 State commerce system in 1950
Source: *PRCERMC, commercial volume 1949–52*, pp. 85–6.

Table 1.1 China's rural SMCs 1949–52

Year	*Number of SMCs (thou)*	*Members of SMCs (mil.)*	*Share in agricultural and sideline products purchased by state commercial sector* (%)	*Share in rural commodity retail* (%)	*Share in rural consumable retail* (%)	*Share in social retail of agricultural producer goods* (%)
1949	20	11	n	n	n	n
1950	39	26	n	8	8	6
1951	35	80	n	14	12	28
1952	33	138	43	33	32	48

Source: *PRCERMC, commercial volume 1949–52*, pp. 329–31.
Note: the state commercial sector includes the state-owned companies and SMCs.

- Expanding interchange of urban and rural products
  This movement aimed to expand sales of rural agricultural and subsidiary products and also to promote urban industrial products. On 15 November 1950, Chen Yun pointed out,

> The measures to increase state revenue determined in this conference, such as the increase of tax grain attached, the increases of some goods tax and import and export tax, will levy an additional several billion

> catties of millet. This will mainly come from farmers. Will the farmers be satisfied? This is a matter we must think about. We must do one thing if we want farmers to be able to pay the tax increase. It is to promote local interchange, national and international interchanges. Farmers will be able to pay the tax as long as they can sell their agricultural, subsidiary and native products ... Helping farmers to sell their products is the prerequisite for the state to obtain the additional tax revenue. Expanding the buying and selling of agricultural, subsidiary and native products is not only a rural problem, but also the key at present to stimulate China's economy. The financial and economic work since the half year has proved completely that urban prosperity is the result of rural economic development ... Therefore, we are able to say that expanding the buying and selling of agricultural, subsidiary and native products is the most important task for China's economy at present. (*ILCSFN*, No. 1, pp. 475–6).

On 4 April 1951, Chen Yun pointed out again that the first thing in finance and economics work was the interchange of urban and rural products.

> Why we should put the interchange in the first place? Because we received a tattered old China, an economy mainly agricultural. The so-called interchange of urban and rural products is, first, to take the agricultural and local products from farmers, then sell urban industrial products to farmers. The interchange benefits to farmers, urban industry and commerce, and also the state ... taking the total grain yield last year as 240 billion catties, the revenue of local products is about 24 billion catties of grain. Last year the tax grain was about 22 billion catties. If we help farmers to sell their local products, their income will be the same as the tax grain. If the local products cannot be sold while they pay the tax grain, farmers will be in trouble. We must make effort to help farmers to sell their local products. (*ILCSFN*, No. 2, pp. 191–2)

1) Method to expand the interchange of urban and rural products

A. Raising a purchase revolving fund

Because of difficulties in state finance, only the state-owned trade sector did not provide sufficient fund for purchases. According to the 1951 initial plan, the native products the state could purchase were valued at about 2 billion yuan. There were native products approximately valuing 2.4 billion yuan waiting to be sold by farmers.

a) The state purchases products partially with cash, partially with barter or on a credit, or on commission basis by the state trade companies.
b) Absorbing farmers' credit deposit with a slightly higher rate in order to use farmers' funds for farmers' problems.
c) Making use of the funds of private firms and encouraging private banks to extend loans to private businessmen for purchasing rural native products (Liu and Wu, 1986, p. 52).

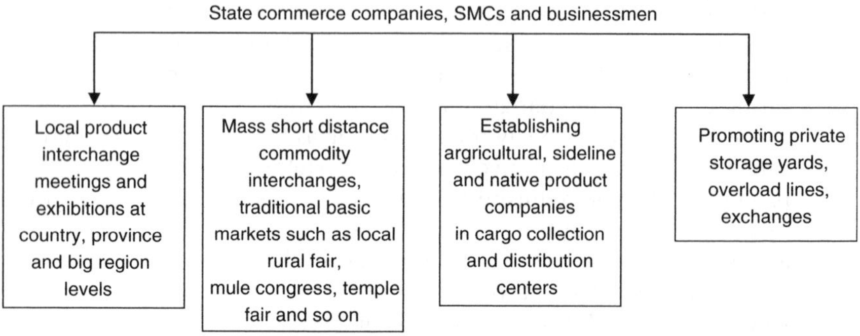

Figure 1.2 China's local product interchange meetings and exhibitions in 1951
Source: Liu and Wu, 1985, pp. 52–3.

B. Holding local product interchange meetings and exhibitions
 In order to sell local products which were difficult to sell, especially the staple native products, local governments made great efforts to open old networks and new channels. Under the state commerce sector's organization and promotion, together with SMCs and private businessmen, many local product interchange meetings and exhibitions were made at county or province level.

C. Expanding transportation
 a) Restoring and establishing transport companies widely
 b) Making full use of existing backward transport means
 Existing backward transport means included wooden boats, large carts, animal-drawn carts, small carts, horse and human labor. Because of the lack of modern transport means, the state made a call to make full use of existing backward transport means. "The most important thing for local product sales promotion is transportation. Under present conditions, transportation should fully use the backward tool. Because there are too few cars in China, motor transport cannot meet the requirement for interchange between urban and rural products. In the North, transportation by large carts surpasses transportation by cars, and in the South transportation by wooden boats surpasses that by steamboats ... so we should still pay attention to and organize transportation by backward tools." (Chen Yun, 4 April 1951, *ILCSFN*, No. 2, pp. 191–2).

 Because of this state push, in 1951 many local products which were very hard to sell before became in great demand. The sale promotion increased farmers' incomes. "From the winter solstice of 1950 to the spring of 1951, local product meetings of North China sold almost all native products equal to 5 billion of catties grain" (Liu and Wu, 1986, p. 53). In three years, the amount of agricultural, sideline and native products purchased increased from eight billion yuan in 1950 to

13.0 billion yuan in 1952, a growing rate of 62 percent (*PRCERMC, commercial volume 1949–52*, p. 7).

- Limiting and making use of private commerce
  In April 1950, Mao said that, "what we should limit and push aside are industry and commerce which do not favor national economy and the people's livelihood, also speculative trade, and the industry and commerce of luxury goods and superstition, but not those which benefit the national economy and the people's livelihood,"(*ILCSFN*, No. 1, pp. 214–15). "Private trade can help the circulation of commodities, and employment. It is of benefit to the people." "The purchase of agricultural products and agricultural sideline products needs be divided. Is it good or not for us to purchase all products? No! ... The interchange of urban and rural products cannot entirely depend on our trade companies, if so, it will harm the farmers" (Chen Yun, 6 June 1950, *ILCSFN*, No. 1, pp. 261 and 263). While limiting private commerce, the state made use of private trade to stabilize the market for a rapid economic recovery.
  1) Methods to limit and make use of private commerce
     The method divides the business fields for public and private commerce. Public commerce controlled the purchase of principal commodities and wholesale markets; private commerce was mainly engaged in the retail market. This was carried out mainly by two commercial adjustments.
  A. Commercial adjustment in June 1950
     In the struggle to stabilize prices in 1950, a large number of speculative private commercial firms were banned and all private firms were strictly limited. Therefore, in June 1950, the state carried out a commercial adjustment.
     a) Reducing the retail business scope and variety of state-owned companies
        The retail business for state companies was only six kinds of daily necessities (grain, coal, gauze, cooking oil, table salt and petroleum). Private firms would be engaged in the retail of other commodities.
     b) Stipulating the purchase scope of state-owned companies
        The state-owned companies could purchase main agricultural products, export commodities and a part of the main agricultural sideline products only. SMCs and private firms had to purchase all other products.
     c) Adjusting price difference
        To adjust wholesale-retail, regional, seasonal and raw materials cost price differences caused private firms to be profitable.
     d) Assisting private firms
        Local government to give full assistance in sale procedures and transportation conditions for private firm and also favorable tax policies and procedures for them (Chen Yun, 15 June 1950, *ILCSFN*, No. 1, pp. 314–15).

B. Commercial adjustment in November 1952
   Because "the three Antis" and "the five Antis" campaigns in 1952 closed many private firms, state-owned commerce increased excessively quickly and private commerce decreased greatly. In order to assist them, in November 1952, the state carried out a commercial adjustment once more.
   a) Adjusting price
      Mainly expanding wholesale-retail, regional, seasonal and raw materials cost price differences in order to enable private commerce to be profitable.
   b) Reducing the public operation scope
      The adjustment mainly was to reduce the scope of retail for state-owned companies and SMCs with a share of 25 percent. The share of private firms in retail businesses was 75 percent. The public sector concentrated on principal commodities, and private firms on secondary commodities.
   c) Relaxing limits to private firms
      Local limits to private firms were canceled and the market monopoly of local public exchanges was forbidden (CPCCC, 12 November1952, *ILCSFN*, No. 3, pp. 413–20).

In 1950, private commerce dominated the national commodity circulation. There were 4.02 million private firms and businessmen in commerce in China with a share of 98 percent in the total number of national commercial firms and businessmen. The commodity sale volume was 18.2 billion yuan accounting for 76 percent in the total amount of wholesale and 84 percent in the total volume of retail sales separately. However, as the state strengthened control over national commerce, the private sector decreased rapidly. In 1952, the share of private commerce in the national wholesale volume decreased from 76 percent in 1950 to 36 percent and the share of private commerce in the national retail volume decreased from 84 percent to 58 percent (*PRCERMC, commercial volume 1949–52*, pp. 343–59 and 414).

Establishing a state rural finance system

In 1951, China began to establish a state rural finance system. The headquarter of the People's Bank of China requested the state bank to establish state bank organizations from top to bottom levels in rural areas and business offices or work teams in markets or towns, as well as organize rural credit cooperatives (RCCs) from bottom to top levels. "Under the state bank leadership, these organizations supplement and mutually assist each other to make a better rural finance ... to widely develop credit cooperative organizations with varied forms in the countryside such as credit cooperatives, credit departments, credit teams and other old Chinese credit organizations" (People's Bank of China general headquarter, May 1951,

PRCERMC, financial volume 1944–52, p. 524). The rural financial activities were under the leadership of the People's Bank of China.

Methods of establishing the state rural finance system

- Establishing the rural system of the People's Bank of China
  1) Setting rural financial management departments in all levels of the People's Bank of China
     The state explicitly stipulated that the county sub-branches of the People's Bank mainly served the countryside.
  2) Setting up business offices and teams in rural market towns
     At the end of 1950, the number of rural business offices (mainly in market towns) was only 457, but at the end of 1953, they had increased to 12,561 (Xu, 1996, pp. 285–6).
- Organizing the RCC
  1) Principles of RCCs (Rural credit cooperatives)
     The RCC is an organization which uses farmers' idle capital to solve difficulty and does not take profit as its main goal. RCC is "organized by local working people to benefit each other and collects funds by shares and deposits to solve its members' difficulties in production and life." All members are responsible for the RCC's profits and losses independently and each RCC "accepts the state bank's leadership and inspection" (Rural Credit Cooperative Regulation (draft), 1951).
  2) Method of organizing RCCs
  A. State promotion
     RCCs were organized mainly by local state banks in the countryside. Local county branches of the People's Bank of China were responsible for impelling, organizing and leading RCCs. In order to promote and instruct RCCs, in 1951 the general headquarters of the People's Bank issued "The Rural Credit Cooperative Regulation (Draft)," "Rural Credit Cooperation Team Joint pledge" and "Service Relation Contract Model of the People's Bank of China and Credit Cooperative (draft)" (Xu, 1996, p. 297).
  B. State support for RCCs
     a) Initially the bank would assign specialists to instruct its office work, and provide it with suitable manpower or financial aid.
     b) Favorable deposit and loan policy.
        When the deposit in a RCC increases, the RCC can redeposit the fund in a state bank according to the contract with a deposit rate higher than personal deposit (no more than 10 percent). When loans increased, the bank would provide loans for it with a loan interest lower than personal loans (no less than 10 percent).
     c) Providing bank business

The state bank would commission the RCC to handle the bank's business as much as possible and pays handling charges such as deposits, loans, and deposits for special use.

d) Helping to establish an accounting system, improving management skills and training for RCCs (PBC general headquarters, May 1951, *PRCERMC, financial volume 1944–52*, p. 549).

3) Forms of RCCs

A. Credit cooperatives

This is the highest form for mass fund cooperation organization. It has certain funds from shares as a foundation for its operation, a set of management systems such as management councils, boards of supervisors, representatives of members and member groups. They use the deposit as their own capital source to carry on rural financing. They cover a large area with only one in each township.

B. Credit departments

Usually a credit department belonged to the SMC. Without payment for shares, it took the deposit as its main capital source. Some SMCs provided the departments with special funds. a department mainly served for the members of its own SMC and operated under the supervision of the SMC. At the end of June 1953, there were 2,137 credit departments nationally with 1,447 in Northeast, 643 in the North China, 14 in East China and 29 in Central South.

C. Credit teams

There were three kinds of credit teams. One did not handle deposits and loan services directly, only the lending service between the members of the team, and was responsible for registers, introductions and guarantees. The second one was based on old Chinese credit organizations to raise funds with a low loan rate for its members. The third engaged in depositing services directly and absorbed a small amount of payment for shares.

4) Features of RCCs

A. A peripheral organization of the state bank and under the state bank's control.

B. Dependence on the state bank.

5) RCC development

In 1947 there were already more than 880 RCCs in the liberated regions. However, because of unsteady prices and hyperinflation from the war, most of them had collapsed or closed down by 1949. Only about twenty were left and were in deep trouble. In 1950 the state began to organize 105 RCCs and some credit departments again. In May 1951, the first national rural finance conference explicitly proposed that both developing and leading rural credit cooperation was one of the important tasks in rural finance. By the end of 1951, China had organized 538 RCCs and many credit teams (Rural finance administrative bureau of PBC, 1953, *PRCERMC, financial volume 1944–52*, pp. 576–80).

Table 1.2 China's RCCs at the end of June 1953 (ten thousand persons)

	National	*Northwest*	*Central south*	*North China*	*Northeast*	*East China*	*Southwest*
Number of RCCs	6,871	228	3,585	2,316	273	403	66
RCC members	427	5	217	111	66	22	6
Number of credit departments	2,137	—	29	643	1,447	14	4 (including northwest)
Number of Credit teams	14,600	7,538	4,150		About 3,000 for four regions		

Source: "Report of credit cooperation work for several years", the rural finance administrative bureau of PBC, 1953, *PRCERMC, financial volume 1949–52*, pp. 576–80.

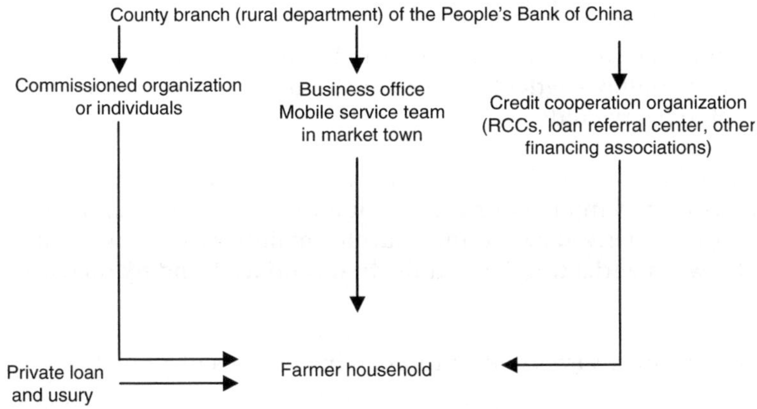

Figure 1.3 China's rural finance system in 1951
Source: "The decision about rural finance organization of the first national rural finance conference," PBC general headquarter, May 1951, *PRCERMC, financial volume 1949–52*, pp. 526–7.

To derive agriculture surplus

Because China is an agricultural country, the countryside was the main source for national capital. At the start of the new nation, the state used rural surplus for national construction, especially after the Korean War, when military expenses increased greatly. At the same time, China was also implementing an industrialization strategy, which needed huge funds. The state intensified its agricultural plunder. Chen Yun on 6 June 1950 acknowledged that, "China is an agricultural country; the investment of industrialization has no alternative but to use agriculture. Industries needs to invest, and agriculture is our only source for funds"(*ILCSFN*, No. 1, p. 267).

Table 1.3 China's fiscal revenue and expenditure in agriculture 1950–53 (billion yuan)

Year	*Total tax revenue*	*Agriculture: various taxes*	*Real agricultural tax (100 million kilograms flour and rice)*	*Share of tax in real agricultural output (%)*	*Agricultural disbursement*	*Share of agriculture in national fiscal expenditure (%)*
1950	4.9	1.9	134.9	12	0.3	4
1951	8.1	2.3	180.8	15	0.4	3
1952	9.8	2.7	178.9	12	0.9	5
1953	12.0	2.8	172.0	12	1.3	6

Source: *New China 50 Years Government Finance Statistics*, Lou Jiwei (ed.) Economic Science Publishing House, 2000.

Methods to derive agricultural surplus

- "Price difference between agricultural and industrial products"
  The state withdraws agriculture surplus through consciously enhancing prices of industry products.
- Depositing
  The state bank raises funds through deposits from the countryside then passes it to industry or the city at a low rate. In the land reform period China derived agricultural surplus mainly by the "price difference between agricultural and industrial products" and by increasing tax.
- Taxing
  To get agriculture surplus direct through increasing agricultural tax.

Liu Ruofeng (1997, p. 45) argued that in 1952, the agricultural surplus derived by the state was 5.57 billion yuan, 43 per cent of the total national income accumulated.

To protect, assist and guide rural handicrafts

Because handicrafts belong to the private sector, not the socialist sector, they were targeted for transformation and for replacement by the state economy. However, in the early years of the new nation, China adopted a policy to protect, assist and guide the handicrafts. On 22 December 1949, Zhou Enlai pointed out, "in order to restore and develop the economy, we needs help and cooperation from private capital." "Private enterprise should be permitted to exist and develop." However, in the relations between public and private economy, "the public and state-owned economy must take a dominant position." In order to increase the share and to keep its leadership of the state-owned economy in the national economy, the "government put 23.9 percent of total budget expenditure into the state-owned economy." "We permit private capitalism, but will guide it away from the old capitalist path." Thus, "it can assist our country step by step towards socialism" (*ILCSFN*, No. 1, p. 82–3).

Methods to protect, assist and guide rural handicrafts

- Protecting the landlord and the rich farmer's handicrafts:
  In the land reform, although landlords and rich farmers were targeted for confiscation, their handicrafts were protected. "We must firmly implement a protection policy for the handicrafts industry and also protect handicrafts run by landlords. We should strictly separate the elimination of landlord feudalist exploitation from protecting the handicrafts run by landlords, and never to apply the struggle against feudal landlords to handicraftsmen ... handicrafts still play a very important role in the entire national economy" (CPCCC, 12 June 1950, *ILCSFN*, No. 1, pp. 282–3).
- Strengthening plans for handicrafts
  A. Making production and sale plans
     Leading handicrafts to make production and marketing plans under the state unified plan.
  B. Guiding handicrafts to operate under state plans
     The state-owned economy guided handicrafts gradually into plans through processing, ordering, exclusive selling rights, and sales on commission.
- Supporting key productions
  A. Principles in choosing key productions
     a) These which have a foundation and can now be restored easily.
     b) These able to assist the people's lives, have economic value, and at present do not need huge investment.
     In 1950, China supported key handicrafts productions such as manual textiles, woven goods, agricultural product processing, farm tools, tools, daily necessities, export production, culture products and raw materials for industry. (The Ministry of Light Industry, 6 April 1950, *PRCERMC, industrial volume 1949–52*, pp. 443–4).
  B. Method of supporting key handicraft productions
     a) Government decides key productions
     b) Government helps to solve material supply and product sales
     c) Making production plans
     d) Government does not provide funds. Funds are raised mainly by the producers.
- Organizing handicraft cooperation
  A. Organizing independent handicraftsmen to establish producer cooperatives
  B. Organizing rural seasonal sideline and family handicrafts to establish production teams

C. Organizing joint operations between small factories and small workshops

- Improving management
- Solving material supply and product sale
  Under the leadership of state-owned economy, local trade organizations and RCCs use the ordering purchase, request processing, and changing product by raw material to help handicraft production.
- Improving technology
  By ordering, request processing, provision of technical guidance, unified specification and standard and strict product examination to improve handicraft technology (The Ministry of Light Industry, 6 April 1950, *PRCERMC, industrial volume 1949–52*, pp. 437–46).
- Loan support
  In order to support handicraft production, in 1951 the People's Bank drew up "The Regulation on Loans for Handicraft Production" and requested the banks to help and extend loans to handicraft production (Xu, 1996, p. 294).

1.4 Restoration of the rural economy

By 1952, China had undergone a comprehensive restoration of rural handicrafts and agriculture. In 1949, the output value of China's handicraft production (including fishing, salt and forest cutting) was 3.2 billion yuan with a share of 23 percent in the total output value of national industry. By 1952, the total output value achieved 7.3 billion yuan, more than double. In the countryside, although there was no rural industry, rural handicrafts obtained a rapid development. In 1952, total employees in rural handicrafts achieved 3.9 million people, 60 percent in national handicraft employees. Its output value was 3.4 billion yuan (not including fishing, salt and forest cutting), 52 percent of national handicraft output value (Ma and Sun, 1981, p. 172).

From 1949 to 1952, rural economy underwent comprehensive restoration. First, agricultural production rapidly recovered. In 1952, the nation agricultural output value was 46.1 billion yuan, an increase of 41 percent compared to that in 1949. Grain yield increased from 110 million tons in 1949 to 160 million tons in 1952, 9 percent more than the pre-liberation maximum yield in 1936. The annual average increment was 16.9 million tons. The cotton recovery was much quicker. Its output increased from 440 thousand tons in 1949 to 1,304 thousand tons in 1952 at an average annual growth rate of 42 percent, 54 percent more than the pre-liberation maximum annual output ("New China 50 Years Statistical Data Assembly," pp. 30, 33–4). The rapid agricultural restoration stabilized the national economy and laid a good foundation for national economic restoration.

In those three years, China started a cultivation improvement campaign and promoted new farm tools and new farm technologies. At the same time, in order to restore production, the state widely mobilized the masses to undertake water conservation and expand rural irrigated areas. The irrigated areas increased to more than 80 million Chinese acres and held a share of 20 percent in the total national cultivated area in 1952. Also, water irrigation for farmlands were improved by more than 180 million Chinese acres (Liu and Wu, 1985, pp. 71–3).

The farmers' livings also improved. Compared to 1949, farmers' lives had a distinct improvement in 1952. Farmers' incomes grew at a rate of 30 percent. The average grain consumption per capita in rural areas was 383 catties, cooking oil 3.4 catties, meat 11 catties, and cotton cloth 13.7 chi,[4] all increased by about 50 percent compared with that in 1949. Many industrial daily necessities such as enamel basins, water cups, thermos bottles which farmers could not afford in the past had already started to enter farmer households generally. Rural electricity consumption also had quick growth, doubling from 21 million kWh in 1949 to 43 million kWh in 1952. China also initiated a mass anti-illiteracy campaign. More than 4 million people got out of illiteracy; most of them were farmers (Liu and Wu, 1985, p. 77). The recovery and development of the rural economy and handicrafts laid a good foundation for China's rural industry.

1.5 Policy effects

Land reforms impelled the restoration of the rural economy with unchanged land systems

Farmers' higher production incentives and unchanged land systems

The land reforms enabled farmers to obtain land, enhanced their status, and enormously stimulated poverty-stricken farmers' production incentive. For a long time, under the feudal landlord land ownership, the landlord's brutal exploitation of and oppression on farmers had seriously fettered Chinese farmers' production incentives and seriously hindered rural economic development. The establishment of new China not only ended the long-term war on the mainland and created a peaceful environment for farmers to carry on production, but also satisfied farmers' requests to get rid of the landlord's exploitation and the desire to have land. The land reform destroyed the feudal landlord land ownership thoroughly, and caused many poverty-stricken farmers to obtain land. It was the first time Chinese farmers became the masters of land for hundreds of years. The reform impelled rural economic restoration and development greatly.

However, although the land reform destroyed the feudal landlord land ownership and caused many farmers to obtain land, it only rearranged land distribution and did not changed the private nature of the land system. Therefore, although after the reform, farmers' production incentive and conditions were improved greatly, the countryside still could not avoid the tendency of a new "polarization." A few farmers getting rich quickly started to buy land and employed labor to expand operations, but some farmers, especially poor farmers, started to sell land to borrow money, and to be hired out to other people because of lack of production tools, and funds. The difference between poor and rich farmers widened and hired labor appeared in the countryside (Chen, Chen and Yang, 1993, p. 88).

Reducing production scale weakened state control

The land reform broke the landlord ownership, which was on a large scale, and formed individual small peasant economies, which decreased the scale return of land utilization. At the same time, it was more difficult to manage land owned by more than 400 million farmers. The difficulty concentrated on grain levying. The land reform caused difficulties for the state to levy public grain. Wen (2000, pp. 153–6) argued that the land reform increased the transaction cost between the state and farmer. The state was unable to get enough public grain from farmers. The land reform broke the old landlord economy and also the large scale grain supply system. The state had to purchase grain from a large number of individual farmers, thus the transaction costs increased. So, although production rose, the grain supply for the state dropped. The land reform weakened state control on rural economy. However, farmers' grain accumulation increased. After the long war, farmers could increase production and improve their lives.

"Industry leading agriculture, city leading countryside" hindered rural development greatly

From the very beginning of the new nation, China put the countryside into an auxiliary status in national economy, led by the city and serving industry and the city. The countryside had to provide all resources to support the city and industry development. This policy greatly promoted national industry development, but was a fatal attack on the rural economy. It had profound effect on the rural economy as well as the entire national economy. For example, the high agricultural tax in the early years of the new nation as a result of this policy stablised the national economy, but weakened the rural economy.

2
Sprouting in the Cooperative Campaign

2.1 Background

Although the Korean War erupted in 1950, from 1949 to 1952 China's economy underwent comprehensive restoration. Its national social product value doubled from nearly 56 billion in 1949 to 102 billion yuan in 1952. In 1952, the agricultural output value was 48 billion yuan, and grain yield 308.8 billion catties, a growth of 43 percent compared with that in 1949. The national gross value of industrial output was 35 billion yuan, an increase of 149 percent compared with that in 1949. All main industrial products surpassed the pre-liberation maximum annual output.

Besides controlling government finance, the state had controlled the national finance and industry. First, China finished the socialist transformation of capitalist finance ahead of schedule. While nationalizing old banks, the state operated a socialist transformation of private financial organizations also and brought them into line with the state bank system. In December 1952, through closing, cleaning up, business changing and merging, the state completed the joint state–private ownership for all private financial organizations. Then, through the business proxy of the People's Bank of China and so on, these organizations completed the financial socialist transformation. State banks and joint state–private owned banks dominated in savings and loan services. The state control over finance strengthened its control on the national economy greatly (*PRCERMC, financial volume 1949–52*, p. 5). Second, the state-owned industry occupied a dominant position in the national economy. In the economic restoration, state-owned industry grew rapidly and took a dominant position with a share of 42 percent in national industry in 1952. On the contrary, private industry dropped and transferred from a share of 49 percent in the industry in 1949 to 31 percent in 1952 (China's industry development, statistical data 1949–84, 1985, p. 45).

China started to make its first Five Year Plan from the spring of 1951, finished in the February of 1955, and passed it officially on 5 July 1955 at the first session of the National People's Congress (Liu and Wu, 1985, pp. 105–6). The first FYP made the "the heavy industry priority" development strategy "to concentrate our main strength to develop heavy industry and build a foundation for national industrialization and modernization of national defense" (*People's Daily*, 1 October 1953). The editorial of the *People's Daily* (3 March 1954) argued:

> To realize the national socialist industrialization by developing heavy industry first is the method to construct a socialist country created by Lenin and Stalin, based on socialist basic laws and the principle that social expansion of reproduction must put the expansion of producer goods in the first place ... In order to reduce the time for industrialization, the Soviet Union adopted the policy to develop heavy industry first. In 15 years after the October Revolution, it completed the course capitalism took several dozen years to finish and changed its own country from a backward agricultural country into an industrialized one. Stalin, when summarizing the experience of Soviet Union socialist construction, once repeatedly pointed out that the most important experience that the Soviet Union therefore could realize rapidly industrialization was to repel the "common" industrialization path and adopt the socialist industrialization path to develop heavy industry first. Obviously, the path the Soviet Union took is precisely the example for us to follow today.

2.2 Policy goals

To transform private into collective ownership

The land reform to abolish the feudal landlord system of ownership was merely the first step for the rural socialist system reform. In 1953, Mao Zedong proposed "the general line for the transition period"[1] which was decided on as the general task for the transition period. This line pointed out, "It is a transition period from the establishment of the People's Republic of China to the completion of socialism. The general task for the transition period is to realize national socialist industrialization gradually, to complete the socialist transformations of agriculture, handicrafts and capitalist industry and commerce gradually" ("The People's Republic of China Constitution", 20 September 1954). In rural areas the socialist transformation is to substitute rural private ownership of producer goods by the collective ownership and establish state control on the rural society. It will achieve two goals: First to bring rural economy into line with the national plan and control the rural economy. Second to change the backward small-scale-production individual economy into an advanced large-scale-production collective economy. In the first FYP period, the basic task in the countryside was "to establish a preliminary foundation for the socialist transformation of both agriculture and handicrafts" (the State Planning Committee, 30 July 1955).

- Establishing large-scale organizational management
  The rural socialist transformation[2] is to bring the small-peasant private economy regulated completely by the market into line with the state plan and to build a rural collective economy under state control. That will strengthen state control on the rural economy greatly. In private economy, the state faces millions of individual farmers directly, which makes the management of farmers extremely difficult. However, a collective ownership system will organize the huge number of individual farmers together and form large-scale cooperative organizations with which the state will manage farmers easily and efficiently.
- Establishing large-scale production
  The CPCCC indicated, "The isolated, dispersed, conservative and backward small-peasant economy is limiting the development of agricultural production. It exposes a very big contradiction in socialist industrialization and cannot both meet the needs of general farmers day by day to improve their life and the need for rapid development of the entire national economy." "We should change the backward small-scale production into the advanced large-scale cooperative one to overcome the contradiction between industry and agriculture, and enable farmers to get rid of their impoverished condition and obtain a common enrichment and prosperous life" (CPCCC, 16 December 1953, *ILCSFN*, No. 4, pp. 661–2).

"Agriculture priority" and "supporting large industry"

"Agriculture priority and supporting large industry" includes not only that agriculture must support heavy industry, but also that the countryside does not develop industry. The support of the countryside for industry was carried out through developing agriculture and providing agriculture products for the industry. The "heavy industry priority" is to put most national resources into heavy industry, especially 156 construction projects with Soviet aid (the first FYP 1953–7). In the first FYP, capital investment in industry was 58 percent, less than 8 percent in agriculture, forestry and water conservation construction. The essential rural target of the first FYP was to promote rural agricultural, handicraft and commerce cooperative campaigns, improve production technology, promote improved seeds for enhancing the per unit yield of land, and build water conservation projects. "Agriculture priority" with no rural industry was Mao Zedong's basic tentative idea for rural development at that time (The National Program for Agricultural Development (Draft) 1956–67, 23 January 1956). So, the role of the countryside in industrialization was to supply agricultural products and rural resources for urban and large scale industry development.

To maintain and transform handicrafts

Although the object of national industrialization was to develop modern industry, the state also adopted a policy to assist, transform and maintain handicrafts for changing them from old and obsolete productions to a modern ones.

- Assisting and maintaining
  Although handicrafts held a very large share in national economy for a very long time, some had already been replaced by modern industry by 1949. The state still wanted to assist and maintain handicrafts because "its declination would not only influence the life of handicraftsmen and increase unemployment, but would affect farmers' production, then also the commercial market greatly" (CPCCC, 31 March 1953).
- Transforming
  The transformation of handicrafts mainly was to organize and improve its production. "We need to organize the handicraftsmen, instruct them to produce according to plans and to enhance their productive ability, which can play a very great role in national economic development" (Zhu, 4 December 1953, *ILCSFN*, No. 4, p. 641).[3] Liu Shaoqi (20 October 1952, *ILCSFN*, No. 3, p. 371) said: "We have to make an effort to help these handicraftsmen to organize producers, cooperatives and to encourage manual workshops to unite to introduce machine production."

2.3 Policy controls

Agricultural producers' cooperative campaign

The agricultural producers' cooperative (APC) is an organization organized by farmers and one of four rural cooperatives in the rural cooperative campaign. In 1951, China had developed farmers' cooperatives, but at that time the cooperative organizations were small, and were at experimental stage (CPCCC, 1951, *ILCSFN*, No. 2, pp. 510–22). In 1953, under "the general line for the transition period", the CPCCC (16 December 1953) decided to establish the agricultural producers' cooperatives nationwide. It argued: "to develop mutual aid and the cooperative campaign for enhancing the agricultural productive force is central for the party to lead the countryside from now on." The CPCCC also requested, "all cadres engaged in rural work must gradually shift their work center to this aspect ... in order to realize the socialist transformation of agriculture gradually."

Main forms of China's agricultural producers' cooperative

- Mutual aid in labor (primary)
  Temporary, seasonal and small
- Year to year mutual aid team (intermediate)
  Starting to unify agricultural and aligned occupations cooperation with certain simple production plans and technical division of labor. Some to have part of the public farm tools and animals and accumulate some public property.

- Agricultural producers' cooperative (senior)
  In an agricultural producers' cooperative, both the land and labor are used publicly, all of the land held by the members is put into the co-operative as shares and the distribution is made according to work to some extent (CPCCC, 16 December 1953).

Methods to promote the cooperative campaign

- Mass and top-down campaign promoted by the state
  1) CPCCC decision-making and all levels of local governments decide the number to build.
     First, the CPCCC decided to establish the cooperatives nationwide. Then, the government in each region decided the number of the cooperatives to build, then the CPCCC checked the numbers from each large region. With a permit from the CPCCC, the number was distributed between provinces in this large region. Again the number distributed to each province was assigned from the province to subordinate counties of this province. The township governments organized cooperatives according to the number assigned.
  2) Merging small mutual aid teams and cooperatives into large ones and at the same time organizing individual farmers to joint the cooperatives.
  3) Promoting elementary cooperatives to form advanced APCs.
- Mao's push and the high tide of the campaign
  1) Mao Zedong's push in winter of 1953
     At the beginning, the APC campaign progressed slowly and mainly concentrated on mutual aid teams. On 30 June 1953, Mao proposed to complete the agricultural socialist transformation in three five-year plans (15 years). However, during a conference, Mao Zedong requested that in newly liberalized regions, each county regardless of size, must try to set up one, two or three APCs that winter or next spring, and the old liberated regions must double their APCs (Chen, Chen and Yang, 1993, p. 145). Under Mao's push, the center of the APC campaign began to shift and started to develop advanced APCs. At the same time, the development started to speed up. Before the third national cooperative conference (October–November 1953) the planned number of APCs was about 35,800, however, after the conference, the number increased to 45,000, about 10,000 up (Chen, Chen and Yang, 1993, p. 147).
  2) Mao Zedong's push in spring of 1954
     By March 1954, only four months later, the number of APCs, which were under construction or already completed was more than 70,000 and surpassed the original planned number. (CPCCC, 12 February 1954). One month later, this number reached more than 90,000, doubling the original plan. In April 1954, the second national rural work conference revised the plan made in the winter of 1953 and doubled the old number to build 700 thousand APCs in 1957. "In 1957 we will build

1.35 million or 1.5 million APCs with a share of about 35 percent in total national farmer households and a share of above 40 percent in national total farming land ... In the second five-year plan period (around 1960), we will strive for the cooperativization nationwide" (Chen, Chen and Yang, 1993, pp. 145–8).

3) Mao Zedong's push in May 1955
On 17 May 1955, Mao Zedong again criticized negative thought and requested a faster development of the cooperation campaign. He even set down the numbers for each province and planned to set up 1 million APCs by 1956. The CPCCC approved Mao's plan.
4) Mao's push in July 1955
On 31 July 1955, Mao once more proposed to develop APCs with great effort and to double the number of APCs from 650 thousand to 1.3 million, an increase of 300 thousand compared with the original plan. On 27 December 1955, Mao urged the completion of the APC campaign by 1960. By the spring of 1958, one half of national farmer households should be in the APC.
5) Mao's push and the completion of the APC campaign in 1956
Mao continued to set high targets for the campaign and on 23 January 1956, requested the realization of Advanced Cooperativization by 1958. The campaign surpassed Mao's target. So in this way, Mao's push and the campaign development promoted each other and finally led the national comprehensive realization of Cooperativization in September 1956, which covered 92 percent of total farmer households. The share of advanced APCs in total farmer households was 63 percent with a share of 29 percent for elementary APCs. Almost all advanced APCs were established from January to September 1956, in only 9 months (Chen, Chen and Yang, 1993, pp. 147–8 and Wen, 2000, p. 188).

Rural credits cooperative campaign

In the rural cooperativization campaign started in 1953, as one of three rural cooperative forms, the RCC's was considered as a link in rural finance between the small peasant economy and socialism and to be able to "promote agricultural production cooperation." The CPCCC pointed out: "in the RCC development, there have been various forms such as credit teams, credit cooperatives and credit departments in SMCs. We should continue to promote and improve this credit cooperation and combine it with the APCs and systematically support the cooperativization campaign" (CPCCC, 16 December 1953). "The development of the SMC, RCC, forestation cooperation, fishery cooperation and handicraft cooperation has become the urgent need for the masses day by day and we must set them up diligently, especially the RCCs, which can be expanded in large numbers and have a most urgent need from the campaign. The RCC development is slow, so we should make greater effort to promote it rapidly and actively (CPCCC, 3 June 1954, *ILCSFN*, No. 5, p. 271).

Methods to promote the RCC campaign

- State push
  In November 1954, the People's Bank requested to start the RCC campaign vigorously. On 7 December 1954, the editorial of the *People's Daily*, "To Develop Positively Credit Cooperatives", made a call for establishing 100 thousand RCCs in the next 3–4 months. "In this winter and next spring, we plan to build 150 thousand RCCs from the present 50 thousand and achieve the goal that 50 percent to 70 percent of total townships nationwide have RCCs and the farmer members increase from 20 million to more than 70 million households ... Although it is very hard to establish 100 thousand RCCs in the next 3–4 months, it will be possible" (Xu, 1996, pp. 284–5). On 14 January 1955, the state formulated officially "The Rural Credit Cooperative Regulation (Draft)" to promote the campaign.
- State bank support
  The RCCs were mainly built by state banks. The banks established a RCC mainly through business instruction and commission business. After the land reform, the People's Bank of China expanded greatly from 457 rural bank business offices (mainly in market towns) in 1950 to 13,846 business offices in the countryside with more than 67,000 cadres in 1956 (Xu, 1996, p. 286). The rapid expansion of the state bank helped and pushed the RCC campaign greatly.

The high tide of the RCCs campaign

- In September 1954, there were 90 thousand RCCs in the countryside.
- By the end of 1954, only 3 months after the state push, the number jumped to 124 thousand, an increase of 34 thousand. There had been one RCC at least in each township for most regions.
- By the end of 1955, there were 159 thousand RCCs with 76 million member households, about 65.2 percent in total rural households.
- By the end of 1956, after merging and restructuring, there were 103 thousand RCCs with nearly 100 million rural households. The rural credit cooperativization was realized (Xu and Deng et al., 1994, p. 42).

The supply and marketing cooperative campaign

The supply and marketing cooperative (SMC) development is one of the important contents in Chinese rural cooperativization. "Half state-operated" is the feature of the SMC. The SMC is in fact a commercial organization under state control and subject to state-owned companies. "The supply and marketing cooperative is one of three forms of rural cooperativization, a socialist mass commercial organization, a bridge for our party and government to contact farmers and consolidate the alliance of worker and farmer" (Cheng, 20 July 1954, *ILCSFN*, No. 5, p. 387). There were three basic tasks of the SMC in the transition period. They were to serve for agricultural production and support national industrialization, to transform small peasant economies and individual handicrafts and to transform rural private commerce and cut off the link between farmer and city capitalism. The link for completing the three basic tasks was to promote the SMC campaign (Cheng, 20 July 1954, *ILCSFN*, No. 5, p. 387).

Methods to promote the SMC campaign

- Providing monopolizing rights
  The state provided SMCs with monopolizing rights through commissioned purchases and sales, especially the state monopoly for purchase and supply of agricultural products. For example, the grain and oils purchased by SMCs was more than 60 percent of the total grain and oils purchased by the state and SMCs were also commissioned for all of the cotton purchased by the state. The state also provided SMCs with exclusive rights in rural producer goods and daily necessaries (Qin and Lu, 1994, pp. 120–2).
- Dividing business fields with state-owned companies
  Although, a SMC is a mass commercial organization, it is under direct state control and had a close relation with the state-owned companies. In order to avoid chaos, during the first FYP period, the state carried out three big adjustments to divide business fields between the state-owned companies and SMCs.
  1) Commodity division on 5 December 1953.
     The center fiscal and finance committee stipulated that the state-owned commercial companies were engaging in the field of industrial products and SMCs for handicraft products.
  2) Division of urban and rural commerce on 24 July 1954.
     The center fiscal and finance committee stipulated that under leadership of the Ministry of Commerce, China's commerce was divided into two parts. State-owned commerce was responsible for the shares held by public and private sectors, price making and the transformation of the private sector in urban areas. The SMC was responsible for rural commerce such as the leadership of rural market, the shares held by public and private sectors, the purchase of agricultural and sideline products and pricing, and the transformation of the private sector.
  3) Division of urban and rural commerce and commodities on 12 April 1955. (Yao and Ji et al., 1995, pp. 53–4).
     The CPCCC requested that state-owned commerce should give more attention to wholesale business and be responsible for united leadership and arrangement of the market. In the agricultural product sector, SMCs were responsible for purchase and wholesale of local raw materials, traditional Chinese medicine and other products (Yaö and Ji et al., 1995, pp. 53–4). At the same time, SMCs were responsible mainly for commodity supply for general farmers and transformation of rural private commerce (Li, 1955, *ILCSFN*, No. 5, p. 165).

- Controlling and transforming rural private commerce
  The state strengthened the SMCs dominant position in rural commerce by controlling and compressing rural private commerce.
  1) Controlling rural private commerce.
     The state controlled rural private commerce by grasping the purchase and wholesale business of commodity through SMCs and private commerce was engaged only in retail sales. So the state controlled the source of commodity. The private commerce could not do its business without the commodity from public commerce and was put into the state plan in this way.
  2) Transforming rural private commerce.
     In the winter of 1954, the SMCs organized some experimental transformations of rural private commerce and in January 1955, the first working conference on rural private commerce was held in Beijing to promote the transformation nationwide.

  A. Method of transforming rural private commerce
     a) Organizing commission sale teams, cooperation teams (shops) and changing private into collective commerce gradually.
     b) Commission purchase and sales. The state-owned companies and SMCs commission private businessmen to sell or purchase goods, and bring them into line with the state plan.
     c) Jointly operating. Under the leadership of the SMC, SMCs and private firms operate jointly.

  B. The end of China's rural private commerce.
     Under state control, China's rural private commerce decreased rapidly. Many private commercial businessmen were organized into cooperative organizations. By the end of 1956, about 1.68 million businessmen had been already brought into various kinds of cooperative organizations: 240,000 people in jointly operated stores, 650,000 people in cooperative shops, 790,000 people in cooperation teams, and about 200,000 people joined SMCs. Because they were too dispersed, or only in seasonal occupations, approximately 380,000 people were unable to organize. Thus, China basically completed the rural socialist transformation of private commerce and formed a united rural socialist market centering on state-owned commerce and SMCs.

As private commerce decreased, SMCs expanded and formed a new commercial network nationwide. In 1953, SMCs held a share of 47 percent in the rural total volume of retail sales. By 1957, state-owned commerce and SMCs had dominated China's commerce with a share of 95 percent in total social commodity retail. There were 19,402 basic units of SMCs with a membership of 157.45 million people and SMC share in rural commodity retail volume was 40 percent (China supply and marketing cooperative historical data collection editorial office, 1988, p. 445).

The handicrafts producer cooperative campaign

Although there had been some handicraft producer cooperatives (HPC) before 1953, they were very few with a share of only 3.9 percent in the total national handicraft. From 1953, China started to organize HPCs massively and initiated the handicrafts cooperative campaign. In December 1953, the CPCCC argued: "we must carry on the socialist transformation of individual handicrafts, guide handicraftsmen to walk along with the socialist path and change individual ownership into a collective one by the cooperative path." It pointed out: "Organizing the handicraftsmen into various types of handicraft cooperatives (the handicraft production team, handicraft SMC, handicraft producers' cooperative and so on) is the only way for the state to implement socialist transformation of handicrafts (CPCCC, December 1953, *ILCSFN*, No. 4, pp. 721–2). However, the state policy for handicrafts is to maintain, not to promote it. So, "we must manage and control its development in order to prevent its output from surpassing need and guarantee its raw material supply" (Chen, 31 December 1954, *ILCSFN*, No. 5, p. 743).

Goals of the handicrafts producer cooperative campaign

- Meeting the farmer's need for producer goods and daily necessaries and assisting national construction.
- Increasing output, improving technology and reducing cost
- Training skilled workers quickly
- Bringing the handicrafts into line with the national plan
- Transforming the handicrafts from small private ownership into public ownership gradually (Liu, 8 December 1953, *ILCSFN*, No. 4, p. 650).

Forms of the handicrafts producer cooperative organizations

- Handicraft production team.
  This is mainly organized by the SMCs in the countryside. Handicraftsmen are organized in joint material supply and product sales. Some teams have a system of collective ownership for tools and united work.
- Handicraft supply and marketing production cooperative.
  This is organized by several individual handicraftsmen or several handicraft production teams for raw materials and product sales. They purchase raw materials from SMCs and SOEs, sell products to SMCs and SOEs and process products for SMCs and SOEs jointly.
- HPC
  This is a higher form for the handicraft socialist transformation. Some of them have a complete collective ownership of main producer goods and a system of income distribution according to work (CPC team of All-China Federation of Cooperative Union, 6 January 1954, *ILCSFN*, No. 5, pp. 327–9).

Methods to promote the handicrafts producer cooperative campaign

- Convincing and demonstrating
  On 31 March 1953, CPCCC (*ILCSFN*, No. 4, p. 122) pointed out that we could not use a compulsory order to organize the handicraft cooperative in order to avoid influencing the handicraftsman's production incentive. "We should instruct, affect and guide them into line with the state planned economy track slowly." "We must enhance the handicraftsman's socialist consciousness and cause them to organize the cooperative voluntarily through convincing and demonstrating" (CPCCC, December 1953, *ILCSFN*, No. 4, pp. 721–2).
- State support
  1) Support of state-owned commerce
     State-owned commerce supported HPCs mainly through instructing their production through material supply and product sale service to make HPCs get rid of the exploitation of commercial capital and go into line with the state plan (CPC team of All-China Federation of Cooperative Union, 6 January 1954, *ILCSFN*, No. 5, pp. 331–3).
  2) Support of state-owned industry
     The main support was to improve technology and management, provide HPCs with old equipment, waste products and materials at low prices as well as processing business.
  3) Support of the state bank
     The state bank should extended loans to HPCs each year with favored low interest (CPC team of All-China Federation of Cooperative Union, 6 January 1954, *ILCSFN*, No. 5, pp. 331–3).
  4) Favorable tax policy
  5) Including HPC production in the state plan.
- SMC support
  1) Supplying raw material and selling product for HPCs
     The CPCCC requested: "the rural SMC should take the sale of handicraft products and the supply of farmer's production and daily necessaries as one of its own primary businesses." "Local SMCs should organize handicraft production vigorously according to farmer need (CPCCC, 12 April 1954, *ILCSFN*, No. 5, pp. 206–7).[4]
  2) Price making
     The SMCs help and control HPCs by making prices and orders with HPCs and put them into state plans.
  3) Assisting dispersed individual handicraftsmen
     (Cheng, 20 July 1954, *ILCSFN*, No. 5, p. 392)

Mao's push and the high tide of the HPC campaign

- Voluntary stage
  At the beginning, the campaign developed voluntarily at a slow pace. By the end of 1953, there were 4,806 HPCs with 300,000 members. The number of HPCs only increased 0.8 percentage points compared to that in 1952.

- Government push to complete the campaign in the second FYP period
  In November–December of 1953, the third national handicraft production cooperation conference was held to promote the HPC campaign and planned that by the end of 1954, the members of HPCs would increase to more than 900 thousand with a output value of more than 1 billion yuan; by 1957, 5 million members with a output value of more than 6 billion yuan. The national campaign would be completed basically in the second FYP period (CPC team of All-China Federation of Cooperative Union, 6 January 1954, *ILCSFN*, No. 5, p. 335). In 1954, the number of HPCs increased by 10 percent and doubled in 1955.
- Mao's push
  1) The push in the second half of 1955 to finish the campaign by 1957
     Mao was unsatisfied at the speed of the HPC campaign from the beginning and started to oppose the "Right-Deviationist and Conservative" in the cooperative campaign (Mao, 31 July 1955, *People's Daily*, 17 October 1955). Under Mao's push, the fifth national handicraft production cooperation conference held in December of 1955 requested that the HPC campaign's speed must fit national industrialization and the socialist transformation of agriculture, capitalist industry and commerce. The conference formulated a development plan to accelerate the campaign and complete the handicraft socialist transformation basically in two years (1956 and 1957). Under Mao's push, the number of HPCs doubled in 1955 and the high tide of the HPC campaign appeared.
  2) Further push in January 1956
     However, Mao was still unsatisfied at the speed and made a further push by criticizing the slow speed of the campaign in January 1956.
  3) Final push on 5 March 1956 to complete the campaign that year
     Mao made a call "to complete the campaign this year." He argued that the speed of individual handicraft socialist transformation was a little slow. "We organized only 2 million people before the end of 1955. However, in the first two months of this year, 3 million people have been organized. We are able to complete the campaign this year. This is very good." Mao also said: "handicrafts are holding a share of 25 percent in the total national industrial output value. Why have not its supply, production and sales be put into the state plan? It is so large and must be brought into the state plan" (Selected works of Mao Zedong, fifth volume, 1977, pp. 264–6).
- The high tide of the HPC campaign
  Under Mao's push, the campaign entered the period of "high tide." By the end of 1956, there were about 100 thousand HPCs (teams) nationwide with 5 million members, about 92 percent in total handicraftsmen and an output value of more than 7 billion yuan, 71 percent in the total handicraft output. China completed the HPC campaign (Liu and Wu, 1985, pp. 141–2). The campaign expanded the handicraft production scale and increased the national output value from 8.2 billion in 1953 to 10.4 billion yuan in 1956.

Table 2.1 China's handicraft industry and its cooperative organizations 1952–56 (ten thousand persons, hundred million yuan, ten thousands units)

	1952	1953	1954	1955	1956
The handicraft industry					
Total employees	645.7	693.1	810.7	758.5	552.1
Urban	259.4	281.2	343.7	327.6	336.2
Rural (share in total)	386.3 (60%)	411.9 (59%)	467 (58%)	430.9 (57%)	215.9 (39%)
Total output value	66.7	82.3	94.5	92.7	104.3
Urban	32.4	39.8	48.7	47.8	64.5
Rural (share in total)	34.3 (52%)	42.5 (52%)	45.8 (49%)	44.9 (48%)	39.8 (38%)
The cooperative organizations					
Organization number	0.27	0.47	4.17	6.46	9.91
Employees	25.25	32.6	121.35	220.58	509.10
Output value	2.55	5.06	11.61	20.16	74.27

Source: *The handicraft industry socialist transformation statistical data* and *PRCERMC*, industrial volume 1953–7.
Note: Cooperative organization number includes both urban and rural number.

State monopoly for purchase and supply

On 10 October 1953, Chen Yun argued: "at present, the national grain issue is very serious, if we do not adopt a suitable means to solve, it will become more serious." "The main problem was that the grain purchased by the state was few, but the grain sold was too much, which has caused chaos in many regions. The grain shortage in some regions such as Northeast region, Beijing and Tianjin seriously affected the national stability and economical development" (*ILCSFN*, No. 4, pp. 446–8). So, Chen proposed "state monopoly for purchase and supply" (SMPS), which was approved by the CPCCC, including Mao Zedong. On 19 November 1953, the State Council issued "The Order on Grain Plan Purchase and Supply" and the "Tentative Method of Grain Market Management." From the beginning of December, except for Tibet and Taiwan, China started to implement the SMPS nationwide.

Basic content of grain SMPS

- State monopoly purchase of grain
  To purchase grain from households which have surplus grain in the countryside. "The farmers who produce grain should sell their surplus grain to the state according to the grain variety, price and planned quantity stipulated by the state. A farmer might freely store up and use the remaining grain after he pays tax grain and completes the grain purchased by the state. He also might continue to sell the remaining grain

to the state, the cooperatives, or transact it at the grain market set by the state, or with other farmers in the countryside" (The state council, 19 November 1953, *ILCSFN*, No. 4, p. 561).

1) Purchase target
   The state purchases grain from the so-called surplus grain households, which have surplus grain. The surplus grain is grain except for the family grain ration, seed, feed and agricultural tax.
2) Purchase quantity
   80%–90% of surplus grain of surplus grain household
3) Purchase price
   The prices are made by the state
4) Purchase time
   Once a year in the regions with one crop a year and twice a year in the regions with two crops a year.
   (The State Council, 25 August 1955, *ILCSFN*, No. 7, p. 127)

- State monopoly supply of grain
  The state monopoly supplies grain for urban inhabitants and the rural inhabitants who lack grain. The grain supply was set at a low price and with different types for different people (CPCCC, 16 October 1953, *ILCSFN*, No. 4, p. 482).
- Two levels of central and local grain responsibility management systems under central control
- Expansion of SMPS
  On 15 November 1953 and 9 September 1954, the state issued orders to implement the state monopoly for purchase and supply of oils, cotton and cotton fabric.

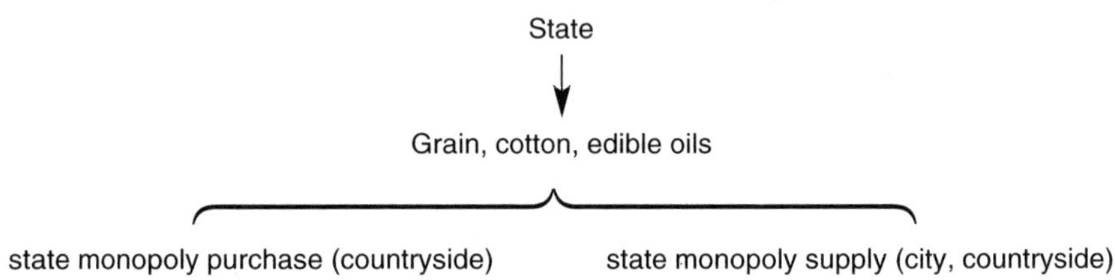

Method for SMPS

- Rural state monopoly for purchase and supply of grain by fixed quotas of production, purchase and sale
  1) To decide on rural surplus grain households (purchase targets), households lacking grain (supply targets), self-sufficient households (no purchase and no supply) and to fix quotas of production output, purchase and sales (abbreviation "three fixings").
  2) Fixing the production quota.
  3) Fixing the purchase quota.

4) Fixing the supply quota.
(The State Council, 5 August 1955, *ILCSFN*, No. 7, p. 125).

- Method of supplying urban and town grain by fixed quota
  1) The state supplied grain rations for urban personnel through institutions such as urban government organizations, schools, enterprises and so on.
  2) The state supplied grain rations for common urban residents by the food supply card or registered resident certificate.
  3) The state supplied grain for the catering trade and service and industry based on fixed quotas. Purchasing secretly was banned.
  4) Private commerce was forbidden to operate the grain business secretly.
  5) Deciding the grain rations of urban and small town inhabitants.
  (The State Council, 19 November 1953 and 25 August 1955)
  6) Grain ration supply card:
  The card is a certificate for common urban inhabitants to buy grain. Without the card, no one was able to buy grain in the state-owned grain store. Every urban household had a grain ration supply card from the government after a strict check based on residence registration (The State Council, 25 August 1955, *ILCSFN*, No. 7, pp. 117–18).

Table 2.2 China's urban grain ration standard for the regions taking rice as staple food (catty / person / per month)

Heavy labor	*Light labor*	*Mental labor or staff of enterprise, institution or organization*	*Middle school and university students*	*Common inhabitants and children above 10 years old*	*6–10 years old*	*3–6 years old*	*Younger than 3 years old*
35–44	26–34	24–29	26–33	22–26	16–21	11–15	5–10

Source: "Tentative method for urban and town grain rationing," the State Council, 25 August 1955, *ILCSFN*, No. 7, pp. 116–17.
Note: processed grain

  7) Grain coupon:
  The grain coupon is mainly for travel or eating away from home. There were two kinds of coupons: the local one used locally and the national one used nationwide.

- The main forms of state purchasing and selling of agricultural products
  1) SMPS
  SMPS are mainly for important agricultural products ("the first grade agricultural product" after 1961) such as grain, cotton and cooking oil. The State Council made the prices and the quotas of SMPS must be completed.

2) Purchasing by assignment.
   Some important agricultural and subsidiary products ("the second grade agricultural products" after 1961) were purchased by the state assignment plan. Purchase by assignment is different from SMPS because only part of these products is purchased generally and it is not managed by the State Council directly.
3) Purchase and sale at negotiated price.
   The state purchases and sells some products at prices negotiated with farmers ("the third grade agricultural products" after 1961). The state makes a contract with the producer or purchases the product at rural fair directly.

Feature of SMPS

The feature is centralized control. The state introduced the grain management system of "the centralized management, command and dispatch," under which, "all of the policy making, all of the volumes to purchase or supply, all of the purchase and supply standards, all of the purchase supply prices and so on must be made or proved by the central government and local governments, under the general policies and principles, to implement the SMPS and guarantee its realization" (CPCCC, 16 October 1953, *ILCSFN*, No. 4, p. 479).

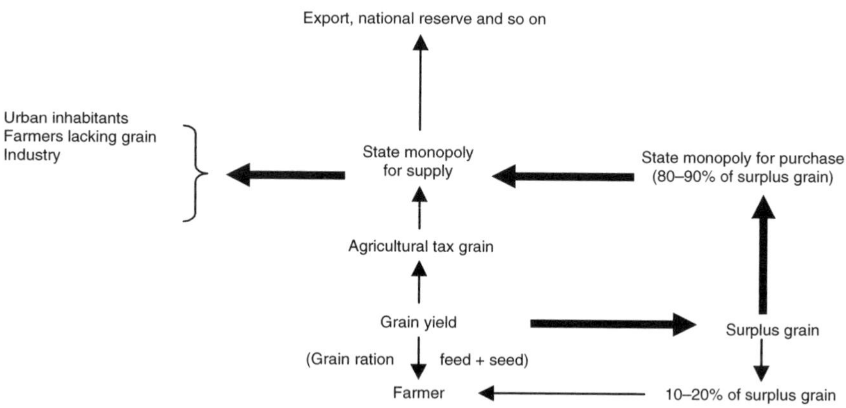

Figure 2.1 China's grain flow under the SMPS in 1955
Source: "Tentative method for state monopoly for purchase and supply of rural grain," the State Council, 25 August 1955, *ILCSFN*, No. 7, pp. 117–20.

The SMPS started at the end of 1953 and obtained the anticipated result through the government's impetus and large-scale propaganda. In the first month of the SMPS, the grain the state purchased increased 38 percent compared to the same time in 1952, and reversed the situation that the grain sold was more than the grain purchased (Chen, Chen and Yang,

1993, p. 182). In 1954 the state purchased 101.78 billion catties of grain, 156.8 million catties more than that in 1953, an increase of 18 percent. The SMPS finally caused the government to get out of the grain crisis.

2.4 Rural industrialization in process

From 1952, China's rural handicrafts experienced first growth, then a drop. Its employees increased from 3.86 million in 1952 to 4.67 million in 1954, an increase of 810 thousand. It then dropped to 2.2 million, a decrease of 2.5 million, about 54 per cent. Its output value increased from 3.4 billion yuan in 1952 to 4.6 billion yuan in 1954, and then fell to 4 billion yuan in 1956, a decrease of 600 million yuan, about 13 per cent. In 1956, rural handicraftsmen were mainly farmers engaged in handicrafts concurrently, who held a share of 56 percent in the total output value of rural handicrafts. Next were the handicraft cooperatives, at 37 per cent, while individual handicrafts only had a share of 7 percent (*PRCERMC, industry volume 1953–7*, p. 939).

China's rural industry, mainly in the SMCs, also appeared in this period. By the beginning of 1954, there had been 11,757 processing enterprises in the SMCs nationwide such as 3,989 oil pressing plants, 1,782 food factories, 1,641 farm tool factories, 588 grain processing factories, 318 cotton ginning mills and 3,439 processing factories for other products. The industry had an average formal staff of more than 200 thousand persons with a fund of 85.02 million yuan and a output value of 1.16 billion yuan. More than 90 per cent of these enterprises were in the countryside (Qiu, Chi and Shi, 1994, in *Economic Cooperatives in China*, Qin Liufang and Lu Longwen, ed., 1994, p. 122). SMC's processing enterprises became one of China's rural industry initial forms.

At the same time, in some regions, many APCs also set up small factories. For example, in the second half of 1955, a factory for tobacco pipes and cigarette holders was set up in the Li xing village of Jie Pai town, Danyang county Jiangsu province. The Chun Lei Senior APC in Dong Tin township, Wuxi county, Jiangsu province formed factories for farm tools and wooden boat repair. By the end of 1956, the APCs in Wuxi county, Jiangsu province had 210 enterprises dealing with processing industries such as twelve enterprises for bricks and tiles, 108 for grain processing (the Jiangsu Province local chronicle compiles the committee, 2000, p. 30).

Through 1952–7, the number of rural telephones increased more than three times from 58 thousands in 1952 to 200 thousand in 1957. The share of the rural population in the total national population reduced unceasingly, from 88 percent in 1952 to 85 percent in 1957, a drop of 3 percentage points.

Although the grain yield maintained an increase, from 167 million tons in 1953 to 195 million tons in 1957, generally, the agricultural growth was quite slow. Except for 1955, the agricultural GDP grew at a pace of no more than 5 percent. Through 1952–57, national cultivated land expanded greatly with an increase of 59 million Chinese acres and amounted to 1.7 billion

Table 2.3 Per capita consumption of farmer households in China 1952–56 (catty)

Year	*Grain*	*Edible plant oils*	*Pork*	*Eggs*
1952	383	3.4	11	2
1953	381	3.1	11	2
1954	380	2.7	11	2
1955	391	3.4	8	2
1956	410	4.2	8	2
1957	409	3.7	9	2

Source: *Chinese Trade and Price Statistical Data 1952–83*, the trade price statistics department of SSB, Chinese statistics publishing house, 1984

Chinese acres by 1957. In the same period, there was an increase of 218 million Chinese acres of irrigated land, equaling 69 percent of the total irrigated land in 1952. Water conservation also developed. The majority of river dikes were maintained and each big river system such as the Huai River, Hai River, Yellow River and so on also were regulated to solve the water problem. Farm tractors also increased from 2,006 in 1952, to 24,629 in 1957 (Liu and Wu, 1985, pp. 183–4). Although farmer household consumption continued to increase, its rate was very slow, about 1–2 percent each year.

2.5 Policy effects

Cooperativization promoted production, strengthened state control and bred rural industry

Expanding agricultural production scale and strengthened state control over the rural areas

The cooperativization centralized fund, improved working conditions and enhanced production efficiency. It made many new things possible, for instance, large farm machinery use and large-scale farmland capital construction. The campaign transformed private ownership and strengthened state control on rural individual economy. Although both of land reform and cooperativization were rural reforms promoted by the state, they had different significance. Although land reform distributed land to farmers, it did not change the private nature of the land system. On the contrary, land reform caused rural economy to be more dispersed and weakened state control on the countryside, thus contradicting the national macro goal. However, cooperativization changed the private nature of the land system to a collective one and eliminated this contradiction. At this point, it had influence far greater and much profounder than land reform. Cooperativization was a new system, under which farmers lost land just got from the land reform and changed the relation between farmers and the state fundamentally. Its completion symbolized the establishment of a centralized control system in the countryside and the formation of a new rural economy, which was brought into line with the national plan. The state controlled the countryside more easily and efficiently through the cooperatives. The APC, SMC and RCCs constituted the basic system of new China's rural economy and completely transformed China's rural traditional structure of the small peasant economy, which had existed for hundreds of years.

Breeding rural industry

Cooperativization expanded the handicrafts production scale, improved working conditions and assisted the handicrafts in funds, raw material supply, product sales and so on, which laid a foundation for the rural industry. At the same time, it concentrated the individual peasant's resources such as funds, labor and other producer goods, which formed the capital primitive accumulation needed for rural industry. In China's countryside, because there was no real industry at all and the economic development level was also very low, making advances for rural industry was extremely difficult, especially for individual farmers. Therefore, rural industry was difficult to start. However, the cooperatives made the essential advances for rural industry.

The SMPS made a agriculture with low return

SMPS were introduced to China as a emergency means for the grain crisis in 1953. However, after the grain crisis, it still continued for more than 30 years in China. This has a profound political and economical root. The compulsory and army supply-style policy had an extremely profound influence upon China's economy and society. The SMPS mainly included three things:

- To lower agricultural product prices (to keep prices down)
- To purchase all of the surplus agricultural product (to expand supply)
- To sell agricultural products at fixed quantity, and fixed prices (to compress demand).

The following takes grain as an example to explain the SMPS influence with supply and demand. It supposes that before SMPS, the demand and supply relation was S_0, D_0, because China's grain could not meet the demand. The low-level balance point of demand and supply is at the E_0 point and the corresponding supply of agricultural product is Q_0 with a price at P_0, where P and Q are price and quantity of grain respectively. Under the SMPS, the state monopolizes the grain market. When the state reduces the price to P_1 (to keep prices down), farmers do not want to sell grain to the state. The grain supply goes down to Qs. However, because the state cannot purchase enough grain, it purchases grain from the SMPS. So the grain supply still is Q_0 (supply expansion). When supplying grain at fixed quantity and fixed price (demand compression), because of price drop, the demand expands from Q_0 to Q_d. however, because of the quota supply, the grain demand compresses from Q_d to Q_0 and makes E as the new balance between supply and demand. The SMPS caused the curves of both supply and demand to become a non elastic level line with fixed price. The price has nothing to do with the supply and demand at all.

The supply and demand relation before the SMPS is:

$S_0 = S(P)$, $D_0 = D(P)$.

After the SMPS the relation is:

$S_0 = S_1$, $D_0 = D_1 = S_1$, (P_1 = the price after the SMPS).

The price has nothing to do with demand and supply (supposing the price for purchase is the same as the sale price). From the analysis above, SMPS have the following influences upon the rural economy:

- Realizing a balance between supply and demand under the shortage of agricultural products and stabilizing national economy.
- Making a low-return agriculture, which reduced farmer incentives. In Figure 2.2, the change of balance point from E_0 to E reduced farmers' income from $P_0 \times Q$ to $P \times Q$, but the grain surplus the state derived is $P_0 \times Q - P \times Q = Q(P_0 - P)$. The lower the price, the more surplus the state derived and the lower the farmers' income is. Purchase at low price reduced the agricultural income of farmers. On the other hand, in the SMPS, both purchase and selling price were fixed. This meant that no matter how much was produced, the purchase price was invariable and always low. Although farmer production increased, income did not increase accordingly, which reduced farmers' production incentives greatly.
- Compressing the people's daily consumption to raise capital for heavy industry

  Liu Shaoqi (1950), on where to collect huge funds for national industrialization, pointed out that the only way was to reduce the Chinese people's own consumption. "Therefore, the means to collect industrial funds was similar to that used by the Soviet Union. That is, to save, by the Chinese people. Without this, we cannot collect large funds needed by Chinese industrialization." Saving means reducing consumption. The SMPS compressed both urban and rural inhabitants' daily consumption to an extremely low level to meet only the daily basic need. Although, under state control, people's basic grain demand was met, it was very far from the actual demand. The SMPS not only hindered agricultural development, but also expanded the potential demand for grain and intensified the shortage of agricultural products. As shown in Figure 2.2, when the price dropped from P_0 to P_1, the demand also increased along with it from Q to Q_d, which enlarged the gap between the demand and supply and formed the huge latent demand.

  It took not only the rural surplus, but also the urban surplus. It also took a part of both the urban and rural inhabitants' daily consumption to support heavy industry. As shown in Table 2.4, while compressing people's consumption, the state supported her industrial development through exporting agricultural and subsidiary products and importing producer goods. So, China's rural developmental strategy did not aim at promoting production through expanding farmers' consumption, but attempted to increase production through a system change from private to cooperative and to promote agriculture though no increase of farmers' income and compressing people's consumption. Then the state, with this surplus and a part of people's daily consumption, pushed her industry. Farmers became a labor army which provided national industrialization with resources, but were kept at survival level. This is the real meaning of "the industry leading agriculture and the city leading the countryside."

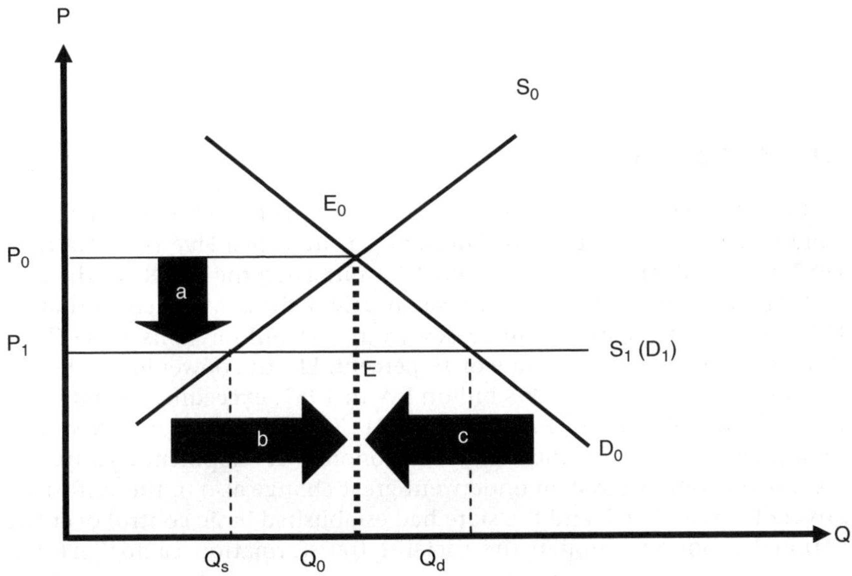

Figure 2.2 SMPS influence upon China's grain supply and demand

Table 2.4 China's import and export 1951–57 (%)

Year	*Share in total export*		*Share in total import*	
	Agricultural and subsidiary products	*Agricultural and subsidiary products processed*	*Producer goods*	*Subsistence means*
1951	55	31	81	19
1952	59	23	89	11
1953	56	26	92	8
1954	48	28	92	8
1955	46	28	94	6
1956	43	31	92	8
1957	40	32	92	8

Source: *Chinese trade and price statistical data 1952–83*, the trade price statistics department of SSB, Chinese statistics publishing house, 1984.

3
Great Leap Forward in the People's Communization Campaign

3.1 Background

By 1957, China's economy had changed greatly, with strong recovery, and rapid growth. China overfulfilled most targets in its first Five Year Plan (FYP 1952–57). Productions in most industries surpassed the targets in the first FYP. The output of steel in 1957 was nearly 4 times as much as that in 1952. The grain yield also increased from 164 million tons in 1952 to 195 million tons in 1957, a rate of 19 percent. Electric power jumped from 7.3 billion kW in 1952 to 19.3 billion kW in 1957, exceeding the target of 15.9 billion kW in the FYP (CSY 1983). The success in the first FYP strengthened China's confidence in its economic development greatly.

China's economic system underwent great change also in the shift from private to centralized, and the state had established basic control over the national economy through the socialist transformation campaigns. On 12 March 1957, Mao Zedong pointed out: "we are now at a stage in which society is changing tremendously ... the change is much deeper than before. We are construing socialism. There are millions upon millions of people who are entering the social transformation campaign ... private economy is becoming a collective one and the capitalist private system is becoming a socialist public one" (*ILCSFN*, No. 10, p. 110). The share of the private sector in total national industry output changed from 51 percent in 1952 to 1 percent in 1957; the share of state and collective owned sectors increased from 41 percent and 7 percent in 1952 to 55 percent and 44 percent respectively in 1957. China's economy had changed and would develop under state direct control.

Although China's economy had great success from 1949, it still was a low-income country with a large rural population. Its natural resources scarcity and pre-modern industry were unchanged. At the same time, China also was a closed country and could not get the necessary resources from the outside world because of the blockade of western countries, which were the main sources of advanced technology, capital and information in the world.

3.2 Policy goals

To surpass England and catch up with America at top speed

The completion of the socialist transformation of China's agriculture, handicrafts and capitalist industry and commerce in 1956 symbolized the end of the private system and the establishment of the centralized public ownership system in China. China would develop her economy under a new centralized command system. On 27 September 1956, the CPCCC pointed out: "The primary mission for our party and people concentrates on developing social productive forces and transforming our country from a backward and agricultural nation to an advanced and industrialized one as soon as possible." The overfulfillment of the first FYP caused people to see the great power of the huge labor army under state control. Bo Yibo (1958, *ILCSFN*, No. 11, pp. 100–1)[1] argued that by 31 January 1958, there had been already a increase in irrigated areas of more than 117 million Chinese acres, surpassing the original target of irrigated areas to increase by 92 million Chinese acres (for water irrigation projects) from October 1957 to the end of September 1958. Namely, the target for the entire year was overfulfilled in only four months. "All of the facts demonstrate fully that farmers who have been organized have confidence so strong and strength so inexhaustible to strive for great development in agriculture!" China, stimulated by the success in the first FYP, abandoned the original second Five Year Plan and set a new plan with much higher targets. In January 1958, Mao made a call for the "Great Leap Forward" (GLF), an overall acceleration of economic growth, "to surpass England and catch up with America."

The core of "surpassing England and catching up with America" in 1958

"Top speed" is the core of the GLF. On 21 June 1958, the editorial of the *People's Daily* entitled "To Strive for Top Speed" emphasized that "speed" was the soul of the General Line for socialist construction. It said: "To develop our country's social productive forces, realize national industrialization and agricultural modernization at the highest speed is the basic spirit and soul of the General Line ... The speed issue deals with the construction line and is an essential policy for socialism in our country." "'Faster' is the center link for 'greater, faster, better, and cheaper' production" (Liu and Wu, 1986, p. 223).

Timetable to surpass England and catch up with America

- To surpass England in 15 years
  China's industrialization strategy to surpass advanced countries had initially formed in the first FYP, however, there was no concrete plan and timetable for realizing the strategy. After overfulfillment of the first FYP in 1957, a concrete timetable to realize industrialization started to form gradually. Mao (17 November 1957) gave a explicit description of the timetable.

He said: "our country has truly won a victory in the socialist revolution in 1957, however, productive forces are still very backward and we must strive for 15 years to surpass England" (*New China Economic Development History 1949–98,* Cong and Zhang, eds, 1999, p. 354). On 1 January 1958, the New Year's day editorial of the *People's Daily* officially proposed that we would take 10–15 years to establish modern industrial and agricultural foundations in our country. "We must catch up with and surpass England in steel, iron and other principal industry products in around 15 years; after that, we have to further develop productive forces and spend another 20–30 years in catching up with and surpassing America in order to gradually transit China from a socialist to a communist society."

- To catch up with England in 10 years
  On 15 April 1958, Mao announced: "the time needed for our country to catch up with large capitalist nations in both industry and agriculture production may not need so long as planned in the past." He believed: "it will take ten years to catch up with England and another ten years to catch up with America." He said: "to catch up with England and America in 25 years or more has retained a leeway of five to ten years. Anyway we will keep the slogan 'to catch up with England in 15 years' unchangeable" (*ILCSFN*, No. 11, p. 276).
- To catch up with England in 7 years
  In May 1958, Mao changed the timetable again. He made a call for "catching up with England in seven years and another eight years to catch up with America" (*New China Economic Development History 1949–98,* Cong and Zhang, eds, 1999, p. 355).
- To catch up with England in 3 years
  However, Mao was still dissatisfied this timetable and announced on 21 June 1958 that we had full assurance to surpass England in 3 years and America in 10 years. He said: "the time to catch up with England is neither 15 years nor 7 years, it is 2–3 years, possibly in 2 years. We here mainly deal with steel production" (*New China Economic Development History 1949–98,* Cong and Zhang, eds, 1999, p. 355).

Table 3.1 The planned targets of national economy for 1959 made on 28 August 1958

Steel (mill. ton)	*Coal* (mill. ton)	*Petroleum* (mill. ton)	*Power* (bill. kwh)	*Railroads* (kilometer)	*Chemical fertilizers* (mill. ton)	*Grain* (bill. kilog.)	*Cotton* (mill. bucket)
27–30	370	8	55	10,500	5.3	400–500	10

Source: *ILCSFN*, No. 11, p. 426–7.
Note: the plan aimed to produce a steel output of 30 million tons.

Table 3.2 **The planned targets of national economy for 1959 made on 10 December 1958**

	Unit	*Output in 1957*	*Output estimated in 1958*	*Planned annual growth rate in 1959 (in 1958)* (%)	*Target of 1959*	*Output of England in 1957*
Steel	Million tons	5.35	11 (including indigenous steel)	82 (106)	20	22
Iron	Million tons	5.86	15.8 (including crude iron)	83 (170)	29	14.5
Coal	Hundred million tons	1.3	2.7	56 (107)	4.2	2.2
Crude oil	Million tons	1.5	2.1	100 (44)	4.2	N
Electricity	Billion kwh	1.93	2.75	92–100 (42)	53–55	105
Machine tools	Ten thousand	2.8	9	44 (222)	13	12
Cars	Ten thousand	0.75	1.45	348 (93)	6.5	105
Locomotives	Set	167	280	650 (68)	2100	1,155*
Chemical fertilizer	Million tons	0.63	1.01	147 (60)	2.5	3.2
Railroads	Kilometer	N	1800	410–468(N)	9400–10400	N
Grain	Billion catties	370	750	40 (102)	1050	N
Cotton	Million buckets	32.8	67	49 (104)	100	N
Edible oils	Million tons	N	3.5	71(N)	6.0	N

Source: "Resolution on National Economic Plan for 1959", CPCCC, *ILCSFN*, No. 11, pp. 631–3.
Notes: The plan was made on 10 December 1958.
"N" is data unavailable.
*The output of locomotives in England was the same as in 1956.

- To surpass England next year!
  On 8 August 1958, the timetable was once more changed. The *People's Daily* indicated: "the problem is if we do think about and want a high speed or not. If we want it, we will have it, if not, there will be no high speed." On 28 August 1958, the CPCCC believed that because of the GLF in 1958, especially the great victory in agriculture, China would have a greater GLF and decided to raise comprehensively national economic targets in 1959. Under the new target, "our country will surpass England in output of steel, iron and other major industries, except for a few products such as electric power" (*ILCSFN*, No. 11, pp. 426–7). At the same time, the targets for both 1960 and 1962 were formulated. According to the plan, the grain yield in 1960 would achieve about 650 billion kilograms, steel about 50 million tons, and in the science and technology field, China would master technologies for atomic energy and jet airplanes. The target in 1962 was to complete the second FYP with a grain yield of 750 billion kilograms or more, a steel output of 80–100 million tons, and to catch up with advanced science and technology. "By 1962 when the 2nd FYP is completed, China will become a great socialist country with modern industry, agriculture, science and culture ahead of time, and create conditions for transiting itself to communism" (*ILCSFN*, No. 11, pp. 426–7). Although on 10 December 1958, the CPCCC made an adjustment to the plan and lowered many targets for 1959 "because if we don't adjust them, it is impossible to realize the targets" (*ILCSFN*, No. 11, p. 643), the targets still retained "top speed." "If we complete this plan, our country will be close to, catch up with or surpass England in the output of industries such as steel, iron, copper, aluminum, machine tools, generating sets and so on (we surpassed England in coal production in 1958)" (*ILCSFN*, No. 11, pp. 629–30). "Top speed" was the core of both the GLF and the industrialization strategy, and had controlled China's policy-making completely.

To establish a centralized public ownership system

Although the state gradually established its control system over the rural economy through cooperatives and state monopoly for purchase and supply of main agricultural products (SMPS), rural cooperatives were a half-socialist system with a private nature and "the color of small-scale peasant economy having a tendency to go for the capitalist system," was still too small to control. Therefore, in order to control and bring the rural economy into line with national plans and make farmers provide agricultural products to support national industrialization at top speed, the state had to have a better system to control the countryside. This was naturally an extension of the cooperatives campaign and also an imitation of the Soviet approach.

The state attempted to achieve this goal through further transforming the rural organizational structure. On 10 December 1958, the CPCCC indicated: "The state-ownership system is more advanced than the collective one because the production materials and goods produced in state-owned enterprises can be distributed directly, reasonably and centrally by the state on behalf of all people according to the need of the entire national economy. However, in collective enterprises ... this is impossible." On February 1959, Mao pointed out: "if the people's commune has strong economical strength, complete communal ownership, and further, ownership of the whole people can be realized" (*ILCSFN*, No. 12, pp. 127–8). At the Shanghai Conference in January 1960, the CPCCC even proposed a tentative plan to "complete the transition of the commune system from basic production brigade ownership to basic commune ownership in eight years" (Liu and Wu, 1986, p. 259).

To abandon "agriculture priority" and promote rural industrialization comprehensively

In order to realize high-speed industrialization, the state started to impel local industry and mobilize all people to develop industry. It called for "the entire party and people to develop industry in order to form a new high tide of industrial development in the shortest time" (CPCCC, 28 August 1958, *ILCSFN*, No. 11, p. 426).

In the countryside, the policy of "agriculture priority" was abandoned and the strategic focus was shifted to industry. An all-round promotion of rural industrialization was put forward. The CPCCC (23 March 1958) requested: "each province, and autonomous region should strive to make their industrial output value catch up with or surpass their agricultural output value in five or seven years." Liu Shaoqi (5 May 1958, *ILCSFN*, No. 11, pp. 310–11) argued that in the first FYP period, we focused on central-managed and large industries, and ignored local, middle and small-scale industries. He pointed out that since advocating middle and small scale industries, the initiative in developing industry had surged upward greatly in each region. "As long as more than 20 provinces, municipalities and autonomous regions, more than 180 prefectures and autonomous prefectures, more than 2,000 counties and autonomous counties, more than 80,000 villages and small towns, more than 100,000 handicraft cooperatives and more than 700,000 agricultural cooperatives can all give a full play to industry development correctly, in a short time, various enterprises will spread everywhere nationwide, and the industry in our country certainly will develop faster." He argued that the future inevitably is: 1) accelerating national industrialization; 2) accelerating mechanization of agriculture; 3) accelerating the process to narrow the difference between town and country (*ILCSFN*, No. 11, pp. 310–11). In November 1958, Mao Zedong wrote: "the task facing our people is, through the people's commune, this kind of social form, to develop productive force at top speed, to impel national industrialization, commune industrialization and factory-style agriculture" (Wen, 2000, p. 222)

Impelling an all-round rural industrialization was not only the need for pushing for industrialization at top speed, but also a result of an exaggerated estimate for the agricultural output in 1958, which violated natural law. The CPCCC (August 1958) pointed: "in 1958, the GLF in agriculture will make a grain yield of 300–350 billion kilograms (real output only 200 billion kilograms), an increase of 60–90 percent compared to that in 1957; cotton about 70 million buckets, an increase of more than 100 percent compared to that in 1957. The annual per capita grain will be about 500 kilograms. The great success in agriculture requires that industry catch up rapidly" (*ILCSFN*, No. 11, p. 465 and 467). The CPCCC estimated that the grain in 1958 would be 375 billion kilograms with a annual growth rate of 102 percent, and 525 billion kilograms in 1959 (real output only 170 billion kilograms) (10 December 1958, *ILCSFN*, No. 11, p. 643). Mao Zedong (8 September1958) indicated: "Due to rapid agricultural development, the pressure on industry is becoming greater and greater and there have been quite stable foundations and mature experience in agricultural production and rural economy. The center of our work must be shifted at the right moment from agriculture and rural areas to industry" (*China's rural society and economy evolution 1949–89*, Chen, Chen and Yang, 1993, p. 319).

As to the relation between rural industry and urban industry, on 7 December 1958, the CPCCC pointed out: "some comrades are worrying that to impel rural industry with great effort may damage urban industry. In fact at present the problem in light industry is that products are insufficient, and too few. It is necessary to make a suitable division of production between rural and urban industries. Urban industry should develop high-level products and advanced techniques; the commune industry should produce low-level but popular products" (*ILCSFN*, No. 11, pp. 582–3). Other goals for developing rural industry were:

- To keep farmers in the countryside and not let them rush into the city
  Unlike other nations where rural surplus labor would go to the cities for a job during the industrialization process, China's industrialization policy was to make rural surplus labor enter rural industry in order to keep farmers in rural areas. Facing the large rural population and small per capita farming land, Mao said in 1959: "if we do not adopt some special means, the country cannot become a good one." "There is a population of more than 500 million engaged in agricultural production in China's countryside, who work every year, but, however, cannot eat their fill. That is the most unreasonable phenomenon." He argued that the rural population must be reduced and proposed: "Do not let them rush into the city! We should develop rural industry with great effort and cause farmers to become workers only in rural areas" (Wen, 2000, p. 222). Mao (1959) also argued: "if the farmers all rush into the city, it will inflate the urban population excessively. That is not a good thing. From now on, we will have to pay attention to this problem. To prevent

this problem we should make the rural living standard approximately equal to or somewhat higher than the urban one." Mao thought that the people's commune would solve this issue. "Each people's commune must have an economic center in future and will develop industry with great effort according to unified planning to make farmers become workers in rural areas. People's communes should establish colleges to train senior intellectuals for their own need. If these are achieved, the rural population will not blindly flow to the towns." "A city in future may not be so large and the people in large cities should be dispersed to the countryside. We should establish many small towns, which is also advantageous even under an atomic war" (Wen, 2000, p. 222)

- To narrow the difference between city and countryside
  On 10 December 1958, the CPCCC argued: "the industry development in communes will not only accelerate national industrialization, but also promote the state-owned system in the countryside, as well as narrow the difference between town and country" (*ILCSFN*, No. 11, pp. 609–10).

To take more and invest less

The state requested the countryside to support the city and national industrialization by taking more from farmers and investing less in rural areas. Liu Shaoqi (5 May 1958) pointed out that it was necessary to mobilize farmers "to contribute their labor, to create wealth, to accumulate massive funds for national industrialization and to develop small-scale industry in rural areas." Some worried that developing agriculture would decrease funds for industrialization. Liu argued that this kind of anxiety is unnecessary and said: "as long as we are good at using the great strength of more than 500 million farmers, even if the state does not increase its investment in agriculture, the scale of agricultural construction can also expand greatly." Liu gave a example: "in eight years, the state has put a total investment of 1.45 billion yuan in to the project for comprehensive control over the Huaihe River and more than 1.6 billion cubic meters of earth and stone have been completed. However, from the winter of 1957 to the spring of 1958, in only a half-year, Henan and Anhui provinces, using farmers' labor, funds and materials, have completed 12 billion cubic meters of earth and stone work" (*ILCSFN*, No. 11, pp. 308–9). In order to achieve rapid national industrialization, farmers had to provide the state not only with agricultural products, but also other resources such as labor, materials, transport means and so on; an all-round support for the city and national industrialization.

3.3 Policy controls

All-round communalization campaign

The emergence of the people's commune in China in 1958 was an extension of the agricultural cooperation campaign and also an imitation of the

Soviet approach aiming at all-round control over rural economy and society to realize "the lofty ideal of communism." On 29 August 1958, at the Bei Dai He Conference,[2] the CPCCC decided to set up people's communes in rural areas nationwide and pointed out: "The people's commune is the best organization to accelerate socialist construction and the transit to communism, and will develop into the basic unit in the communist society" (*ILCSFN*, No. 11, pp. 466–7). On 10 December 1958, the CPCCC pointed out: "from now, the task facing our people is, through the people's commune, the form of social organization, based on the 'General Line' for socialist construction proposed by the party, to develop social productive forces, to promote national industrialization, commune industrialization, mechanization of agriculture, electrification at high-speed, and to gradually transit the socialist collective ownership system to the socialist state ownership one, thus to establish the system of state ownership in our entire socialist economy fully in order to make our country a great socialist nation with highly developed modern industry, modern agriculture, modern science, technology and culture" (*ILCSFN*, No. 11, pp. 601–2). Mao (1959)[3] said: "the establishment of people's communes in rural areas enhances the old collective ownership of producer goods with some ingredient of state ownership, expands scale, and realizes the union of industry, agriculture, commerce, education and military, and the union of farming, forestry, animal husbandry, side-line production and fishing, which will powerfully impel agricultural production and the entire rural economic development" (*ILCSFN*, No. 12, pp. 127–8).

The standard pattern of people's communes promoted by the CPCCC in 1958

- Commune ownership of producer goods
  All main producer goods such as land and large tools belong to the commune. Each member of a commune hands over all his producer goods such as draught animals and forest, including the private foundations of the houses to the commune, and will be allowed to retain a few domestic animals and domesticated fowls only.
- Wage and grain supply system and public welfare
  There was a wage system or piece-rate wage system and free grain supply system for members according to the standard made by the state and the commune. The welfare facilities in a commune include dining halls, nurseries, tailoring teams, hospitals and so on. Each commune also would introduce a universal compulsory education system and gradually make all school-age children go to school and all young adults study until senior primary school level.
- Management system controlled by government
  The management system in a commune is "to integrate government administration with commune management." A commune was also the local government in the township (Xiang). Although the highest regulatory body in a commune was the commune congress, it did not have the

right to operate the commune. The local government and commune party committee held the real power. This was a system in which all managerial personnel were appointed by the higher government and government controlled everything in the commune such as labor, production and investment.

- Centralized leadership and the level-to-level administration system
  There is a system of centralized leadership and a three-level administration in a commune. The commune is in charge of everything and is responsible for profit and loss, and manages large-scale production, such as enterprises, mines, the supply and sale departments (state-operated basic commercial unit in rural areas) and credit departments (state-operated basic financial offices in rural areas). The administrative district (or production brigade) was in charge of all affairs and was the basic unit in economic accounting. The production team was the fundamental unit to organize farmers directly for production and distribution, that is, farmers worked collectively and obtained grain and wage in the teams (the Zha Ya Shan Satellite People's Commune, 7 August 1958, *ILCSFN*, No. 11, pp. 387–99).

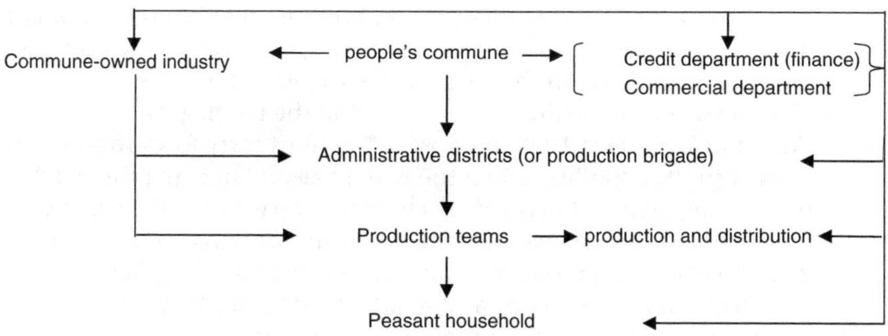

Figure 3.1 Organization structure of the people's commune in 1958

Method to promote the communalization campaign

- Government impetus
  Firstly, the CPCCC made the decision to establish communes nationwide and formulated specific stipulations on the procedure, scale, and steps to establish a commune, related policies and general regulations such as the General Regulations of the Zha Ya Shan Satellite People's Commune. Then, local governments at various levels mobilized and organized farmers to establish people's communes.
- Integrating government administration with management of economic organizations
  A people's commune is not only an economic organization, but also a government body, which makes the commune hold dominant power in

rural areas and enhances the incentive of local governments to further the communalization campaign.

- Deciding on the commune scale
  The state stipulated that a commune generally would consist of one township (xiang), with a population of about 2,000 households and may also include several townships (xiang) with a population of about 6,000–7,000 households or 20,000 households even more. Otherwise, "the tendency of the commune development might be to form one large commune only in one county, which combined all communes in the county."
- Merging small into large cooperatives and transferring them into a commune
- Communism education campaign:
  1) Disseminating to farmers communism's magnificent prospect of "taking everything you need" and "eating without paying" in order to mobilize, and impel farmers to join the commune. The CPCCC (29 August 1958) announced with confidence, "it seems that communism will be realized in our country soon; we should utilize the form of the people's commune and try to find a concrete way to take our country to communism" (*ILCSFN*, No. 11, p. 450). The future ideal Utopian society propagandized by the government drove millions upon millions of poor and illiterate peasants who trusted the new government, because they obtained lands freely in the land reform, to join communes.
  2) "Pulling down the white flag and hoisting the red flag"[4]
     The CPCCC (August 1958) proposed: "we must carry forward the communist spirit of 'pulling down the white flag and hoisting the red flag' in this campaign and make every effort to propagandize the superiority of the socialist system over the old one by innumerable examples of the great increases in production output, in order to strengthen farmers' confidence in taking the socialist road" (*ILCSFN*, No. 11, p. 452).
- Reforming rural finance and commerce management systems
  1) "Two transfers"
     This is to transfer both personnel and property of all state-owned rural branches of grain, commerce and finance to the commune, except those which served for several communes or broader areas. The commune was in change of business management and all personnel and properties, including their fixed assets and floating capital (CPCCC and the State Council, 20 December 1958, *ILCSFN*, No. 11, p. 667).
  2) "Three unities"
     This is to unite policy, plans and floating capital management. Policy unity means that each commune must obey national policy. Secondly, plan unity requests each people's commune to obey national plans such as purchase and plantation plans. Finally, each commune must strictly manage floating capital to guarantee that funds from the state be put into production and commodity circulation in industry and agriculture only, not in capital construction or for other purposes.

3) "One contracting"
   Each commune must make a contract with the state for its budgetary revenue and expenditure in order to increase its incentive for increasing revenue and controlling expenditure (CPCCC, 20 December 1958, *ILCSFN*, No. 11, p. 667).

Features of the people's commune

- Large scale
  Three years of the APC campaign did not organize all farmers into the cooperatives; however, in the communalization campaign in 1958, nearly all farmers joined communes. Before communalization, there were 798 thousand advanced agricultural producer's cooperatives nationally with an average of 151 households per cooperative. But by the end of September 1958, there were 23.4 thousand communes nationally with an average of 479 households per commune, three times as large as the advanced cooperatives (Chen, Chen and Yang, 1993, p. 309).
- All-round control over the rural areas
  Because the commune was an economic organization and also local government, it covered everything such as rural industry, agriculture, the military, education and commerce. All rural resources and activities were controlled by the commune.
- Militarization
  The commune was requested "to militarize organizationally" and "to act in a soldierly way." That is, to organize the peasants into an army. Farmers would act just like an army in a battle according to any order from the state. In this system people at lower levels must be subordinated to those at higher levels, which guaranteed the state's control over farmers. The CPCCC (10 December 1958, *ILCSFN*, No. 11, p. 618) indicated:

> The so-called "military organization" is also called "factory-style organization." Labor organization in a commune must have strict discipline like that in a factory or an army. Large-scale agricultural production, just like large-scale industrial production, is an industrial army. The modern industrial army is organized by the bourgeoisie and a factory is equal to a military camp ... The industrial army in a socialist society belongs to the working class only. We now apply this system to the countryside and establish a socialist industrial army of agriculture with a democratic and centralist mechanism, which does away with any exploitation from landlords and rich farmers and also the small-scale agricultural production.

In order to realize militarization, "all levels of production organizations in the commune should correspondingly establish a militiaman organization." The commanding officers at all levels of militiamen organizations "must become members of the management administration of the communes." They will receive dual leadership from the management and the

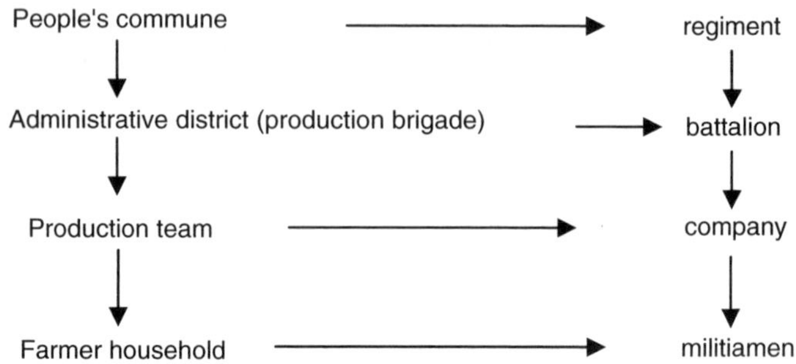

Figure 3.2 The people's commune and rural militias organization structure in 1958

higher authority of militiaman" (CPCCC, December 1958, *ILCSFN*, No. 11, p. 619). "Taking one people's commune as one unit, based on production organization and the number of militiaman, the militiamen, mainly the primary militias, should be organized into militiaman brigades, squadrons and squads ... These armed people are not only civilian, but also soldiers. They are a team for production, a team for study, a team for work and also a team for fighting." At the same time, the militiamen were divided into two kinds. "The ordinary militia were composed of male or female citizen of 16–50 years old and the primary militias are male citizens at 16–30 years old" (CPCCC, 1958, *ILCSFN*, No. 11, p. 469). The commune became a half-military organization and an effective tool for the state to control the countryside. The militiamen were often used to implement tasks from the government, especially arduous ones.

- Collectivization

  The commune must realize the collectivization of life such as the dining hall, nursery and other social welfare undertakings, which guarantee the commune "to organize militarily" and "to act in a soldierly manner."

Mao's push and the "high tide" of communalization

- Outset stage

  On 1 July 1958, the *Red Flag* published an article advocating "to change cooperatives into a basic units with not only agricultural cooperation, but also industrial cooperation. In fact, this is a people's commune combining agriculture with industry." In August, Qiliying people's commune in Xinxiang County, Henan province was established.
- Mao's push

  At the beginning of August 1958, Mao Zedong pointed out that it was good to name these as the "people's commune;" its advantage was that it combined industry with agriculture, commerce, education and the military all together. He believed that the people's commune was both "large and public" and would speed up agricultural development and create conditions for transferring the countryside to communism.

- High tide of the campaign
  Under Mao's push, the CPCCC (29 August 1958) decided to establish people's communes nationwide. This created enormous impact and enthusiasm in both local governments and farmers. Vast number of farmers requested to join communes, which led to "a high tide of the people's communalization campaign in rural areas." In only one month, many provinces announced they had realized rural communalization. "From the summer of 1958, in only a few months, more than 740 thousand agricultural producers' cooperatives have been, under the strong request of vast number of farmers, changed into more than 26 thousand communes. There are more than 120 million farmer households participating in the communes already, more than 99 percent of the total farmer households nationally" (CPCCC, 10 December 1958, *ILCSFN*, No. 11, p. 598). The communes with more than 5,000 households accounted for 30 percent in the total communes, and there were 94 counties which had organized a commune at county level or a united commune leading all communes in the entire county (Chen, Chen and Yang, 1993, p. 310). Communalization changed not only the rural economic organization form, but also the rural social structure.

Rural organization structure change around 1958

Before 1958

- county government
- township government
- cooperative
- (mutual aid group)
- farmer household

After 1958

- county government
- people's commune
- production brigade
- (administrative district)
- production team
- farmer household

Mass steel campaign

In order to attain the goal "to surpass England and catch up America" at top speed, China initiated its first industrialization wave centering on a mass steel campaign. "We must guarantee the key production of industry first. The key in industry is steel, iron and machinery production, and the development of machinery also depends on steel and iron production" (CPCCC, August 1958, *ILCSFN*, No. 11, pp. 465–6). "If the entire industry is a net, the iron and steel industry is the key link. As long as we take the key link, the entire industry will be brought forward" (*People's Daily*, 8 August 1958).

Reasons to launch the mass steel campaign

- Industrial development in 1958 would greatly surpass any year in history both in scale and at speed and would need massive steel and iron resources.
- The mechanization and electrification of agriculture also relied on steel and iron.
- There would be billions of funds to purchase producer goods due to a great agricultural harvest and rapid development of the rural industry.
- There could be a rapid development next year and more steel and iron would be needed (*People's Daily*, 1 September 1958).
- China was rich in coal and iron mineral resources.
- There were 600 million people in China. These 600 million people were an "invincible strength," "the more the people, the stronger the strength." "They can not only attain a grain harvest in a drought year, but also build plants, look for mineral resources, develop mines, construct rail roads" (*People's Daily*, 8 August 1958).

High steel output target for 1958

- 6.2 million tons with a annual growth rate of 16 percent (February 1958)
- 8–8.5 million tons with a annual growth rate of 50–59 percent (end of May 1958)
- 10.7 million tons with a annual growth rate of 100 percent (August 1958)
  (CPCCC, 31 August 1958, *ILCSFN*, No. 11, pp. 465–6)

In order to realize top speed, the CPCCC raised the target of steel production continually and finally decided to double the steel output from 5.35 million tons in 1957 to 10.7 million tons in 1958. In fact, by the end of August 1958, national steel output was only 4.5 million tons. So, China had to produce more than 6 million tons of steel and iron in the remaining four months in 1958.

Method to promote the mass steel campaign

- "Steel production priority"
  "From now to the end of this year, only 122 days, the target of 10.7 million tons of steel must be realized, one ton short is not allowed." "Guaranteeing with all strength the attainment of doubling steel output is the most important political task currently for our entire party and all people" (*People's Daily*, 1 September 1958). In order to guarantee the completion of the high target, the entire country, all people and all industries were to support and serve for steel production. Because so much coal, electricity and transportation was needed for the steel industry, many non-steel factories had to stop or half stop their production. For example, "light industry has stopped some production

to support the steel industry. Because of the shortage in electric power in the Northeast region, two-thirds of electric power in light industry plants have been cut" and "in Jinan paper mill, five of eight paper-making machines have been stopped" (the Ministry of Light Industry, 7 December 1958, *ILCSFN*, No. 11, pp. 578–9).

- "Small, indigenous and mass" (SIM):[5]

1) Building small backyard furnace in large quantities
In the countryside, local governments had to organize farmers to built small backyard furnaces manually for producing iron and steel.

A. 30 thousand small backyard furnaces newly built in the countryside by July of 1958.
B. The number suddenly increased to more than 170 thousand in August,
C. 600 thousand small backyard furnaces nationally by September of 1958.
D. After October, there were more people put into steel and iron production and they formed battlefields for steel and iron-making in fields, streets and everywhere (Liu and Wu, 1986, p. 223). "The mystery to develop iron and steel was broken" and "iron ores, poor or rich, dispersed in more than half the counties nationally were found and excavated. The army of the steel industry expanded from several hundred thousand to several million people" (*People's Daily*, 1 September 1958).

2) "Indigenous method"[6]
On 8 August 1958, the *People's Daily* argued: "we support the position to take small and indigenous methods as the main way to produce steel" because "at present it is impossible to build large and medium-scale modern plants of iron and steel generally." It indicated that although small and indigenous backyard furnaces were low technology, they actually had merits modern steel and iron plants did not have. "They need little investment, simple equipment and local technology, are easy to learn and construct for the masses in a short time. Taking small and indigenous methods as the main way to produce steel, we may, at the present situation of lacking technicians, steel supply, advanced equipment and funds, mobilize the entire party and people to develop the steel industry ... Not only plants can produce steel, but also institutions, the army, schools, residential districts, handicraft and agricultural cooperatives are able to produce steel."

3) Mobilizing the masses
Mobilizing the masses is mainly to mobilize farmers, who held a dominant share in China's population. The commune provided an extremely good tool for the state to launch the mass steel campaign in the countryside by mobilizing farmers, male and female, old and young rapidly and successfully. For instance, in order to guarantee the ore supply for steel and iron making, the government mobilized all people

> to seek for ores in the mountains. There were many leaders of the party committees who led the masses to go to remote mountains for ores. Teachers and students in elementary and middle schools, People's Liberation Army officers and solders, even 70, and 80 year-old people all went into this campaign. In some provinces, there were even several million people climbing mountains to seek ores. In order to solve the coal shortage, from September 1958 there were about 20 million people with hoes and pot stoves going to the high mountains for coal. By the end of 1958, there were more than 100 thousand small coal pits built nationwide. In order to solve the transportation problem, millions upon millions of people were mobilized to form a vast transportation army with not only modern transportation vehicles such as trains, automobiles, steamboats, airplanes, but also backward tools such as wooden sailboats, mules and handcarts. Even bicycles were used to transport goods in some regions (Liu and Wu, 1986, p. 233).

According to the need of the mass steel campaign and the GLF, an all-round "SIM" campaign was launched by the state in mines, coal, electric power, machinery and transportation industries. It was said that if there were a need, a mass "SIM" campaign would be organized and all people would be put into the campaign (Liu and Wu, 1986, p. 233).

In the second half of 1958, millions upon millions of farmers were put into the mass steel campaign. According to an investigation in 17 provinces, more than 600 thousand furnaces of steel and iron smelting, and 59 thousand coal pits had already been established, which produced more than 500 thousand tons of crude iron. In the same period, the government also mobilized about 20 percent of animal-drawn and handcarts and 30 percent of wooden sailboats to participate in the transportation for the mass steel campaign. The volume of goods transported accounted for about 20 percent of the total national transport in the same year. A huge number of farmers were organized to construct roads and railroads too. In 150 thousand kilometers of roads newly built nationally in this year, about two-thirds were constructed by the people's communes" (Liu and Wu, 1986, p. 238).

To promote rural industry with great effort

While launching the mass steel campaign, China also impelled rural industry with great effort. "The commune must go in for rural industry in a big way and gradually transfer a suitable number of the labor force from agriculture to industry to develop, according to the plan, light and heavy industries such as agricultural and products processing tools and machines" (CPCCC, 10 December 1958, *ILCSFN*, No. 11, pp. 609–10). "The current shortage of product supply and agricultural product processing can be solved only by going in for commune industry in a big way." "Each commune should make 80%–90% of the industrial products used by the commune itself." "Communes have everything for developing industry. They have enough funds, labor and whatever for industrial development. There is nothing the communes may not or cannot develop successfully." "We should go all out to mobilize the masses into communes to develop industry" (CPCCC, 7 December 1958, *ILCSFN*, No. 11, pp. 581–2)

Methods to impel rural industry

- The government organizing and promoting
  Government makes plans to determine the number of rural enterprises. For example: Gansu provincial government in December 1959 requested that each commune in 1960 must build nine factories (farm tool factories, power plants, chemical fertilizer plants, agricultural chemical factories, comprehensive processing factories, grain and cooking oil processing factories, garment factories, brick, tile and stone and lime-making factories, coal mines or mining plants) and one building team (Gansu provincial committee of the CPC, 1960, *ILCSFN*, No. 13, p. 736). The feature of these plans is that the quotas formed by lower government levels will be larger than those formed by higher government levels for the same level. For example, in a county plan, a commune will build five enterprises. However, in the commune plan, the number usually was more than five.
- The government providing resources
  In the GLF in 1958, the majority of increase in China's rural industry came from the state.
  1) Transferring 25.5 thousand urban handicrafts cooperatives with 1.28 million members into commune-run industries.
  2) Transferring part of state-owned enterprises in rural areas into commune-run enterprises.
  3) In the first half of 1960, more than 500 thousand small-scale handicraftsmen and merchants in cities were moved to rural areas and traffic sectors.
  4) Some state-owned industrial sectors such as the Ministry of Light Industry used their own funds and technology to help the communes to build enterprises in the same industry.
  5) Transferring state-owned rural basic units of commerce, grain, finance and banks into communes, except those which served for several people's communes.
  6) State investment for supporting the commune.
- "The equalitarianism and indiscriminate transfer of resources" (EITR).[7]:
  The EITR made primitive accumulation for rural industry.
  1) Transferring all industrial equipment, funds and other properties of small factories, workshops, sideline production teams (groups) of agricultural producers' cooperatives to communes.

2) Transferring household sideline production, handicrafts, small family factories, personal workshops, private plots, domestic animals and fowls of farmers to the communes.
3) Transferring more than 35 thousand handicraft cooperatives (groups) in rural areas and small towns to the commune industry.
4) Transferring planters and breeding farms of cooperatives to the communes (Hu and Zheng, 1996, p. 37 and 39)

- Doing the job with local methods
  Although there was a massive labor supply in China's countryside, most of them received no education, and even were illiterate. Developing rural industry in China lacked not only funds, technology and management but also skilled workers. The communes had to "do the job with local methods." "To develop industry in the commune we may start first from SIM, then gradually change to half SIM and half modern" (CPCCC, 7 December 1958, *ILCSFN*, No. 11, p. 577 and 583). "For production technology, we should combine handicrafts with machine industry, indigenous with modern production ... to change gradually from native to modern methods, from small to large scale, from low to high level" (CPCCC, 10 December 1958, *ILCSFN*, No. 11, p. 610). The features of commune-owned industry in the GLF were:
  1) Small scale with few workers
  2) Low technology such as manual technology with some simple tools and little investment
  3) Poor quality, many of them were so poor that no use could be found for them.
- Decentralization
  1) Forming large regions
     At the beginning of June 1958, the state decided to divide the nation into seven cooperative regions: Northeast, North China, East China, South China, Central China, Southwest, and Northwest regions. Each region was requested to establish large-scale backbone industry and economic centers as soon as possible in order to enhance local incentive.
  2) Transferring the central-run enterprises
     In order to speed up industrialization, "all of the enterprises run by central industry ministries and part of non-industry ministries of the State Council should be transferred to local governments and be under local management, except some special ones as well as enterprises for experimental purpose" (CPCCC, 11 April 1958, *ILCSFN*, No. 11, p. 264). At the beginning of June 1958, the state requested the completion of the transition of the majority of these central-run enterprises. In less than twenty days, by 15 June, more than 880 enterprises and institutes were transferred to local management, accounting for 80 percent of the entire central-run enterprises and institutions.

3) Transferring recruiting rights
   At the end of June 1958, the state transferred the rights of labor recruiting, adjusting and planning for state-owned enterprises to local governments.
4) Transferring the rights to examine and approve projects
   In September 1958, the state stipulated that the majority of large and middle scale construction projects would be examined and approved by local governments and central ministries directly.
5) Lifting the ban on issuing local construction bonds by provinces, cities and autonomous regions in 1958 (Liu and Wu, 1986, p. 226).
6) "Two transitions" in the countryside
   The state transferred both personnel and properties of rural state-owned enterprises and institutes to the people's commune.

Decentralization enhanced greatly the incentive of local governments to develop local industry, including rural industry. For example, in the backward Gansu province, "from January to March of 1958, there were approximately 1,000 factories built there. From March to May, about 3,500 new enterprises were put up ... From May to June, there were more than 220 thousand factories newly built. The counties, townships, communes, schools, as well as various institutes all went into the hot wave of local industrialization" (Liu and Wu, 1986, p. 226).

- Favorable tax policy
  Such as exemption from income tax of industry and commerce.
- Mobilizing the masses
  Rural industry was developed to build small enterprises everywhere in the rural areas. The CPCCC (7 December 1958) argued that the important thing was to go all out to mobilize farmers of communes, and the main barrier for impelling both industry and agriculture simultaneously and developing commune industry was whether to mobilize the masses or not (*ILCSFN*, No. 11, pp. 583–4). Under the government's impetus, rural industry, centering on agricultural industry, rapidly developed, and nearly every commune set up small factories and workshops.

Features of the rural industry in the GLF

The main characteristic is that rural industry had communes, and production brigade-owned enterprises (CPBOE) only. In 1958, the state permitted rural industry to develop only at commune level, that is, all rural enterprises were run by the commune. Individuals, and even the production brigades were unable to run enterprises. In February 1959, production brigades were allowed to develop industry. The duty for a commune was "to operate and manage, under national plans, industry, transportation, commerce and finance for the entire commune; which are not suitable for disperse management." Production brigades could "develop and manage some small-scale factories for their own uses such as farm tools, chemical fertilizer made by local methods, brickyards, tailoring and shoe-making, grain processing factories etc., and also simultaneously organize and manage, under national plans, various sideline and agricultural products processing, which are suitable for disperse management" (CPCCC, February 1959, *ILCSFN*, No. 12, p. 135 and 137). However, the state still forbade private enterprise to develop.

Common dining hall and free welfare services campaign

One of the important contents in China's rural GLF was the free welfare services campaign, centering on the common dining hall (CDH). The *People's Daily* editorial entitled "To Run the Common Dining Hall Well" (25 October 1958) pointed out that distribution was the key issue for the people's commune after the basic completion of communalization nationally. "At present we must develop collective welfare undertakings, especially the CDH and the nursery for realizing a military-style organization, action in a soldierly way and collectivization of life." "To run the collective welfare undertakings well, especially the CDH, already becomes an extremely important work in the current people's communalization campaign, and a key for consolidating the commune." At the same time, the CPCC also made a call to develop kindergartens, nurseries, clothes groups, haircut rooms, public bath halls, happiness homes, middle schools, red-and-expert schools and so on to lead farmers to a happier collective life. "We will gradually reform the existing old-style houses and construct new botanical garden residential centers in villages and townships, including houses, CDHs, nurseries, kindergartens, happy homes for the elderly, factories, threshing floors, animal sheds, stores, post and telecommunications offices, warehouses, schools, hospitals, clubs, movie theaters, stadiums, bathrooms, restrooms and so on" (CPCCC, 10 December 1958, *ILCSFN*, No. 11, pp. 615–16).

Method to promote the CDH campaign

- State push
- Controlling the grain ration
  There was a grain supply system in the commune. If a CDH were established, the grain ration for farmers' daily life would be sent to the CDH directly. So, the farmers had to join the CDH for meals as soon as a CDH was formed.
- Deciding the scale of a CDH
  Generally a common dining hall for a production team or an enterprise or an institute.
- Establishing temporary CDHs
  A temporary CDH might be established for a shock mission.
- Establishing production bases
  A CDH should have its own production base to raise pigs, sheep, fish, domesticated fowl, and process part of agricultural products for its own use. (*People's Daily*, 25 October 1958)

Features of the rural common dining hall

The largest feature of a rural CDH is "to eat without paying." "From this time on, families who in the past worried frequently about food and daily necessities, might 'eat without paying,' in other words, they obtained a most important and reliable social security" (CPCCC, 10 December, 1958, *ILCSFN*, No. 11, p. 599).

There were a huge number of people who participated in the rural common dining halls. The percentage of farmers who joined a common dining hall in rural areas reached an astonishing level in many provinces. For example, in Henan Province, the rate was as high as 97. 8 percent. Almost all farmers in the province participated in the common dining halls.

The GLF also developed many rural public warfare undertakings. "The communes implemented a distribution system combining wages with the grain supply system and vigorously promoted 'eating without paying,' and tried to form a free system covering everything or the majority of the people's lives. By the end of 1958, more than 3.4 million common dining halls and various nurseries as well as 150 thousand happiness homes were established in China's countryside" (Liu and Wu, 1986, p. 238). In some regions communes were even "taking on seven things" or "taking on ten things" for commune members. The "taking on seven things" provided the members with free meals, clothes, housing, education, free services for child-bearing, weddings and funerals, medical care and so on. Compared to the seven things, the "taking on ten things" included three more things such as free heating in winter, haircuts, play or film-seeing and so on" (Liu and Wu, 1986, p. 238). Mao in February 1959 indicated with surprise: "There are unexpectedly thousands of people not engaged in production, even ensembles in some large communes" (*ILCSFN*, No. 12, p. 129).

Table 3.3 The percentage of farmers participating in common dining halls in the total commune population by the end of 1959

National share (%)	*Provinces with a share of more than 90%*		*Provinces with a share of 70%–90%*		*Provinces with a share of 50%–70%*		*Provinces with a share below 50%*	
72. 6	Henan	98	Beijing	87	Hubei	68	Gansu	48
	Hunan	98	Xinjiang	85	Fujian	67	Shandong	36
	Sichuan	97	Zhejiang	82	Jiangxi	61	Qinghai	30
	Yunnan	97	Guangxi	81	Shaanxi	61	Jilin	29
	Guizhou	93	Guangdong	78	Jiangsu	56	Heilongjiang	27
	Shanghai	95	Hebei	74	Ningxia	53	Liaoning	23
	Anhui	91	Shanxi	71			Inner Mongolia	17

Source: "On strengthening common dining halls", CPCCC, 18 March 1960, *ILCSFN*, No. 13, p. 89.
Note: by the end of 1959, there were 3.9 million common dining halls and about 4 hundred million people participating in common dining halls in China.

The irrigation work campaign

The irrigation work campaign was launched throughout rural areas in the GLF. "Since last winter, irrigated areas have increased by 450 million Chinese acres. Adding the original 970 million Chinese acres of irrigated area, the irrigated area already occupies 57% of the existing farming land in China, more than one-third of the world existing irrigated areas. So, if we work hard for two winters and two springs, we will realize the goal to bring all of China's existing farmlands under irrigation" (CPCCC, 29 August 1958, *ILCSFN*, No. 11, p. 455). In order to realize the goal, in 1958 China made a grand plan for farmland water conservancy construction. On 29 August 1958, the CPCCC instructed: "both strengthening the party's leadership and giving free rein to the spirit of communist large-scale cooperation since last winter are the keys for completing smoothly the water conservation campaign in 1959" (*ILCSFN*, No. 11, p. 458).

Target for water conservation campaign in 1959 (made in August 1958)

- To increase the irrigated area of 490 million Chinese acres
- To control the waterlogged area of 72.81 million Chinese acres
- To complete 96.1 billion cubic meters of earth and stone work (the state plan)
- To complete 100 billion cubic meters of earth and stone work (local plans) (CPCCC, 29 August 1958, *ILCSFN*, No. 11, p. 456).

Plans for national water conservation systems

- To move water from the South (mainly the Yangtze River system) to the North, to unify the Jiang, Huai, He, Han and Haihe basins as one water system
- To unify the Song and Liao basins as one water system
- To make local plans by local governments respectively.

Methods to promote the irrigation work campaign in 1958

- State plan
  First, the Ministry of Agriculture held the Xiangyang Conference (twelve provinces and regions in the South) and the Zhengzhou Conference (provinces and regions in the North) in May and June (of 1958) respectively and made plans for water conservation projects. Then, according to the plans, the quotas were distributed to each province and region.
- Large-scale mass communist cooperation
  1) Regardless of the regional boundary between communes, townships, counties, and even provinces, to construct trans-region and trans-department projects.
  2) To mobilize farmers with their own tools and food to construct water and soil conservation projects in mountainous areas, construct reservoirs, drill wells, and so on.

- "Three priorities"
  1) The "small scale project priority"
  2) The "water storage project priority"
  3) The "commune-run project priority"
- Self-reliance
  Relying on farmers' own strengths with state aid as a subsidiary to construct the projects.
- Using different methods to solve water conservation issues in different areas
  1) Methods suitable for plains and low-lying easily waterlogged areas
  2) Methods suitable for mountainous, half-mountainous and hilly and plateau areas
  3) Methods suitable for serious leakage areas
  4) Methods suitable for soil erosion areas
  5) Methods to combine construction with use of water conservation works
- Reforming tools and improving operations technology

(CPCC, 29 August 1958, *ILCSFN*, No. 11, p. 456 and 457)

Because the water conservation projects mainly depended on labor for their completion, they became the best demonstration to show the superiority of the commune. Under the state's impetus, a huge number of farmers were organized into "a construction army for water conservation" and completed many large projects in the GLF. However, "in the three years of great development, the center of development was on the construction of new projects and neglected the maintenance and management of projects completed in many regions. So, construction divided management and led to a reduction of benefit from these projects, even to a serious destruction of the projects completed" (Leading Team of CPC of the Ministry of Water Resources and Electric Power, 25 November 1961, *ILCSFN*, No. 14, p. 860).

High procurement of grain

The high procurement of grain in the GLF was not only a necessity for the GLF, but also a direct result of the "exaggeration wind." The "heavy industry priority" strategy led not only to a mass steel campaign in the countryside, but also to the flow of large numbers of farmers to cities to support industry. So the demand for grain in the cities rose greatly, which required a high procurement of grain. On the other hand, the GLF fomented an "exaggeration wind"[8] in China, especially in the rural areas. Reported grain yields increased rapidly, created new records and finally achieved an unimagined level which made the high procurement reasonable.

Due to communalization, agricultural products procurement became easier and simpler than before. Instead of collecting grain from huge numbers of individual farmers, through the communes, the quotas of grain procurement

Table 3.4 China's grain purchase and its share in total grain output in the GLF (million tons)

Year	*Estimated output*	*Real output*	*Purchase volume*	*Net purchase volume*	*Share of purchase in the yield* (%)	*Share of net purchase in the yield* (%)
1956		193	45	29	23.6	14.9
1957		195	48	34	24.6	17.4
1958	375	200	59	42	29.4	20.9
1959	525	170	67	48	39.7	28.0
1960		144	51	31	35.6	21.5
1961		148	40	26	27.4	17.5

Source: *CSY* 1984, p. 370 and the "Resolution on 1959 National Economic Plan", CPCCC, 10 December 1958, *ILCSFN*, No. 11, p. 633.
Notes: 1) The estimated output comes from the "Resolution on 1959 National economic planning," CPCCC, 10 December 1958.
2) The net purchase volume is the total volum of purchase that subtracts the grain back to rural poor farmers.

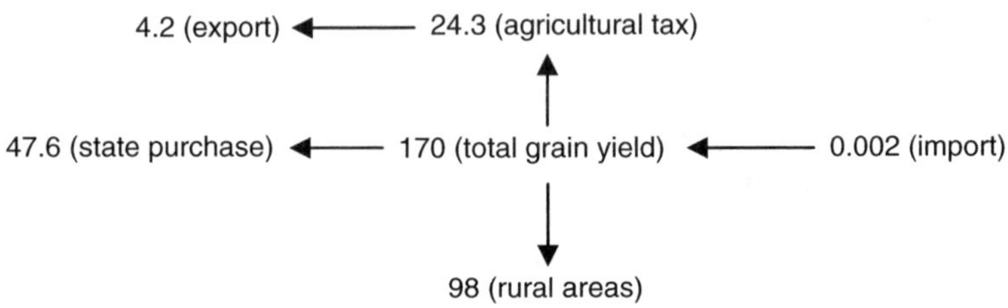

Figure 3.3 China's grain distribution in 1959 (million tons)
Source: *CSY* 1984.
Note: the agricultural tax is calculated on its share in total grain yield in 1959 (14 per cent) from "New China 50 years Government Finance statistics," Lou Jiwei, Economic Science Press, 2000, p. 74.

would be distributed from communes to production brigades, then to production teams level by level. Therefore, according to the procurement quotas, production teams directly offered grain to the commune, then to the state. Because the communes controlled all grain, it was unnecessary for government to deal with individual farmers directly about grain procurement.

Although the commune was helpful for grain procurement, the procurement in 1958 was not an easy one. Procurement plans of grain, cotton, edible oils and other agricultural products in 1958 were not completed until March 1959. As Mao said in February 1959: "farmers are carrying on a 'firm resistance' to grain procurement. Nearly all production brigades and production teams under-report real output and distribute the grain among farmers secretly." Mao did not mention (possibly did not think about) the influence of the "exaggeration wind" on procurement. In fact, in many rural areas, there was not much grain reported in 1958 at all, it was not that farmers did not want to hand over the grain to the state, but that they really had no grain to offer the state. As shown in Table 3.4, the grain procured was 59 million tons in 1958, with a rate of 22 percent compared to that in 1957. However, the actual total output of grain only grew at a rate of 2.5 percent in the same year. The share of the grain procured in the total output increased from 24.6 percent in 1957 to 29.4 percent in 1958 and 39.7 percent in 1959.

Popularizing the rural education campaign

The CPCCC (10 December 1958) indicated that a profound significance of the commune system was to eliminate finally the differences between mental and physical labor. "The commune will implement universal compulsory education combined with labor and set up elementary and spare time schools to enable school-age children to enter school. Young and mature adults can study in continuation schools to reach the degree of senior primary school. Each production brigade should set up an after-work agricultural middle school to make all young and mature farmers study to the level of high school. If possible, training schools or universities which meet the needs of the commune should be established" (Cha Yashan Satellite People's Commune, 7 August 1958, *ILCSFN*, No. 11, p. 390).

Target of the campaign in the GLF

- Eliminating rural illiteracy in young and mature people in twelve years from 1956 (CPCCC, 25 October 1957, *ILCSFN*, No. 10, p. 653)
- Striving to eliminate rural illiteracy in 5–7 years (CPCCC, 8 April 1958, *ILCSFN*, No. 11, p. 255)
- Striving to eliminate rural illiteracy before 1962 (CPCCC, 2 April 1960, *ILCSFN*, No. 13, p. 214)

Methods to promote the campaign

- To realize rural universal education at elementary school level ahead of time and to make great efforts to develop commune-run primary schools.
- To popularize secondary education by developing commune-run agricultural middle schools and other professional middle schools, and to manage full-time and part-time agricultural middle schools or other secondary vocational schools.
- To promote commune-run agricultural middle schools.
  1) The people's communes, not the state, would organize and run the schools and the people who studied there would pay the fees for running the schools. These schools introduce a part time study system and serve for local production.

2) 3-year program. Generally the agricultural middle schools had a 3-year program.
3) Curricula in the schools were politics, Chinese, mathematics and agricultural knowledge (or related technical knowledge).
4) Teachers in these schools came from graduates of senior middle schools who did not enter college; cadres who were transferred to rural area from cities; teachers doing some teaching in addition to their main job at elementary or middle schools, and cadres at the agricultural technology extension stations.
5) Rural schools could use accommodation such as ancestral halls, temples, public buildings, and private houses.

- Popularizing spare time education and literacy classes to eliminate adult illiteracy
  Each commune must form literacy classes everywhere and organize farmers to learn in their spare time. (CPCCC, 8 April 1958, *ILCSFN*, No. 11, pp. 255–61)

Features of the rural education campaign

- Large-scale
  The campaign went everywhere with huge number of farmers participating in it.
- High speed
  Many schools were set up rapidly. For example, to set up one school took only four days in Shuang Lou township (xiang), Haian county, Jiangsu province, and seven days for two schools in Shi Qiao township (xiang), Hanjiang county in the same province (CPCCC, 8 April 1958, *ILCSFN*, No. 11, p. 257). It was said that in only a few months, several hundred thousand schools were established nationwide.
- Simple
  Most of the agricultural middle schools established by the communes had no facilities except rooms or houses used as classrooms. Each student paid a few yuan for tuition each term. It was reported that the township government spent only a few jiaos (1 jiao =1/10 of a yuan) for chalks to construct an agricultural middle school in Shuang Lou township (xiang), Haian county, Jiangsu province (CPCCC, 8 April 1958, *ILCSFN*, No. 11, p. 258).

China's rural education expanded greatly during the GLF. The Ministry of Education (4 March 1960) reported that only four months after the CPCCC authorized the report of the Ministry of Education titled "On further eliminating rural illiteracy and developing spare-time education" of October 1959, the eliminating rural illiteracy and spare-time education campaign had progressed very quickly. By February 1960, the number of people participating in the eliminating illiteracy and spare-time study campaign reached more than 132 million, about 66 percent of total rural young adults. It was an increase of 150 percent compared to 50 million people in October 1959. Among these, participation in eliminating illiteracy was over 60.5 million people, more than 63.8 million in spare-time elementary school, more than 7.7 million in spare-time secondary school and more than 43 thousand in spare-time college. In 1959, the number of rural residents who overcame illiteracy, nationally achieved 24 million (including some urban residents). At the same time, there were also many persons who graduated from spare-time secondary schools (CPCCC, 2 April 1960, *ILCSFN*, No. 13, p. 215).

3.4 Rural industrialization in process

On 19 December 1958, China officially announced that the target to double its steel output had been attained twelve days ahead of time. Its iron and steel industry realized a great leap forward (Liu and Wu, 1986, p. 235). In the countryside, in little more than four months after the communes were established in 1958, many small industrial enterprises suddenly emerged and developed rapidly. Most of them were for agricultural production and daily life. For example, in Hebei province, the share of enterprises for agricultural production and daily life in the total number of commune-run enterprises was 93 percent with a share of 80 percent in the total output value in 1958 (Zhang, 1990, p. 14). Although rural industry, strengthened by the communes made a great leap forward in 1958, it dropped afterwards, especially in the number of its enterprises, which fell from 2.6 million in 1958 to 117 thousand in 1960. Its output value experienced a rise from 6.25 billion yuan in 1958 to 10 billion yuan in 1959, followed by a fall to 5 billion yuan in 1960 and less than 2 billion yuan with only 45 thousand enterprises in 1961.

Rural infrastructure also developed rapidly during the GLF. A number of houses, roads and hospitals were built. Rural telephone subscribers increased from 200 thousand in 1957 to 920 thousand in 1960, with

Table 3.5 Commune-owned industrial enterprises in the GLF 1958–61

Year	*Number of enterprises (ten thousand)*	*Annual growth rate of enterprises (%)*	*Output (billion yuan)*
1958	260		6.25
May 1959	87	–67	7.34
1959	70	–20	10
1960	11.7	–83	5
1961	4.5	–62	1.98

Source: *The hard course of TVE*, Zhang Yi, Law Publishing House, 1990, p. 16

Table 3.6 China's rural labor structure 1957–61 (million persons)

Year	*Rural population*		*Rural labor*								
	Total	*Share in national population* (%)	*Total*	*Industry*	*Construction prospecting*	*Farming, forestry water conservation meteorological*	*Transportation communications*	*Catering commerce service*	*Science, culture, health, education*	*Government associations*	*Other*
1957	547	84.6	206	3.2	4.5	192.0	1.5	1.6	1.2	1.5	0.3
1958	553	83.8	213	18.5	20.0	151.2	5.0	11.5	4.5	2.0	0.3
1959	548	81.6	208	5.8	18.4	158.2	3.1	11.6	4.6	2.5	3.7
1960	531	80.3	198	4.6	4.10	163.3	3.0	12.9	4.0	2.4	3.3
1961	532	80.7	203	1.9	2.0	191.3	1.0	0.7	1.3	2.5	1.9

Source: *China labor and wages statistical materials 1949–85*, the social statistical department of SSB, China Statistical Publishing House, 1987.

Table 3.7 China's industry and agriculture development 1957–60

Year	*Index of primary industry GDP*	*Index of secondary industry GDP*	*Primary Industry GDP (bill. yuan)*	*Share of primary industry in national GDP*	*Average per capita grain (Kg/person)*	*Grain yield (mil. tons)*
1957	103.1	108.0	43.0	40.3	306	195.1
1958	100.4	152.9	44.6	34.1	306	200.0
1959	84.1	125.8	38.4	26.7	255	170.0
1960	83.6	105.6	34.1	23.4	215	143.5

Source: *New China 50 Years Statistical Data Assembly*, the national economy synthesis statistics department of SSB, Chinese Statistics Publishing House, 1999.

Notes: 1) GDP and the share are calculated at current prices.
2) The indices are based on comparable prices and the previous year = 100.
3) Secondary industry contains industry and the construction industry.

Table 3.8 China's household and per capita consumption 1957–61 (kilograms, yuan)

	Household consumption			*Per capita consumption*				
Year	*Rural*	*(index)*	*Urban*	*Urban*	*Rural*			
				Grain	Grain	Vegetable oil	Pork	Eggs
1957	82	(102.0)	222	196	205	2	4.5	1
1958	86	(102.5)	212	186	201	2	4.5	1
1959	70	(80.8)	224	201	183	2	2.5	0.5
1960	73	(95.5)	236	193	156	1.5	1	0.5
1961	87	(101.3)	248	180	154	1.5	1.5	0.5

Source: *New China 50 Years Statistical Data Assembly*, the national economic synthesis statistics department of SSB, Chinese Statistics Publishing House, 1999 and *Chinese Trade Price Statistical Data 1952–83*, the trade price statistics department of SSB, Chinese Statistics Publishing House, 1984.

Notes: 1) The grain is trade grain.
2) Index is previous year=100.

Table 3.9 Population statistics in China 1957–61

Year	*Population (million persons)*		*Death rate (person per thousand)*			*Death increase (million persons)*
	urban	*rural*	*national*	*urban*	*rural*	
1957	99	547	10.8	8.5	11.1	
1958	107	552	12.0	9.2	12.5	0.8
1959	123	548	14.6	10.9	14.6	2.6
1960	130	531	25.4	13.8	28.6	9.7
1961	127	531	14.2	11.4	14.6	2.3

Source: *CSY* 1984 and 1991. The data of death increase is from *The Political Economy of Agro-Industrial Relations in Contemporary China*, Katsuji, Nakagane, University of Tokyo Publishing House, 1992, p. 231.

an increase in rural post offices from 38 thousand to 54 thousand. Rural electricity consumption jumped from 108 million kW in 1957 to 692 million kW in 1960 (*CSY* 1983 and "Modern China Electricity Industry", 1994).

The rapid rural industry development promoted farmer movements nationally. Firstly, a number of farmers moved to the cities. The share of the rural population in the national population decreased from 85 percent in 1957 to 80 percent in 1960, a drop of about 5 percentage points. Secondly, a huge number of farmers rushed into non-agricultural industries in the GLF, which changed the rural labor structure rapidly. As shown in Table 3.6, the labor supply in non-agriculture sectors increased greatly in

1958, especially in industry, in which the labor supply suddenly jumped from 3 million in 1957 to 19 million in 1958, more than five times as much as that in 1957. On the contrary, the labor supply in farming and related sectors decreased from 192 million in 1957 to 151 million in 1958, a reduction of around 21 percent.

Compared with rural industry, China's agriculture experienced serious damage in the GLF. The grain yield decreased from 195 million tons in 1957 to 148 million tons in 1961 and the per capita grain level went down to 215 kilograms in 1960, a drop of 30 percent compared with 1957. As shown in Table 3.8, in the GLF the rural annual consumption of the average family dropped sharply and the rural annual per capita grain consumption had a great reduction too. Compared with 1957, grain consumption dropped 24 percent in 1960. In 1961 the rural annual per capita consumption of cooking oil and eggs was only one half as much as that in 1957.

Because of the lack of grain, a panic famine spread in the GLF nationwide. Many people starved to death. Nakagane (1992, p. 231) argued that the non-normal death in the GLF was about 15 million people. Table 3.9 indicates that the annual per capita grain consumption in urban areas was more than in rural areas and the rural mortality rate was very high, more than twice as high as the urban one in 1960, which shows that the state mainly guaranteed the urban grain supply only, which made the great famine spread mainly in the countryside.

3.5 Policy effects

The GLF impelled rural industrialization greatly but damaged agriculture seriously

Although the GLF impelled rural industrialization through 1958–60, it resulted in a serious reduction of agriculture, which brought about a strong conflict between rural industry and agriculture from the very beginning of China's rural industry, namely, developing rural industry would harm agriculture. The conflict had a huge and profound influence on China's rural economy and industrialization as well as national economy. It changed China's industrialization strategy and damaged rural industrialization greatly. This will be discussed in the next chapter.

A theoretical frame work for growth in the GLF

A two-sector model with only industry (i) and agriculture (a) sectors will be applied to an analysis of economic growth in the GLF. Therefore, its C-D production function is as follows:

$$Y = F\,(L, K) \qquad (1)$$

$$Y_i = F_i\,(L_i, K_i) \qquad (2)$$

$$Y_a = F_a\,(L_a, K_a) \qquad (3)$$

where Y = total output, Y_i = industrial output, Y_a = agriculture output, L = total labor, L_i = labor in industry, L_a = labor in agriculture, K = total capital, K_i = capital in industry, K_a = capital in agriculture. Therefore, we may obtain:

$$Y = Y_i + Y_a = F_i\,(L_i, K_i) + F_a\,(L_a, K_a) \quad (4)$$
$$L = L_i + L_a \quad (5)$$
$$K = K_i + K_a \quad (6)$$

This model shows that industry and agriculture are highly related, that is, under a certain amount of labor and capital, any change in labor or capital in a sector will affect the labor or capital in another sector, then the corresponding output.

Effects of the GLF on the input in each sector

- A massive increase in labor and investment of industry
  The state invested not only the surplus from industry, but also the agricultural surplus and part of private consumption in industrial reproduction. Not only did a number of farmers transfer from rural to urban areas for industry, but also many farmers mobilized to join rural and national industry.
- A massive reduction of agricultural labor and a very small increase in agricultural investment
  From equation (5), we can get:

$$L_a = L - L_i \quad (7)$$

  Because the total national labor (L) was constant, an increase in industrial labor would certainly lead to a decrease in agricultural labor correspondingly. In the same way, there was very little increase in agricultural investment.

Growth pattern of the GLF

- Expanding the industry sector
  Rapid industry expansion in the GLF came from two sides. First, along with a rapid increase in industrial capital, the industrial production function curve shifts rapidly to the upper left side unceasingly. As shown in Figure 3.4, the curve moves from F_{i1} to F_{i2} and to F_{i3} ... This meant that even if labor stays invariable, industry output still increases continuously. Secondly, the increase in industrial labor pushes the output curve to the right side. As a result of the increase in both labor and investment, the industrial output grows not along one production function curve, but jumps along several different curves. As shown in Figure 3.4, when the labor force increases from L_1 to L_2, and to L_3, the industrial output also jumps continuously. Therefore, the total effect of the GLF on the industry should be a growth from point O_1 to O_2, and to O_3 ...

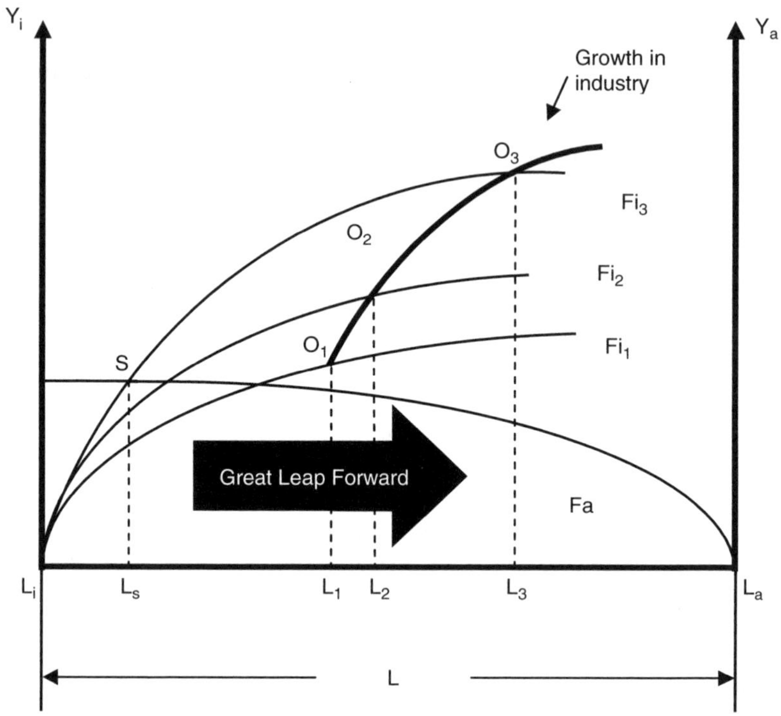

Figure 3.4 The growth pattern of the GLF

- Contracting the agriculture sector
  When there is no new investment, the agricultural production curve F_a keeps invariable, that is, the growth of agriculture is along one production curve. At the same time, the massive labor reduction in agriculture puts the output to the right side too, which leads a drop in the agricultural sector.
- Causing the national economy to grow at high speed
  Although there was a reduction in agriculture, the total national economy grew at high speed because the increment of industrial output was much larger than the decrement in agricultural output, $\Delta Y_i > \Delta Y_a$.

Great developments in rural industry and a serious drop in agriculture

- Great and comprehensive development of rural industrialization
  The GLF completed the primitive accumulation of industry and rapidly established rural industry. At the same time, it also developed large-scale education and public welfare services in rural areas. The GLF led a great and earth-shaking change and had a strong impact on the feudal, conservative and backward countryside.

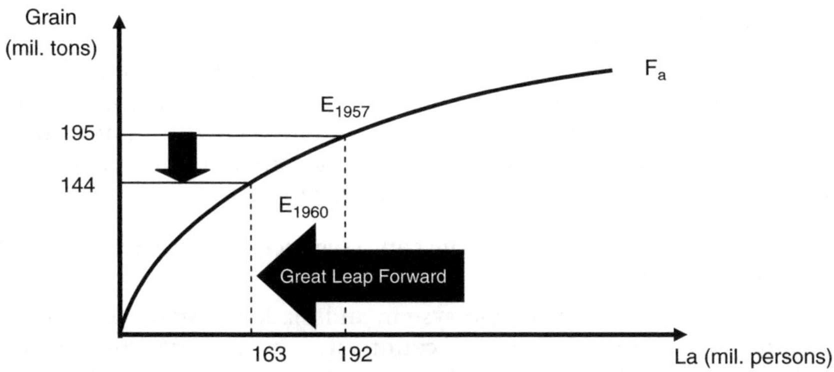

Figure 3.5 China's grain drop 1957–60

- A serious drop in agriculture
  Because the agriculture at that time depended heavily on manual labor, the massive reduction of labor in agriculture damaged agriculture seriously and led to a great drop in grain yield.

The puzzle of Lewis's theory for the rural GLF

Lewis (1954) put forward the theory that there is labor with negligible marginal productivity in developing countries and there would be no influence on agriculture in transferring labor from the agricultural to the industrial sector, on the contrary, the transfer would promote economic growth. However, the shift of labor from agriculture to industry in the GLF had an unfavorable influence on agriculture. Why cannot Lewis' theory explain the growth? In fact, the growth of the GLF was very similar to the development pattern described by Lewis' theory to expand industry by transferring rural labor to industry. The GLF should be consistent with Lewis' theory. The key to the puzzle lies in the labor that was transferred from agriculture: that is, if it was surplus with a negligible marginal productivity or not. If yes, the transfer would not affect agriculture. If no, agricultural production would be affected. As we indicated above, a huge number of farmers were put into mass steel and other industries, so there was no one to harvest the crops in the fields in many regions. Certainly the labor transferred from the agricultural to the industrial sector included non-surplus farmers, which caused the agriculture to drop. In the GLF, the condition for Lewis' theory was not met. So we cannot prove that Lewis' theory is wrong. On the contrary, the growth pattern of the GLF, in which China's economy developed through transferring farmers and expanding industry, proved to some extent that Lewis' theory is correct. However, why did the GLF not act like Lewis' growth theory? The mechanism of labor shift is the key. In the GLF, government made the shift, but in Lewis' theory, market is the decisive force. The market mechanism is able to prevent non-surplus labor from leaving agriculture by labor price, but a central command mechanism cannot do it at all. The shortcoming of Lewis' theory is that it only describes the growth in market economy and neglects government interference in economic development, which is a common thing in developing nations. That leads to a limitation for its application.

Communalization constructed the campaign economy with a huge labor army and no plan

Communalization broke the old system and made the state complete its comprehensive control over the countryside, which brought a earth-shaking change to China's self-sufficient small peasant economy. Although the form of the people's commune was changed several times, its basic structure and function remained essentially unchanged.

Huge labor army

The cooperative campaign only transformed the private ownership system, but communalization completely eliminated private ownership and established a centralized public one. It organized farmers into a vast labor army. Under commune control, the labor army would do every thing according to state policy, which provided China with a guarantee to expand its economy through inputting massive low-cost labor to make up its funds and technology shortages.

Campaign economy with no plan

- No plan economy

  Although the state exerted highly centralized governing on the rural economy, it was unable to make a complete and scientific plan because of the majority of leaders at various levels were farmers or military officers with no secondary education, and some of them were illiterate. They had been farmers for generations under the small peasant economy and did not have the ability to formulate a strict plan and manage the huge labor army. Also there were no suitable conditions and environment to carry on a large-scale and planned production in the rural areas. So the so-called plans did not have binding force and could be changed at will. The following are some examples of the so-called plans:

  1) The first "five-year plan"

     China started to work out the plan in the spring of 1951 under the Soviet Union's help and did not complete it until February 1955 (Liu and Wu, 1986, p. 105). The reason for the long time was mainly that the targets in the plan did not conform to the reality. For example, in the initial plan, the annual average growth rate in agriculture was 7 percent. However, because the real rate in both 1953 and 1954 did not attain the target continuously, the plan was adjusted to 4.3 percent (Liu and Wu, 1986 p. 109). Even though the plan was revised several times, there was still a big gap between the final plan and actual results.

2) Steel output plan in 1958
The steel output plan in 1958 showed the features of the so-called plans much more clearly. The target of steel output in 1958 was raised continuously and groundlessly, and finally achieved the high peak of 10.7 million tons. However, the CPCCC in August 1958 suddenly decided to double the steel output in 1958, with only four months left and more than half of the new target, six million tons of steel to make. In fact, this kind of plan is no plan at all.
3) Grain yield plan in the GLF
In the grain yield plan, "exaggeration winds" and "confused orders" emerged one after another everywhere. The paddy yield per mu reported even amounted to more than 65 tons unexpectedly (Liu and Wu, 1986 p. 227). The difference between the grain yield estimated by the CPCCC (300–350 million tons) and real yield (200 million tons) in 1958 was 100–150 million tons, 50–75 percent of the real yield! It is impossible to make a real plan without basic scientific knowledge.

- Campaign economy concentrating on "one target only"
Without a plan, it is impossible to organize an economic activity under the centralized system with a huge labor army. Therefore, there are two features in the system:
1) Changing the center for development unceasingly
Because the center decided has to adapt to the changeable economic situation continually.
2) Concentrating on "one target only" (high target)

The centralized system with a huge labor army and no plan led to the wave-like development in China, that is, "to rush headlong into mass action and to pull out in mass action too."

Communization promoted rural industrialization and also the famine in the GLF

One of Communalization goals initially was to organize the GLF easily. It quarantined the GLF development. The commune established the commune and production brigade-run enterprises directly and promoted a comprehensive rural industrialization in the undeveloped countryside though rural industry was not a success. On the other hand, communization promoted famine from two sides. Firstly, the low level public welfare services made by communalization damaged the rural economy seriously, especially "eating without paying" and "opening your stomach to eat as much as possible" in CDHs, which caused a sharp increase in grain consumption and became one of the main reasons for the famine (Chang and Wen, 1997). Secondly, it also guaranteed high grain procurement and reduced the rural grain supply greatly.

4
Great Leap Backward in the Panic Famine

4.1 Background

Under the promotion of the GLF, China had a high-speed growth rate of 21 percent in GDP in 1958. Its industry even had an astonishing growth rate of 53 percent. This high-speed growth was realized not only by concentrating on the steel industry but also by a high accumulating rate. Through 1958–60, the accumulation rate in the national income achieved 34, 44 and 40 percent respectively, surpassing that of 23 percent in 1953. The share of productive accumulation in total accumulation increased from 49 percent in 1953 to 82 percent in 1958, 87 percent in 1959 and 97 percent in 1960 (*CSY* 1984, p. 32 and 34). The GLF concentrating on steel output only brought chaos to the national economy. It caused a serious imbalance between industry and agriculture and between light and heavy industries. The output value of industry increased from 70 billion in 1957 to 164 billion yuan in 1960, about 1.3 times as many as that in 1957. However, the output value of agriculture in China decreased greatly from 54 billion in 1957 to 46 billion yuan in 1960, a drop of 23 percent. The "steel priority" strategy also caused an imbalance in the interior of the industry. Because of the shortage in coal, mineral excavation, transportation and electric power, many industries had to stop and to support the steel production in order to complete the target of steel and iron production which led to a stagnation in many other industries. For example, light industry development was very slow in the GLF. The share of light industry in the total industrial output decreased from 55 percent in 1957 to 33 percent in 1960, a drop of 22 percentage points. Conversely, heavy industry had a strong expansion with a share of 67 percent in the total industrial output in 1960. The high-speed economic growth lasted one year only in the GLF, and then started to slow down. In 1960, China's GDP had negative growth. Even in industry promoted by the state, the growth rate of output decreased greatly also, to only 6 percent, a cut of 23 percentage points compared with the previous year. The national economy faced an overall crisis.

At the same time, the great reduction in agricultural yield made by the GLF and communization led to a serious and widespread famine. The state was unable to control these oversized communes. The so-called "five winds"[1] were popular everywhere in the rural areas. The out-of-control state caused chaos in the rural economy.

4.2 Policy goals

To give up the GLF and take up "grain priority"[2]

Although Mao Zedong argued that it was because of farmers' "firm resistance to the state purchase," not because of a lack of grain, that the state was unable to get enough grain, the serious grain crisis soon came clear. From the second half of 1960, the grain shortage increased, and finally the CPCCC had to reluctantly acknowledge the reality that the crisis was made by the great reduction in grain yield. That is, the farmers did not produce so much grain as reported! Facing the nationwide serious economic crisis centering on the famine, the policy goal was changed immediately.

Increasing the grain supply while continuing the GLF

Although as the GLF went forward, the grain crisis became more serious, and the CPCCC had been managing to solve it, the grain problem was still dealt with under the GLF before 1961. The CPCCC wanted to increase grain production while insisting on the GLF and the mass steel campaign. The CPCCC (10 August 1960) said that grain shortages happened in both 1958 and 1959 and continued in the summer of 1960, though the summer harvest of 1960 had already been completed. There were serious food shortages in some cities and the agricultural and subsidiary products exportation was also not completed. "This kind of serious situation cannot continue in any event ... therefore, the CPCCC requests that the entire party and all the people make great efforts to develop both agriculture and grain"(*ILCSFN*, No. 13, p. 517). However, it still persisted with the GLF and requested: "we must guarantee steel and iron production." In other words, the CPCCC still did not give up the original "steel priority" and the "catching up and surpassing at top speed" development strategy, and still wanted to continue the GLF. On 3 November 1960, the CPCCC acknowledged a reduction in grain production in many areas and a grain crisis started. The CPCCC requested to increase the labor supply in agricultural production. "Guaranteeing enough labor in agricultural production is the key for guaranteeing the current grain production." However, it still wanted to continue the GLF, and the supply and dining hall system in the communes. "We must keep the dining halls in good condition" (*ILCSFN*, No. 13, p. 671). When the famine spread nationwide, the crisis was still thought a temporary one. Mao (15 November 1960), filled with lofty sentiments, announced: "in five months, we must change all this. The Communist party must be able to transform the situation in five months and to strive for a big agricultural harvest in 1961" (*ILCSFN*, No. 13, p. 695).

However, the crisis became worse. The CPCCC (7 September 1960) admitted: "in some areas of Shan dong province, after the wheat harvest, swelling sickness, abnormal death and population outflow is continuing to occur ... the same things are also appearing in many provinces such as Henan, Shanxi, Anhui, Jiangsu" (*ILCSFN*, No. 13, p. 565). The deepening grain crisis day by day pushed the CPCCC to adjust its policies. From August 1960, the CPCCC continuously issued orders in order to improve the grain crisis, such as the "Instruction on Guaranteeing the Completion of Grain Transportation Plan" (15 August 1960), the "Urgent Instruction on Cleaning up Labor Firmly and Earnestly to Strengthen Agricultural Production" (20 August 1960), and the "Instruction on Decreasing Grain Ration of Dwellers in Both Countryside and City" (7 September 1960). At the same time, the CPCCC took some measures to solve the problem. For example:

- Launching the campaign to make food substitutes such as tree leaves and grass
  On 16 October 1960, the CPCCC requested: "all regions must earnestly implement a 'low grain ratio,' use melons and vegetables as a substitute for grain and manage dining halls and grain in good condition" (*ILCSFN*, No. 13, p. 643). It (14 November 1960) issued the "Urgent Instruction on Launching Immediately Large-scale Campaign of Gathering and Manufacturing Food Substitutes" and indicated: "it is a vital and emergent task currently for our entire party and all the people to mobilize the masses to launch a large-scale campaign of gathering and manufacturing food substitutes immediately. In recent years, agricultural production has suffered large natural disasters continuously ... The serious disasters have brought temporary difficulty to us ...except for increasing grain, melon and vegetable production, we should also increase each kind of food substitute by any means possible." "Each region must mobilize the masses on a large scale, making use of every chance and minute, to rapidly gather tree leaves, grass and wild plants, which can be used as a food substitute, as far as possible, to preserve straw stalks and plant roots, which may be made as a substitute for food as far as possible. We should not burn them down but make them into food substitutes step by step in a planned way" (*ILCSFN*, No. 13, p. 688).
- Accelerating grain transportation to the city
  Insufficient transport in China also aggravated the crisis when the grain procurement increased. In order to guarantee the urban grain supply, the CPCCC (17 November 1960) requested that the top leader in each region must be in command of the transport directly and to "inspect and command the transport everyday just like commanding a military battle" (*ILCSFN*, No. 13, p. 702).

However, the crisis continued to worsen and spread to the production of commodities for daily life. The Ministry of Light Industry (7 January 1961) reported: "recently in many regions the output of industry for daily life is decreasing and products are in short supply. Even essential items for daily life such as table salt, matches, pots, troughs, bowls and chopsticks, are also unobtainable" (*ILCSFN*, No. 14, p. 11).

Giving up the GLF and increasing the grain supply

The worsening of the crisis forced the CPCCC to give up the GLF and mass steel campaign. From the very beginning of 1961, China started to change its policy. The New Year's Day editorial of the *People's Daily* announced that in 1961, the entire party, all the people, and the whole nation must "concentrate our strength to change our weak agricultural foundation with low technology and limited anti-natural disaster ability in our country fundamentally." Li Fuchun[3] (14 January 1961) indicated: "the national economic planning in 1961 must implement the policy to take agriculture as a foundation, give agriculture the most important status and strive for an abundant agricultural harvest, specially for an abundant grain harvest." "The experience in current years has proved more and more the extremely important status of agriculture in national economy. Speeding up agricultural development is the center link to develop the national economy rapidly and proportionally." He requested: "the entire party and all the people must make great efforts to develop agriculture and grain and each sector must strengthen its support for agriculture." In the national economic planning, "we must put agriculture at the top of national economy and arranges economic development in the order of agriculture, light industry and heavy industry" (*ILCSFN*, No. 14, p. 36). Zhou Enlai (3 April 1961) pointed out: "there are several tasks in our current construction. The first is agricultural development ... if agriculture cannot grow, there will be no consolidated foundation for the industry to develop" (*ILCSFN*, No. 14, p. 238) and he concluded the five aspects of agriculture for industry development:

- How much commercial grain farmers can supply for the city
- How many laborers agriculture can provide to industry in the city
- How much raw materials agriculture can produce for industry
- How much market agriculture can provide to industry
- How many people agriculture can provide to develop transportation.

He argued: "we must take agriculture as the center of the economy and produce commercial grain, so that we are able to build our industry foundation rapidly ... in order to develop industry, we must understand the relations between industry and agriculture, between city and countryside, this is a main issue ... in one word, we are only able to build industry which is based on the commercial grain the countryside can provide to the city. We have a disaster, which has changed the situation. A part of the farmers' grain ration has been taken as commercial grain to the city. In fact it is not commercial grain, the farmers themselves have not enough grain to eat!" (*ILCSFN*, No. 14, pp. 239–40).

Under the nationwide famine threat, from 1961 China started to give up the radical GLF and took a "grain priority" policy. In order to support agriculture and adjust the imbalance in industry, the target of steel output growth in 1961 decreased a great deal, only 0.3 million tons more than the output in 1960. In the countryside, the development center was changed to agriculture and grain was the key link in rural development.

To halt rural industry

Limiting and reorganizing rural industry

The state started to reorganize its industry comprehensively. The CPCCC (19 August 1960) urged the reorganization, consolidation and improvement of commune-run industry. "They must serve agriculture and produce traditional export products as much as possible. Any rural enterprise which is competing for raw materials with large enterprises (state-owned enterprises) must halt construction if it has not been completed or be canceled if it has not begun its construction" (*ILCSFN*, No. 13, p. 540). At the same time, (15 June 1961) it imposed many restrictions on the material sources and investments of commune-run enterprises. Also commune-run enterprises could not hinder agricultural production and their share in the total labor of the production brigades must be less than 2 percent (*ILCSFN*, No. 14, pp. 389–90).

Stopping rural industry

Finally, in order to shift the center of rural development and concentrate resources on grain production, the CPCCC (27 September 1962) decided to halt rural industry. "Generally the communes will not develop enterprises for several years and all the enterprises which have been established but are unable to subsist or have not been supported by the masses should be closed down" (*ILCSFN*, No. 15, p. 621).

To reduce grain demand and guarantee the urban grain supply

As the crisis deepened, the measures to solve the crisis expanded from increasing the grain output to decreasing the demand for grain. The CPCCC decided to reduce the supply of state commercial grain while making great efforts to produce grain to guarantee the urban grain supply because the state controlled all of the commercial grain in China. Chen Yun (31 May 1961) put forward four measures to solve the grain crisis:

- To adjust the policy in the countryside continuously
- Industry must support agriculture vigorously
- To import grain

- To mobilize the urban population to go to the country to reduce the urban grain supply by the state

"There are two roads for us to choose: one is to dig from the farmer's grain ration continuously, another is to move the urban population to the country. We must choose one of them. I think that the only road we can choose is to compress the urban population" (*ILCSFN*, No. 14, pp. 364–6). He believed that if the urban population was not compressed, the state would have to procure more grain from farmers, which would have serious results:

- Lowering the incentive of farmers to produce grain
- Causing draft animals to continue to die in great numbers
- Making industrial output continue to drop
- Increasing grain imports.

However, what is the difference between personal grain consumption in urban and rural areas? Chen argued: "Some people say that a worker moving from the city to the countryside will eat food too. If he does not eat in the city, he must then eat food in rural areas. In fact, to eat in rural areas is totally different from that in a city. How different? Quite a lot. In the first year from the city to the rural area, the annual grain supply will decrease by 150 catties per worker generally. If 10 million workers are moved to rural areas, the grain supply decreased will be 1.5 billion catties, 3 billion catties for 20 million workers. This is the difference in the first year. A more remarkable difference lies in the second year. The workers originally from the countryside return to their hometown and the workers originally in the city settle down in the countryside. Both participate in collective production and grain distribution, adding the grain from their private plots and will not need the grain supply from the state. Thus, moving 10 million people to the countryside will reduce the grain supply to 4.5 billion catties; 9 billion catties for 20 million people" (*ILCSFN*, No. 14, p. 374). The reduction of demand for state commercial grain is one of the emergent goals for China to solve the famine crisis.

To strengthen control over the people's communes

The gigantic and powerful communes brought earth-shaking changes to the small peasant economies in China's countryside, and the inadaptability between the backward countryside with huge numbers of illiterate farmers and the powerful communes needing a high level of management skills resulted in great chaos in the rural economy. The state could not carry on an effective control over the commune itself. To strengthen its control and eliminate the chaos the CPCCC (3 November 1960) urged a campaign for reorganizing the communes nationwide. "We must mobilize the masses to launch a campaign to rectify the style of work and to reorganize the commune this winter" and must firmly oppose the commandism, blind direction of production, cadre specialized winds, thoroughly correct communism and exaggeration winds focusing on embezzlement, waste and bureaucratism. "Any behavior of party members or cadres which breaks the law or party discipline will be punished strictly according to the party discipline and state law." "Through the campaign of rectifying and reorganizing, we could transform backward regions, communes and production brigades, and purge all levels of leading administrations of the commune and rural CPC organizations."

4.3 Policy controls

To cut commune power

In order to relieve the serious crisis, the state began to reorganize the people's communes centering on cutting the huge power of the communes and giving the farmers more rights, on the other hand, to take back the power which had been released to the communes by the state in the GLF to weaken the communes.

Methods to cut commune power

- Transferring the basic accounting unit4 to the production team
  1) At the commune level
     In the initial period of the people's commune in 1958, Mao's tentative plan was to build three levels in the people's commune and make the commune level the basic accounting unit. This was a system of commune ownership. However, this plan was only realized in some regions.
  2) At the production brigade level with some at commune level
     Because it is difficult to implement the system of people's commune ownership the CPCCC in April 1959 decided on the system of "the three-tie ownership, the production brigade as the foundation" and made the brigade the basic accounting unit. This system enlarged the power of the production brigade. However, some regions still had a system of basic accounting unit at the commune level because the CPCCC wanted to develop the rural economy in order to overcome the "temporary" difficulty and launch a new GLF, then again transfer the commune to the commune ownership system nationwide (*ILCSFN*, No. 12, pp. 129–30).
  3) All at the production brigade level
     As the crisis worsened, the CPCCC (3 November 1960) emphasized the production brigade basic ownership system and expanded the power of the production team. "The three-tie ownership system based on the production brigade is the fundamental system in the commune at present and is unchangeable for at least seven years from 1961." It proposed that existing communes and brigades with the commune owner-

ship or state ownership system should cease if they operated badly (*ILCSFN*, No. 13, p. 661). "The labor, land, farm animals and farm tools must be 'four fixations' and must be used only by the production team. They must be registered and no one can use them casually." Further, the state allowed commune members to hold small private plots and to do family sidelines. "The commune economically is a union of the production brigades. The production brigade is the basic accounting unit and the production team is a unit to directly organize production and collective welfare undertakings" (15 June 1961, CPCCC, *ILCSFN*, No. 14, p. 385). The CPCCC stipulated that the people's commune management committee "could not use or transfer labor, producer goods and other materials freely." "All of the land in the scope of a production brigade belongs to the production brigade and is used solely by production teams fixedly in the brigade."

4) At production team level
On 7 October 1961, the basic accounting unit was changed again. "Taking the production team as the basic accounting unit is good because its best merit is that it can solve the contradiction that the basic production unit is the production team, but the unified income distribution unit has been the production brigade in the collective economy for a long time" (*ILCSFN*, No. 14, p. 738). The CPCCC (27 September 1962) explicitly stipulated: "the production team is the basic accounting unit in the people's commune. It carries out independent accounting, is responsible for its own profits and losses, organizes production and distributes income. The system will remain unchangeable for at least 30 years as soon as it is decided" (*ILCSFN*, No. 15, pp. 625–6). The regulation also stipulated that all lands in a team belonged to the team and the labor in a team is controlled by the team. No person or unit could use them without ratification from the members or the people's committee at county level or above.

- Reducing the commune scale

When the people's commune was established in 1958, its large scale was one of its main characteristics and received Mao's appreciation. However, in 1961, as one of the causes for the crisis, this "large scale" had to be reduced. "The commune's scale was too large in many regions ... Generally communes control production brigades over too many things and too tightly and production brigades control production teams over too many things and too tightly" (CPCCC, 22 March 1961, *ILCSFN*, No. 14, pp. 221–2). "The scale at all levels of the people's commune should be beneficial to production, to management, to unity and should not be oversized. In particular, the production brigades should not oversize" (CPCCC, 15 June 1961, *ILCSFN*, No. 14, p. 386). As a result, the scale of the commune was reduced greatly from more than 5,400 households per average commune in 1958 to about 1,800 households on average in

1962, only 32.9 percent of the scale in 1958 (Wei, 1994, *Economic Cooperatives in China*, Qin and Lu, eds, 1994, pp. 23–4).

- Closing the CDH
  Although the common dining hall in the commune had many problems and was very difficult to run, as one of the superiorities of the commune and the symbol of the socialized and ideal communist society, it was maintained by the state. During the serious crisis, the CPCCC (March 1961) still insisted on the common dining hall. However, in June of the same year, the CPCCC changed its policy and indicated: "whether or not a production brigade runs a CDH depends on the members in the brigade" rather than requesting to persist with the CDHs. At the same time, the method to distribute grain was changed too. "The grain should be assigned to farmer households directly and controlled by the commune members no matter whether to run a dining hall or not" (CPCCC, 15 June 1961, *ILCSFN*, No. 14, p. 411). The CDH was closed down as soon as farmers held the decisive right. In fact, the CPCCC was very reluctant to make the decision. It also reflected the serious difficulty the CPCCC faced.
- Abandoning the free supply system
  The system of partial free supply for commune members was changed into the work-points system, in which the income of a member will be distributed according to the work-points he earns. Thus, the commune members must work for the work-points, then they can obtain the return on the work-points.
- Restoring the handicraft co-operatives
  On 20 January 1961, the CPCCC urged the concentration of the power of economic management on central government. "All rights of personnel administration, finance, commerce and industry transferred from provinces (cities, autonomous regions) and central ministries to prefectures, counties, communes and enterprises since 1958 should be taken back if improperly transferred" (*ILCSFN*, No. 14, p. 102).

  In order to cut the commune's control over rural industry, the CPCCC decided to restore the handicraft cooperatives, which were transferred into commune-run enterprises in the GLF, and to separate the handicraft producers' cooperatives from the commune again. The CPCCC (19 June 1961) stipulated that the handicraft producers' cooperatives already transferred into the commune-run industry, if not favorable to production development, must return to the original types of handicraft cooperatives or cooperation teams. "The handicraft producers' cooperatives and cooperation teams belong to the members collectively in these cooperative organizations. The rural handicraft cooperatives are a unit to operate independently in the people's commune and to receive dual leadership from both the commune and the county federation of handicraft industries" (*ILCSFN*, No. 14, pp. 437–8). At the same time, the state stipulated that no one could force the handicraft cooperatives to accept any plan and could adjust their production only through a consultation.
- Taking back the state commercial branches and restoring the SMC

Although the state commercial branches were transferred to the commune in 1958, the state took them back in 1959 because the transference resulted in chaos in which the commune was able to take commodities freely and pay less tax or even no tax at all (Xu, 1996, p. 310). The CPCCC (19 June 1961) decided to restore the SMC. "The SMC may be established according to a commune or region ... the cooperatives will operate under the dual leaderships of both the union of SMCs at higher level and the commune management committee (or regional administrative institute)." "The SMCs carry on independent accounting, and are responsible for their own profits and losses ... the cooperative union at higher level and the people's commune management committee (or regional administrative institute) have no right to use the funds and materials of these SMCs" (*ILCSFN*, No. 14, pp. 455–6). The experiment of restoring the cooperatives started from May 1961 and extended gradually in July. Finally, the rural SMCs had great development. Later, the cooperative shops and cooperative teams were also restored. In 1962, there were 33,294 SMCs at grass-roots level with 148 million members. Also there were 25 provinces and 2,042 counties which had restored SMCs (Qiu, Chi and Shi, 1994, *Economic Cooperatives in China*, Qin Liufang and Lu Longwen, eds, 1994).

- Taking back the state bank branches and restoring the RCC
  The state bank branches were taken back several months later in April 1959 after they were transferred to the people's commune on 20 December 1958 because the transference made the commune able to use funds arbitrarily which caused a great financial confusion (Xu, 1996, p. 309). On 9 November 1962, the CPCCC decided to restore the RCC and separate it from the commune. The shares, accumulated fund and property in a cooperative belong to all members in the cooperative collectively. The RCCs would

Table 4.1 Total savings deposits and loans of rural credit cooperatives in China (billion yuan)

Year	*Savings deposits from*			*Loan for*		
	Total	*Collective agriculture*	*farmer*	*Total*	*Collective agriculture*	*farmer*
1960	4.3	2.8	1.5	2.2	1.3	1.0
1961	4.7	3.1	1.6	1.8	1.0	0.8
1962	2.8	1.8	1.0	1.6	0.8	0.8
1963	3.1	2.1	1.0	1.4	0.6	0.8
1964	4.3	3.2	1.1	1.4	0.4	1.0
1965	4.8	3.5	1.3	1.4	0.3	1.0
1966	6.1	4.6	1.5	1.5	0.4	1.1
1967	7.3	5.9	1.4	1.5	0.4	1.1
1968	7.6	6.0	1.6	1.7	0.4	1.3
1969	7.3	5.8	1.5	1.8	0.5	1.3

Source: *China Finance Yearbook 1993*, the China Finance Society, China Finance Yearbook Editorial Department, 1993.

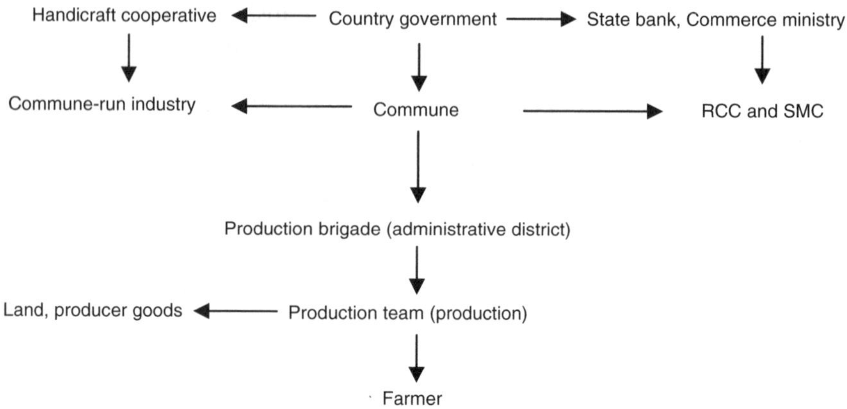

Figure 4.1 The people's commune control system in 1962

operate and account independently, and be responsible for their own profits and losses. No person or unit had the right to reassign or divert the funds and saving deposits in a RCC. The RCC may be established according to the structure and scope of the commune and also in a market or small town. A credit station may be set up in one or several production brigades. The saving deposit rates of a RCC were consistent with that in the state bank; however, its loan interest rate may be higher than the agriculture loan interest rate in the state bank (Xu, 1996, p. 331 and 334).

The anti-"equilitarianism and indiscriminate transfer of resources" campaign

In restructuring the commune, the state launched an anti-"equilitarianism and indiscriminate transfer of resources" (EITR) campaign by returning property taken during the GLF. The CPCCC (3 November 1960) argued: "we must firmly oppose and correct the communist wind of EITR thoroughly" and stipulated that any kind of belongings such as houses, furniture, land, farm tools, domestic animals and building materials taken by the government and enterprises at the county level or above from the commune or by the commune from production brigades or teams as well as by the county, commune, production brigade and teams from farmers since the establishment of the people's commune all must be cleaned up and firmly returned to the original owners. The return must be the original objects with a reasonable rent, and depreciation or repairing fees for their use (*ILCSFN*, No. 13, p. 662). The CPCCC (19 June 1961) further emphasized: "the party organizations at all levels must be determined to carry out the instruction made by the CPCCC and Comrade Mao Zedong repeatedly to firmly correct the EITR and return the property completely and thoroughly. Only by doing so, can we promote agricultural production development" (*ILCSFN*, No. 14, p. 431).

The timetable of the campaign

The campaign to be completed by 1961. If it cannot be completed in one or two years, it should be solved in three years and must be solved completely in five years (CPCCC, 19 June 1961, *ILCSFN*, No. 14, p. 432).

Methods to return property

- Mobilizing the masses
  "Those who did the EITR should carry out the returning and return the properties to where they came from. We will consolidate the people's commune system with three levels of ownership based on the production team through the returning." "Both clearing up the EITR and returning the property must take mass line."
- Returning original goods
  The CPCCC urged the return of original goods if they still existed and to pay a fee for their use. "If the original has been lost or consumed, you can use other things equal in value to redeem ... county, commune or production brigades should use their own offices or other public buildings, even the boarding houses of the county to redeem member's houses which have been torn down." (CPCCC, 19 June 1961, *ILCSFN*, No. 14, p. 432)
- Compensating with cash
  If not enough original properties were returned, cash would be paid to compensate for them. The order to use cash for compensation was:
  1) Production brigade or team funds,
  2) Enterprise and institution funds,
  3) The funds from the overall plans of the province, city and autonomous region, if needed,
  4) State aid if still needed. The state was prepared to subsidize 2.5 billion yuan for the return of property, which would be distributed according to the rural population. (CPCCC, 20 January 1961, *ILCSFN*, No. 14, pp. 95–6).
- Expanding the scope of property return
  On 19 June 1961, the state not only defined explicitly the scope of property return but also expanded it to labor. "Except for labor used in the mass steel campaign, which may be excluded with a ratification from the masses, other labor used should be cleared up and paid." The scope was:
  1) Producer goods and subsistence means
  2) Domestic animals
  3) Lands
  4) Forests
  5) Labor
  6) Houses
  7) Other
  (CPCCC, 19 June 1961, *ILCSFN*, No. 14, p. 431).

- Establishing special agency and making plans for property return
  In order to guarantee that the property return worked smoothly, the CPCCC (19 June 1961) requested the set up of committees: teams and special administrative agencies for the property return at all levels of the central, provincial, city and autonomous regions; especially, county, commune and production brigades. Planning committees and government departments were to put the goods for the property returns into economic plans in order to guarantee the production and supply of these commodities.

As a result of the campaign, a lot of producer goods and materials were returned to production teams and farmers, which raised farmers' incentives for production and also did damage to the rural industry. Because, as said above, the commune and production brigades collected funds and producer goods through the EITR to establish their enterprises, the property return could hurt many rural enterprises, especially small ones. Some of them even had to close due to shortages in the producer goods or funds suddenly made by the property return.

Ceasing rural enterprises

From the second half 1960, the state started to reorganize and limit the commune and production brigade-run enterprises. Because rural industry was mainly composed of commune and production brigade-run enterprises, restricting rural industry means limiting the commune-run and production brigade-run enterprises. As the crisis deteriorated, the restriction became stricter. The CPCCC (27 May 1962) indicated: "the rural commune-run enterprises have more than 1.26 million employees, are engaged across broad fields and consume too much commercial grain. They should be closed down generally. Personnel should return to production teams ... if really needed, the industrial enterprise should, after reorganization, be changed into an independent accounting unit or into a handicraft co-operative, which is under the management of the commune. From now on, in the adjustment stage, the rural people's commune will not develop industrial enterprise generally" (*ILCSFN*, No. 15, p. 464).

Methods to stop rural enterprises

The first stage began in 1961, focusing on limiting the labor and operating scope of the rural enterprises.

- Limiting the commune and production brigade to develop enterprise strictly
  When the economic crisis started, the CPCCC (15 June 1961) still persisted in permitting the commune and production brigades to develop industrial enterprises, but with some restrictions (*ILCSFN*, No. 14, pp. 389–0 and 395).
  1) Labor cuts and share restrictions for rural enterprises in total rural labor
     The CPCCC (10 August 1960) argued that because commune-run industries and diversified economies such as forestry, sideline and other non-production sectors employed too many workers, we should "implement a

simplification from each aspect. We will stop those enterprises or institutes which should be stopped, postpone those which should be postponed, cut those which should be cut and transfer those which should be transferred (replacing a man by a woman and strong labor by weak), and squeeze out labor as much as possible" (*ILCSFN*, No. 13, pp. 517–18). On 15 June 1961, it made a clear restriction on the labor share of commune-run and production brigade-run enterprises in total rural labor.

A. No more than 2 percent
The share of the production brigade labor used by commune-run enterprises cannot surpass 2 percent of the total labor of the production brigades in the commune generally.

B. No more than 5 percent
"The share of production team labor used by the production brigade-run enterprises cannot surpass 5 percent of the total labor of the production teams in the brigade generally.
(*ILCSFN*, No. 14, pp. 389–90 and 395)

- Half industry, half agriculture
The CPCCC (10 August 1960) urged that the commune and production brigade-run enterprises must be half agriculture and half industry. "Except those which have to maintain production continually yearly. They should combine with the agricultural seasons to do more in the slack season, less in the busy season and close down in the very busy season" (*ILCSFN*, No. 13, p. 518). "The production brigade may run enterprises, but should observe the principle of doing more in the slack farming season and less or none in the busy season" (CPCCC, 15 June 1961, *ILCSFN*, No. 14, p. 395).
- Limiting business scope
The CPCCC (25 November1960) explicitly stipulated the business scope of the commune and production brigade-run enterprises. The stipulation divided the scope into three catalogs.

A. Industries to run resolutely
Agricultural industry, such as farm machinery (mainly repairs), agriculture chemicals, feed and grain processing, tailoring, shoemaking and industry for export

B. Industries to run with certain conditions
Small mine excavation, smelting, building materials and so on

C. Industries unable to run resolutely
These industries have to compete with major industries for raw materials; were not to have close relations with agriculture or commune members' lives; to use more labor, and had a bad affect on agricultural production such as native spinning and weaving, soap and leather (Hu and Zheng, 1996, p. 41). Major industry refers to city industry, especially state-owned industry.

The second stage started in 1962, and the policy changed from limiting rural enterprises to halting them.

- Stopping CPBOEs
  On 27 September 1962, the CPCCC stated that the communes and production brigades would not run enterprises for several years, and all enterprises which had been established would be closed down if they were unable to survive or had no support from the masses (*ILCSFN*, No. 15, p. 621).
- Stopping sideline production of the communes and production brigades
  Later, the CPCCC (22 November 1962) explicitly stipulated: "in the collective sideline production, we will concentrate on the development of the production team's sideline production. The commune and production brigade should not develop sideline production ... The commune and production brigade should not run an enterprise generally and should not establish a specialized production team engaged in sideline production" (*ILCSFN*, No. 15, pp. 702–3).
- Transferring the commune-owned enterprise
  Although in 1961, the CPCCC still permitted the people's communes to run enterprises, it imposed many limits on them. In 1962 it did not allow the commune and production brigades to run enterprises, except for a few, and it started to reorganize the existing commune-run enterprises. It urged: "the enterprises to be retained must be decided by the commune congress. According to the different situations, they will be transferred to handicraft cooperatives, production teams or private handcraft and family sidelines. A few enterprises with the commune congress agreement and ratification of the county people's committee may be run by the people's commune continually, or transferred to the production brigade. Each commune-run enterprise should directly serve for agricultural production and farmers' lives. They may not hinder agricultural production, increase commune members' burdens or affect the state purchase of agricultural products ... the policy for the production brigade-run enterprises is the same as that for the commune-run enterprises" (CPCCC, 27 September 1962, *ILCSFN*, No. 14, p. 621 and 625). On 22 November 1962, the CPCCC stipulated again: "all of the commune and production brigade-run enterprises which were established originally by merging the sideline teams of the production team should be transferred to the production team" (*ILCSFN*, No. 15, pp. 702–3).
- Promoting rural handicraft industries and sideline production
  While stopping rural industry, the state urged the communes to develop handicraft industries and side occupations. The CPCCC requested that the commune management committees should promote rapid development of rural handicraft industries. The rural handicraft industries may be of various types such as those run by the commune, production brigade or team directly. Handicraft producer's cooperatives and cooperative teams, and individual handicraft industry are to operate independently. On 27 September 1962, the CPCCC not only persisted that the people's communes must positively promote the rural handicraft industry, but also emphasized that the rural handicraft producers' cooperatives and cooperation teams were independent units and under the dual leadership of both the handicraft

federation at county level and the commune (*ILCSFN*, No. 15, p. 622). At the same time, the CPCCC (27 May 1962) decided the respective business scopes for both the handicraft industry and major industry and limited rural handicrafts to hand production only (*ILCSFN*, No. 15, p. 465). This policy did not allow communes to develop rural industry, but only to develop rural handicraft industries and household sidelines.

Through depressing rural industry, China wanted to speed up agricultural development and protect state-owned industries. The policy change caused rural industry to conflict with the major industries, which damaged the rural industry and made rural industry decline greatly. However, although the CPCCC placed a strict limit on rural industry, it did not completely put a ban on the industry's development. State policy was in fact ambiguous. It wanted to stop rural industry's development to concentrate strength on agriculture, but did not completely forbid the industry. So, a few rural industrial enterprises were able to survive and become the foundation for the future rural industrialization.

Farmer-making to increase agricultural labor with all effort

In order to realize the goal to develop agriculture, the CPCCC took measures to increases labor input in agriculture and grain production. First they concentrated labor on the agricultural front. The CPCCC (10 August 1960) called: "the CPCCC requests the entire party and all the people to make great efforts to develop agriculture diligently, and go in for grain in a big way ... we must squeeze out labor from various aspects as much as possible and thus replenish the agricultural front; firstly the grain production front" (*ILCSFN*, No. 13, p. 517).

Methods to increase agricultural labor

- Ensuring more than 80 percent of agricultural production shares in total rural labor
  On 10 August 1960, the CPCCC defined a concrete share of the agricultural production in total rural labor and argued: "we must squeeze labor out from the city and countryside, from the inside and outside of the commune as far as possible to strengthen agricultural production, especially grain production and to ensure that the share of labor of agricultural production in the total rural labor is at least 80 percent in the busy season" (*ILCSFN*, No. 13, pp. 517–19).
- "Three criterions"
  In order to concentrate the labor force on grain production and the agricultural front, the CPCCC (3 November 1960) made three concrete quantitative criterions for agricultural labor.
  1) The rural full and half labor (excluding auxiliary labor) should account for about 40 percent of the rural population. Full labor should be two-thirds of the total rural labor.

2) Taking the total rural full and half labor as 100, the labor used by the people's commune and production brigade (basic accounting unit) cannot surpass 5 percent. The production team should use 95 percent.
3) The labor on the agricultural production front in a busy farming season must achieve 80 percent. The total labor in non-agricultural industries such as commune-run industry, local transportation, forestry, animal husbandry, side-line production, fishery, welfare, culture and education cannot surpass 20 percent.
(*ILCSFN*, No. 13, pp. 669–70).

- A ban on transferring rural labor
On 3 November 1960, the CPCCC made a call for "ensuring enough labor on the agricultural production front is the key to currently guaranteeing grain production" and explicitly stipulated: "in five years, all units at a level above county cannot transfer labor from the countryside. If necessary, the transferring must get ratification from the party committee at the level of province or city or autonomous region. If a commune wants to use the labor in production brigades or teams, it must get ratification from the party committee at the level of prefecture. A production brigade can use the labor of production teams when approved by the party committee at county level" (*ILCSFN*, No. 13, pp. 669–70).

From the second half of 1960, China began to increase the agricultural labor supply with all effort nationwide. The increase mainly came from two sources; one from the non-agricultural industry and non-production departments in the commune interior, another from commune outside such as city. This mobilized labor in cities by reducing staff and mobilizing the urban population to the countryside. According to reports at the beginning of February 1961 from 26 provinces, cities and autonomous regions (exclud-

Table 4.2 The national increase of agricultural labor in 1960

Time	*In the first half*	*At the end of November*
Rural population	545 million	551 million
Rural labor	209 million	215 million
Agricultural labor	120 million	145 million
Share of rural labor in rural population	38%	40%
Share of the labor used fixedly by production teams in rural labor	82%	89%
Share of agricultural labor in total rural labor	57%	67%

Source: "Report on Adjusting Rural labor and Simplifying the State Staff" made by the five-person team of the CPCCC and authorized by the CPCCC on 9 April 1961, *ILCSFN*, No. 14, pp. 276–7.
Note: 1) the share of rural labor in the rural population was a statistical investigation in 11 provinces.
2) The agricultural labor in 1957 was 153 million.

ing Xinjiang and Tibet), from autumn to the end of November 1960 (in several month only!) the labor supply transferred from various aspects to the agricultural front had reached 29.1 million people; 21.9 million people from the commune interior and 7.2 million people from outside (the five-person team of the CPCCC, 9 April 1961, *ILCSFN*, No. 14, pp. 275–7).

The report of the five-person team authorized by the CPCCC on 9 April 1961 pointed out: "the figures show that the labor supply on the agricultural front has improved, but has not achieved the 'three criterions' stipulated by the CPCCC ... Now this has not been realized in many regions, but

Table 4.3 The sources of the agricultural labor increase in the second half of 1960

Commune interior source and the share in total labor increased from the interior (%)		*Commune outside source and its share in total labor increased from the outside* (%)	
Commune-run industry	15	State staff	45
Over-age student	17	Farmers working in city	30
Life welfare	16	City commune-run factories, enterprises	5
Forestry, animal husbandry, side-line production and fishery	19	Other urban labor (including farmers in city)	20
Capital construction	11		
Commune management	4		
Culture, education and hygiene	3		
Other	15		

Source: as Table 4.2.
Note: this data is from an investigation in 11 provinces, cities and autonomous regions.

Table 4.4 Labor structure in China 1958–64 (million persons)

Year	*Labor in agriculture and industry*	*Labor in agriculture*	*Share of agriculture in total labor*	*Labor ratio of agriculture to industry (industry=1)*
1958	199	155	77.8	3.5
1959	192	163	85.0	5.6
1960	200	170	85.1	5.7
1961	220	197	89.9	8.9
1962	230	213	92.6	12.5
1963	236	220	93.1	13.5
1964	245	228	93.1	13.5

Source: "China Labor and Wage Statistical Data" 1949–1985, the department of social statistics, the State Statistical Bureau, China Statistics Publishing House, 1987, p. 9 (share and ratio calculated by Shi Cheng).
Note: Agriculture includes agriculture, forestry, animal husbandry, sideline production and fishery.

we must achieve the criterions firmly ... Only to do so the adjustment is advantageous to the striving for a good agricultural crop this year" (the five-person team, 1961, *ILCSFN*, No. 14, pp. 277–8). Under the government's impetus and compulsory measures, the agricultural labor supply increased quickly. As shown in Table 4.4, the share of agricultural labor in total national labor increased rapidly from 85 percent in 1960 to 93 percent in 1963, 8 percentage points up. The ratio of industry to agriculture labor increased from 1: 5.7 in 1960 to 1: 13.5 in 1963.

To transfer the urban population to the countryside for farmer-making[5]

Chen Yun (31 May 1961) indicated: "we must make our mind up firmly to mobilize the urban population to the countryside. To make the decision early is better than later. In my opinion, each person having come from the countryside in the last three years must return to where they came from." "For three years we recruited a staff of more than 25 million people and made the urban population achieve 130 million. But this is not suitable. We did not have experience, moreover we over-estimated the grain yield" (*ILCSFN*, No. 14, pp. 373–4). He argued that at present there was not enough grain and industry was too large with more hands than needed. So staff and workers must be cut. In order to solve the famine, the CPCCC launched a campaign to transfer part of the urban population to the countryside.

Plans to cut urban population

- The plan of 1961 to cut more than 20 million
  On 16 June 1961, the CPCCC made the "Nine Measures to Reduce Urban Population and Grain Sales in the City" and decided, on the base of the 129 million urban population, to reduce more than 20 million of the urban population in three years and at least 8 million in 1962. According to the plan, the reduction should be finished in the first half of 1963 (*ILCSFN*, No. 14, pp. 412–13).
- The plan of 1962 to cut 20 million again
  On 27 May 1962, both the CPCCC and the State Council together made "the Decision on Further Simplifying Staff and Reducing the Urban Population" and decided again to reduce 10.56 or 10.72 million staff and workers and 20 million of the urban population respectively, based on the urban population of 120 million with a staff and workers of 41.7 million at the end of 1961. The reduction of both the staff and workers and urban population should be mainly completed in 1963 and finally ended in 1964 (*ILCSFN*, No. 15, pp. 462–3).

Methods to transfer the urban population to the countryside

The CPCCC urged local party committees to launch a full large-scale campaign to cut urban population step by step in a planned way. The committees were to ensure the completion of the urban population plans.

- Cutting the number of people but no increase
  The cities and towns were to reduce number of people, not to increase. If an increase was really needed, it must have ratification from the CPCCC or the central bureau of the CPC. Cutting the urban population must go with a decrease of grain supply (CPCCC, 16 June 1961).
- Verifying the urban population thoroughly
  The CPCCC established special teams for verifying the urban population and food supply together with local governments to verify the population in cities, especially in the large and medium cities. They were to check disguised urban dwellers and residence cards in order to make the urban population consistent with the grain supply and strictly prohibit fraudulent claims and corrupt practices (CPCCC, 16 June 1961). It urged: "to carry out a thorough population and food supply verification in 183 large and medium cities nationwide." The concrete request is: "to verify the number of residents, to supply grain for them strictly according to the real resident number in order to make one urban dweller with only one quota of grain decided by the state and to put an end to the false population receiving grain fraudulently."
  (*ILCSFN*, No. 14, pp. 412–18).
- Reducing staff and workers in urban enterprises
  1)The targets of simplification
  A. Staff and workers in urban enterprises newly come from the countryside after January 1958 (including temporary, contract, apprentice and regular workers).
  B. Workers who came to the city before the end of 1957 but want to go back to their home village voluntarily. The old ones may be allowed to retire or resign from the enterprise if they want to.
  2) Treatment and arrangement for the redundant staff and workers
  The state would provide the redundant staff and workers with funds to help them to immigrate to the countryside. At the same time, the CPCCC urged local party organizations, communes, production brigades and teams to help them to settle down and solve the problems in their life and work.
  3) Verifying the grain and wage reduction
  After the staff and worker reduction, each unit must strictly verify the number of staff and workers reduced. Reducing a worker must cut the grain and wage he had correspondingly to strictly prohibit fraudulent claims
  (CPCCC, 28 June 1961, *ILCSFN*, No. 14, pp. 505–9).
- Simplifying government organizations, domestic parties and people's organizations
  On 22 February 1962, the CPCCC made a plan to simplify the government organizations, domestic parties and people's organizations. Redundant staff would be sent to the countryside to strengthen the local government and commune system.

Table 4.5 China's plan to simplify its government, parties and people's organizations in 1962

Administration level	*Original staff (mill. persons)*	*Staff to reduce (mill. persons)*	*Percentage of reduction in original staff* (%)
Total staff	2.68	0.94	35
Central	0.06	0.03	41
Province and autonomous region	0.20	0.07	36
Prefecture	0.19	0.11	61
City	0.50	0.14	28
County and commune	1.72	0.58	34

Source: "Suggestion on simplifying state organizations, parties and people's organizations at all levels" of the CPCC team for simplifying and authorized by the CPCCC on 22 February 1962, *ILCSFN*, No. 15, pp. 198–203.

- Transferring the educated youth to the countryside
  The state mobilized not only staff and workers, but also a large number of educated youth to the countryside. On 6 October 1962, the CPCCC requested that all large or medium-scale cities must, if feasible, mobilize educated youths and technicians to the countryside in a planned way. "The total educated youth going to mountain and countryside in 1962–1966 are 1.3 million persons" (China Labor and Wage Statistical Data (1949–85), p. 110).

From the second half of 1960, China started to cut its urban population on a large scale. In the national plan made in November 1960, China planned to simplify 5.02 million staff and workers; however, under local plans, the total cut was 5.28 million from September 1960 to the end of 1961, 260 thousand persons more than the national plan. By the end of February 1961, the real staff and workers simplified was 2.24 million (CPCCC, 9 April 1961, *ILCSFN*, No. 14, pp. 279–80). From January 1961 to June 1963, China in two and half year altogether cut about 26 million urban residents (Liu and Wu, 1986, p. 296). The CPCCC (6 October 1962) announced: "Because of the reduction of staff and urban population, from this January to August, the total wage paid by the state is 2.6 billion yuan less than that in the same time last year. The commercial grain supply in cities is 3.23 billion catties less than that in the same time last year, which enabled the state to reduce the grain procurement and lighten the farmer's burden. At the same time, from last year to the present, the labor from the city to the countryside altogether reaches more than 12.6 million persons. All of them have played and will play a remarkable positive role not only in improving the urban economy, but also in developing agriculture and strengthening the collective economy" (*ILCSFN*, No. 15, pp. 660–1).

Table 4.6 China's population structure and employees in state-owned section 1960–63 (million persons)

Year	*Urban*		*Rural*		
	Total	*Share in national* (%)	*Total*	*Share in national* (%)	*Employees in state-owned section*
1960	131	19.7	531	80.3	50.4
1961	127	19.3	532	80.7	41.7
1962	117	17.3	556	82.7	33.1
1963	116	16.8	575	83.2	32.9

Source: *CSY* 1984, pp. 81–2 and 110.
Note: the population includes natural growth.

To compulsorily restrict farmers' movements to the city

Although Mao proposed to prevent farmers from entering the city in the GLF, his tentative idea was to keep farmers in the countryside through raising rural development and the level of life. However, after the failure of the GLF, the rural economy went back wards and Mao's original plan could not be realized. So, the goal to prevent farmers from entering the city had to be realized by compulsory administrative means. The CPCCC (4 February1959) had pointed out, "if farmers blindly flowing to the city continues, it will greatly hinder the development of both agriculture and industry, and be disadvantageous to consolidating the people's commune too … Therefore, we must take effective measures to stop it immediately" (*ILCSFN*, No. 12, p. 28).

After the GLF, both the CPCCC and the State Council (6 October 1962) urged: "various regions and sectors must pay attention more carefully to saving labor after completing the plan to cut staff. Recruiting staff or workers from the society, including temporary workers, must have ratification from the State Planning Commission or the Ministry of Labor. In the next few years, recruiting staff from the countryside is not allowed with a ban on changing temporary workers into regular ones." "From now on, we must strictly control the increase in the urban population, especially the population in large cities … we must limit farmers' immigration to the city" (*ILCSFN*, No. 15, p. 666 and 677).

Methods to restrict farmers' movements to the city

- Establishing the household registration system and dividing the population into two sectors

  From the beginning of the 1950s, China established a household registration system and divided its population into the "agricultural and non-agricultural population," that is, the urban and the rural population. On 9 January 1958, the "People's Republic of China Household registration Regulation" was passed and China began to control population immigration through the residence card. The city residence card is for the non-agricultural population and the rural residence card for the agricultural population. According the regulation, the rural population's immigration to the city "must have a hiring proof from a labor department in the city or an entrance proof from a school or immigration proof from a city household registration institute." In other words, without such proofs, it is illegal for a rural dweller to immigrate to a city. Because the state controlled all schools, labor departments and household registration institutes, so it controlled immigration from country to city completely.

- Controlling grain supply by the residence card

  1) No grain in the city without a city residence card

     According to the SMPS, the state was responsible for only the grain and cooking oil supply for the non-agricultural population in the city. The "Tentative Method of Grain Rationing in the City and Town" made on 5 August 1955 explicitly stipulated the supply of grain for the non-agricultural population only according to the city residence card. In other words, the SMPS system banning private markets and the trade of main products and the household register system completely eliminated the possibility for a rural dweller to obtain grain in the city.

  A) No grain from the state without the city residence card

  B) No grain to purchase under the SMPS

  C) No grain from other people because the grain ration for each person only meets his own basic requirement for a city life.

     Certainly, the city residence card also ensured many other basic things for daily life in the city. For example, from 1962 China started to issue the "Shopping Ticket" in more than 130 large and medium cities for purchasing the majority of daily necessities such as matches, soap, sugar and so on. However, the tickets were distributed according to the city residence card too.

  2) No grain without working in the rural commune

     Rural grain was distributed under the system of basic ration plus work-point grain in most regions. The basic ration was based on the rural residence card and decided according to the basic requirement for the daily life of an old person or child, which is not enough for adult rural labor. The work-points grain was distributed according to the work-points earned by a rural laborer through his work. In other words, a rural laborer must meet his grain needs through his work. Also a rural laborer must work in the production team where he lived to get the work-points and was unable to earn work-points in other teams. So, a rural laborer had to work in his own production team for his grain needs. This system restricted not only farmers' immigration to the city, but also rural farmers' movements between rural regions.

- Controlling housing by the residence card

  1) No city housing without an urban residence card

Except for a small quantity of private housing, the urban real estate had been completely nationalized or collectivized, so most urban dwellers and their families enjoyed housing at an extremely low price, provided by the state-owned or collective enterprises and organizations, and also the housing was inheritable. The nearly free housing was a welfare offered to urban dwellers only by the state and anyone with a rural residence card was unable to enjoy it. It was impossible for a rural dweller to get housing in the city privately because of the state's monopoly.

2) No house without local rural residence card
In the countryside, each commune member could obtain a piece of land for a house from the production team he belonged to. However, the farmer had only a right to use the land to build a house and was unable to sell it because the land still was owned collectively. Under this system, not only was an urban dweller unable to obtain rural land, but also a rural dweller similarly could not get a piece of land from other teams. Without a local rural residence card, no one was able to obtain a pierce of land to build a house. The housing system restricted farmers' immigration, not only to the city, but also between rural regions.

- Controlling social welfare by the residence card
Urban dwellers also enjoyed other social welfare provided by the state such as employment, medical care, pensions, social security and education, all of which the rural dwellers were unable to enjoy.

Although China set up the household register system at the beginning of 1958 to control its population, it did not strictly limit its farmers at that time.

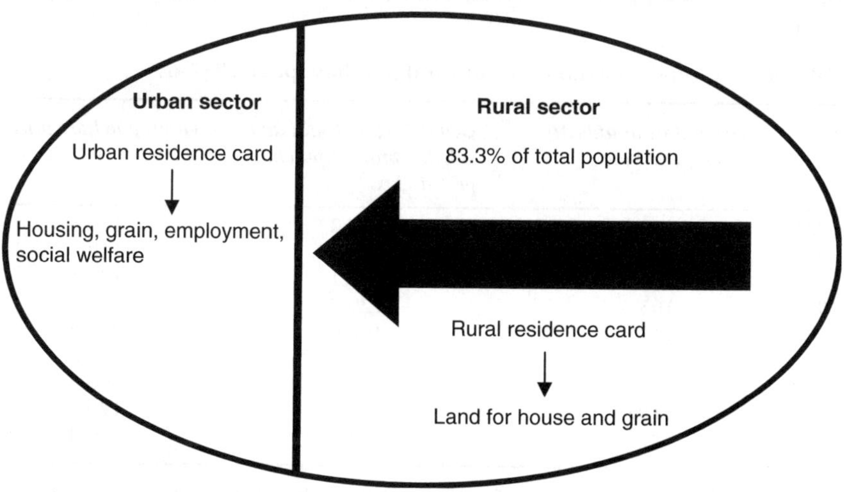

Figure 4.2 China's population division by the household register system in 1963

On the contrary, as a result of a labor need for the GLF, a large number of farmers rushed into the city. The real restriction on farmers entering the city started from the failure of the GLF. The compulsory restriction of farmer immigration combined with the transfer of the urban population to the countryside became China's basic measures to relieve the crisis. The "farmer making" on a large scale made the rural share in the total national population change from 80 percent in 1960 to 83 percent in 1963, a increase of 3 percent points, though a number of farmers were reported to starve to death in the same period. The city residence card became a dream for millions of Chinese farmers to change their lives of poverty.

To raise the purchase price of agricultural products

On 9 January 1961, the CPCCC team for grain price reported: "the present grain purchase price should be enhanced," because "the natural disaster has continued for two years and farmers' incomes are quite low and decreasing due to the poor harvest." Therefore, enhancing the grain price was "advantageous to farmers' production incentives." The CPCCC (15 January 1961) decided to raise the grain purchase price. "From this summer harvest, the national average grain purchase price will increase by 20 percent, simultaneously along with the increase of 5 percent in average grain price, as a reward to the main grain-production regions already implemented in 1960, the total increase in the grain purchase price is 25 percent (keeping the retail price unchangeable temporarily), and in this and the next year we will enhance the prices of meat, birds, eggs, cooking oil, cotton, tobacco, hemp, tea, sugar, lumber, bamboo and so on step by step in a planned way" (*ILCSFN*, No. 14, pp. 59–60). As shown in Table 4.7, the grain purchase price

Table 4.7 China's general index of rural purchase price 1957–64

Year	*General rural industry retail price index*	*General agricultural and sideline product purchase price index*	*Grain purchase price index*
1957	102.2	120.2	116.5
1958	101.5	122.9	119.5
1959	102.5	125.1	121.1
1960	105.3	129.4	125.0
1961	110.5	165.6	216.6
1962	115.4	164.6	228.8
1963	114.2	159.9	190.4
1964	112.0	155.8	170.4
1965	107.9	154.5	170.4

Source: *China Trade and Price Statistical Data 1952–83*, the trade and price statistics department, of SSB, Chinese Statistics Publishing House, 1984, p. 358 and 402.
Note: 1952 price =100.

and other agricultural product prices increased rapidly in both 1961 and 1962 and started to fall later. However, compared with the industry retail price, the aggregate level of agricultural product purchase prices rose greatly.

Reducing agricultural tax

On 23 June 1961 the CPCCC authorized the report made by the Ministry of Finance and agreed to cut agricultural tax. The report pointed out that in 1959 and 1960, because of the natural disaster, the actual agricultural output was much lower than the one estimated originally, however the agricultural tax was not reduced correspondingly and promptly. In those two years the agricultural tax burden was too heavy and was out of balance between regions. Some regions had too heavy a tax, especially the regions with a high grain output. In addition, the state did not deduct tax for lands used in the water conservation and capital construction projects and private plots. So it decided to cut agricultural tax (*ILCSFN*, No. 14, pp. 491–2).

Methods to reduce grain purchase

- Reducing the general tax rate
  The actual agricultural tax rate cannot surpass 10% at national average level.
- Cutting local tax
  The share of local extra-charges in agricultural regular tax should be cut from 15–30 percent in the past to no more than 10 percent.
- Stabilizing the tax rate
  Agricultural tax should be levied according to the new rate nationally and be stabilized for three years. No extra tax would be levied for the increment in agricultural output (CPCCC, 23 June 1961, *ILCSFN*, No. 14, p. 493).

From 1961, the agricultural tax rate was reduced from 14 percent in 1959 to 9 percent in both 1961 and 1962 (*New China Fifty Year's Government Finance Statistics*, pp. 74–5).

Relieving control over the rural market

In the 1950s, China's rural market included regular rural fairs, commodity exchange and non-periodical small trade fairs. The communalization in 1958 eliminated the rural markets. Although in order to promote rural economic development, the rural markets were organized again in 1959, the state implemented a strict control over the rural market and many products could not trade freely in rural markets (CPCCC, 23 September 1959, *ILCSFN*, No. 12 p. 580). In order to enhance the incentive of farmers' production and increase supply, the CPCCC decided to loosen control over rural markets and let more commodities enter the market freely (CPCCC, 15 January 1961, *ILCSFN*, No. 14, p. 72).

Methods to relieve control on rural markets

- Reclassifying commodities to reduce the commodities controlled or purchased by the state
  Through the classification of goods, different categories of commodity had different transaction methods.
  1) The classification in 1959
     There were three categories of commodities. The first category was the commodities under state monopoly purchase and marketing such as grain, cotton and cooking oil; the second category covered the commodities with the state unified purchase; the commodities in the third category included all commodities not in the first and second categories
  2) The classification in 1961 and the difference between the classifications in 1959 and 1961.
     There were three categories. The first category was the same as that in 1959. The second category was the commodities purchased by the contracts assigned by the state. The third category was traded freely in market and included all of the commodities out of the first and second categories. The CPCCC on 15 January 1961 emphasized: "at present, the second category should be reduced and the third one should be increased in order to activate rural economy quickly."
  A. Permitting part of the commodities in the first category to enter the market after completing the state purchase plan, though they were permitted to sell only to the state.
  B. Increasing the commodities in the second category to sell at markets. The nature of the second category was changed from the state unified purchase to the state contracts assigned purchase. That is, the surplus could be sold at market after completing the contracts, which was purchased completely by the state according to the rule in 1959. Also, the second category commodities to sell at market were increased, such as private surplus, products from private plots and family sidelines.
  C. Opening the third category commodities completely
     The original rule for commodities in the third category was: "if there is a state purchase plan or a contract with the state, after completing the plan or contract, the surplus can be sold at market. If there is no state plan or contract, the commodities can be sold at market" (CPCCC, 1959). In 1961, all of the third category commodities were permitted to trade at market freely with no assigned contract purchase for them," (*ILCSFN*, No. 14, p. 69).
- Expanding the scope of trade at market prices
  1) Permitting all goods in the second category to trade at market prices
     In 1959, all the commodities in both the first and second categories had to trade at the prices made by the state. However, in 1961, all of

the second category goods and materials were permitted to trade at market prices, even for the state purchase.

2) Permitting all commodities in the third category to trade at market prices
According to the stipulation in 1959, the third category commodities must be traded at the prices made by the state, however the new rule in 1961 permitted farmers to trade their commodities in the third category at market freely (CPCCC, 1961).

3) Relieving price control
The price policy in 1959 was to stabilize market price of the commodities in the third category in order to avoid too large a change in prices. In 1961, price control was relaxed and a change in the prices allowed. The CCPC argued that the price change benefited developing production, promoted rural economy, expanded material exchange between city and countryside, improved material supply in the city and industrial areas, and increased exports.

- Adjusting personnel for rural market access
  1) Permitting nearby urban dwellers to enter the rural market.
  In 1959, only the people's communes, production brigades and teams and their members were permitted access to the rural market. In 1961, the market access scope expanded to state-owned commercial enterprises and departments, and nearby urban dwellers.
  2) Forbidding factories, mines, government organizations, institutions and associations, the army, schools, state-owned farms and so on access to rural market unless having ratification from the state commercial authority in 1961.
  3) Forbidding the people's communes, production brigades and teams, and their members to open a shop in rural markets and transport commodities.
  4) Forbidding the people's communes, production brigades and teams to trade in rural markets before completing the state purchase plans.
- Continuing the ban on distant transportation and trade, and handing over resales
  In 1961, everyone in the rural market was permitted to sell only the commodities he produced himself or purchase the commodities for his own needs only. The state forbade changing hands to resell for money, abandoning farming for commerce and engaging in speculation and profiteering. The sale of commodities must be in one or several nearby markets and distant transportation and sales were forbidden (*ILCSFN*, No. 14, pp. 70–1).

From 1961, relieving control over the rural market caused a reduction in the purchasing volume of agricultural and subsidiary products by the state and collective commercial sector from 97 percent in 1959 and 94 percent in 1960 to 79 percent in 1961 and 77 percent in 1962 (CSY 1984, p. 364).

4.4 Rural industrialization in process

In order to get rid of the serious crisis, China carried out a comprehensive reorganization of the rural economy centering on "grain priority" and "farmer making" (GPFM), and compressed rural industry. Both the number and output value of rural enterprises dropped greatly, in particular, the commune-run enterprises. In 1959, the enterprises' output value amounted to 10 billion yuan, however, by 1963, the output value was only 0.4 billion yuan. The production brigade-run enterprises were better than the commune-run ones, though they also decreased.

Table 4.8 China's commune and production brigade-owned enterprises 1958–65 (billion yuan)

		Commune-run enterprise		
Year	*Gross output value of rural industry*	*Number (ten thousand units)*	*Output value*	*Output value of production brigade-run enterprise*
1958	6.3	260	6.3	—
1959	More than 10.0	70	10.0	—
1960	—	11.7	5.0	—
1961	5.2	4.5	2.0	3.2
1962	4.1	2.5	0.8	3.3
1963	4.0	1.1	0.4	3.6
1964	4.5	1.1	0.5	4.0
1965	2.9	1.2	0.5	2.4

Source: *The hard course of TVE*, Zhang Yi, the law publishing House, 1990, and *China's TVE and village development*, Hu Biliang, Zheng Hongliang, Shanxi Economic Publishing House, 1996.

After the GLF, not only did the rural population increase, but there was also a big change in the distribution of rural labor. The employment in rural industry decreased greatly from 5 million in 1960 to 2 million in 1961, a drop of 58 percent. By 1963, the employment was only 0.4 million, less than 10 percent of that in 1960. The employment in other industries such as construction, commerce and services also decreased greatly. At the same time, labor in agriculture increased rapidly, from 160 million in 1960 to 230 million in 1965, 65 million up, an increase of near 40 percent.

Agriculture began to stop decreasing from 1961. First the grain yield grew from 148 million in 1961 to 160 million in 1962 and 170 million in 1963. The cotton and oil-bearing crops started to level off. The entire agriculture seemed to get out of the crisis with a growth rate of 5 percent in 1962 and 11 percent in 1963 (*New China 50 Years' Statistical Data Assembly*, 1999).

Table 4.9 Rural employment in various industries and sectors in China 1960–65 (million persons)

Year	*Industry*	*Construction and prospecting*	*Farming, forestry, water conservation and meteorology*	*Transportation, post and telecommunications*	*Commerce, catering service, material supply and sale*	*Science, culture, education and hygiene*	*Government organization association*	*Other*
1960	4.6	4.1	163.3	3.0	12.9	4.0	2.4	3.3
1961	1.9	2.0	191.3	1.0	0.7	1.3	2.5	1.9
1962	0.6	0.7	207.6	0.6	0.6	0.8	2.4	0.5
1963	0.4	0.8	214.3	0.6	0.6	1.0	2.3	0.4
1964	0.4	0.9	222.7	0.6	0.6	1.3	2.2	0.4
1965	0.5	1.0	228.5	0.6	0.6	1.5	2.1	0.5

Source: *China labor and wage statistical data 1949–85*, the social statistics department of SSB, China Statistics Publishing House, 1987, p. 80.
Note: the labor number of industry includes the labor in production brigade-run or team-run enterprises. The labor in the table is divided according to the main profession a labor was engaged in, regardless of the concurrent profession.

Table 4.10 Rural consumption in China 1960–65 (yuan, kg.)

Year	*Per household consumption*		*Rural resident consumption*	*Urban per capita grain consumption*	*Rural per capita consumption*			
	Rural	*Urban*	*Index*		*grain*	*edible plant oil*	*pork*	*egg*
1960	73	236	95.5	193	156	1.5	1.0	0.5
1961	87	248	101.3	180	154	1.0	1.5	0.5
1962	93	248	106.9	184	161	1.0	2.0	1.0
1963	94	240	107.5	190	160	0.5	3.5	1.0
1964	99	253	105.8	200	179	1.0	4.5	1.0
1965	104	259	110.0	211	177	1.0	5.5	1.5

Source: *New China Fifty Years Statistical Data Assembly*, the national economic synthesis statistics department of SSB, China Statistics Publishing House 1999 and *China Trade and Price Statistical Data 1952–83*, the trade and price statistics department of SSB, China Statistics Publishing House, 1984.

Notes: 1) The indices are calculated at previous year = 100.
2) The grain is trade grain.

Average farmer consumption increased gradually from 1961. The per capita consumption of main foods such as grain, pork and eggs also started to grow. The big rural famine was alleviated gradually. However, the rural consumption level was far lower than that in 1957. For example, the per person grain consumption in 1965 was merely 354 catties, less than the 409 catties of 1957. In general, because other foods were very scarce, the grain could not meet farmers' daily food need. As shown in Table 4.10, the urban inhabitant's grain consumption was far more than the rural one. China mainly guaranteed its urban food supply. Rural telephones decreased significantly. In 1960, on average every 578 persons held one telephone, however, the number of people for one telephone doubled to 1,214 persons in 1965. In 1965 the share of the communes with one telephone in the total communes was 96 percent, however, the share of the production brigades with one telephone in the total brigades was only 53 percent, about half of the brigades without any telephone at all. The number of post offices also reduced. Although the rural electricity consumption grew rapidly, its growth rate also decreased from 135 percent in 1960 to 44 percent in 1963 (*CSY* 1984 and *Electric Industry in Modern China*, 1994, pp. 372–3).

4.5 Policy effects

The GPFM caused the reversing-Lewis model and led to the poor rural economy

The blow brought about by the failure of the GLF and the famine was extremely heavy on China's ambitious industrialization strategy which forced China not only to give up its radical plan to "surpass Britain and catch up with America" immediately, but also to implement a series of compulsory policies to alleviate the crisis. These policies centering on the GPFM had a profound influence on China's rural and national economy. As an emergency measure in the famine, the GPFM enabled China to get rid of the famine gradually. However, unlike the short term "concentrating on steel only" in the GLF, the GPFM "concentrating on grain only" became the top rural policy and controlled China's rural development for about 20 years. The GPFM not only did not solve the problem of "eating a meal" in China, but also hindered the development of rural economy and industry as well as China's national industrialization seriously. It resulted in a poor countryside with backward agriculture and poor farmers.

The GPFM constituted a reversing-Lewis model as shown in Figure 4.3. Contrary to the GLF, under the GPFM not only did not labor in the agricultural sector shift to industry, but also a part of labor transferred from industry to agriculture, with most rural labor concentrating on agriculture. Because of the great reduction of labor and capital in rural industry, the production

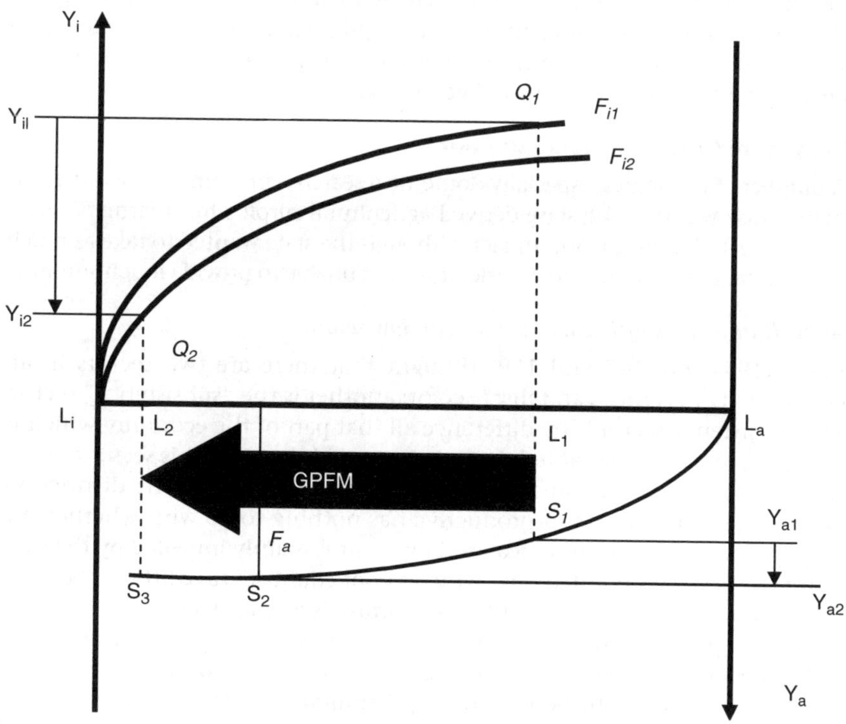

Figure 4.3 The effects of "grain priority" and "farmer making" on the rural economy

Note: Where *Y*, *L* and *F* are output, labor and production function respectively. *i* and *a* represent industry and agriculture.

function curve shifts from F_{i1} to F_{i2}; correspondingly the output of rural industry Y_i also drops from Q_1 to Q_2, thus rural industry output went down comprehensively. In the agricultural sector, which had only a small capital investment and mainly depended on labor input, it is supposed that the sector has an invariable production function curve. When the GPFM pushed huge amounts of labor into the agricultural sector, from point S_1 to point S_2, the agricultural output Y_a increased unceasingly. However, because of the invariable production function, the labor marginal return dropped continually at the same time. Supposing the critical point is S_2, at which the marginal return of labor is zero. So, from point S_2, if labor increases continually, the labor with a zero of marginal return will appear, which Lewis (1954) regards as labor surplus. Obviously, the excessive increase in agricultural labor will cause the labor marginal return in agriculture to drop to zero and the labor increase will not make any contribution to the total output. The GPFM pushed more than 83 percent of China's labor into agriculture in the 1960s, which in fact resulted in a drop in agricultural efficiency and a waste of labor resources. In general, although the agricultural labor increase promoted agricultural production, the increase in agricultural output was much less than the drop in rural industrial output; $Y_{i2}–Y_{i1}$ is much larger than $Y_{a2}–Y_{a1}$. So overall, the reversing-Lewis model kept the rural economy from developing and led to a poor rural economy.

Why were China's farmers so poor?

A number of researches, especially domestic researches in China, argued that the main cause was that the state derived agricultural surplus from farmers excessively (Liu 1997, pp. 44–50). In fact, although the state wanted to take as much agricultural surplus as possible, agriculture was unable to provide much surplus.

Agriculture as a "subsistence" sector with low return

Lewis (1954, pp. 147 and 159) thought that there are two sectors in an economy. One is the "capitalist" sector; another is the "subsistence" sector. The subsistence sector is by difference all that part of the economy which is not using reproducible capital. Output per head is lower in this sector than in the capitalist sector, because it is not fructified by capital. The distinction between productive and unproductive has nothing to do with whether the work yielded utility. Economical development is mainly impelled by the capitalist sector. Lewis pointed out "why do poor countries save little"; "because their capitalist sector is so small." Agriculture is a "subsistence" sector, so it has a low return. Besides, China's state monopoly for the purchase and marketing system forced prices of main agricultural products down to a very low level and further cut the benefit from agricultural production.

Huge labors in agriculture made poor farmers

Obviously, the fact that agriculture is a low return sector cannot explain the Chinese farmers' poverty. For example, in developed countries farmers

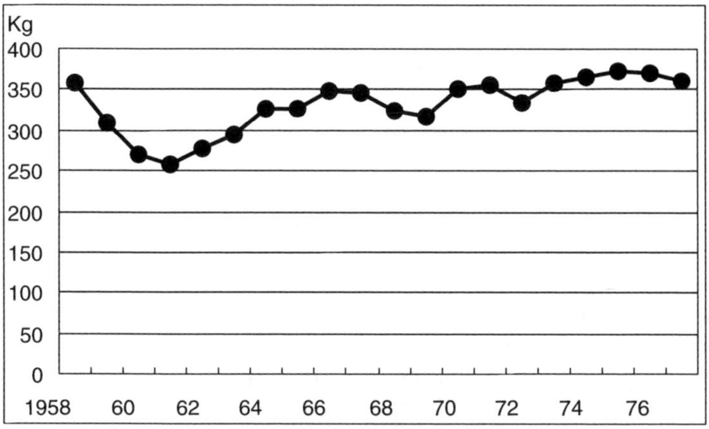

Figure 4.4 China's rural per capita grain yield 1958–77
Source: *CSY 1984*.

are not poor, because developed countries enhance labor efficiency to maintain farmers' incomes by reducing the number of farmers. In developed countries, only a few farmers are engaged in agriculture. The most important condition for a country to keep farmers out of poverty may be to reduce the number of farmers. However, under the GPFM, farmers were not reduced, instead, they increased a great deal and forced the marginal labor return and labor efficiency down artificially. In 1963 the rural population achieved 83 percent of the total population and led to an unbelievable scene of nearly "600 million people working only for China's own food supply." It was the massive numbers of farmers engaged in low return agriculture that caused farmers' poverty. As shown in Figure 4.4, from 1958 to 1977, about twenty years, China's rural per head grain yield did not increase basically.

"Second-class citizen" in China's dual structure model

The dual-structure model

Although after the failure of the GLF, China gave up the "concentrating on steel" policy, the development center was still heavy industry. The "heavy industry priority" combined with the GPFM created China's dual structure development model, which is to develop industry in the city only and to develop agriculture in the countryside only. That is to put most capital into the city and industry and most labor into rural areas and agriculture by the GPFM. The countryside in the dual structure model is a production base of agricultural products to meet industry and national needs. Except for daily necessaries, farmers provided all agricultural products they made to industry and city construction. The dual structure model produced not only a poor countryside, but also a backward agriculture because the cost for anything such as technology and machines to replace labor was too high due to the vast cheap labor supply in the countryside.

The GPFM made farmers "second-class citizens"

Under the GPFM, farmers became "second class citizens" in China's dual structure model.

- They had to carry out agriculture with low return and were unable to undertake high return industry.
- They had stay in the poor countryside and could not move to the city.
- They were unable to enjoy social welfare the state provided such as employment, housing, education and medical care.
- The next generation of a farmer was still a farmer.

The GPFM not only damaged the rural industry and economy, but also harmed China's industrialization and national economy. Because the GPFM limited labor to move to the industry sector, industry had to develop mainly through the increase in investment and was unable to grow through labor increase. That is, industry could not use enough labor to expand, especially for labor-intensive industries. The GPFM hindered the full-scale development of industry. The reversing-Lewis model with a huge labor supply concentrating on low return agriculture could not give full play to China's labor superiority and resulted in labor waste, which constrained China's industrialization and national economic development.

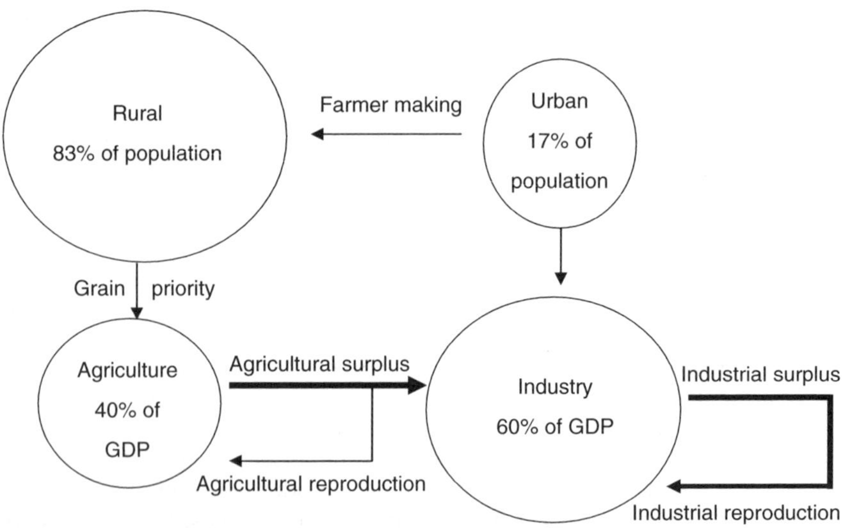

Figure 4.5 China's dual structure model in 1963
Source: *CSY 1984*.

5
Recovery in the Campaign to Accelerate the Mechanization of Agriculture

5.1 Background

China's economy recovered strongly in industry, but agriculture stagnated, with a grain shortage in 1970. In the Great Cultural Revolution started by Mao Zedong personally, the army controlled China comprehensively and directly. All government departments, social enterprises, business units and mass organizations were governed completely by the revolutionary committees headed by military representatives of the Chinese People's Liberation Army. The original administrative personnel at all levels for economic management were deprived of authority, enterprises' rules and regulations were cancelled, and anarchism was popular throughout the entire nation. Large number of workers left their production posts, which led many enterprises to suspend production. From 1967 to 1968, China's economy was in great chaos. Similarly rural economy was out of order. The administrative institutes at all levels of people's commune were unable to carry on their normal work. All this damaged China's economy tremendously, and caused both industry and agriculture to jump back comprehensively, especially industrial production, which dropped continuously for two years. In 1969 the drop stopped and the economy started to recover again. Industry showed strong resilience with an annual growth rate of 33 percent, reaching or surpassing the level in 1966. Although industry was strong, agriculture was still stagnant. The grain yield was only 211 million tons, 3 million tons less than that in 1966. The national annual per capita grain was still down, only 265 kilograms, about 91 percent of that in 1966. The cotton output was 2 million tons with an annual drop of 12 percent. At the same time, as the population increased and national arable land reduced, the average per capita cultivated land decreased unceasingly. China was facing a stronger press of grain supply.

By the end of the 1960s, under the blockade of both the West and Eastern European countries headed by the Soviet Union, China had shut off nearly all relations with world economy. The rate of her total imports and exports to GDP decreased from 12 percent in 1955 to only 5 percent in 1969. Because of the sealed and blockaded condition, China had to develop the economy completely upon her own strength.

5.2 Policy goals

To raise efficiency and expand production for self-sufficiency in grain locally

After the GLF failure, China continued the "grain priority" policy, which put most rural resources, especially labor, into grain production and strictly prohibited other industrial development. However, this policy did not change the grain shortage and backwardness in agriculture. Although the total grain yield increased, the per capita grain yield had been stagnant for many years. "At present, our grain yield per unit area is low comparatively, the ability to resist natural calamities is not strong with small grain reserves and low levels of mechanization of agriculture, especially in 14 north provinces, cities and regions. Their population approaches almost one half of the national one, however, their grain dependence upon the southern region has not changed. This does not suit rapid national economic development and also the 'big contribution' China should make to humanity" (the State Council, 11 December 1970). The CPCCC requested that party organizations and governments at all levels, especially at the two levels of prefecture and county, must take rural production as the center of their work and the regions with a grain shortage must speed up agricultural development for a self-sufficient grain supply as soon as possible. Each department must positively support agriculture. In order to solve the grain shortage, the state made a call for farmland transformation and farm capital construction on a large scale, mainly by changing dry farmland into paddy fields and unsuitable land into that suitable for grain production. The North Conference in December 1970 requested: "if the basic condition for agricultural production cannot be changed, the output cannot be stable and the passive aspect of agriculture cannot have a rapid change. In the fourth FYP, each rural person must have one Chinese acre with a high and stable yield regardless of drought or flood incidents through transforming land and constructing water conservation" (The State Council, 11 December 1970).

At the same time, in order to change the way to promote agricultural production by massive labor input only, and solve the grain shortage thoroughly, the CPCCC proposed to promote agricultural development by raising agricultural production efficiency. "Not to promote mechanization of agriculture and only to depend on manual labor will not enhance agriculture labor productivity quickly, will not change the situation of '600 million farmers working only for their own daily food supply and also will not save labor for speeding-up the industry'" (the State Council, 11 December 1970).

To develop agriculture through farmer self-reliance

Although the state wanted to speed up agricultural development, it did not want to invest much in agriculture and wanted to develop agriculture by depending on farmer funds with only a small amount of state aid. The state asked farmers to criticize their dependency on both "the weather and the state"[1] and to persist in "relying on their own strength and arduous effort" to develop agriculture. "Agricultural development depending either on the poor and lower-middle peasants and their own efforts or on natural conditions and state aid is an important struggle between two political lines on the agricultural front" (the State Council, 11 December 1970). The State Council gave an example that the Jiuyuangou people's commune of Suide County, Shanxi Province was in the past a typical case of "farmers developing agriculture, the state providing funds." From 1953 to 1963, the state invested 960 thousand yuan there, however, the commune built only 2,600 Chinese acres of terraced fields and five dams. However, "Since last winter, they did not spend one penny of state funds but have built 2,450 Chinese acres of terraced fields and more than twenty dams." Two kinds of policies led to two different results. "The more that agricultural development depends on the state, the lazier the people become, and the more the grain yield reduces. However, if farmers rely on their own efforts and learn from Dazhai, agriculture will develop rapidly." Yan An County was also given as another example. With a backward agriculture for a long time, "they built only 18,000 Chinese acres of irrigable fields in twenty years. This year, inspired by Yanan spirit, they built 10 thousand Chinese acres of irrigable fields and 30 thousand Chinese acres of Dazhai-style fields in only about half a year. What took twenty years to finish in the past can be completed in only one year now!" (the State Council, 11 December 1970). The CPCCC asked that local governments realize a self-sufficient grain supply by self-reliance and to reverse the situation of "shipping southern grain to the north" (the State Council, 11 December 1970).

To strengthen the collective economy and raise the level of public ownership[2]

Because of the economic crisis, the transition of communes to ownership by the whole people in the GLF was suspended and the basic accounting unit had to be released to production teams, but the policy-makers did not give up the goal to realize ownership by all the people through the people's commune system. On the contrary, they believed that only through a high level of public ownership could China solve its agricultural and grain issues. Raising the level of basic accounting unit gradually "from the incomplete communal ownership to the sole communal ownership" was Mao's basic plan to transform the rural economy system (Mao, 27 February–5 March, 1959, *ILCSFN*, No. 12, p. 127). Therefore, after the crisis, the economy was stable and became better gradually, raising the level of the rural basic accounting unit to expand public ownership became the essential target for China's rural policy. The CPCCC tried very hard to raise the basic accounting unit level through strengthening the collective economy, especially the economies at commune and production brigade levels, namely, to raise the basic accounting unit from the production team to production brigade level, then to commune level, then finally complete the system of ownership by all the people in the countryside. Mao believed that in order to eliminate the differences between the three levels of ownership and to change the three-level system into a one level system, namely sole communal ownership, the commune must have stronger economic strength and a consistent economic level for all production teams. Therefore, to consolidate and expand the collective economy became an important goal for realizing the ownership transition.

To ban private economy

The North Conference wanted to eliminate both the capitalist tendency of "more private plots, more free markets, more independent responsibility for profits and losses and household output contracting" and the "freedoms for employment, trade, finance and land tenancy," and to prohibit the private sector to continue on the socialist road. The conference believed that the capitalist tendency which represented landlords and rich farmers would weaken and disintegrate the collective economy, and restore capitalism. The conference pointed out that, "Currently there is an intense struggle between these two lines and the capitalist tendency in some communes and production brigades is serious. Embezzlement, stealing, speculation and abandoning farming for commerce are destroying the consolidation and development of the collective economy." The conference stressed that we must criticize the capitalist tendency unceasingly and must eliminate its influence thoroughly (the State Council, 11 December 1970).

5.3 Policy controls

"Constructing Dazhai-Type County" campaign

From 25 August to 5 October 1970, the State Council held the national conference for agricultural development in North China. Its main content was to start the "Constructing Dazhai-Type County" (CDTC) campaign. Although Mao Zedong set up the Dazhai Production Brigade as a model and called to "in agriculture, learn from Dazhai" in 1964, the CDTC campaign in 1970 caused the "learn from Dazhai" to become a large-scale national mass movement, which formed not only tens of thousands of Dazhai-Type communes and production brigades, but also hundreds of "Dazhai-Type" counties. The "Learn from Dazhai" campaign was not only popular in the countryside, but also expanded to all industries nationwide. On 11 December 1970, the CPCCC forwarded "the Report of the Agricultural Conference for the Northern Region" of the State Council and made a call for learning from Xiyang County, the first Dazai-type County where there was a Dazhai

Production Brigade. From 1967 to 1970 Xiyang County had constructed a Dazai-type county according to the Dazhai Production Brigade's experience. On 23 September 1970 the *People's Daily* editorial "In Agriculture, Learn From Dazhai" announced that Xiyang County had already become the Dazhai-type county, had doubled its grain yield in three years and had surpassed the target for the average yield per Chinese acre in the "Program for Agricultural Development." The North Conference decided to launch the CDTC campaign and called for "mobilizing the entire party to make great efforts to develop agriculture and to strive to popularize the Dazhai-Type County" nationwide (the State Council, 11 December 1970).

Main content of the CDTC campaign

Zhou Enlai (21–22 December 1964) called the Dazhai Production Brigade as the advanced model of developing agricultural production by depending upon the people's communes' collective strength and self-reliance. He concluded that "learning from Dazhai" was primarily to persist "the principle of politics in command and thought first, the spirit of self-reliance and arduous effort, and the communist style of loving the nation and the collective." However, the content of the CDTC in 1970 changed greatly.

- "Poor transition" to expand the scale of the basic accounting unit[3]
  The most important thing in "Learning from Dazhai" was to continue the people's commune system and expand its ownership level unceasingly from the production team to the production brigade and then the commune. Although after the GLF, many regions reduced the basic accounting unit to the production team level, Dazhai still persisted in taking the production brigade as the basic accounting unit while 94 percent of production brigades in Xiyang county took the production team as the basic accounting unit.
  However, Xiyang County learned from Dazhai and expanded the basic accounting unit to the production brigade. From 1967 to 1968, in one year only, all its 413 production brigades restored the production brigade basic accounting unit system completely. Afterwards it implemented the communal basic accounting unit system in the Dazhai people's commune, and even proposed to practice a county-basic accounting unit system (Chen, Chen and Yang, 1993, p. 428). One of the important contents of the CDTC was to expand the basic accounting unit. The CPCCC requested rural development to realize the basic accounting unit transition from the production team to the production brigade.
- "Cutting off the capitalist tail"[4]
  The CDTC wanted to continue on the collective economy and socialist road, restrict private economy and criticize the "capitalist tendency" (the State Council, 11 December 1970). For example, Xiyang county had private plots of 22,899 Chinese acres in 1967 and by 1970 they were cut completely. At the same time, the rural diversified economy was restricted

Table 5.1 The basic accounting unit's change in Xiyang county 1966–70

	1966	*1967*	*1968*	*1969*	*1970*
Number of production brigades	415	415	413	413	412
Number of production teams	1,449	1,407	967	918	919
Number of basic accounting units	1,366	1,320	413	413	412
Number of production brigade basic accounting units	64	79	413	413	412
Share of production brigade basic accounting unit in total basic accounting units (%)	4.7	6	100	100	100

Source: "Report on Introducing Production Brigade Basic Accounting Unit in the People's Commune", the Revolutionary Committee of Xiyang County, 1977, *China's rural society and economy evolution 1949–89*, Chen Jiyuan, Chen Jiaji and Yang Xun, eds, 1993, p. 431.

strictly. All commercial production and trade was regarded as capitalist activities and prohibited. Not only individuals but also commune and production brigades could not be engaged in commercial production and trade. The commune and production brigade-run enterprises were also restricted. In some regions farmers even were prohibited from participating in local fairs (Chen, Chen and Yang, 1993, pp. 435–6).

- Labor management centering on egalitarianism
- Self-reliance and arduous effort.
  1) Relying on farmers' own efforts to develop production and carry on large-scale farmland capital construction.
     As a poor ravine village with hilly fields making up 80 percent of total fields, Dazhai in the 1960s carried on large-scale farmland capital construction and turned the ravines into fertile, drought and rain-resistant farmland. They used the people's commune collective strength and received no funds from the state. "Learn from Dazhai" means asking farmers not to want state investment and subsidy, but to depend on their own strength for large-scale farmland capital construction and production (the State Council, 11 December 1970).
  2) Self-reliance to solve difficulties.
     From 2 August 1963, the Dazhai Production Brigade experienced a heavy rain and flood lasting seven days and seven nights unceasingly. Almost all the houses were shattered and farmland washed away. But, facing the difficulty, the Dazhai Production Brigade made a decision of "three no's" and "three no less." That is, it did not want state food, relief funds and relief materials. And the grain ration for its members was to be no less than before, the production investment for next year was to be no less than before, and grain sold to the state was to be no less than before. This is called the Dazhai spirit.
- Loving the nation and the collective[5]

Methods to promote the CDTC campaign

- Mobilizing rural cadres by large-scale national conferences
  1) The North Agriculture Conference.
     From 25 August to 5 October 1970, the conference held by the State Council under Zhou Enlai's direction lasted 41 days with more than 1,200 participants from various levels. The conference was divided into three stages. The first stage took place in Dazhai, Xiyang County to visit and study. The second stage was to summarize and exchange the experience of "Learning from Dazhai" between regions. The third was to discuss measures and policies for realizing the "Program for Agricultural Development", to promote Xiyang County's experience of the CDTC and to request each county to construct a "Dazhai-Type County" according to Xiyang County's pattern.
  2) The first national conference on "in agriculture, learn from Dazhai."
     From 15 September to 19 October 1975, the conference lasted 36 days with 3,700 participants.
  3) The second national conference on "in agriculture, learn from Dazhai."
     From 10 to 27 December 1976, the conference lasted 18 days with more than 5,000 participants.
- Formulating the standard for the Dazhai-Type County
  The first national conference on "in agriculture, learn from Dazhai" in 1975 formulated six standards for the Dazhai-Type County.
  1) A leadership of the party committee at county level to firmly implement CPCCC policy.
  2) Poor and lower-middle peasants in dominance and to firmly struggle against capitalist activity.
  3) Cadres at county, commune and production brigade levels to participate in collective production.
  4) Fast development in farmland capital construction, mechanization of agriculture and scientific farming.
  5) The collective economy to expand unceasingly; both the production and income of poor communes and production brigades to achieve or surpass the local present medium level.
  6) All-round development of farming, forestry, animal husbandry, sideline production and fishery with more output, more contribution to the state and improvement of commune member life gradually (Chen, Chen and Yang, 1993, p. 442).

  Although the state called for an all-round development of agriculture, in fact, the center was still the "grain priority" because self-sufficient grain was a hard target which had to be completed.
- Making plans, increasing the quotas at each level, and competing mutually
  Like other mass campaigns, the state made an overall plan for the CDTC campaign first, and then local governments formulated their own plans based on the national plan. For example, in 1975 the CPCCC called the

nation to strive hard for five years to construct one-third of total counties into Dazhai-type counties by 1980. The remaining two-thirds of the total counties should also build more Dazhai-type production brigades and communes (Chen, Chen and Yang, 1993, p. 443). The CPCCC plan target was decomposed to various provinces, and then to each county. The quotas planned by the higher level were increased at each lower level, so each level competed mutually.

"Poor transition," "transforming nature" and "concentrating on grain only" under the CDTC campaign

Under state impetus, the CDTC campaign progressed rapidly. By the end of 1977, China announce that it had already built 723 Dazhai-type counties and realized the goal to construct one-third of her total counties into Dazhai-type counties ahead of time. The CDTC campaign mobilized hundreds of millions of farmers to carry on large-scale transformations of nature in order to increase grain yield. The center of the transformation was "changing dry farmland into paddy fields," that is, to increase the sown area of rice. Therefore, the national rice sown area expanded and its share in the total grain sown area rose unceasingly.

Table 5.2 China's Dazhai-type county construction 1975–77

	1975	*1976*	*1977*
Number of Dazhai-type counties built annually	316	123	284 (plan)
Total number of Dazhai-type counties built	316	439	723 (plan)

Source: "Report Compendium of Symposium on Several Issues on the Popularization of Dazhai-Type County", CPCCC, 19 November 1977.

In transforming nature, farmers created many miracles, especially in many poor mountainous regions. In order to introduce water uphill, farmers completed many large projects by only their own hands and shoulders because of no machines. The share of rice in the total grain sown area increased from 26 percent in 1969 to 29 percent in 1974 nationally (*CSY* 1984). However, the man-made nature transformation had a great influence on not only on agriculture but also on China's nature. To become self-sufficient in grain, many regions made great efforts to change non-grain fields such as cotton, cane, and vegetable fields into grain fields, which led to an imbalance of agricultural products. Moreover farmers encircled lakes, filled in seas and cut down trees to make fields, which destroyed the natural ecology and environment.

Under the government's impetus, the CDTC campaign evolved into a formalist movement. The exaggeration wind was again in vogue. In order to complete the target, local governments, taking no account of actual conditions and economic return, increased investment in a few model counties and changed them into abnormal "Dazhai-Type Counties." Even the Dazhai Production Brigade itself was not excepted and exaggerated too. For a long time, people had suspected the high grain yield per mu of Dazhai was false because the actual farming land could be larger than the statistical one. In addition, after Dazhai become a model, it got aid from the state. For example, the state invested 500,000 yuan in the brigade for mechanization of agriculture. As a result, if state aid is divided by the grain Dazhai sold to the state, the state got nothing but had to pay 0.226 yuan for one catty of grain. That meant Dazhai made no contribution but was a burden to the state (Wu and Liu, 30 September 1987). Chen, Chen and Yang (1993, p. 456) argued that if China had built 723 Dazhai-type counties, according to the standard, China's grain should have had a very big growth. However, by 1977, the grain output had no remarkable increase, nor did commercial grain. China had to import not only grain, but also cotton, edible oil and sugar. The CDTC campaign did not accelerate agricultural development.

The "Accelerating Mechanization of Agriculture" (AMA) campaign

The mechanization of agriculture was another way for China to raise production efficiency, solve her grain shortage and promote agricultural development. At the beginning of the 1950s, Mao had proposed a tentative plan to realize the mechanization of agriculture in twenty-five years (1956–80) and in April 1959, he pointed out: "the fundamental solution of the agricultural issue lies in mechanization" and requested that the mechanization of agriculture must have a small progress in four years, medium progress in seven years and a big progress in ten years (Cong and Zhang, 1999, p. 246). In July 1966, the State Council held the first national conference on mechanization of agriculture and made a plan to realize the mechanization of agriculture by 1980. However, the CPCCC did not truly take mechanization seriously and formed no concrete measures to achieve mechanization at all. It still attempted to replace funds and technical increase with simple labor increase. Since the GLF failure, although China had strictly carried out the policy of "grain priority" and invested massive labor in grain production, her grain yield, especially the average per capita grain yield, not only had not increased, but dropped. Finally in 1970, the CPCCC decided to accelerate the mechanization of agriculture and raise agriculture labor productivity and pointed out: "if we don't develop mechanization of agriculture, and only depend on manual labor, it will be impossible to raise agriculture labor productivity quickly and be impossible to change the situation that 600 million farmers work only for their food; also be impossible to send in more labor to speed up industry construction." "Chairman Mao proposed to realize the mechanization of agriculture in twenty-five years. Now fifteen years have already passed. We should really grasp the next ten years to achieve the goal that in the fourth FYP, the cultivation mechanization level will be about 50 percent of total cultivatable land and the irrigation and drainage mechanization level about 60 percent of the total cultivatable area" (the State Council, 11 December 1970). The State Council (3 December 1971) requested that in the next five years, from raw material to manufacture, from manufacture to repair and service, from main engine to parts, most provinces, cities and autonomous regions should strive to form a complete and self-sufficient system. The state also proposed a ten-year goal.

Table 5.3 China's ten-year target for mechanization of agriculture 1970–80

Mechanization level for main work in farming, forestry, animal husbandry, sideline production and fishery	*Number of farm tractors*	*Number of walking tractors*	*Power of irrigation and drainage*	*Chemical fertilizer used per Chinese acre*
More than 70%	about 800,000	about 1.5 million	about 60 million horse power	about 80 catties

Source: *China rural finance epitome of history*, Xu Tangling, China Finance Publishing House, 1996, pp. 346–7 and *New China Economic Development History1949–98*, Cong Shuhai and Zhang Heng, eds, Shanghai Finance and Economy University Press, 1999, p. 247.
Note: In 1970, the share of tractor-plowed areas in national cultivated areas was 18 percent, 3 percent for the machine sowing area, 1 percent for the machine harvesting area, less than 0.2 percent for the machinery transplanting and seedling paddy rice area.

Methods to promote the AMA campaign

- "Taking locally-made and medium-small scale machinery as the mainstay"
  The state requested: "farm machinery should be mainly made locally and should be medium-small mainly" (the State Council, 3 December 1971). This was to develop the farm machinery industry mainly by local provinces, cities and autonomous regions relying on their own efforts. At the same time, the state tried to implement the "walking on two legs" policy, that is to form a manufacture network including state-owned enterprises and local provinces, cities and autonomous region-owned enterprises. The farm machinery industry should use both indigenous and modern methods, and both mechanization and semi-mechanization simultaneously. It must develop from raw materials, make efforts to promote the county-owned five-small-industrial enterprises diligently and continue to serve agriculture (the State Council, 11 December 1970).
- Constructing a three-level farm machinery net work of "county, commune and production brigade"
  In August 1971, the State Council requested: "to establish the three-level farm machinery repair and manufacturing network at county, commune

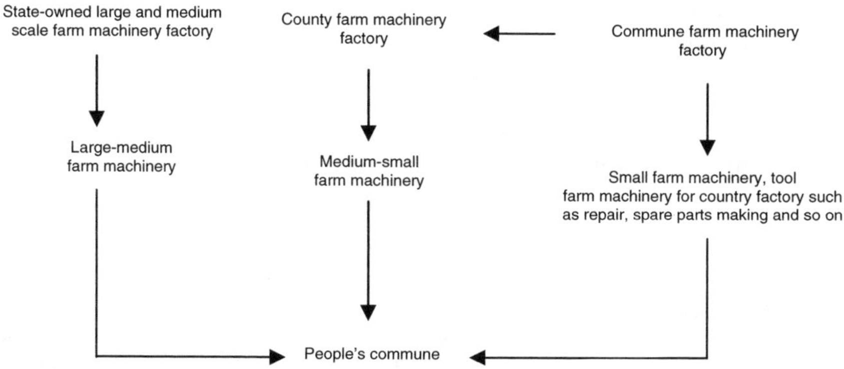

Figure 5.1 China's farm machinery industry network in the 1970s

and production brigade levels." It requested an overhaul to be completed in the local county, a medium repair in the local commune and a minor repair in local production brigades and teams (Zhang, 1990, pp. 19–20). The county, people's commune and production brigades would form a three-level repair network. Local governments at all levels including communes made the farm machinery network.

- Centering on farm industry
  The center of farm machinery development was farm industry serving for agriculture, mainly including agricultural irrigation and drainage, agricultural products processing, transportation and so on.
- Collecting funds by the state, commune and production brigades
  Main fund sources for developing mechanization of agriculture were:
  1) The state fiscal funds, state bank and RCC loans.
  2) Funds collected by communes and production brigades. They collected funds for the mechanization of agriculture through developing agriculture and subsidiary production such as raising pigs.

Main features of the campaign

This was "relying on communes and production brigades to collect funds while making state assistance subsidiary." Although the state wanted to accelerate the mechanization of agriculture, it did not want to fund the mechanization and still requested farmers to collect funds. "The capital source for the mechanization of agriculture must earnestly implement the policy of relying on commune and production brigades' own efforts to collect funds while making state assistance subsidiary ... Do not rely on state assistance, and do not use unsuitable means to collect funds" (the People's Bank, 9 January 1970).

Funds for the mechanization of agriculture included two parts. One for purchasing farm machinery; another for developing small farm machinery by farmers. The purchasing fund was the key factor for the campaign. The

State Council on 3 December 1971 explicitly pointed out: "farm machinery purchases must be made by the collective economy primarily." In other words, the collective had to fund the purchases. From 23 June to 12 July 1974, the People's Bank held the national rural finance conference in Beijing and argued that whether or not the communes and brigades could collect funds to buy machinery was the key to realizing the mechanization by 1980.

Table 5.4 China's mechanization of agriculture development 1965–74 (ten thousand)

Year	*Total farm machinery power (mil. kw)*	*Irrigated areas (mil. hectares)*	*Chemical fertilizer used (pure) (mil. tons)*	*Large and medium tractors*	*Small tractors*	*Machine threshers*	*Farm trucks*
1965	10.99	33.1	1.94	7.3	0.4	11.4	1.1
1970	21.65	36.0	3.51	12.5	7.8	45.5	1.6
1971	n	36.4	3.65	15.0	13.4	62.4	1.8
1972	n	38.0	4.21	19.0	20.8	87.2	2.1
1973	47.83	39.2	5.11	23.4	30.2	103.2	2.5
1974	59.30	41.3	4.86	28.1	42.1	129.7	3.1

Source: *New China 50 Years Statistical Data Assembly*, the national economy synthesis statistics department of SSB, Chinese statistics publishing house, 1999, p. 32 and *New China 50 Years Agricultural Statistics Material*, the rural social economy investigation team of SSB, Chinese statistics publishing house, 2000, pp. 22–5.

The AMA campaign development

After the Northern Conference in 1970, from 16 August to 15 September 1971, the second national conference of mechanization of agriculture was held to push the campaign further. By the end of 1971, more than 90 percent of counties had at least one farm machinery manufacturing and repairing factory (the State Council, 3 December 1971). The gross national farm machinery power developed rapidly, from 21.7 million kW in 1970 to 47.8 million kW in 1973. Farm machinery, chemical fertilizer and rural electricity consumption all increased greatly, especially small tractors, which increased by nearly three times from 1970 to 1973.

To promote the "Five-Small Industries" (FSI)[6]

From February to March 1970, China drew up its national economic planning for 1970 (draft) and requested to develop the FSI and targeted at least one farm machinery repair factory in each county (Liu and Wu, 1985, pp. 371–2).

Methods to promote the FSI

- The state special fund
  In order to help local governments develop FSI, the state decided that from 1970 special funds of 8 billion yuan could be used by provinces, cities and autonomous regions (Wang, 1998, p. 456).
- Transferring the central enterprises
  In order to raise the incentive of local governments to promote local industry and expand the local industry scale, the CPCCC began to reform its economic management system and transfer the enterprises managed by central government directly to local governments. In June 1970, the CPCCC decided that all suitable enterprises and institutions owned by the departments and committees of the State Council should be transferred. The majority of them should be transferred to local governments. A few would be managed by the dual leadership of both central and local government. The transferring should be done by stages and finished in 1970. By September 1970, 2,237 of 3,082 enterprises and institutions managed by central ministries had been transferred, about 73 percent of the total (Liu and Wu, 1985, pp. 372–3).
- Favorable financial and tax policies
  60 percent of profit obtained by the newly built FSI enterprises may be left to the local county in 2–3 years. The FSI enterprises in a temporary deficit would get a government subsidy and enjoy a tax exemption for certain period, with a permit from the local province or city or autonomous region. The banks and RCCs would extent loans to support the FSI enterprises in difficulty (Liu and Wu, 1985, pp. 370–1).

Under state impetus, the FSI in 1970 had rapid development. Nearly 300 counties and cities established a small iron and steel plant. More than twenty provinces, cities and autonomous regions built walking tractor plants, small power machine factories and other small farm tool and part factories. Ninety percent of total counties established their own farm machinery repair and manufacturing factories. In 1970 the production capacity of local small iron and steel plants increased 1.5 times compared to the previous year, and the share of small fertilizer and cement plants in national chemical fertilizer and cement output reached 40 percent. Some underdeveloped provinces and autonomous regions also built a batch of spinning and weaving, daily chemical, hardware and other light industry factories. 1970 was a leap forward for China's local industry after 1958 (Liu and Wu, 1985, p. 371). FSI development gave a strong impetus to China's rural industry not only in raw materials, and spare parts supply, but also in technical training and markets.

To control rural commodity trade and prohibit private commerce

In 1970, China exerted severe control on its commercial circulation and launched the "three opposings" campaign (opposing embezzlement and stealing, opposing speculation[7] and profiteering and opposing extravagance and waste) (CPCCC, 6 September 1970). "All underground factories, stores, contracting work teams, transport teams and clubs must be firmly banned" (CPCCC, 5 February 1970). In the countryside, one of the important contents of the North Conference and CDTC campaign was to control the rural commodity trade strictly and oppose free markets in order to avoid "going along the capitalist road."

Methods to control rural commodity trade

- Controlling SMCs directly
  1) Merging SMCs
     In July 1970, the national federation of SMC, the Ministry of Commerce, the Ministry of Grain and the Central Industrial and Commercial Administration Bureau merged together and form a new ministry, the Ministry of Commerce. SMCs at province, city and county also merged with state-owned commercial enterprises at the same level, however below county level, the basic unit of SMCs did not change and still kept their collective ownership (Qin and Lu 1994, p. 146). Although the SMCs below county level are still collective, the SMCs at higher levels have become state-owned and in fact the basic SMCs have also become a part of state-owned commerce. With the sole state-owned commercial system, the CPCCC is able to govern SMCs directly, so it controlled rural commerce completely.

  A. Controlling SMC's operating rights.
     SMC's operating rights belonged to the state.

  B. Stipulating SMC business fields and channels.
     SMCs were to purchase agricultural and subsidiary products for the state (the SMPS products) and supplied agricultural means of production and manufactured products for daily life. As the purchase channel for agricultural products, the basic SMCs purchased the products and offered them to higher SMCs level by level (county and provincial level). Industrial products were distributed from high to low company level by level. SMCs were retail only (Xu, Deng et al., 1994, pp. 145–6).

  C. Overall control on SMC funds and personnel.

  2) Providing funds for basic SMCs
     The state provided funds for basic SMCs and subsidy for their loss.
  3) Providing the power to monopolise the market through administrative methods such as the operating right for important commodities.
- Limiting rural fair trade
  In order to oppose free trade, the CPCCC created strict control over rural trade fairs and many rural fairs were closed.
- Prohibiting non-commercial units and individuals to deal with commercial activity

While limiting rural fairs, the CPCCC also prohibited people's communes and individual commercial activities. All non-commercial units, even collective organizations, were unable to carry on commercial activity. The CPCCC on 5 February 1970 stipulated: "Except for state-owned and cooperative shops and private retailers with a license of commerce, no unit or individual is permitted to carry on commercial activity," "the management of local fairs must be strengthened, all commodity which is not permitted to go to market must be banned. Without a local authority permit no unit is able to purchase products from rural communes and brigades at rural fairs, nor to exchange goods with rural communes through cooperation nor to use personal relations for rural products."

Table 5.5 SMC shares in total social commodity retail sales and the purchase of agricultural and sideline products in China 1968–73 (%)

Year	*SMC share of commodity retail in*		*SMC share of consumable product retail in*		*SMC share in national agricultural and sideline products purchase volume*
	Total social volume	*Rural volume*	*Total social volume*	*Rural volume*	
1968	29.7	60.1	25.5	60.0	88
1969	33.8	66.3	29.3	67.2	88
1970	35.4	66.4	30.9	68.6	90
1971	35.6	67.1	31.1	71.1	90
1972	35.3	68.5	30.8	73. 5	89
1973	34.8	67.0	30.4	72.3	89

Source: *China Supply and Marketing Cooperative Chronicle and Development Survey 1949–85*, China supply and marketing cooperative historical series editorial office, Chinese finance economical publishing house, 1988, p. 453. The data of agricultural and subsidiary products purchase volume includes state-operated business and comes from *CSY* 1984, p. 364.

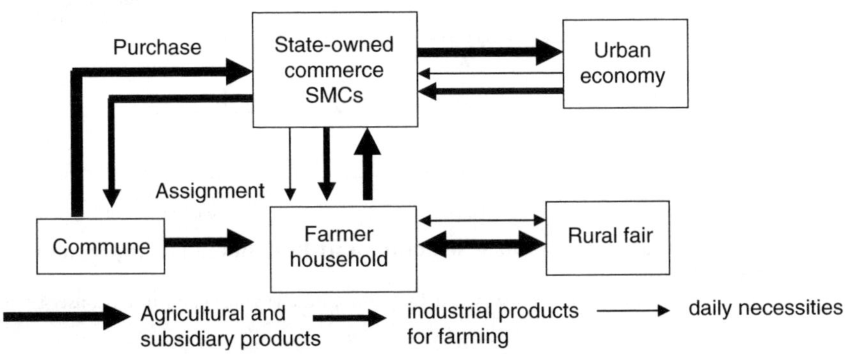

Figure 5.2 China's rural commodity flow in 1971

Transferring the RCC

On 7 January 1970, the military representative of the Chinese People's Liberation Army of the People's Bank decided that RCCs must be operated by poor and middle-lower peasants. This was to establish a management committee (group) dominated by poor and middle-lower peasants. The committee also included members from the local revolutionary committee and RCC. Under the leadership of local commune and brigade revolutionary committees, the RCC management committee would implement the party's line and policy and manage the personnel, political thinking, development direction and funds (including extending, using and taking back) of the RCC. The RCC management by poor and middle-lower peasants in fact is to transfer the RCC right of personnel, estate and funds from the state to communes and brigades.

Methods to transfer RCCs

- Cutting RCC councils and boards of supervisors and establishing the "poor and middle-lower peasant management committees."
- Abolishing RCC rules and regulations
  After the transfer many RCC rules and regulations were abolished.

The number of China's RCCs at the end of 1973 was 91 thousand with 41 thousand owned by communes and 40 thousand by production brigades or several production teams jointly. Also there were 230 thousand credit service stations established by production teams (The Rural finance Bureau of the Ministry of Finance, 11 May 1974).

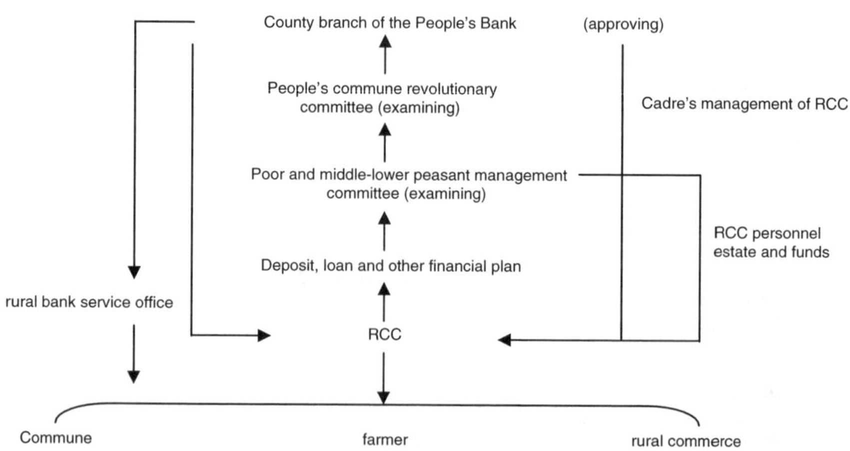

Figure 5.3 China's rural finance structure and RCC financial implementing procedure in 1970

Source: *China rural finance epitome of history*, Xu Tangling, China Finance Publishing House, 1996, p. 357

"Educated Youths Going to Mountain and Countryside" campaign (EYGMC)[8]

Although as early as the 1950s and 1960s the state began to mobilize urban educated youths to go to the mountain and countryside, organizing urban educated youths to the countryside massively started after 1968. On 22 December 1968, the *People's Daily* published Mao's instruction: "it is very necessary for educated youths go to the countryside and accept poor and middle-lower peasant's reeducation. We should persuade urban cadres and other people to send their own children who have graduated from junior middle school or high school or university to the countryside. We should make this mobilization. Rural comrades should welcome them." Zhou Enlai on 6 August 1973 pointed out that all of the youths going to the countryside were educated middle-school students who had received a ten-year education in city. They would help farmers develop agricultural production.

Goal of the EYGMC campaign

Ye Jianying[9] (6 August 1973) concluded the goal of the EYGMC campaign as follows:

- Preparing for a possible war with the former Soviet Union.
  The youths to go to the countryside, especially to the border areas, to strengthen national defense and also strengthen the countryside.
- Training the revolutionary successor.
  The EYGMC was considered as an important strategic plan for China to move towards communism. In the near future, there would be millions of proletariats revolutionary successors in politics, production, culture and technology who had worked and transformed their world outlook for many year in the countryside.
- Constructing the countryside and eliminating three big differences.
  The EYGMC would help rural construction, narrow the gap between the city and countryside, worker and farmer, and physical and mental labor, and eliminate these differences.
- Alleviating the urban employment press.

Methods to promote the EYGMC campaign

- Mao Zedong made a call for the campaign personally.
- Mobilizing the guardians and youths.
- Self-application for EYGMC
- Stopping urban recruitment of the urban industrial enterprises, institutions and governmental organizations for high school graduates.
- Determining the places to go and preparing for settling down.
  First, the youths choose which commune to go to then the communes make preparation for the youths to settle down there. The state will provide the funds needed for a life in the countryside such as a simple house, basic life apparatus and production tools. The state is responsible

for the grain and cooking oil needed for the youths in the initial months. Local communes will prepare other apparatus and tools for the youths to work there.

The feature of the EYGMC campaign

"Accepting the poor and middle-lower peasant's reeducation." The educated youth in the countryside must work under the farmers' surveillance. In other words, the educated must be controlled by the uneducated.

The rise and fall of the EYGMC campaign

Under Mao's call, a hot wave of the EYGMC campaign surged immediately nationwide. In some regions, because all the junior middle school graduates went to the mountain and countryside, some high schools were closed down. Large quantities of high school students who were studying in school also went to the countryside for work. Many of the educated youths going to the mountain and countryside were 15–16-year-old children and could not support themselves. In the countryside, they not only had to be engaged in arduous physical labor, but also had to take care of themselves. They experienced an extremely difficult life both physically and mentally. Although the EYGMC campaign brought about many social issues and wasted people's youth, the large quantities of urban educated youths with scientific knowledge and technology for the countryside strengthened the city and countryside relations and promoted rural industrialization greatly. In fact, the EYGMC campaign did not alleviate the urban employment pressure, but carried on an urban and rural labor exchange because the state recruited more than 10 million farmers from the countryside to make up the urban labor shortage while sending the urban youths to the countryside. This exchange replaced educated labor with uneducated. The national working conference for the EYGMC campaign from 31 October to 10 December 1978 decided to end the campaign finally.

Table 5.6 The educated youths going to the countryside in China 1967–75 (ten thousand persons)

Year	*1967–68*	*1969*	*1970*	*1971*	*1972*	*1973*	*1974*	*1975*
For production team	166.0	220.4	75.0	50.2	50.3	80.6	119.2	163.5
For state-owned farm	33.7	46.9	31.4	24.6	17.1	9.0	18.7	23.7
Total	199.7	267.4	106.4	74.8	67.4	89.6	172.5	236.9

Source: *Chinese Labor and Wage Statistical Data 1949–85*, the society statistical department of SSB, the Chinese statistics publishing house, 1987, p. 110.
Note: "for production team" includes the persons returning to home village. "For state-owned farm" includes the persons going to state-owned forestation and so on.

5.4 Rural industrialization in process

In the 1970s the CPBOEs were restored, and by 1978, the communes and brigades had 1.5 million enterprises with 28.3 million persons; about 9.5 percent of the total rural labor, and an output of 49.3 billion yuan, about 21 percent of the total rural social output value. These enterprises centered on industry primarily, which had a share of 78 percent in their total output value. The rural enterprise development promoted the entire rural economy greatly. It provided funds not only for agricultural development, but also for rural collective welfare undertakings and constructions. At the same time, it provided tax to the state to support national economic development. In 1978, rural enterprises provided 2.6 billion yuan for agricultural development, 4 hundred million yuan for rural collective welfare undertakings, 2.7 billion yuan for rural constructions and 2.2 billion yuan for tax (*CTVEY* 1978, p. 87 and 569).

The rural industrial development promoted the shift of farmers from agriculture to non-agricultural industries. In fact, many farmers concurrently were engaged in non-agriculture industries. They did farming in the busy season and worked in industry in the idle season, the so-called "part in agriculture, part in industry." In 1978, employees in CPBOEs numbered 28 million persons with more than 17 million persons engaged in industry (*CTVEY* 1978, p. 87 and 571). However, the share of the rural population in the national population basically kept unchanged, at around 83 percent.

Although China's grain yield kept growing unceasingly, its agriculture grew slowly with a negative growth in both 1976 and 1977. The national

Table 5.7 China's rural industry development 1970–78

Year	*Number of enterprises (ten thousand)*			*Output value (hundred million yuan)*		
	Total	*Commune-run*	*Brigade-run*	*Total*	*Commune-run*	*Brigade-run*
1970	n	4.5	n	64.0	26.7	37.3
1971	n	5.3	n	77.4	39.1	38.3
1972	n	5.6	n	93.8	46.0	47.8
1973	n	6.0	n	107.3	54.8	52.5
1974	n	6.5	n	129.0	66.8	62.2
1975	n	7.7	n	169.4	86.8	82.6
1976	111.5	n	n	243.5	123.9	119.6
1977	139.2	n	n	322.7	175.3	147.4
1978	152.4	32.0	120.4	382.0	211.9	170.1

Source: *China's TVE and village development*, Hu Biliang and Zheng Hongliang, Shanxi economic publishing house, 1996.

Note: the number of commune-run enterprises in 1970 is 4.47, which is different from 4.74 in the original text. The original text is the same as that in *The Hard Road of TVE*, Zhang Yi, p. 21, which is not correct originally.

per capita grain still increased slowly from 293 in 1970 to 300 kilograms in 1977, an increase of only 7 kilograms in seven years. In 1970–7, the farmer family consumption level undulated greatly with a slow growth in the average per capita expense from 119 yuan in 1970 to 130 yuan in 1977, an increase of 11 yuan only in seven years. Food consumption bogged down similarly. The rural dweller grain consumption increased from 369 catties in 1970 to 377 catties in 1977, only 8 catties up in seven years!

Although the number of telephones in the countryside increased, from 1,294 people per telephone to 1,082 people per telephone, the telephones mainly belonged to collective organizations and farmers personally did not have a telephone at all and had to communicate with each other by traditional means.

5.5 Policy effects

The puzzle of the rural industry recovery since 1970

The huge population and relatively scarce land resources made the grain supply hold an extremely important status in China. In particular, the famine caused China to pay much attention to the grain issue. However, the solution of the grain shortage was restricted not only by the domestic economic system and land resource shortage, but also by the closed situation, which made China unable to use international resources. The long-term grain shortage made China persist with "grain priority" and restrict rural industry strictly until the economic reform at the end of 1978 in the countryside. However, after the Northern Conference in 1970, rural industry started to recover, and not only reached the level in 1959, but also surpassed it. This is difficult to understand because as we know, the main goal of both the CDTC and AMA was to solve the grain shortage, not to develop rural industry. On the contrary, rural industry was severely restricted (except farm machinery). Some cadres in communes and brigades were criticized and fired because of leading farmers to establish enterprises. Also some cadres, managers and salesmen in enterprises were landed with various sorts of charges, arrested and even put in prison. In some regions, rural enterprises had to do transactions secretly (Zhang, 1990, p. 22). The recovery and development of rural industry under the policy of "grain priority" is contradictory and difficult to understand.

"Self-raised funds" made the policy contradictory

Both the AMA and CDTC campaigns aimed at increasing grain yield, continuing the people's commune system and expanding the collective economy for the transition of the higher ownership system through continuing with "grain priority", improving agricultural efficiency, restricting household sideline production and rural industry and commerce.

However, developing farm machinery and expanding the collective economy needed massive funds. Where and how do the funds come from? Although the CPCCC implemented "grain priority", its principle was more labor input and less investment. Therefore, the communes had to collect most of the funds themselves to develop farm machinery and expand the collective economy. It is precisely the "self-raised funds" that made the central policy contradictory. Although the state asked communes to raise the fund themselves, it did not indicate where and how to collect the funds. In fact, the answer is obvious. Because these funds cannot be collected directly from farmers' private estates, the only way to collect the funds is by developing the collective economy. In other words, communes can obtain the funds only through developing agriculture or non-agricultural industry. However, because agriculture in China was a low return industry and almost the entire agricultural surplus was taken by the state, it was extremely difficult, if possible, to collect funds through agricultural income, especially for the regions with little land and large populations. The fund collection had to depend on non-agricultural industry with a higher return. In other words, only by developing high return sideline production and industry, could communes collect enough funds. However, "grain priority" is actually a policy to restrict rural industry. Strictly implementing "grain priority" made communes unable to collect the funds and unable to speed up the mechanization of agriculture, or to expand the collective economy. It was a contradiction of central policy to aim at both "grain priority" and the "acceleration of mechanization of agriculture and expansion of the collective economy", and both "self-raised funds" and restriction of rural industry.

"Self-raised funds" induced rural industry development

Because developing rural industry can collect funds for both the AMA and expanding the collective economy, which conformed to central policy, developing rural industry was consistent with central policy to some extent and had a legal or half-legal status. It is precisely on this point that many local governments had to relax control and permit communes to develop industry and other non-agricultural industry. Certainly, funds were for grain production and collective economic expansion. This is an extremely important reason for the recovery and development of the rural industry under the strict "grain priority" control. Both the AMA and the expanding collective economy promoted rural industrial development.

The ambiguity of policy made regional differences in rural industry development

However, the policy relaxation was extremely ambiguous and non-public. The CPCCC didn't publicly and directly allow communes to develop rural industry (except farm machinery industry) and still emphasized "grain priority." Therefore, each region adopted different measures for rural industry, which made some regions make use of the contradictions in central policy and develop their own rural industry: however, some regions didn't make use of the policy contradiction and still wanted to get funds from agriculture, which led to a backward rural industry. Although there are many reasons for regional unbalance of rural industry development, whether or not to make use of policy contradictions and ambiguity to develop rural industry under state restriction is an extremely important factor. The reason for a strong rural industry in many regions is because these regions developed rural industry early, continued to develop the half-legal "underground" industry and strived tenaciously for its survival and development, which caused them to become leaders in the later economic reform. For instance, in the southern part of Jiangsu Province, "the Northern Conference was a turning point for rural industry, which made commune and brigade-run industry rise and obtain a half-legal status." After the conference, there were many farm machinery tool factories in the Jiangsu countryside. However, most of these farm machinery factories were in loss as a result of the price system. Wuxi County proposed the method "to raise the farm machinery by developing industrial machinery." "Paying the loss of the farm machinery with the profit from industrial machinery to support the mechanization of agriculture" expanded the variety of production in fact and exceeded the limit to develop farm machinery only. It is on precisely this foundation, that the commune and brigade-run industries began to develop (Wu, 1999, p. 34).

Because no one knew if the method "to raise the farm machinery by developing industrial machinery" is legal or not, some regions did it and some not, some dared to do it, some did not dare to do it and some wanted to do, but had no suitable conditions. So, a difference in rural industry appeared between regions. In particular, in many poor regions with bad natural conditions, in order to be self-sufficient in grain, farmers still concentrated on agriculture and on large-scale farmland capital construction and didn't develop rural industry. Thus, both the AMA and the expanding collective economy by the "self-raised fund" caused a policy relaxation, which caused rural industry to recover.

Case study: the mechanization of agricultural development in Xu Hang people's commune in the 1970s

The Xu Hang people's commune of Jiading County, Shanghai was one of the communes with a higher level of agricultural mechanization in the suburb of Shanghai. At the end of 1973, it had 25,400 Chinese acres of collective land with a output value of 6 million yuan from agriculture and sideline production and an output value of 14 million yuan from commune-owned factories (the investigation team of the Shanghai Revolutionary Committee, 1974, p. 114).

The slow development of mechanization mainly depended on state investment before 1970

"Developing mechanization needs massive funds, however, where do the funds come from? ... Many cadres put their hopes on state investment to realize the mechanization, not on the foundation of their own strength." Because the state didn't invest enough, "as a result, the commune cannot afford to buy large farm machinery and electric pumping station." From 1960 to 1964, depending on state investment completely, "the commune only constructed four electric pumping stations and could not afford to buy a large tractor until 1965." The area irrigated by electricity in the total cultivated areas was only 30 percent (the investigation team of Shanghai Revolutionary Committee, 1974, pp. 114–15). Because it depended on state funds, mechanization developed very slowly.

The rapid development of mechanization depended on rural industry for funds after 1970

- Making great efforts to develop rural industry for the fund
  The commune developed twelve enterprises such as farm tool factories, farm machinery, irrigation stations, chemical plants, light bulb factories, grass textile mills, hardware repair and parts factories, towel factories, paper carton factories, engineer brigades, stock farms, aquatic product teams. Each production brigade also had a farm machinery repair and part shop, grain and feed processing, small chemical factory, small hardware and a mushroom room. At the same time, it developed sideline production such as raising pigs, fish, cows, mushrooms and pearls, weaving yellow grass hand baskets, and sandals (the investigation team of Shanghai Revolutionary Committee, 1974, p. 116).
- Self-raising all funds without any state investment
  "Since the Great Proletarian Cultural Revolution (1966–76), the production team's average accumulation per year has been more than 500 thousand yuan and the average accumulation of the commune-run industry has amounted to 800 thousand yuan each year. Since 1970, the production brigade economy has developed gradually. In 1973, its accumulation fund is 220 thousand yuan." Thus, funds for mechanization were strengthened gradually. Besides several electric pumping stations built by state investment at the start, the entire communes did not ask the state for funds. It was reported that since the Great Cultural Revolution, the commune had put more than 3.5 million yuan in to its mechanization of agriculture. By the end of 1973, 60 percent of the investment of mechanization of agriculture in Xu Hang commune came from the accumulation of production brigades and teams, and 40 percent from the accumulation of the communes (the investigation team of Shanghai Revolutionary Committee, 1974, pp. 116–17).

- Rapid development of mechanization of agriculture after 1970
  By the end of 1973, the share of irrigating and draining areas by machines in total farming lands was 100 percent in Xu Hang commune with 28 large and medium tractors, 73 walking tractors, 17 agricultural tugboat, 810 motors and 35 rice transplanters as well as other small machines such as water pumps and sprayers. "The commune has also made 56 bridges for tractors, and subsidized its production brigades to build 11 electric irrigation stations and 88 kilometers of channels, with nearly 35 kilometers of underground channels" (the investigation team of Shanghai Revolutionary Committee, 1974, pp. 115–17). "On average 3 Chinese acres have one horsepower and about 195 Chinese acres have one tractor (standard unit). All grain threshing, grain and feed processing and plant disease protection basically have realized mechanization" (the investigation team of Shanghai Revolutionary Committee, 1974, p. 115).

This investigation argued that the mechanization development in Xu Hang commune indicated that "developing the mechanization of agriculture can never rely on state investment. So long as we earnestly excavate the potential of collective economies at people's commune, production brigade and production team levels, the fund issue can be completely solved by own strength." "Just as the poor and middle-lower peasants said, 'if we don't develop commune-run industry, mechanization will not develop so quickly'" (the investigation team of Shanghai Revolutionary Committee, 1974, p. 117).

Part II

Rural Industrialization in the Transition to Economic Liberalization

6

Rise under the Household Responsibility System

6.1 Background

Mao Zedong's death in 1976 symbolized the end of the Chinese traditional socialist system, but the Mao-style highly centralized system continued until the end of 1978. In the post-Mao time, what China faced is a highly centralized economy with sole public ownership. Through various campaigns, China eliminated private ownership comprehensively in all fields of its economy and established the sole public ownership system. In its industry, the majority of enterprises were owned by the state with no private enterprise at all. In 1978 the share of state-owned enterprises in national industry output value was 78 percent, the share of urban and rural collective enterprises 22 percent. In the countryside, except for a few private plots, the people's commune, RCC and SMC controlled completely all farmers and the entire rural economy.

Under the dual structure model, China formed initially an independent and complete economic system with high accumulation, which met mainly urban people's basic living needs, and established an independent and preliminary modern industrial system with a high-speed growth in its industry, especially heavy industry. On the other hand, the model also constructed a highly abnormal economic structure centering on heavy industry, which led to slow development of its light industry. The quantity, quality, color and varieties of light industrial products were unable to meet people's daily needs (Liu and Wu, 1985, p. 443). High speed but extensive industrial development with military management created not only an unbalanced structure, but also chaotic management, low efficiency and bad quality. At the same time, the high accumulation ratio in the national income, which was as high as 37 percent in 1978, compressed consumption and made people unable to improve their living for a long time. In 1978, China also faced an unprecedented urgent employment press and there were 20 million people needing to find a job (Liu and Wu, 1985, p. 444).

Although under the long-term "grain priority," farmers "completed massive large and medium scale hydraulic projects and constructed a large number of high yield farming fields with a great increase in chemical fertilizers, farm machinery, irrigation and drainage machinery and agricultural electricity compared to the past," which led to a comparative growth of grain output (CPCC, December 1978), China's grain shortage could not be solved and agriculture was unable to develop quickly and the countryside was unable to get rich. "Generally, our agricultural for nearly 20 years has not had quick development ... although both the yield for per unit area and total grain output had grown, the national per capita grain in 1978 was only equal to that in 1957. The annual per capita income of the national agricultural population was only around 70 yuan and there were nearly 25 percent of the production teams of which the annual per member income was below 50 yuan. The average collective accumulation fund for each production brigade was less than 10 thousand yuan. In some regions a simple reproduction could not be maintained." In 1978 there were 250 million rural residents, 31 percent of the total rural population, living below the poverty line. After a 30-year high-speed industrial development, China still faced a poor countryside with a huge poor rural population and still faced the basic issue "to solve its own daily food supply."

6.2 Policy goals

To abandon equalitarianism and enhance farmers' incentives

China started to seek a new development path after Mao Zedong died. In December 1978, the Third Plenum of the Eleventh CPCCC decided to shift its work center from political struggle to economic development, reform the highly centralized system, and adjust its economy. This decision symbolized the start of China's reform and open policy to get rid of Mao Zedong's Utopia development pattern replacing economic law by political ideology. The focus of the conference was rural economic development. Its main goal was to raise farmers' production incentives, based on the people's commune collective economy, to accelerate agricultural development and change the poor countryside. The CPCCC argued: "the most important starting point for determining agricultural and rural economic policy is the full display of socialist system superiority and the fully display of 800 million farmers' incentives. We must take care of their material interest economically; really protect their democratic rights politically while strengthening socialist thought education for farmers." It emphasized: "leaving aside certain material interests and political rights, any incentives coming from any social class won't appear naturally. Whether or not all of our policies conform to the need to develop productive force depends on whether or not the policies are able to raise workers' incentives" (CPCCC, December 1978). Here, the CPCCC emphasized the importance of farmers' incentives, material interests and political rights to accelerate agricultural development and change the poor countryside.

To give up the egalitarianism of the people's commune

"All levels of economic organizations in the people's commune must earnestly carry out the principle to work according to ability and to distribute according to the work. The more the work, the more the pay is, the little the work, the less the pay is ... We must firmly correct egalitarianism" (CPCCC, December 1978).

To expand farmers' independent production rights

"Under the premise of continuing the socialist direction, executing state policies, laws and regulations and accepting state plan instructions, all basic accounting units in the people's communes' have the right to choose the crops to plant as conditions permit, to decide the measures for increasing production and the pattern to manage, to assign their own products and cash and to resist any blind direction from any leading body and leader" (CPCCC, December 1978). In other words, most production teams will have an independent operating right. Certainly, these reforms must be carried on under the premise of continuing the people's commune system.

To abandon "grain priority" and develop rural economy from all sides

To abandon "grain priority" is to change the policy from concentrating on grain production only and to promote rural economy on all sides simultaneously. The CPCCC enumerated seven "main experiences and lessons, which should be remembered firmly." The sixth one is: "in the past, it was right to vigorously promote grain production, but we neglected and harmed economic crops, forestry, animal husbandry and fishery and paid no attention to ecological equilibrium. This is a very big lesson. We must make full use of our superior natural conditions, fully excavate various potentials, and enable farming, forestry, animal husbandry, sideline productions and fishery all to have a big development." The CPCCC made a call for "changing the situation to only promote grain production and neglect industrial crop production and forestry, animal husbandry and sideline production" (CPCCC, December 1978). At the same time, the CPCCC pointed out: "commune and production brigade-owned diversified economies are socialist economy, private plots and livestock, household sidelines and rural fairs are an attachment and supplement to socialist economy and we do not allow them to be criticized and banned as capitalist economy." "They cannot be treated as the so-called capitalist tail and be criticized." It emphasized: "On the contrary, we should encourage and support farmers to carry on household sideline production, to increase personal income and active rural economy while guaranteeing, consolidating and developing collective economy" (CPCCC, December 1978). In other words, the CPCCC relaxed its control on the rural economy and allowed farmers to develop full-scale rural economy.

To develop rural industry for strengthening farmers' material ability of reproduction

The CPCCC decided to officially relax the restrictions on rural industry, mainly the commune and production brigade-owned industry (CPBOI). It emphasized that developing farmland capital construction and rural commune and production brigade-owned enterprises played an important role in the transformation of agricultural production natural conditions, and enhancement of farmers' material ability to expand reproduction. "The commune and production brigade-owned enterprises (CPBOEs) must have a big development. We should raise the share of these enterprises in the economic income at three levels of the people's commune gradually. Every agricultural and subsidiary product suitable for rural processing must be transferred to these rural enterprises gradually" (CPCCC, December 1978). This indicated that the CPCCC changed its ambiguous policy for rural industry and allowed it to develop officially. But this is only a policy relaxation, and does not completely abandon restrictions. In fact, the state still put a restriction on rural industry.

The goals to develop rural industry (the State Council, 3 July 1979)

- Serving for agricultural production, collecting funds for the mechanization of agriculture and enhancing farmers' material ability to expand reproduction
- Expanding collective economies at people's commune and production brigade levels to create conditions for developing the people's commune from a small to a large collective body, again transiting it from the large collective body to the ownership system of the whole people in the future.
- Solving the rural employment issue created by mechanization
- Increasing collective income and raising farmers' living standards
- Accelerating nation industrial development
- Reducing the differences between city and countryside and between urban worker and farmer, and avoiding the over-concentration of industry in large cities
- CPBOE share in the gross economic income of the people's commune at three levels should be raised from 30 percent in 1978 to about 50 percent by 1985

Obviously, the goal for rural industry is mainly to develop agriculture, expanding the collective economy and solving rural employment. This is totally different from the AMA campaign. It is not simply and purely to impel agriculture by increasing farm machinery directly, but to promote agricultural development through developing non-agricultural industry for accumulating funds and strengthening the whole rural economic power. This policy change indicated that the CPCCC no longer considered rural industry as an opposition to agriculture which would harm agricultural development. On the contrary, it would benefit and impel agricultural development. At the same time, rural industry could benefit rural economy, and could strengthen the collective economy without harm to big industry. This is a decisive policy transformation.

To continue the commune system and ban sharing out land and private farming

Although the CPCCC decided to reform its old economic system and relax its control on the rural economy for raising farmers' incentives, it still continued with the people's commune system and wanted to implement reforms and impel agricultural development under the collective system frame. "The collective economy is an unshakeable foundation for our agriculture to advance to modernization. It has a superiority with which the private economy cannot compare. This has already been proved by our 20-year agricultural development history." The CPCCC argued: "although our collective agriculture experienced some winding and had some faults, generally speaking, its achievement is greater. After more than 20-years rural collective economy has been consolidated in most regions and the agricultural collectivization direction has been supported by most farmers ... there is no doubt that the agricultural collectivization direction is correct and must be continued" (CPCCC, 27 September 1980). When correcting egalitarianism and implementing distribution according to the amount of work, the CPCCC (December, 1978) emphasized: "Distributing land to farmers is not allowed, except for some sideline productions, and some regions with inconvenient transportation such as mountainous areas and isolated households. The guarantee-output contract with household is also not allowed in order to avoid harming and disintegrating the collective economy."

From the very beginning, China's rural economic reform had dealt with rural industry as well as its relations with other industries. In the relation of the rural industry to agriculture, the CPCCC changed the old policy from regarding their opposing each other to benefiting each other. As to its relations with major industry, major industry was the center for the national economy and rural industry cannot harm its development. The CPCCC also solved the issue between collective and private economies by developing collective enterprises only.

6.3 Policy controls

To introduce the household responsibility system (HRS)[1]

Although the people's commune was reorganized after the GLF failure, as an organization form, it continued and had become the only government tool and rural economic organization to control rural economy, political activity and resources in China's countryside for twenty years. The rural reforms aimed to reform the people's commune. However, because the CPCCC wanted to implement the reform under the frame of the people's commune system, any reform, which might weaken the commune system would not be allowed. So although as early as Spring 1979, the Xao Gang production team, Fengyang County, Anhui Province, the smallest and poorest team county-wide, spontaneously started the HRS, the contract system did not go nationwide until the policy change in September 1979.

The main content of the HRS

- Contracting collective land to individual farmers.
- Individual farmers holding the use and operative rights of the land contracted
- Individual farmers possessing other producer goods personally, except land.
- Individual farmers responsible for own profits and losses
- Individual farmers responsible for tax, state purchase and the part for the collective
- The remaining part belonging to the contractor completely, which may enter market freely.

Stages for the introduction of the HRS

- Two "Not Permitteds" at the end of 1978
  One is that contracting the output of collective land by individual households is not permitted. The other is that sharing out the collective land by farmers is not permitted. Although the rural reform centered on enhancing farmers' incentives, the CPCCC continued the people's commune collective system, strictly prohibited both the "contracting output by individual households" and "sharing out collective land by individual households," which in fact is to oppose the HRS.
- Hesitating in September 1979
  However, the two "not permitteds" made at the end of 1978 were changed at the Fourth Plenary of the Eleventh CPCCC in September 1979. Although the CPCCC still continued "not permitting" sharing out collective land by farmers, the control on "not permitting contracting the output of collective land by individual households" was lifted a little, which reflected a policy change and hesitation for the HRS and sent a signal to farmers that the CPCCC allowed local governments to try the HRS. This hesitation encouraged not only farmers but also local governments greatly (Chen, Chen and Yang, 1993, pp. 483–4).
- Not opposing and not supporting in 1981
  The emergence of the HRS brought about a great and intense debate nationwide. At the symposium on rural management held by the State Agricultural Committee in January 1980, a heated debate was made

between the two sides to support or oppose the HRS. However, the state kept a neutral position between them (Chen, Chen and Yang, 1993, p. 491). In 1981 the HRS developed rapidly not only in poor regions but also expanded to the regions with medium level. By July, the share of production teams with the HRS in total production teams was already 32 percent and at the end of October, the share achieved 45 percent.

- Recognizing HRS legal status in 1982
  In 1982, the CPCCC officially recognized the HRS as one of the collective economy forms. The CPCCC (1 January 1982) pointed out: "the establishing the HRS has progressed so rapidly, which reflected the strong desire of hundreds of millions of farmers to develop socialist agriculture according to China's actual rural condition." It also recognized that all of the HRSs were of the "socialist collective economy production responsibility form," which was based on the foundation of land public ownership and accepted state plan instruction. They were different from private economy and a part of socialist agriculture and would develop into a more perfect collective economy gradually. The CPCCC recognition impelled the HRS to develop greatly. By June 1982, the share of production teams implementing the HRS in total production teams had reached 72 percent, 79 percent by November.
- Supporting and promoting in 1983
  The No. 1 CPCCC document (2 January 1983) praised the HRS highly: "Since the Third Plenum of the Eleventh CPCCC, our countryside has had many tremendous changes, of which the HRS is the one with the most profound influence and is becoming the main form increasingly ... its consummation and development will certainly cause the concrete path of the agricultural socialist cooperatives to conform even more to our country's reality." It appraised: "this is our farmers' great creation under party leadership, a new development of Marxism agricultural cooperativization theory in the practices of our country."

Features of introducing the HRS

- Created and impelled by farmers
  Although the CPCCC wanted to implement rural reform, it did not want to change the commune system and didn't support the HRS at first. Under farmers' creating, experimenting and promoting, the CPCCC began to change its policy for the HRS from opposing and watching, to recognizing, supporting and promoting. Unlike other massive campaigns, the HRS introduction is not a campaign promoted by government, but by farmers.
- Poor regions impelling rich regions
  The HRS was created by farmers in one of the poorest regions first and later got popular in other poor regions. The introduction of the HRS in rich regions was promoted by the poor regions where the HRS had had government support.

The HRS started from poor regions, expanded to rich regions gradually and covered the whole nation rapidly. In January 1980, the share of basic accounting units contracted in total basic accounting units was 85 percent and by the end of 1980, the share had achieved 91 percent. In June 1982, the share was 99 percent, and the HRS controlled the rural areas completely (Wei, 1994, *Economic Cooperatives in China*, Qin and Lu, eds, 1994, p. 30). This was a rural revolution in China and finally led to the disintegration of the "big and public" people's commune system, which had controlled the countryside for twenty years.

To expand business scope and control operations of rural enterprises

Before the reforms, rural industry was defined in the field of agricultural industry serving the mechanization of agriculture. However, on 3 July 1979 the State Council expanded the business scope of CPBOEs and explicitly requested them to serve the people's lives, major industry and exportation while focusing on agricultural industry. The main fields were as follows:

- Agricultural industry
- Fuel, raw materials, power industries, spare parts and partial products for major industries
- Small chemical industries, smelting, daily articles, hardware and so on
- Traditional handicraft and exportable and compensation trades
- Urban and rural capital construction and transportation
- Tailoring, daily repair, catering trades and other services

Although the state relaxed control on the business scope of the CPBOE, it controlled their business activities such as production, material supply and product sale, and wanted to strengthen government instructions to rural enterprises. "All levels of planning and related departments, especially the industry sector, should manage both state enterprises and the CPBOEs and adopt various plans to strengthen CPBOE production and sales and link them up with national economic plans at all levels" (the State Council, 3 July 1979).

Methods to control CPBOE operations

- Controlling production
  The State Council requested that the people's communes must make a productive plan for the CPBOEs to control their production and also divided their products into three categories:
  1) The products put into line with all levels of state plans directly by planning committees.
  2) The products put into line with all levels of state plans indirectly through contracts with other enterprises in a state plan.

3) The products not put into line with all levels of state plans but necessary for society with reliable raw materials and power supply. The communes should make a plan for their production.

- Controlling material supply
  1) The government production departments and planning committees at all levels responsible for the material supply for the production directly in line with plans at all levels.
  2) The enterprises or departments contracting with the CPBOEs responsible for the material supply for the production indirectly in line with plans at all levels according to the contracts.
  3) Controlling supply channel
  A. Local planning committees responsible for the materials allotted by the state for capital construction, equipment maintenance and technological transformation, essential transport means and local recycling steel products and other materials.
  B. Supplying the second and third class materials and labor protection materials through the application of the managing departments of the CPBOEs.
  C. Purchasing the second and third class materials and labor protection materials voluntarily by the enterprises and their managing departments.
  D. Supplying some of the second and third class materials and labor protection materials by local material offices at the same level.
- Controlling product sale
  1) Purchasing the production directly in line with plans at all levels by the related state departments according to contracts.
  2) Purchasing the production indirectly in line with plans at all levels by the related enterprises according to contracts.
  3) Selling the products out of plans at all levels by the CPBOEs themselves or with aid from their management departments.
- Controlling price

  CPBOEs must carry out state price policy. The products purchased by the state in principle should have the same price as that of state-owned enterprises. Other products should have a market price but must be below the highest price stipulated by the government pricing department.

  (The State Council, 3 July 1979).

Although the state wanted to control the CPBOEs by the state plan and the CPBOEs also requested to put their production and sales into the state plan so they could get raw materials and sales market from the state, the majority of CPBOEs were not in China's industrial plans and their production, supply and sales mainly depended on markets because the state wanted to concentrate resources on SOEs and didn't want to provide resources to the CPBOEs.

Table 6.1 Growth of state-owned, collective and private industries in China 1978–83 (%)

	1978	*1979*	*1980*	*1981*	*1982*	*1983*
Growth rate of state-owned industry	14.4	8.9	5.6	2.5	7.1	9.4
Growth rate of collective industry	10.6	8.6	19.2	9.0	9.5	15.5
Growth rate of private industry	n	n	n	134.6	79.0	120.6

Source: *CSY* 1996, p. 403.
Note: Collective industry including both urban and rural collective industry, but primarily the rural one.

Being market-oriented helped the CPBOEs get out of the state control and promoted their development. On the other hand, to expand CPBOE access to industries, especially the industries with high return, helped it develop from a small to a widespread domain and made more profit, which impelled the rural industry greatly. They developed with a much higher speed than that of the state-owned enterprises after the policy lift.

To take self-raised funds as the mainstay

Developing rural industry needs massive funds. The State Council on 3 July 1979 explicitly urged the CPBOEs to raise funds mainly depending on their own efforts and stipulated the fund sources as following:

- Accumulation of the enterprises
  The enterprise accumulation is the main fund source for the CPBOEs.
- The public accumulation funds of the production brigade and production teams
  Withdrawing suitable funds from the production brigade and production team's public accumulation funds in stock form.
- Local government finance
  The funds allotted by local government finance to the managing department for supporting local CPBOEs.
- State fiscal funds
  The state fiscal funds allotted every year to support the CPBOEs. The Agricultural Bank of China (ABC) was responsible for the management of both state and local government funds
- State bank loans
  Loans with low interest from the ABC every year to support the CPBOEs.

Although the state requested to develop CPBOEs with great effort, its policy for CPBOEs was mainly to relax control, and allow it to develop.

Table 6.2 The loans of the ABC and RCC for the CPBOE (year-end) (billion yuan)

	1979	*1980*	*1981*	*1982*	*1983*
Total	4.4	8.1	9.8	11.5	14.0
ABC	3.0	5.3	6.2	7.3	8.0
RCC	1.4	2.8	3.6	4.2	6.0
Share of ABC loans for CPBOEs in total state bank loans	0.01	0.02	0.02	0.02	0.02

Source: *China Rural Finance Statistics 1979–89*, the Agricultural Bank of China, China statistics publishing house, 1991, pp. 1047 and 1276.

Notes: 1) The state bank loan data in 1979 comes from *New China 50 Years Statistical Data Assembly*, the national economic synthesis statistics department of SSB, Chinese statistics publishing house, 1999, p. 64.

2) Before 1984, the ABC was the only state bank to extend loans to the CPBOEs.

The state didn't want to provide much funds. In the sixth FYP (1981–85), the share of government fiscal funds (both state and local government) in the total investment of CPBOEs was only 0.6 percent. At the same time, the loans from the state banks for the CPBOEs were also very few. Although state bank loans held a certain proportion in total CPBOE investment, the share of these loans in total loans extended by state banks was only about 0.02 percent (Xu, Deng et al., 1994, p. 174).

Favorable tax policy with limited favorable loans

Favorable tax policy

On the foundation of the self-collecting fund by rural enterprises, the state implemented favorable tax policies for the CPBOEs, especially for those in industry supported by the state. The favorable policies included both tax reduction and exemption. "The state implements a low tax or tax-free policy for the CPBOEs ... these enterprises that serve directly for agricultural production and commune members' lives may enumerate the concrete products and services and can enjoy the exemption of industry and commerce income tax[2] according to the local actual situation after an examination and authorization of the province or city or autonomous region revolutionary committee." From 1978, small iron ore, coal, power and cement factories could enjoy the exemption of industry and commercial tax and income tax for three years. "From now these newly set up enterprises will enjoy a tax-free for three years." The favorable policy also included other enterprise, which had difficulty in paying tax such as those in the frontier and minority nationality regions, which would from 1979 enjoy an exemption of income tax for five years (the State Council, 3 July 1979).

Opening the CPBOE loan and providing a few favorable loans

Before 1978, there was no item for the CPBOEs in state bank loan plans and the state bank extended all loans to the CPBOEs in the name of agriculture loans. In order to support CPBOE development, the state requested the ABC to extend some low-interest loans to these enterprises. The ABC (10 November 1979) set up the rural CPBOE loan project and started to extend loans to the CPBOEs.

- The method of extending favorable loans to the CPBOEs:
  1) For collective enterprises only.
     The ABC loans were only for collective enterprises such as the CPBOEs and enterprises owned by both the commune and county. Other types of enterprises such as private enterprises could not obtain the loans.
  2) For production turnover and production facilities only.
  3) One-year and three-year loans generally with a few five-year loans.
  4) Favorable interest rate.
     To support CPBOE development, the state bank made favorable loan interest rates less than that for the SOEs, especially for the CPBOEs serving for agricultural production (the ABC, 19 May 1980).

The CPBOEs enjoyed favorable tax policies not only from the state, but also from local government at various levels. They basically enjoyed a more favorable interest rate than the SOEs. But, as indicated above, the loans were very few. In fact, the state provided mainly a low tax policy for the CPBOEs.

Restricting rural industry to protect agriculture, collective and state-owned industries

Although the CPCCC permitted rural industry to develop and hoped to promote agricultural development by the rural industry, it strictly limited rural industry in order to prevent possible harm to agriculture, collective economy and state-owned industries.

Main content of the restriction

- Developing collective enterprise only
  First, the CPCCC allowed only collective enterprise to develop, in other words, to develop collective industry vigorously, not private industry. One of the goals in developing the CPBOEs was to expand the collective economy. The ban on private industry was not relaxed. Therefore, the State Council (3 July 1979) stressed that the CPBOE was a socialist collective ownership economy. "The enterprise run by a commune will belong to the commune and the one run by a production brigade will belong to the brigade." The State Council explicitly pointed out that the rural industrial enterprises generally should be established from now on by the people's communes. Local counties would send cadres to lead the enterprises, which should operate in the form of county-owned enterprises.

- Supporting agriculture
  Rural industry must support and not hinder agricultural production. Because the main goal in developing the CPBOEs was to expand farmers' production ability to promote agriculture, the state requested that rural industry must support agriculture. There were two ways for rural industry to support agriculture. One was to concentrate on agricultural industry, which could support agriculture directly. The other was to take some profits from rural industry and put it into agriculture. It was not permitted to harm agriculture due to the development of rural enterprises.
- Not competing with the SOEs or destroying natural resources
  The state stipulated that the CPBOE development couldn't compete with and harm the development of major industry. "The rural enterprises cannot set up processing industries with a surplus production ability, cannot compete with the advanced large industrial enterprises for raw material and power, and cannot destroy national resources" (the State Council, 3 July 1979). Here the surplus production ability deals with the production ability of the state enterprises. In other words, the CPBOEs couldn't develop industries in which the state enterprises had a surplus production ability. In addition, the CPBOEs couldn't compete with the state enterprises for raw materials and power. For instance, because of rural enterprises, some SOEs often could not obtain agricultural and subsidiary products as raw materials, and had to stop production. The state requested that CPBOEs act as circumstances permitted and carried on production according to local resources and social need. They couldn't violate local natural conditions or develop blindly. At the same time, because of the backward technology and equipment of the CPBOEs, which was wasteful and destructive of resources, the state stressed that the rural enterprises couldn't destroy national resources and bring loss to the country.

Methods to restrict the CPBOEs

- Controlling funds
  Because funds were the essential condition for rural enterprises, the state controlled the enterprises not conforming to the policy through limiting the flow of funds. The fund control was mainly as follows:
  1) Controlling government expenditure.
     In order to avoid rural enterprises competing with major industry, the state controlled government finance and allotted massive funds to the SOEs to guarantee enough funds for major industry, while the CPBOEs obtained very few government financial allocations. The fund shortage was the main impediment for them to develop rapidly.
  2) Controlling bank loans.
     The banks implemented different loan policies for different enterprises and industries according to state developmental strategy. For example, bank loans were mainly extended to the SOEs, which made non-state-

owned enterprises unable to compete with the SOEs. Also the ABC stipulated that only collective enterprises could obtain favorable loans. Thus, they could develop more rapidly than non-collective enterprises, which were unable to obtain bank loans. State banks also implemented industry control through different loan policies for different industries.

- Controlling labor
  In order to prevent a labor decrease in agriculture due to the development of rural industry, the State Council stipulated, that "The CPBOE implements the work system to work partially in industry and partially in agriculture. If an enterprise needs labor, under the premise to guarantee enough labor in agriculture, both the people's commune and production brigade will consult with the basic accounting unit and assign the labor to the enterprises. The enterprises cannot hire labor privately and randomly" (the State Council, 3 July 1979). This meant that a commune must guarantee enough labor in agriculture before assigning labor to rural industry.
- Controlling profit
  A CPBOE cannot use its own profits and the profit use must be decided by the congresses of both the people's commune and production brigade, approved by the county and commune authority separately. Besides being used for expanding reproduction of the enterprise and for setting up new enterprises, the profit must mainly be used in farmland capital construction, mechanization of agriculture and support for poor production teams (the State Council, 3 July 1979).
- Controlling the tax rate
  Through different tax rates for different industries, the state carried on its industrial guidance and controlled each rural industry development. For example, the Ministry of Finance on 19 April 1982 decided to cut all favorable tax rates for products such as tobacco or liquor made by rural enterprises. They could no longer enjoy a tax exemption. Products such as wristwatches, clocks, electronic products, bicycles, sewing machines and domestic electric appliances sold by rural enterprises also couldn't

The structure of administrative setup for CPBOEs in 1980

Rural people's commune enterprise administrative bureau
(of the Ministry of Agriculture and Forestry)

↓

Provincial people's commune enterprise administrative bureau (or other institutes)

↓

Prefecture, city and county people's commune enterprise administrative bureaus
(or other institutes)

↓

Commune enterprise office (company or other institutes)

↓

CPBOEs

enjoy tax reduction. Thus, in this way, the state restricted the development of those rural enterprises it did not support.

- Controlling raw materials and products
  Regarding the rural enterprises brought into line with the state plan directly or indirectly, the state controlled their operation through the raw material supply plan and product purchase and made them develop according to the state plan.
- Establishing administrative setup
  In order to manage the CPBOEs, the state established an administrative setup at all levels of governments.

To introduce the government finance contract system

In February 1980, the State Council decided to reform its government finance management system and introduce a new system, the "eating by dividing cooking stoves" system from 1980.[3]

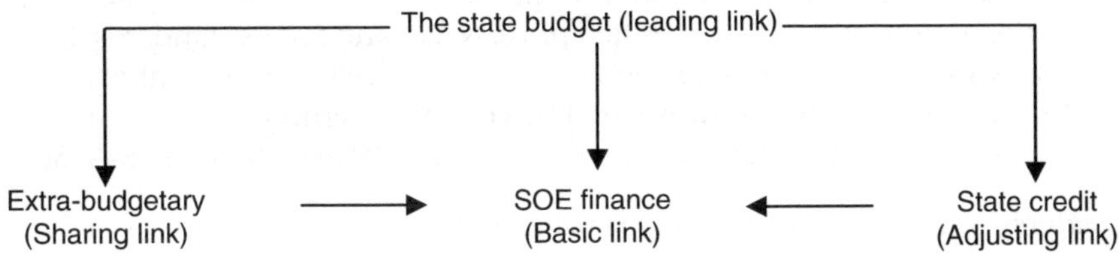

Figure 6.1 China's government finance system (four links) in the 1970s

The features of the government financial system before the reform in 1980

- "Unified leadership, administrating at all levels separately"
  China implemented a level-to-level administration system of government finance under central unified leadership. Central government completely controlled both the total financial revenue collected by both central and local governments and the expenditures of central and local governments. Local governments would implement a concrete fiscal budget after central government decided the government fiscal revenue and expenditure scale at all levels.
- "Distributing on total revenue, and changing each year"
  In government financial revenue and expenditure, the central government takes all the revenue collected by both central and local governments first then distributes them among local governments proportionally based on the revenue and need. Local quota is not fixed but changeable each year on central government adjustment.

Under the old system, the central government held too much power with a monotonous fund channel, which made local governments and enterprises lack independent economic rights with no incentive for their revenue and fund use efficiency.

Government finance system reform in 1980

- Adjusting financial revenue and expenditure scope of central and local governments.
  The way to collect the revenue was still the old one with classification and division at all levels. The expenditure introduces a contract system at each level.
- Expanding local power on financial revenue and expenditure.
  The share of local revenue offered to central government, the share of adjusting income and the subsidy for local government are invariable for five years in principle after the central government approved. Local governments arrange and adjust, based on their own revenue, their own revenue and expenditure for the balance between them independently in the scope decided. Central government no longer issues local expenditure quotas.
- Central unification.
  In order to maintain a national unified government finance system, the national fiscal systems such as tax, price, wages and bonus standards, bond issues and enterprise cost expenditure scope, as well as important expenditure standards must be formulated by central government and cannot be changed without central government approval (Wang, 1995, pp. 849–50).

Features of the government finance system reform

- "The more collected, the more to spend; the less collected, the less to spend"
  1) Before reform
     Under the old system, any increment of local government revenue must be delivered to central government and cannot be used by the local government that collected it. After the central unified balance nationwide, this part was to be distributed among regions. In other words, regions with increased new revenue cannot have an increase in their expenditure.

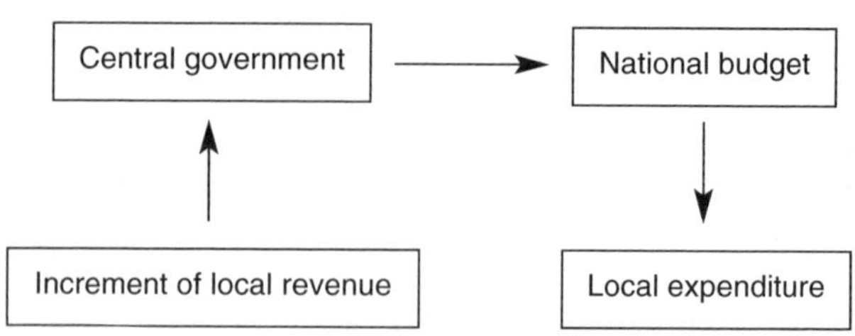

  2) After the reform
     The main change of the new system is to relate local government's financial revenue with their expenditure. If there is an increase in the revenue of a local government over the quota, the local government can spend the part increased. Similarly, if there is a decrease in the

revenue to less than the quota, the local government must reduce its expenditure by the same amount.

- Unchangeable for five years
  The quota period of both local government revenue and expenditure increased from "one year" to "five years." In other words, after the new quota was decided, a local government would control all of the increment revenue over the next five years.
  (Wang, 1995, p. 851)

The introduction of the government finance contract system caused local governments to obtain more rights in their financial revenue and expenditure, especially to expand their right to spend new revenue increment, which raise their incentive for increasing new revenue greatly. In order to obtain more revenue, local governments at various levels impelled local economy diligently. In the countryside, as the main source of government revenue, the rural industry was pushed by local governments at all levels vigorously.

To raise the purchase price of agricultural products and reduce grain procurement

Raising the purchase price of agricultural products

From 1979, China decided to raise the purchase price of agricultural products greatly. "The price of grain purchased by the State Monopoly will rise 20 percent from summer grain in 1979. The price of grain purchased after the State Monopoly Purchase will increase another 50 percent from this foundation. The purchase prices of cotton, edible oils, sugar, livestock products, aquatic products and so on should also rise correspondingly based on different situations" (CPCCC, 28 September 1979). For example, the purchase price for eggs rose by 30 percent on average and live pigs by 25 percent in 1979 (Liu, 1997, p. 186). "The industrial products for agriculture such as farm machinery, chemical fertilizer, agricultural chemicals and plastic should reduce their prices gradually through cutting costs to benefit farmers. After the rise of the purchase price of agricultural products, the grain retail price must remain unchanged" (CPCCC, 28 September 1979).

Reducing the amount of grain procurement

In December 1978, the CPCCC also decided to reduce the grain procurement and requested that the grain quota for state purchase should stabilize at the level made for the period of 1971–5 over the next several years and should decrease by 2.5 billion kilograms from 1979 in order to relieve the farmers' burden and develop production. The grain purchase must be exempted in the paddy rice regions with a grain ration less than 200 kilograms and in the miscellaneous grains regions of less than 150 kilograms.

In 1979, the state reduced the grain purchase by 2.8 billion kilograms to relieve the burden on old commodity grain regions with high quotas. In 1980 the State Council agreed to cut 0.5 billion kilograms of grain quotas for thirteen provinces and autonomous regions such as Sichuan, Yunnan, Inner Mongolia and Heilongjiang and exempted Tibet from the grain state monopoly for purchase and supply completely. The share of average grain procurement in the total annual average grain output decreased from 25 percent in 1953–78 to 22 percent in 1979–84 (Cong and Zhang, 1999, pp. 652–3).

To relax control and allow collective commerce to develop

Although the CPCCC in 1979 requested rural commerce to promote the exchange of goods between city and countryside, the old commercial system was unable to adapt the rural economy after the reform. The No. 1 document of the CPCCC (1 January 1982) argued; "one of the current prominent issues is that the rural commerce is unsuitable to the development needs of commercial economy, which led to an impediment to rural commodity circulation and a difficulty in both buying and selling products when the rural diversified economy had just started to develop." The economic transformation brought about by the HRS forced the CPCCC to reform the old rural circulation system and to change its original policy, strictly prohibiting non-commercial organizations and units from operating commerce. The state, on the one hand, continued the policy of "taking planned economy as the mainstay, making market regulation subsidiary" and the SMPs, on the other hand starting to relax its control on rural commerce and allowed new circulation channels to open. The CPCCC requested "all possible means to dredge and open circulation channels," "to break local blockades, organize circulation of commodities and vigorously promote product sales according to economic law. At the same time, we must try to set up and develop the collective trade of both commune and production brigades."

The State Council (17 June 1982) further relaxed control over rural commerce, changed the old system of dividing urban and rural commerce, in which the state-owned companies dealt with urban commerce and rural SMCs with rural commerce. The state decision removed the impediment of commercial exchange between urban and rural areas and promoted the exchange of industry and agriculture products between city and countryside.

Methods to relax control on rural commerce

- Restoring the cooperative commercial nature of the SMCs

  The CPCCC decided to restore the original cooperative nature of the SMCs and strengthen their massive, democratic and flexible management. "The SMCs must gradually carry on an organizational reform ... Its basic units must restore the nature of cooperative commerce, and expand stocks from production teams and farmers on voluntary principles ... relate the SMCs operations with farmers' economic interests" (CPCCC, 1 January 1982).

  1) Restoring the cooperative nature of the basic units of the SMCs.

2) Changing the SMCs at county level into a federate cooperative of the basic units and separating them from state-owned commerce.
3) Both the county federate cooperatives and basic units of SMCs to account independently, be responsible for their own profits and losses, and for paying income tax to the state.

- Developing commune and production brigade collective trades
  "We must try and develop commune and production brigade collective trades in a planned way, such as trade warehouses, united supply and sales departments and agricultural and industrial integrated complexes, and gradually realize a system that is multi-ingredient, multi-channel and with few links" (the same as above).
- Breaking local blockades and allowing cross-region commodity flow and exchange and product promotion
- Breaking the blockade between city and countryside commerce
- Developing industrial and commercial synthesis
  The commercial sector may process the purchased agricultural and subsidiary products by itself or with communes and production brigades and teams, and may commission farmer families to process the products. "We must develop the industrial and commercial synthesis which is able to purchase, process and sell products" (CPCCC, 1 January 1982).

Table 6.3 China's rural fair trade value and SMC share in rural markets 1978–83 (%)

	Trade value of rural fair (billion yuan)	*SMC share in social commodity retail*	*SMC share in rural commodity retail*	*SMC share in social agricultural and subsidiary products purchased*
1978	12.5	35.4	68.2	32.6
1979	17.1	34.3	62.7	26.2
1980	21.1	31.7	57.0	26.1
1981	25.3	29.5	52.3	24.7
1982	28.8	27.7	48.2	23.6
1983	33.0	24.8	42.4	23.7

Source: *China Trade and Price Statistical Data 1952–83*, the trade and price statistics department of SSB, Chinese statistics publishing house, 1984, and *China Supply and Marketing Cooperative Chronicle and Development Survey 1949–85*, the editorial office of China supply and marketing cooperative historical series, Chinese financial and economic publishing house, 1988.

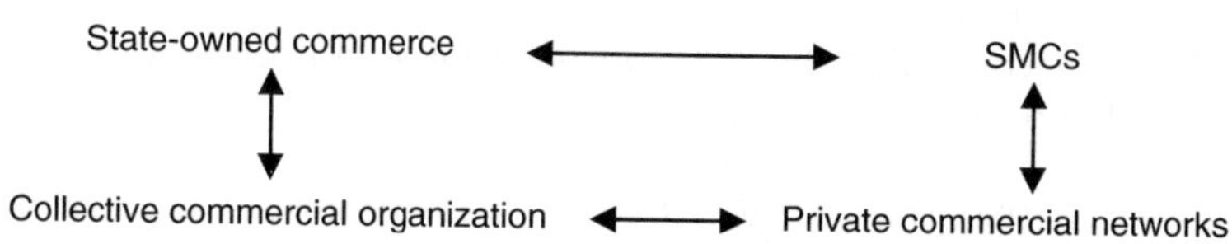

Figure 6.2 China's rural commercial circulation system in 1980s

The features of relaxing control on rural commerce

Both the reform of the SMCs and opening new circulation channels essentially broke state monopoly on rural commerce and introduced non-state-owned commercial mechanisms. Policy relaxation led not only to a number of collective commercial enterprises, but also caused many private commercial enterprises to appear. At the same time, many commercial specialized markets started to develop. The development of the non-state-system commercial sector caused the share of SMCs in rural commodity markets to drop greatly.

To restore the Agricultural Bank of China and relax control on rural finance

To restore the Agricultural Bank of China

In February 1979, the State Council decided that the ABC would establish all levels of organizations from the top downward and lead both rural business offices of the people's bank and the RCCs. On 13 March 1979, the ABC officially restored and became the only state specialized bank in China's countryside. The state simultaneously indicated that the central task of the rural finance was to support the development of rural commodity economy and the full-scale development of rural economy, not just grain production and the collective economy.

- Main business scope of the ABC
  1) Supervising the funds from government finance for supporting agriculture, commune collectives and individual farmers.
  2) Extending loans to state-owned agricultural departments and enterprises, the SMCs, rural collectives and individual farmers.
  3) In charge of accountant training of rural people's commune basic accounting units

  (Xu and Deng et al., 1994, pp. 33–4).
- The influence of the ABC on rural finance
  1) Expanding rural credit scope.
     In the past, the rural credit business of the People's Bank of China was mainly agriculture loans to support grain production. The ABC broke through this and expanded the scope to the whole rural economy including rural industry and individual farmers (Xu and Deng et al., 1994, p. 21).
  2) Expanding the credit object from rural collective economy to both the collective and private economy.
  3) Leading the RCCs.
     The ABC controlled the RCCs organization establishment, personnel, credit and revenue and expenditure.

At the end of 1980, there were 27,828 ABC organizations with a total staff of 285,000 persons, 2,211 county branches and 25,164 business offices nationally. Also there were 59,507 RCCs with a formal staff of 272,000 persons[4] (*China Rural Finance Statistics* 1979–89 and 1991).

To relax the restrictions on rural private finance

Before the reform, the state strictly forbade any form of rural private finance. But along with the policy relaxation on rural economy, some rural private lending also started to appear. In many regions, the commune collectives raised funds through high interest rates. The funds raised came primarily from individual farmers. There was also lending between collectives, and between individual farmers. After the reform, the policy for rural private lending experienced two stages.

- A ban on rural private lending in 1979
  In September 1979, the ABC indicated the main harm of rural private lending:
  1) Weakening the collective economy because of high interest rates.
  2) Encouraging speculation for economic benefit and corroding the masses.
  3) Reducing the deposit of the RCCs.
     Because of the high interest, many loans of private lending came from the RCCs, which led a big drop in RCC deposits.
     (Xu, 1996, p. 381)
- Allowing rural private lending to develop in 1981
  The ban on rural private lending didn't stop the high interest lending at all. On the contrary, lending developed very quickly in the countryside, especially in the developed regions with strong CPBOEs. As the reform went, the state started to change the policy for rural private finance. The State Council (8 May 1981) lifted the ban and indicated: "under the domination of the state bank and RCCs, we allow a proper lending between collectives and their farmer members, and between farmers, and take the lending as a subsidiary of the bank and RCC. That will benefit agricultural development. But we must guide and strengthen the management for rural private lending." Although the state officially lifted the ban on rural private lending, it opposed rural usury.

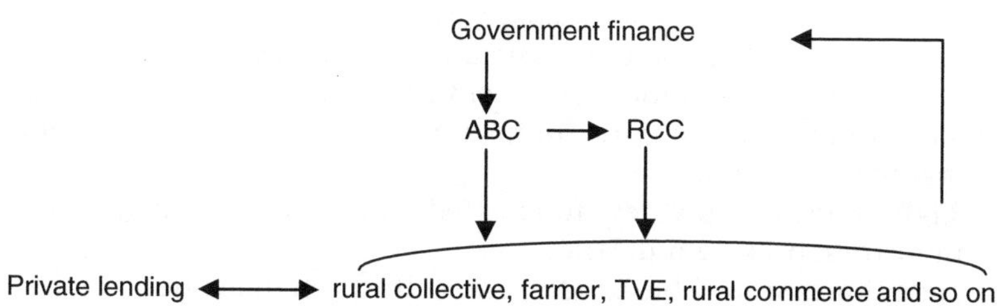

Figure 6.3 China's rural finance structure in the 1980s

Relaxing rural finance control, expanding the credit scope and object of the state bank and RCCs and permitting private lending changed rural fund flows and promoted the redistribution of rural production factors. As a result, the relaxing pumped rural funds to rural industry and other non-agricultural industries greatly. Although the state wanted to increase agricultural investment, the state fiscal expenditure in agriculture decreased unceasingly from 15.1 billion, 13 percent in total state fiscal expenditure in 1978 to 1.1 billion yuan, 10 percent in total state fiscal expenditure in 1981 (*New China 50 Years Finance Statistics*, 2000). In fact the policy change helped rural industry to solve its fund shortage.

Opening to the world

In the reform, China started to end its long-term isolation from the world, especially from western developed countries, and to open to the world aiming at making use of foreign capital, developed technology and equipment through various bilateral economic cooperations. The CPCCC (22 December 1978) pointed out: "we must positively develop, based on self-reliance, equality and mutual benefit economic cooperation with various countries, diligently use the world's advanced technology and equipment, and vigorously strengthen the science and education needed for realizing our modernization."

Methods to open up to the world

- Attracting foreign capital
  In July 1979, the People's National Congress of China made a law to allow foreign capital to enter China. The introduce of foreign capital aimed at the "expansion of international economic cooperation and technological exchange," and simultaneously the law requested that "all activities of the joint venture enterprises must abide by all of the People's Republic of China laws, related rules and stipulations." This law also stipulated favorable policies for enterprises such as tax reduction. The state (20 September 1983) stipulated the industrial fields in which to invest for the joint venture enterprises:
  1) Energy development, building materials, chemical and metallurgical industries.
  2) Mechanical manufacture, instrument and measuring appliances, marine petroleum mines equipment and manufacturing industries.
  3) Electronic and computer industries, communications equipment manufacturing industries.
  4) Light industry, textiles, food, medicine and medical instrument industries, packing industries.
  5) Agriculture, animal husbandry, and cultivation industries.
  6) Tourism and services.

- Setting up special economic zones (SEZs)
  In order to explore opening up, China established SEZs as experiment bases. In 1980, the CPCCC approved Shenzhen, Zhuhai, Shantou and Xiamen as SEZs with favorable policies for foreign firms investing in the SEZs, and expanded the SEZ governments' economic rights simultaneously with favorable policies for the construction of SEZs.
- Providing favorable policies
  The CPCCC on 15 July 1979 authorized Guangdong and Fujian provinces to implement special policies and measures, mainly to expand their economic management rights and provide financial aid.
- Reforming the foreign trade system to promote export
  The reform mainly entrusted some local government, administrative departments and commodities the license of import and export to break the state monopoly on national foreign trade. For example, the state authorized Beijing, Tianjin, Shanghai, Guangdong, Fujian and Liaoning provinces and cities to establish local foreign trade companies (other regions only had state-owned foreign trade companies) and some central government ministries such as the Ministry of Metallurgy and the Ministry of Machinery the import and export license.

The opening up policy played an important role in China's rural industry development, especially in the coastal regions. For example, because of geographic convenience widespread overseas relations and huge cheap labor supply, the joint venture processing industry in both Guangdong and Fujian countryside developed greatly. Before 1980, rural enterprises for export production in thirteen provinces and cities such as Jiangsu, Zhejiang, Guangdong, Beijing, Tianjin and Shanghai were less than 1,500, but by 1985 the number of the enterprises was more than 8,500 and increased to more than 10,000 in 1986 (CTVEY 1978–1987, p. 453). Exportation greatly promoted rural industrial development.

6.4 Rural industrialization in process

Through 1978–83, rural industry rose suddenly. The total output value of the CPBOEs grew at a rate of 11 per cent from 1978–79. By 1983, the output was 102 billion yuan, more than double compared to that in 1978. The CPBOE concentrated mainly on industry and the share of the industry in total CPBOE output value was 77 per cent in 1979. In 1983, the share of rural industry in the national gross value of industrial output was 12 per cent.

The rise of rural industry powerfully supported the agriculture, rural and national economy. The share of CPBOEs in total rural social output value was 24 percent in 1980. It provided 2.3 billion yuan for agricultural production, 6.8 hundred million yuan for collective welfare and 4.2 billion

Table 6.4 Rural enterprise's development (the CPBOE) 1978–83

Year	*Number of enterprises (mill. units)*	*Number of staff and workers (mill. persons)*	*Total output value (billion yuan)*	*Share of industry in total CPBOE output value (%)*
1978	1.5	28.3	49.3	78.1
1979	1.5	29.1	54.8	77.2
1980	1.4	30.0	65.7	77.6
1981	1.3	29.7	74.5	77.7
1982	1.4	31.1	85.3	75.7
1983	1.4	32.4	101.7	74.5

Source: *CTVEY*, 1978–87.
Notes: 1) This is for the CPBOEs only.
2) The output value in both 1978 and 1979 is at 1970 price.

yuan for various rural enterprises such as building bridges, roads, schools and theaters in 1980 (*CTVEY*, 1978–87). Because of higher returns of the CPBOEs than in agriculture, rural industry became an important source for farmers to increase their income. At the same time, the tax paid by the CPBOEs increased from 2.2 billion yuan in 1978 to 5.9 billion yuan in 1983, more than doubled. In 1983, the share of the CPBOE tax in total national tax revenue achieved 8 per cent. The rural industry development also changed the rural labor structure and about 9 percent of rural labor shifted from agriculture to non-agricultural industry.

During this period, not only rural industry had rapid development, but also agriculture got a good harvest. Except for 1980, the agricultural part of the GDP had an annual growth rate of 4 per cent or above and even achieved 12 per cent in 1982. The grain also kept up quick growth and had

Table 6.5 Rural economic development 1978–83

Year	*Index of primary industry GDP*	*Share of primary industry in national GDP*	*Per capita grain (kg/person)*	*CPBOE share in total rural labor*
1978	104	28	319	9.5
1979	106	31	343	9.3
1980	99	30	327	9.4
1981	107	32	327	9.1
1982	112	33	352	9.2
1983	108	33	380	9.3

Source: *New China 50 Years Statistical Data Assembly*, the national economic synthesis statistics department of SSB, Chinese statistics publishing house, 1999 and *CTVEY* 1978–87.
Notes: 1) GDP is at current year price.
2) The share of the primary industry in GDP is calculated at current year price.
3) The index is at previous year =100.

a big harvest with a national per capita grain increase from 319 kg in 1978 to 380 kg in 1983.

In the five years 1978–83, farmer average net income increased by 120 per cent (*CSY*, 1984), surpassing the total increment in the past twenty years (Liu and Wu, 1985, p. 458). Farmers' living standards had a comprehensive rise too. In 1983, the per capita annual net income of rural households was more than doubled to that in 1978, and the per capita annual grain consumption also increased from 194 kg in 1978 to 228 kg in 1983, a rise of 21 percent. Rural consumption of other agricultural products such as edible vegetable oil and pork meat all increased. The Engel coefficient for this period had an obvious drop, from 68 percent to 59 percent. Rural infrastructure had also a distinct improvement. For example, the number of rural telephone subscribers increased from 730,000 to 820,000 and rural electric consumption from 29 billion to 48 billion kW (*CSY*, 1984 and 2001, and *China's Contemporary Electric Industry*, 1994, p. 373).

6.5 Policy effects

The HRS broke down state overall control and liberalized the rural economy

The introduction of the HRS symbolized the conclusion of Mao Zedong's military economic system and the beginning of economic liberalization. In China's economic reform, the HRS is the most important one, and was originally an experimental measure to correct the egalitarianism to enhance farmers' incentives. It was thought as a "very commonplace" one. However, its introduction caused not only the countryside to have an earth-shaking change, but also the entire national economic system to have a big transformation. The profound influence it brought about for the rural economy as well as national economy goes far beyond people's imaginations. The most important role the HRS played in the reform was to break the overall state control on China's economy, which then promoted economic liberalization. Rural liberalization thus went to cities and all industries, which caused China's entire economy to transit to liberalization.

Although the economic efficiency of the people's communes was low, as an organization system, it was effective in controlling the countryside and hundreds of millions of individual farmers. Therefore, although in 1958 the communalization created national famine, the communes were retained and continued another twenty-five years. The people's commune system involved not only political ideology, but also state control on the countryside and farmers, which made the CPCCC unwilling to reform it for a long time. The HRS supported by farmers ended overall state control and made rural production factors flow more freely.

The rural partial liberalization of production factors made by the HRS can be shown in Figure 6.4. In the figure, Y_a, Y_0 and F_a are agricultural output,

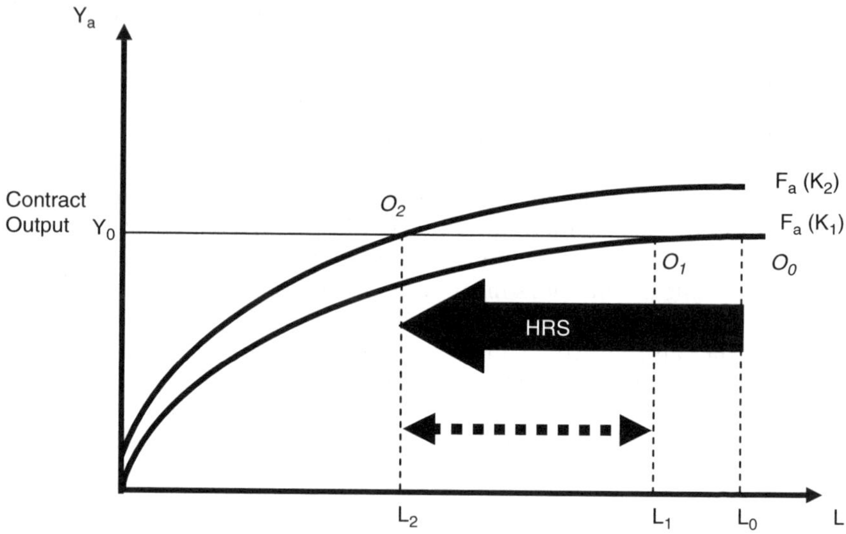

Figure 6.4 The partial liberalization of the rural economy made by the HRS

contract output and the production function of agriculture respectively. L is rural labor.

- Liberalizing the labor surplus
  Supposing before the HRS, the rural output was Y_0 and the corresponding labor supply was L_0. Because of "the grain priority" and "the farmer making" policy, the majority of national labor concentrated in agriculture, which caused a labor surplus in agriculture. After the HRS, the contract output was Y_0 equal to that before HRS. Under similar working conditions, the labor to complete the contract task was still controlled by the state. But because the surplus labor did not affect the contract task, they got out of state control. So this part of the labor supply is controlled by farmer themselves. As shown in Figure 6.4, this part is L_0–L_1.
- Liberalizing more labor by efficient improvement
  At the same time, because the HRS raised farmers' incentives, capital including human capital increased, which made the production function curve move to the upper left side and change from F_a (K_1) to F_a (K_2). Therefore, the labor needed to complete the contract reduces to L_2. The labor change is L_1–L_2. This part is also out of state control because it does not affect the contract. Therefore, as a result of the HRS, the total labor out of state control will be L_0–L_2; in other words, the HRS caused the liberalization of rural production factors. This was only a partial liberalization because the part to complete the contract is still under state control. Here, surplus labor is not necessarily the one with zero marginal return,

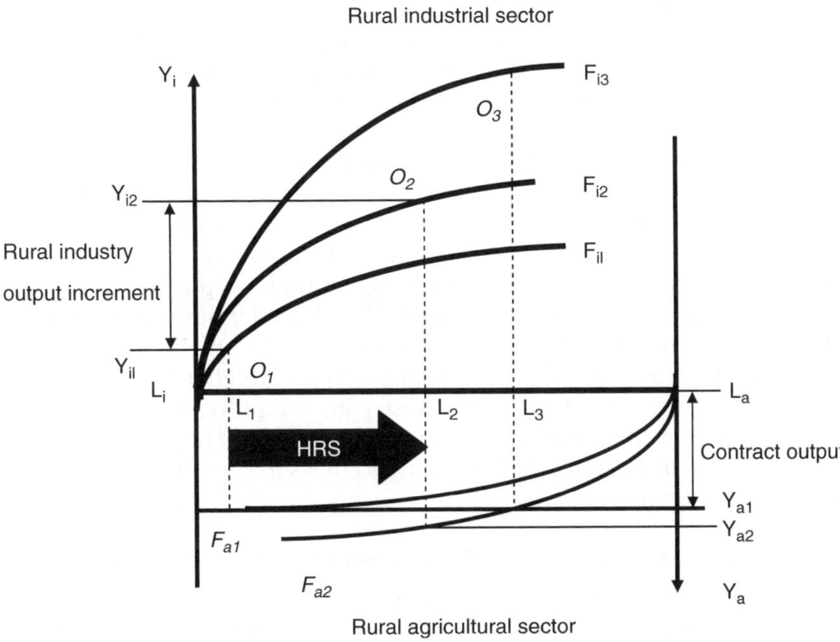

Figure 6.5 The rise of rural industry after the HRS and ban lifting

but the one who does not affect the contract if getting out of agriculture. At the same time, the HRS also reduces non-production activity in people's commune and saves labor. Other elements of production are also affected by the HRS similarly.

Therefore, after the HRS, a common phenomenon in the countryside was the huge labor surplus that suddenly appeared everywhere, becoming a serious employment pressure for China and also a huge labor supply for rural non-agriculture industry. The appearance of the free production factors caused a fundamental change in the rural economy. Although the state prohibited rural private economy at that time, rural private economy appeared very naturally in the countryside because of the free production factors.

Lifting the ban led to the rise of China's rural industry in Lewis-style

Although the HRS liberalized partial factors and made the redistribution of rural factors possible, if the ban on rural industry was not lifted, the liberalized factors would be unable to flow to rural industry. The HRS and ban-lifting led to a Lewis-style development in the rural areas and the rise of rural industry. So, abandoning "the grain priority" and lifting the ban was another main reason for the rise of rural industry. Although this transformation had an experimental nature, it was the first time that the state officially permitted rural industry to develop since the GLF in 1958. The policy change impelled rural industry greatly and led to its rapid rise. As shown in Figure 6.5, Y_i, Y_a, F_i, F_a and L are the rural industry output, agricultural output, rural industry and agricultural production function and labor respectively.

The HRS liberalizes partial factors of production and changes labor from L_1 to L_2. Because the farmer incentive rises, the reduction of labor does not necessarily affect agricultural output; instead the production function moves from F_{a1} to F_{a2} with an agricultural output at point Y_{a2}. Thus, although agricultural labor is reduced, agricultural output increases from Y_{a1} to Y_{a2} surpassing the contract output Y_{a1}. The labor out of agriculture is able to flow into rural industry because of the lift on the ban on rural industry. Therefore, the labor in rural industry with higher return increases continuously, which makes rural industry grow rapidly. There is another way to promote rural industry. In the same way, the HRS also liberalizes part of capital from agriculture, which also flows to rural industry because of the higher return.

Why did the liberalized rural factors flow to rural industry, not urban industry?

Because there was still a ban on farmers immigrating to the city, farmers were unable to go to the city. Therefore, the new capital pushes the industry production function curve to move from F_{i1} to F_{i2} and F_{i3} ... huge rural resources flowed into rural industry, causing its rise in the reform.

Government finance contract raising local government incentives for rural industry

The government finance contract system raised local governments' incentives to develop rural industry greatly, especially rural governments at basic levels. Previously, local governments had no funds except their basic life expenditures and some of them had to depend on state aid to survive in poor countryside. All local governments took every means to impel local economies, especially rural industries with high returns for local development and also their own extra revenue. On the other hand, although the state lifted the ban on rural industry, it was very difficult for farmers to develop industry privately, not only because of the restriction on private economy, but also the difficulty in collecting funds and other factors needed for starting an enterprise. At the same time, because rural resources were not able to enter city, local industry development become the first choice for investment for rural local governments. In order to impel local industry, rural local authorities formulated many favorable policies such as providing free land and guarantees for bank loans. Local governments directly organized innate rural resources for local industrial development, which promoted rural industry greatly. The important role of local governments in China's rural industry development is one of the major characteristics of China's rural industry.

The "out of the plan" led to the "market oriented" rural industry and dual industry structure

Rural industry in the "second-class citizen" position

The ban-lifting on rural industry in 1978 was not to develop the industry itself but for accelerating agricultural development. State policy was still "agriculture first and SOEs first". The policy change merely offered a legal status for industry and agriculture still took first place. The CPCCC didn't abandon the policy of the countryside supporting the city and urban industry, and the dual economic structure centering on city industry. On the contrary, rural industry was still considered to be contradictory to agriculture and major industry and to be restricted. So, the CPCCC didn't regard rural industry as a real industry, and did not put it into the national industrial development plan. It was defined as rural diversified economy, even as a part of the agriculture. Unlike urban industry, its central administrative bureau belonged to the Ministry of Agriculture, not to the Ministries of Industry and the state planning committee as usually. Rural industry was neither industry nor agriculture in China's economy and was unable to enjoy planned investment, raw materials, energy and product sales in order to guarantee agriculture and major industry from the competition of rural industry. In China's basically planned economy system, being "out of the plan" caused rural industry to become a "second-class citizen."

Being "out of the plan" forced rural industry to be "market oriented"

Being "out of the plan" led to the "market oriented" mechanism of rural industry. In fact, because being "included in the plan" meant funds, and raw materials as well as product sale guarantees, all CPBOEs wanted to be "included in the plan" and being a part of the plan became an urgent desire of the CPBOEs. However, the rural enterprises certainly did not enjoy the treatment of "in the plan." They had to seek production factors such as funds and raw materials from markets. In other words, they had to adopt a "market oriented" mechanism, which is the main feature of China's rural industry in the partial planning system.

Being "out of the plan" forced rural enterprises into labor-intensive consumer goods industries

Both fund and technology shortages meant rural enterprises were unable to develop capital-intensive and high-tech industry. Simultaneously, the heavy industry was under severe state control, rural enterprises were also unable to enter. In addition, the countryside had a massive labor surplus, and rural enterprises had to replace funds and technology by labor, and concentrate on labor-intensive industry. Labor-intensivity is one of the main features of rural industry. Rural enterprises also concentrated on daily consumer goods industries. It is well known that, China's "heavy industry priority" policy compressed national consumption, weakened its consumer goods industries, which led to a serious consumer goods shortage in China. The commodity shortage formed a huge market with several hundred million consumers, which provided a huge development space for the "market oriented" rural enterprises. Also the consumer industry was labor-intensive, low-technology, and had a quick capital turnover with raw materials centering on agricultural products. Through developing the consumer industry, rural enterprises obtained a high-speed and continuous development.

Being "out of the plan" broke down the old dual structure and created a new one

The emergence of rural industry broke the overall state control on industry and liberalized China's industry, changing the industry structure from the sole city industry structure to the dual structure of both urban and rural industry. At the same time, it also transformed the rural economy from the sole agriculture to the dual structure with both agriculture and rural industry. Although China's dual industry structure formed naturally in the reform, it brought a huge influence to China's industry as well as to the entire economy.

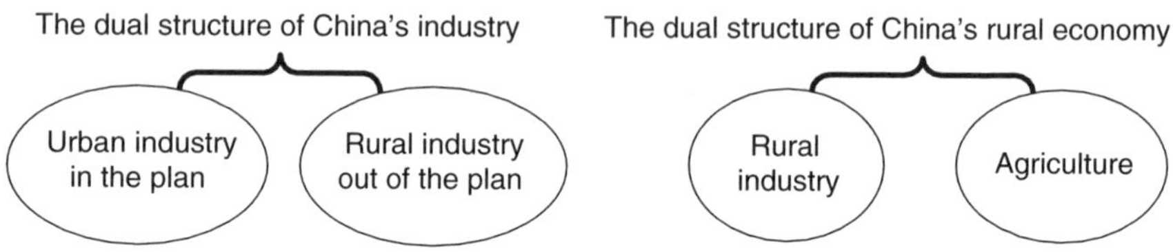

Figure 6.6 China's dual industry structure and dual rural economic structure in 1980

7
Great Expansion in the Disintegration of the People's Commune System

7.1 Background

After the reform and opening up in 1979, China's economy had a great development and many targets of the sixth FYP (1980–5) were completed by 1983, two years ahead of time. The gross output value of industry and agriculture in 1983 was 1.8 percent more than the target in 1985 and the steel output 2.6 percent more. Thirty-three kinds of products such as hydraulic electric generators, synthetic ammonia, chemical fertilizers, automobiles, engine beds, walking tractors, washers, and tape recorders achieved the target in 1985, two years ahead of time. In 1983, agriculture had a record harvest with a gross output value 6.2 percent more than the target planned in 1985. The grain yield was 387 million tons, 7.6 percent more than the target in 1985. Cotton was 4.6 million tons, 28.8 percent more than the target. This was a great and unprecedented growth in China's history (Liu and Wu, 1985, pp. 460–1).

Although 600 thousand CPBOEs were closed down or merged in 1981–83, rural industry still grew rapidly. In 1983 the annual gross income of the CPBOEs increased at an annual rate of 120.6 percent, net profit by 101.6 percent, and tax by 130.9 percent (*CSY*, 1984, p. 185). The tax paid by the CPBOEs already surpassed that of agriculture and the share of the CPBOEs in national industry achieved 12 percent. Rural industry had played an important role in the national economy. In 1983 there were 5.9 million production teams implementing the HRS, 99.5 percent of the total national production teams covering 97.1 percent of the total national townships (communes). At the same time, there were 25 million specialized and key households, about 13 percent of the total farmer households and other forms of economical cooperatives.

Private enterprises had a rapid development too after the introduction of HRS. "Now there are more than 500 thousand private enterprises, more than half of which are engaged in industry, with an estimated annual output value of more than 3 billion yuan" (the Ministry of Agriculture,

26 December 1983). These non-collective enterprises were set up by farmers spontaneously. Non-collective enterprises broke through central government control to develop only collective enterprises, and symbolized that rural industrialization had entered a new stage.

7.2 Policy goals

To relax control comprehensively to impel rural economy

Although the CPCCC in 1978 decided to reform its old system, it was not clear on how to carry out the reform, nor what was the real goal of the reform. Driven by the success in the rural reforms since 1978, the CPCCC (20 October 1984) proposed to establish a planned commodity economy system as the goal of the reform. Although it still continued a planned economy, "namely a planned commodity economy, not a market economy regulated completely by the market," the CPCCC divided the plan into two parts. One is the command plan dealing with only the important products and economic activity affecting the entire national economy. The other is the instructive plan regulated by economic levers or by the market. "We should suitably reduce the scope of the command plans and expand the scope of the instructive plans step by step." That is, to relax state direct control on the economy. The No. 1 document of the CPCCC in 1984 (1 January 1984) pointed out that since the reform, rural policy "has obtained tangible results, which prove that the basic goals and policies of reform proposed by the CPCCC are correct." It argued that "both the agricultural record harvest and the inspiring progress of rural economy" caused us to believe more firmly that "so long as we keep the party's policy stable, summarize new experiences and solve new problems, we can unite and lead hundreds of millions of farmers to develop rapidly." The CPCCC requested: "to stabilize and consummate the HRS, to raise productivity levels and dredge the circulation channels"; and to raise farmers' incentives, promote the flow of rural production factors and develop the commodity economy through relaxing state control more widely.

To promote rural industry comprehensively for agriculture and rural development

The CPCCC (1 March 1984) indicated that rural industry was an important part of the rural diversified economy, an important pillar of agriculture, an important way to make farmers rich and a new important source of national tax. "At present, rural enterprises have become an important strength of national economy and an important complement of SOEs." It decided to change the name of rural enterprises from CPBOEs to "township and village enterprises" (TVEs) to cover rural private enterprises and requested local governments to help and support TVE development. "We must put attention heavily to TVE survival and development." The policy aimed to promote rural and agricultural development through rural industrial development. That is, to develop TVEs for:

- Collecting funds to support agricultural and rural development
  The TVEs will collect funds for developing the rural economy such as mechanization of agriculture, rural infrastructure construction and collective welfare undertakings. "The production costs in regions with high grain yield or vegetables is very high. If there is no subsidy from CPBOE profits, these productions will be difficult to continue." The CPCCC requested: "all levels of party committees and governments must positively guide rural enterprises to complete the task to support agriculture." The TVEs also provided funds "for collective welfare undertakings and other collective expenditure such as rural teacher wages, subsidy for birth control, building bridges, roads, schools, and theaters." "Realizing agricultural modernization needs massive funds and must depend upon the CPBOEs to a great extent" (CPCCC, 1 March 1984).
- Increasing farmer income
  The TVE was also an important source for farmers to increase their income. "In the regions with a strong CPBOE, a farmer's income has already changed from mainly depending on agriculture to mainly depending on the CPBOE. In 1982, the average labor productivity in the CPBOE was 2,700 yuan, far higher than that in agriculture " (CPCCC, 1 March 1984).
- Increasing state financial revenue
  This is a new contribution of the TVE to the national economy and also a new goal for the state to develop rural industry. The rapid development of rural industry was becoming "the main source of the new increment of state tax revenue." "Along with rural enterprises' development, its tax will increase, which is needed for national construction" (CPCCC, 1 March 1984). The CPCCC urged the support of TVE development in order to increase the financial revenue continuously and lastingly.
- Solving the rural employment of surplus labor

To lift the ban on private enterprise under taking collective enterprise as the mainstay

For a long time, the main target of CPCCC rural policy had focused on "expanding collective ownership and eliminating private ownership." Therefore, since the reform, only collective enterprises were permitted to develop. However, the HRS made many non-collective enterprises, especially private enterprises, appear. After waiting and watching, experimenting and tacitly consenting, the CPCCC finally lifted the ban and acknowledged and permitted private enterprises to develop. In 1984, the CPCCC used the name of TVE to include rural private enterprises in rural industry. The CPCCC pointed out: "we should also warmly support the enterprises joint-operated by farmers, family industries and individual enterprises." But although the CPCCC permitted rural private enterprises to develop, it still persisted primarily in developing collective ones and requested to "positively guide and control private enterprises and make them healthily develop." In other words, the CPCCC wanted to guide private enterprises to become collective ones. "After the HRS, the joint venture enterprises by farmers developed very quickly ... most of these enterprises were cooperative ones or could be guided into cooperative ones ... we should positively instruct their operation, guide them to develop into collective ones and not discriminate against them" (CPCCC, 1 March 1984).

To develop TVEs in coordination with SOEs

In order to prevent rural industry from harming SOEs, after lifting the ban on rural industry in 1979, the CPCCC emphasized that rural industry must not harm state-owned industry. However, in 1984, the CPCCC defined the rural enterprise as the "state enterprise's important complement" and pointed out that there was both "crowding out and making-up to each other" between TVEs and SOEs, but that the making-up was greater than the crowding out. "Looking at the overall situation, that is a benefit to both sides and basically a cooperative relation." The CPCCC requested "to treat the TVE in the same way as the SOE and give necessary support" and wanted to enable both enterprises to develop more quickly in the competition, and gradually to form a national industry with large, medium and small enterprises with both high and low technology, in which both the city and countryside displayed its own superiority (CPCCC, 1 March 1984). Certainly, this mutual development centered on SOEs and rural industry was only a complement to the SOEs.

"To leave the land but remain in the countryside"[1]

Although after the reform China gave up the "grain priority" policy, Mao's policy "preventing farmers from entering the city" was not changed. China still persisted in limiting farmer immigration to the city. After the HRS, and facing massive surplus, the CPCCC no longer kept labor in the countryside compulsorily, and wanted to solve employment through developing rural industry. So one of the important goals to develop rural enterprises was to shift farmers from agriculture and prevent them from entering the city. This was called "to leave the land but remain in the countryside." To solve rural employment through developing rural industry and small towns was China's basic rural industrialization policy after the reform. "TVE development will promote town development, speed up the construction of rural economic and cultural centers, be advantageous to realizing the 'leaving the land but remaining in the countryside' and prevent farmers rushing into the city" (CPCCC, 1 March 1984).

7.3 Policy controls

Abolishing the people's communes to separate rural governments from economic organizations[2]

After the reform, the HRS had an enormous impact on the universal management system of the people's communes and directly changed their organizational structure. Because farmers obtained the right to operate production and gradually became relatively independent producers, the two levels of production brigade and team lost their rights and gradually become paralyzed. The No. 1 document of the CPCCC (January 1982) argued: "recently, because of many reasons, a part of rural basic-units of the communes has become lax, even in a paralyzed or half paralyzed condition." On 4 December 1982, the "People's Republic of China Constitution" newly passed explicitly stipulated that the township or village government was the local administrative body and the rural people's commune was "the socialist working masses collective ownership" economic organization. Thus, rural government was separated from rural economic organization by law. The CPCCC (31 December 1982) pointed out that the people's commune's system should be reformed from two aspects. One was to implement the HRS; another was to separate rural government from economic organization. The CPCCC (12 October 1983) requested each region to carry out the reform of separating rural government from the commune and strive to complete the reform before the end of 1984.

Methods to separate rural governments from economic organizations

- Establishing township government and party committees
  The CPCC (12 October 1983) stipulated that taking the township as basic unit, the township party committee and government could be established. The township scale was generally based on the original people's commune's jurisdiction scope. If the original people's commune was too large, it may also be reduced suitably.
- Establishing town government
  In towns with certain conditions, the town government may be established to promote rural economic and cultural development.
- Establishing the villager committee
  The villager committee may be established in original production brigades. The villager committee is the basic unit of mass autonomous organization responsible for community public affairs and public utility and not for production. The villager committee implements democratic election system.
- Establishing the villager group
  The group may be established within the original production team's scope.

- Establishing economic organization
  In the original people's commune scope, various economic cooperation organizations may be established. Agricultural and industrial integrated corporations, agricultural technology service companies, industrial corporations and commercial companies may be established to manage original commune-owned enterprises. The original production brigades generally establish agricultural producer cooperatives or economic federations of communes.
- Implementing by stages
  1) Small experiment stage.
     In March 1979, the Xiang Yang people's commune, Guanghan County in Sichuan province started to carry out the experiment to separate rural government from economic organization and to establish the township government, and on 18 June 1980 the farmers under government support replaced the commune by township government and industry and commerce companies (*Farmer Daily*, 4 November 1998). Afterwards the experiment was carried out in other regions.
  2) Widespread experiment stage.
     In December 1982 after the new Constitution was made, the experiment was carried out nationwide.
  3) Implementing comprehensively stage.
     After the CPCCC decision in October 1983, the reform extended to all regions nationally. By the spring of 1985, the reform had been completed nationally.

  Before the reform, there were more than 56,000 people's communes; after the reform, in 1985, there were more than 91,000 township and town people's governments with more than 940,000 villager committees (*New China 50 Years Agricultural Statistics Material*, 2000). "Separating rural government from economic organization" symbolized the final disintegration of the people's commune which had existed for more than twenty years and were used by the state to implement a comprehensive political and economical control on farmers and rural economy.

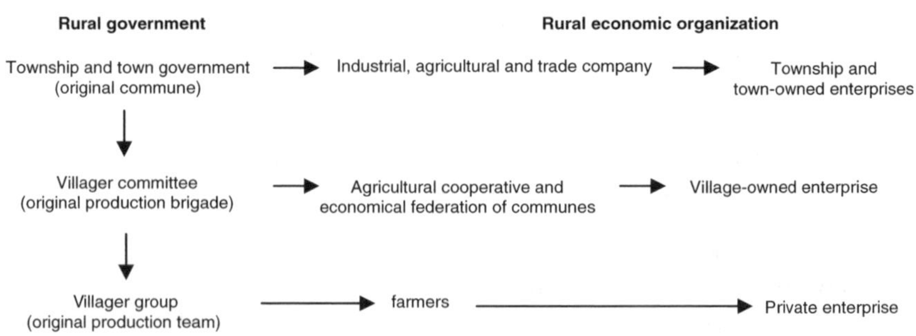

Figure 7.1 China's rural basic organizations after "separating rural government from rural economic organization"

Lifting the ban and encouraging rural private enterprises

From strictly forbidding farmers to be personally engaged in industry and commerce to acknowledging the validity of rural private industry and commerce, China experienced a complex, argumentative, hesitant and experimental process. The ban on rural private industry and commerce had not been lifted until the big success of the HRS in 1984.

Processes in lifting the ban on rural private industry and commerce

- Banning on rural private industry and commerce in 1979
  Although in the reform, the CPCCC permitted and encouraged rural industry to develop, this permission was only restricted in the collective industry of commune and production brigades. The CPCCC defined that "the CPBOE is socialist ownership economy." One of the important goals to develop the CPBOE was to expand collective economy. The development of the CPBOE also would create the conditions "for developing the people's commune from small to big collective then to the ownership system of the whole people gradually in the future" (the State Council, 3 July 1979). Developing rural industry meant expanding collective economy and realizing the ownership system by the whole people, not for developing private economy. So rural private industry and commerce was unable to develop.
- Relaxing the limit on private economy with "Three-Nots" in hiring labor in 1983
  However, the widespread introduction of the HRS weakened state control on rural economy gradually, which caused rural private economy to grow. The CPCCC didn't immediately take a stand for the private economy, but only adopted a policy to wait and see. In 1983, the state started to relax the limit on private industry and commerce. Hu Yaobang on 1 September 1982 requested: "we should encourage the individual worker economy to develop suitably in the scope of state stipulation and under the management of industry and commerce administration as a necessary and beneficial supplement to public ownership economy." The No. 1 document of the CPCCC (2 January 1983) proposed the "Three Nots" policy of "not to advocate, not to propagate openly and not to ban eagerly" for hiring labor privately, which exceed the labor number stipulated by the State Council for rural private economy.
- Encouraging private industry and commerce in 1984
  In 1984, the CPCCC policy started to change. The State Council (27 February 1984) positively encouraged farmers to be engaged in industry and commerce. "Developing rural private industry and commerce has a positive role in promoting rural commodity production, stimulating the interchange of urban and rural products and making use of rural surplus labor." It encouraged "rural surplus labor to be engaged in professions needed urgently by the society." At the same time, the CPCCC expanded the definition of the rural enterprise from CPBOE to the TVE, which covers both rural collective and private enterprises. The CPCCC (1 March

1984) explicitly permitted farmer private enterprise to develop and announced: "from now on we will no longer carry out the ownership transition level by level, but we still need the CPBOE to support agriculture and promote agricultural modernization." These policy changes showed CPCCC encouragement and support for rural private enterprises.

Methods to encourage rural private industry and commerce

- Favorable policy
  According to the stipulation of the State Council, farmers engaged in the professions such as handicraft production, repair, service, catering and business needed by society and truly in difficulty could enjoy state favorable policies in loans, prices, tax and so on and have necessary technology assistance.
- Permitting farmers to do business at rural towns and markets
  Farmers were also permitted to do business such as setting up stalls at small towns and markets with their own grain rations. They may also open a shop there, but could not randomly occupy farming land.
- Expanding the scope of the cooperative economy
  The CPCCC expanded the scope of the cooperative economy and put private economy in the scope of the cooperative economy in order to avoid the blame on private economy. For example, the CPCCC (1 January 1984) put some private enterprises hiring more workers than the stipulation out of the scope of the capitalist hiring.
- Permitting individual farmers to be engaged in transport and agricultural and subsidiary products traffic
  The State Council (27 February 1984) permitted individual farmers to purchase vehicles and tractors for transport business. Individual farmers may be engaged in freight transportation, also passenger transportation and the transportation of local agricultural and subsidiary products and goods for rural production and construction. At the same time, the State Council (25 February 1984) stipulated that besides the state-owned commerce and the SMCs, the state permitted other cooperation commercial organizations and individuals to traffic agricultural and subsidiary products.
- Limiting hiring labor
  Although in 1984, the CPCCC relaxed its control and encouraged rural private economy to develop, it still limited the hiring of private economy. "Rural individual industry and commerce is generally run by a person or a family. If necessary, after the approval of the county, and city industry and commerce administration, it may hire one or two, or three persons but five hands at most."

Under state encouragement, rural private enterprises obtained a rapid development. As shown in Table 7.1, rural private enterprise development had a high tide in 1985, and its total output value increased nearly two times compared to that in 1984.

Table 7.1 China's rural private enterprise development (million units, million persons, billion yuan, %)

Year	*Number of the enterprises*		*Employees*		*Output value*	
	Total	*Share in total TVEs*	*Total*	*Share in total TVEs*	*Total*	*Share in total TVEs*
1984	4.2	69	12.3	24	24.4	14
1985	10.4	85	26.5	38	67.8	25
1986	13.4	89	34.0	43	102.5	29
1987	15.9	91	40.9	46	152.7	32
1988	17.3	92	46.5	49	213.3	33
1989	17.2	92	46.5	50	257.3	35

Source: *CTVEY* 1992, CTVEY editorial committee, agricultural publishing house, 1992
Note: the output value is at 1980 prices.

To abrogate the state monopoly for the purchase system of agricultural products

Along with agricultural product output increase and the purchase price enhancement, state funds for purchasing agricultural products increased greatly while the state sale price of agricultural products basically kept unchanged. That caused the state fiscal price subsidy for grain and cooking oil to rise rapidly from 8.4 billion yuan in 1979 to 18.9 billion yuan in 1983. In order to get rid of the heavy fiscal burden, the CPCCC (1 January 1984) decided to abrogate the state monopoly for the purchase system of agricultural products.

Methods to abrogate the state monopolizing purchase system

- Reducing monopoly purchase and assignment purchase in 1984
  On 30 June 1984, China adjusted its agricultural and subsidiary products purchase policy on a large scale and reduced the agricultural product varieties of the monopoly and assignment purchases. The varieties of both first-class and second-class agricultural and subsidiary products managed by the Ministry of Commerce were reduced from twenty-one to twelve. The varieties of assignment purchase were cut from eighteen to nine. Simultaneously the state relaxed its control on traditional Chinese medicine, forest and aquatic products. The State Council (19 July 1984) requested a fundamental reform in the rural commercial system.
- Abrogating the state monopoly for purchase system and establishing a contract and market purchase system in 1985
  The CPCCC (1 January 1985) announced that from this year, except for a few varieties, the state no longer issued the purchase quotas of the agricultural products to farmers and officially cancelled the state monopoly for agricultural product purchase system. So the state monopoly for the agricultural purchase system of thirty years finally come to an end. At the

same time, the state grain supply system in the countryside was also cancelled and the contract and market purchase system was established.

1) Contract purchase.
   Grain and cotton purchase was changed from the state monopoly to a contract one. The state-owned commercial departments made a purchase contract with farmers before the sowing season. The grain not in the contract may freely go on the market. If the grain price on the market is lower than the original state monopoly purchase price, the state will still purchase the grain at the original price in order to protect farmers' interests. The cotton not in the contract is also allowed to go on the market freely.
2) Market purchase.
   Market purchase means to buy products directly from the market. The state requested that live pigs, aquatic products and vegetables for large and medium cities, industry and mining areas should gradually cancel assignment purchases and go freely on the market. All agricultural product processing, consuming and trade enterprises and units were allowed to sign a purchase contract with farmers, and farmers could also sign a sale contract with a unit through cooperative organizations or producer associations. The CPCCC emphasized that no one could issue a compulsory productive plan to farmers (CPCCC and the State Council, 1 January 1985).

Although the rural state monopoly purchase system was abrogated, the state monopoly for supplying the city was not cancelled and the state still supplied low price grain, cooking oil and other agricultural products to urban residents, which made the state grain purchase price higher than its sale price. This was called "the buying and selling to hang upside down," which led to a heavy fiscal subsidy burden for the state.

To break the state monopoly and establish a multi-style and multi-channel commercial system

The State Council (19 July 1984) requested that the rural commodity circulation system must be thoroughly reformed to change the inconsistency of circulation with production as soon as possible. It pointed out that the reform must liberalize rural commerce from too strict state control and must break the state monopoly to develop a "multi-style, multi-level joint commercial system."

Methods to break the state monopoly and establish a multi-style, multi-channel commercial system

- Changing the SMC from "government-run" into "farmer-run"
  The CPCCC stressed that the SMC was a independent collective commercial enterprise and the core of the SMC reform was to change it from

"government-run" into "farmer-run," otherwise, the SMC could wither day by day. The main measures were:

1) Giving a free hand in absorbing farmer stock and expanding the share of farmers in the total funds of the SMC to relate the SMC with farmers' interests closely.
2) Expanding business and service scope. In the scope permitted by state policy, the SMC may be engaged in any business.
3) Changing the personnel system from government appointment to member election and competition system (contract system.)
4) Introducing contract responsibility distribution system.

- Encouraging collective and private commerce

  1) Encouraging collectives and farmers to develop commerce.

  The State Council (19 July 1984) argued that it was difficult for the rural circulation of commodity to only depend on state-owned commerce and the SMC and we must develop multi-form, multi-channel and multi-operation of state-owned, collective and private commerce, encourage and attract them to be engaged in the commodity exchange and make them an important supplement to state-owned commerce and the SMCs.

  2) Making competition between state-owned, collective and private commerce equally
  (the State Council, 19 July 1984).

- Relaxing control on price and commodity

  1) Relaxing control on agricultural product price.
  The agricultural product prices were divided into three kinds. The state decisive price, the state instructive price and the market price

  A. Agricultural products at state decisive prices were grain, cotton, cooking oils, flue-cured tobacco, silkworm cocoons, sugar and so on.
  B. Agricultural products at state instructive price were live pigs, lumber, tea and so on.
  C. Agricultural products at market price were the majority of agricultural products not in the state decisive and instructive prices.

  The share of agricultural products sold by farmers at the state-decisive price decreased from 76 percent in 1983 to 24 percent in 1988; on the contrary, the share of agricultural products sold by farmers at market price increased from 11 percent in 1983 to 57 percent in 1988 (Yao and Ji et al., 1995, p. 444).

  2) Relaxing the control on non-agricultural products (such as industrial products)
  Non-agricultural products were divided into two categories. One was distributed by the state plan with state decisive prices and purchased from state-owned wholesale departments. Another was purchased out of the state plan with prices made by enterprises themselves.

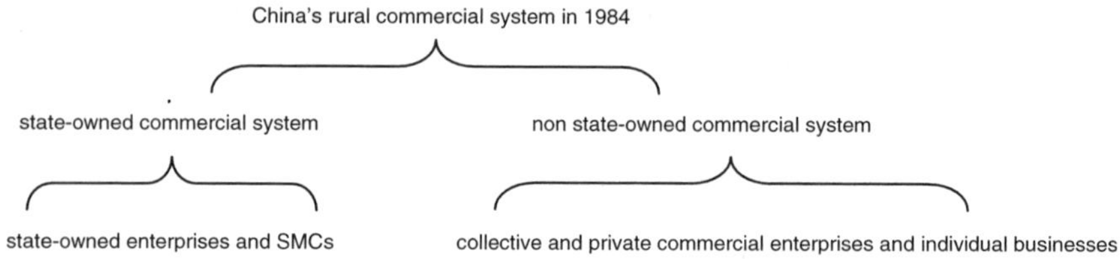

Figure 7.2 China's rural commercial system in 1984

A. Rural enterprises must strictly implement state price policy and every product produced by the raw material and fuel distributed by the state plan must sold at the state price (CPCCC, 1 March 1984).

B. Rural enterprises may make prices by themselves for the products purchased out of the state plans. The products produced by the raw materials and fuel purchased at market with higher price may be sold at a price higher than the state price (the State Council, 19 July 1984). At the same time, the state also cut commodities controlled by the state plans, especially industrial raw materials, and increased commodities regulated by market. For example, the share of steel products allocated by state plan in the national steel output decreased from 77 percent in 1979 to 57 percent in 1985; lumber from 85 to 31 percent; cement from 36 to 19 percent and coal from 59 to 49 percent (Gui et al., 1994, p. 9).

- Establishing trade centers and wholesale trade markets
  The State Council (19 July 1984) requested to gradually establish agricultural and subsidiary products trade centers and wholesale transaction markets in large and medium cities and commodity collection and distribution centers. The agricultural and subsidiary products comprehensive trade centers, and specialized trade centers were engaged in providing market information and organizing future delivery.
- Developing transportation and trade facility vigorously
  Because of the transportation and commercial facility shortage in rural areas, the State Council (19 July 1984) requested to develop rural transportation and speed up rural commercial facility construction, especially to develop and support collective and private transportation in purchasing transportation vehicles and fuel. While constructing large or medium scale state projects for commercial facilities, the state encouraged "farmers to collect funds and construct processing and preserving facilities themselves."

To relax the prohibition and allow farmers with their own grain supply to work in small towns

The CPCCC (1 January 1984) began to relax its control on farmer movement to the city and pointed out: "the farmers going to work or business in small towns should be allowed to settle down there if they take their own grain ration." This means that farmers may freely move to small towns and markets to work or do business. The State Council (13 October 1984) requested local governments at all levels to support farmers with business ability or technique to do business in small towns.

Methods to allow farmers to work in small towns

- Opening up small towns to farmers
  Every farmer and family member applying for work or doing business for a long time in small towns and having a fixed residence there should be permitted to settle down there. The public security department would register them as regular residents with constant address and issue them the registration card "taking care of own grain ration resident" and the card "grain and cooking oil supply at high price."
- Permitting the farmers who have moved to small towns to settles down in their native village once they return to the countryside (Chinese Agriculture Yearbook, 1985, pp. 470–1)
- Introducing the "temporary residence card" and "lodging residence card" system in 1985 and permitted farmers to temporarily reside in cities
- Not supplying grain and cooking oil for farmers moving to small towns. After settling down in small towns, the farmers were unable to enjoy the grain supplied by the state at a low price and had to take care of their own grain ration. Farmers were still under a strict control on immigration to large or medium cities and were unable to enjoy urban welfare, including housing and regular employment opportunities

To reform the RCCs and permit the establishment of non-bank system financial organizations

While continuing the rural state financial system centering on the ABC and the RCC, the CPCCC began to reform the RCC and cause it to return to the original mass cooperative finance organization. At the same time, it also permitted the establishment of non-bank system financial organizations and "suitable private credit." The CPCCC (1 January 1984) requested: "to permit farmers and collective funds to freely or organizationally flow without regional limit and to encourage farmers and collectives to collect funds to invest in or set up various enterprises. The state protects the investors' legal rights and interests."

Methods to reform the RCCs and permit the establishment of non-bank system financial organizations

- Reforming the RCCs
  1) Independent operating and responsibility for own profits and losses. The CPCCC (1 January 1984) pointed out: "The RCC must become a real mass cooperation financial organization. It should independently operate savings and credit services in observing state financial policy and being under the leadership and surveillance of the ABC." The ABC should

gradually cut its subsidy to RCC loss and no longer make instructional business targets for the RCC. The RCC should operate independently. Its profit should relate to its gain closely. All of the funds collected by the RCC, except paying the drawing reserve fund to the ABC, will be used by itself completely (the State Council, 13 October 1984).

2) Permitting to extension of loans for rural industry and commerce.
For a long time, the RCC was mainly engaged in agricultural loans. In 1984, a RCC could extent loans to rural industry and commerce with the remaining credit as long as it met the agricultural loan requirement of its members.

3) Permitting floatable interest rates
According to state stipulation, the RCC may fluctuate its interest rates based on the datum rate of banks. Some of them may approach the market rate.

4) Permitting cross-region business.
The RCC was unable to do cross-region business before the reform. In 1985, the RCC could do cross-region business between the cooperatives and specialized banks in different regions (CPCCC, 1 January 1985).

• Increasing bank loans for rural industry and other non-agricultural industries
The ABC loans for rural non-agricultural industry increased continually, not only in the overall sum, but also in the varieties. The ABC (9 December 1985) expanded the extension of loans from the CPBOE only in 1979 to foreign-funded and multi-household enterprises. The state began to relax loans for private enterprises. The reform made both the ABC and RCC increase the loans for TVEs unceasingly.

Table 7.2 The remaining loans of the ABC and RCC at year-end for TVEs (billion yuan, %)

Year	*ABC loans to TVEs*		*RCC loans to TVEs*	
	Total	*Share in total ABC loans*	*Total*	*Share in total RCC loans*
1982	7.3	15	4.2	23
1983	8.0	14	6.0	27
1984	15.8	13	13.5	29
1985	18.8	13	16.4	30
1986	28.8	18	26.6	35

Source: *China Rural Finance Statistics* 1979–89, the Agriculture Bank of China, Chinese statistics publishing house, 1991.

• Permitting the establishment of local financing organizations not in the state bank system:

1) Establishing commune and production brigade-owned funds (CPBOF).
The CPCCC (1 March 1984) proposed to establish the CPBOF for supporting CPBOE development. The fund had two sources to collect

capital. One is 1% of CPBOE profit after tax managed by the management department of local government for the TVE. The other comes from government fiscal expenditure for supporting TVEs.

2) Rural cooperative foundation[3]
3) Rural management and service company
4) Rural management station
(Xu, Deng et al., 1994, p. 69)

- Relaxes control on the rural non-bank system credit

1) Permitting non-bank system fund collection
The main forms of rural non-bank system fund collections were farmer private fund collections, collective and enterprise fund collections, and local government fund collections. The ABC (26 October 1984) requested that the rural fund collection was one of the rural credit forms and an important way to promote rural economy, and should permit farmers to gather capital for rural development.

2) Allowing private lending
The ABC in May 1984 point out that along with rural commodity production and circulation development, rural free lending was inevitable. Therefore, lending with no interest or a rate slightly higher than that of banks or RCCs was a supplement to banks and RCCs and should be permitted to exist and develop. However, usury and illegal operations must be banned. The state control on non-bank system lending concentrated on interest rates and strictly prohibited usury funds (Xu, 1996, p. 388).

Tax reduction for TVEs

Although the state adopted favorable tax policies for TVEs in the initial period of reform, in order to adjust and control TVEs and collect funds for key construction, the Ministry of Finance (3 September 1983) cancelled the original favorable income tax policy for TVEs. All of the TVEs competing with the SOEs for raw materials were unable to reduce or be exempt from income tax. Meanwhile the enterprises enjoying favorable tax policies were reduced also. In 1984, after No. 1 and No. 4 CPCCC documents were issued, the state reduced TVE tax once more and expanded the scope for TVE to enjoy favorable tax policies. The Ministry of Finance (25 March 1984) requested: "according to CPCC No. 1 and No. 4 documents," some TVEs can enjoy industry and commerce income tax reduction.

- A periodic tax reduction for those TVEs not competing with modern industry for raw materials and having difficulty paying the industry and commerce income tax.
- Levying the industry and commerce income tax only when the income surpasses 3,000 yuan for the TVEs in frontier counties or national autonomous region counties.

- Exempting the industry and commerce income tax for five years from the production starts for the profit of the TVEs making use of their own waste water, waste gas, and waste residue for their main production materials.
- Exempting the industry and commerce income tax for two–three years from the production starts for rural cold storages and warehouses established by TVEs, communes and individual farmers.

To permit TVEs to compete with SOEs

TVE development inevitably competed with SOEs. Although TVEs were small with low technology and low efficiency, their low cost and nimble market mechanism made SOEs inferior in competition. In light industry using agricultural and subsidiary products such as the textile industry, because of the competition from TVEs, many SOEs with advanced equipment and machines were unable to obtain enough raw materials and had to suspend their production. On the contrary, TVEs had a rapid development. In order to guarantee SOE development, the CPCCC, always through administrative means, limited TVE development. On 1 March 1984 the CPCCC changed its policy and permitted TVEs to compete with SOEs. "Although TVEs have a low labor productivity, they can gain from some products, which will make SOEs lose if producing them." It urged the TVEs to develop with SOEs coordinately and enable both sides to develop quickly in the competition.

Methods to permit TVEs to compete with SOEs

- Putting TVEs into the plan
  1) Bringing into line with the plan directly.
     TVE products requested by the state will be included in the national economic plans.
  2) Bringing into line with the plan indirectly.
     TVEs will cooperate with SOEs in supply and sale, which bring TVEs indirectly into line with the plan.
- Joint venture with SOEs:
  SOEs to provide equipment and technology with TVE workshops and labor to set up joint ventures together.
- Forming a complete set with the SOEs
  The CPCCC requested TVEs to be engaged in the necessary parts, appurtenance and initial processing for SOEs. The SOE should in its product renewal expand some products to TVEs.
- Dividing fields between TVEs and SOEs
  1) Dividing the resource fields.
  2) Dividing the agricultural and subsidiary product processing fields.
     In every industry where the SOE holds surplus production ability, the TVE cannot enter and expand processing ability. Every indus-

try that uses agricultural and subsidiary products as raw material and is suitable for rural processing should let TVEs undertake more processing gradually centering on assisting collective TVEs. The raw materials needed by the original processing industry in large and medium cities, including the part made by technical improvement, should be guaranteed continually. In addition, the large and medium cities may not expand their processing ability (CPCCC, 1 March 1984).

3) Allowing TVEs to access the city construction market.
On 1 March 1984, the CPCCC relaxed its restriction and allowed TVEs to enter the city construction market. The TVEs satisfying the regulation of construction may contract city construction projects with an approval from the city government. Zhao Ziyang[4] (15 May 1984) argued: "we must allow rural construction teams to participate in city bids, contract city construction projects" and compete with SOEs.

- Restricting the TVEs competing with SOEs for raw material, energy and market through credit, tax and price

Although the state still protected and supported the SOEs, relaxing the restriction and permitting TVEs to compete with SOEs powerfully promoted TVE development and raised the TVE share unceasingly in national economy, especially in industry.

Table 7.3 China's ownerships structure and the share of rural enterprises in national industries (%)

Year	*Share of each ownership in industry*			*The share of rural enterprises in national industries*				
	SOE	*Collective*	*Private*	*Raw coal*	*Cement*	*Bricks*	*Paper and cardboard*	*Silk fabrics*
1982	n	n	n	21	13	78	19	16
1983	77	22	0.1	23	14	83	21	20
1984	n	n	n	26	16	81	21	25
1985	65	32	2	26	20	81	24	38

Source: *Chinese Rural Statistics Yearbook*, 1990, the rural social economy statistics department of SSB, Chinese statistics publishing house, 1994, *CSY* 1984, p. 194 and *CSY* 1996, p. 403.

Notes: 1) The share of each ownership in national industry is calculated according to the data in CSY.

2) Both collective and private industry include both urban and rural collective and private industry, and the collective industry centers on rural collective industry primarily.

3) The nation gross value of industrial output also includes other type industries such as foreign-funded enterprise.

To promote food, feed, building materials, construction and energy industries first

The State Council (25 February 1984) pointed out that developing comprehensive utilization of agricultural and subsidiary products was advantageous to promotion of commodity production, stimulation of both urban and rural markets, increase of farmer income, realization of agriculture modernization and construction of a socialist new countryside with Chinese characteristics. "After the adjustment, TVE agricultural and subsidiary products processing industries, specially the food, feed, building materials and construction industries, and more importantly the energy industries, should have a greater development."

Methods to promote the food, feed, building materials, construction and energy industries first

- Processing agricultural products locally. The new expansion of processing ability for agricultural and subsidiary products should be put into the countryside as much as possible
- Dividing the agricultural and subsidiary product processing industries between different enterprises and TVEs should be in the suitable fields and promote economic cooperation with SOE.
- Allowing TVEs to access city construction markets
- Encouraging farmers to mine. The mining scope included small ore, debris of big ore and the places around big ores (CPCCC and the State Council, 1 January 1985)
- Favorable finance and tax policies
  The investments in food, feed and small energy industries were able to enjoy favorable policies in loan, interest rates and tax (CPCCC and the State Council, 1 January 1985).

Although the CPCCC gave priority to food, feed, building material, construction and energy industries, the shares of these industries in total TVE output did not rise distinctly, except for the construction industry, the share of which in total TVE output had a big increase from 7.1 percent in 1978 to 13.4 percent in 1983. The share of TVEs in national construction industry also had a big increase from 6.1 percent in 1978 to 26.6 percent in 1987 (*CTVEY* 1978–87, pp. 55–6).

Spark program (SP) to improve the TVEs technologically

The SP was proposed in 1985 by the National Science Committee and proved by the CPCCC in 1986. It is the first science and technology program in China to promote rural economy and is organized and implemented by the National Science Committee aiming to promote agriculture, rural industry and economy through science and technology. Its core is to develop advanced and also suitable technology and promote technological progress of the rural economy. In 1985 the experiment of the program started. In 1986 the SP started officially focusing on developing technology for TVEs.

SP targets in the seventh FYP (1986–90)

- Developing 100 complete sets of technical equipment suitable for TVEs and organizing mass production.
- Establishing 500 technical models of TVEs and providing them with a complete set of technology, management regulations, product design and quality control methods.
- Training rural educated youths and cadres in basic units in the short-term and teaching them to grasp one or two advanced techniques suitable for local use every year.

Methods to implement the SP

- Cooperation of local government, scientific research institutes and enterprises under the state leadership. The State Science Committee to be responsible for SP organization and implementation
- Deciding the project
  First the enterprise and related research institute jointly apply to local Science Committees for a project, and then the committee examine the project. The project will be decided as a SP project after passing the examination. There are two ways to decide a project.
  1) Deciding a project according to administrative level such as the state level, provincial level and county level. By 1988, there were 1,459 SP projects decided at state level, 10 percent in the total, 4,774 at provincial level, 33 percent in the total and 8,394 at prefecture-county level, 57 percent in the total (the State Spark Program Office, April 1989).
  2) Deciding a project according to technical field.
  In 1988 there were 320 projects with a total investment of 1.4 billion yuan decided according to technical field at state level, 59 projects relating equipment with an investment of 110 million yuan, and 14 projects in electronics with 27 million yuan investment.

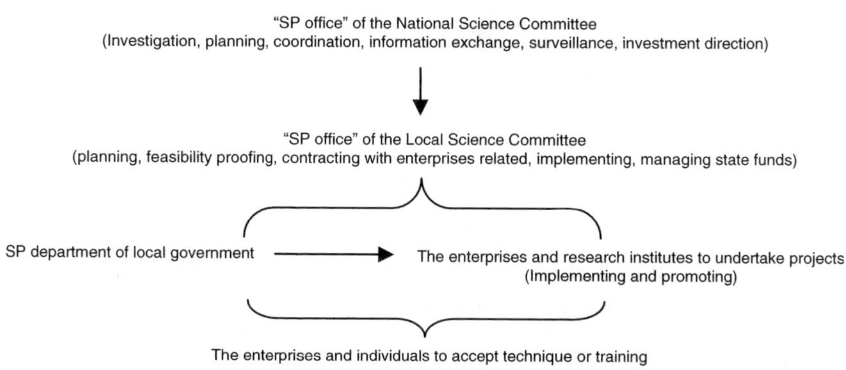

Figure 7.3 SP organization system

- Establishing training bases
  An important content of the SP is to train rural educated youths and management staff at basic units. The SP established many training bases to help farmers study and grasp science and technology. By 1988, the SP had established 60 training bases and trained 4.0 million farmers (the State Spark Program Office, April, 1989).
- Self-raising funds
  SP fund sources are "mainly gathering funds, mainly enterprise self-collecting and mainly loans with state guidance." The fund for SPs at state level defers to the principle of "locality with large share and the state with small share." The state investment for the SP includes fiscal funds and loans. Local government investment for SPs mainly comes from local special development funds.
- Setting national SP prizes for promoting medium and small-scale enterprises and general rural technical progress (23 June 1987).

SP features

- Centering on TVEs:
  80 percent of development projects in SPs directly face TVEs and 60 percent of SPs are undertaken by TVEs.
- Governments provide necessary support and research institutes make technical backing
- Small government investment:
  Both central and local government investment in SPs is low. The financial support of the governments for SPs is mainly bank loans. As shown in Figure 7.4, bank loans occupy a very important share in SP investment.

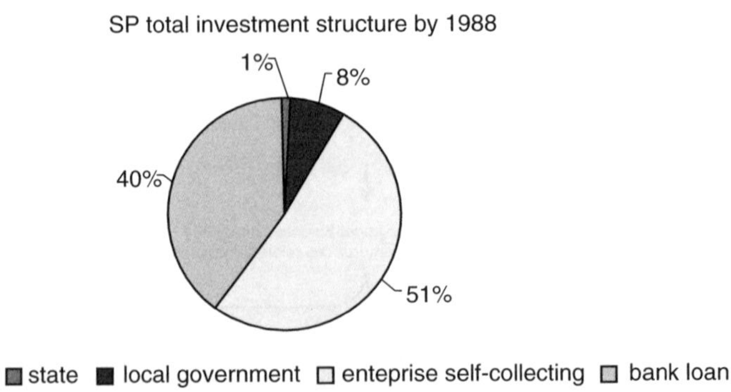

Figure 7. 4 SP total investment structure by 1988
Source: *The Spark Program Report* 1988, the Spark Program Office of the State Science Committee, April 1989.

By the end of 1988, there were 14,627 SP projects with total investment of 8.75 billion yuan and 5,353 projects were completed, 36 percent in total projects. Simultaneously SPs also promoted 100 kinds of technical equipment suitable for TVEs and trained 3.97 million technicians and management staff for the countryside. The SP target in the seventh FYP was fulfilled ahead of schedule according to the report of China's SP Office in April 1989.

Although the SP played a positive role in improving and promoting TVE technical progress, its effect is very limited because of the small number of the projects. He, Gu and Yan (1996) argued that in Jiangsu province, there were 230 SP projects on average every year throughout 1986–90. Except for agricultural projects as well as the projects for industrial enterprises above county level, the SP projects only covered a little more than 1/1000 of the TVEs at township and village levels. During the seventh FYP, the share of SP projects in total industry construction projects at township and village levels was only 1.18 percent.

Pollution control

On 27 September 1984, the State Council pointed out that because of unreasonable products and layout, low technical equipment, a lack of labor protection and pollution preventing and controlling facilities, TVEs caused serious pollution to the urban and rural ecological environments. The State Council asked for prompt control over pollution and energy waste.

Methods to control TVE pollution

- Forbidding the TVEs to make serious pollution
  TVEs could not be engaged in productions making serious pollution such as native asbestos and sulfur production, native galvanization, leather making, papermaking, coking, refining oil, phosphate fertilizer, dye and other small chemical industries as well as noise and vibration industrial projects which disturbed people's lives seriously. The TVEs engaged in these productions must be stopped or closed or reorganized or transformed.
- Planning enterprise layout reasonably
  The state stipulated that polluting TVEs could not be set up in regions such as town winning side areas, densely inhabited areas, water source protectorates, scenic spots, historical sites, scenery tour areas, hot spring convalescent and nature protection regions and must be closed or moved to other regions if already established.
- Controlling new pollution sources strictly
  All newly built TVEs or those rebuilt or transitted for different production must fill in a "Report of Effect on the Environment," which must be examined and approved jointly by the authority and environmental protection departments at county level. For those TVEs

without examination and approval, local planning committees, agricultural offices and other related departments could not allow them to construct; banks could not provide funds and loans to them; industrial and business administrative department could not issue business licenses to them. For those TVEs which did not follow state stipulation and caused environmental pollution, the government must investigate and affix both economic and legal responsibility of the departments, enterprises or individuals concerned.

- Prohibiting shifting poison or harmful products to TVEs without an ability to prevent and control pollution. The concerned enterprises and individuals, who shift pollution must be investigated and punished.

Although the state formulated a strict policy to control the pollution made by TVEs, "in most regions TVE pollution protection was very bad. For example, In 1985, in Tongshan County, Xuzhou city, Jiangsu Province, TVEs built 202 new projects. Only seven projects really carried out state pollution protection standards" (the investigation team of TVE environmental pollution, the Ministry of Farming, Forestry, Animal Husbandry and Fishery, 1985).

To lengthen land-contracting times and stabilize the HRS

On 1 January 1984, the CPCCC urged "to stabilize and consummate continually the HRS, help farmers to expand production scale, based on family operations, and enhance economic efficiency."

Methods to stabilize and improve the HRS

- Lengthening land-contracting time
  The CPCCC (1 January 1984) requested that land contracting time should generally surpass fifteen years and longer for projects with a long production cycle or newly developing projects such as fruit trees, forestry, barren hill and land. Lengthening the contract time would encourage farmers to increase investment, raise soil fertility and carry on intensive farming.
- Permitting the subcontraction of land
  During the contract period, being incapable to cultivate or transferring to other business, a farmer may give the land or a part of the land he is contracting back to the collective for unified arrangement. The contract land may be subcontracted, but the contracted land and private plot could not be sold or rented. It was also banned to make the land get out of cultivation or to change it into a homestead or other non-agriculture uses.
- Supporting specialized farmer households
  The CPCCC highly praised the specialized farmer households for "getting rich through hard work firstly, developing commodity produc-

tion firstly, and improving production technology firstly" and urged their protection and support. It also encouraged concentrating farmland gradually on farming experts (CPCCC, 1 January1984).

To lengthen the land-contracting time, permit land subcontracting and support land centralizing promote further the free flow of production factors in the countryside, which then accelerated rural industrial development.

The "Two-Track System" (TTS)[5] for prices of producer goods

In 1984, China started to introduce the TTS for prices of producer goods to aim at breaking the state monopoly on prices and to enhance producers' incentives.

Methods to introduce TTS

- Permitting enterprises to fix prices of producer goods in 1984
  Before the TTS, producer goods in China were mainly made by SOEs and were controlled by the state. Their prices were fixed by the state. The State Council (20 May, 1984) permitted the enterprises to have a right to fix the prices of the industrial producer goods which were produced and sold by them (about 2 percent in their planning output) or the part beyond the planning output.
- Permitting the "out of plan" prices to fluctuate in a scope of 20 percent of the plan prices in 1984.
- Canceling the original price fluctuation limit of 20 percent of the plan prices and permitting enterprises to sell the products at prices slightly lower than local market prices in 1985.

Usually, because producer goods are scarce in China, the prices out of planning were much higher than the planning prices. The TTS raised production incentives, especially SOEs' and stimulated the production of scarce goods and materials, and optimized the element of production disposition. But the TTS also had a great impact on state control on the producer goods and made chaos in the producer goods supply. "In fact, except in the first two years, the two-track price difference generally was more than one time, some were three to four times as high as the planning prices (Zhang, 1995, *China's Path 1978–94*, the expert team of China Reform and Development Report, 1995, p. 128). The TTS affected state plans because in order to pursue high profit, many enterprises didn't want to complete the state plan on time, but wanted to sell their products at prices much higher than the planning ones.

To expand the opening up to the world

The CPCCC (20 October 1984) pointed out: "closing the country to international intercourse would prevent modernization" and as China's basic long-term policy, the open-door policy had already obtained remarkable benefits. The CPCCC requested to "expand positively the economic and technological exchange and cooperation with foreign countries."

Methods to expand opening up to the world

- Opening fourteen coastal port cities
  In May 1984, the CPCCC decided to open Dalian, Qinhangdao, Tianjin, Yantai, Qingdao, Lienyungang, Nantong, Shanghai, Ningbo, Wenzhou, Fuzhou, Guangzhou, Zhanjiang and Beihai comprehensively to foreign countries.
- Special favorable policies for export and advanced technology foreign-funded enterprises. The policies mainly include tax reduction, favorable loans, infrastructure use, export license, examination and approval procedure simplification and so on.
- Lengthening the operating period of the foreign-funded joint ventures
  1) The operating period was 10–30 years for general projects and more than 30 years for projects with large investment, long construction period and low profit rate in 1983.
  2) The operating period was changed to "10–30 years for general projects, 50 years or longer for projects with large investment, long construction period, low profit rate and advanced or key technology offered by foreign investors to produce highly sophisticated or competitive products internationally in 1986.
  (The State Council, 20 September 1983 and 15 January 1986).
- Eight billion US dollars target of TVE exportation by 1990 made in December 1987.

Under the expansion of opening up to the world, TVE outward-oriented economy developed quickly. The delivered value of export products increased from 10 billion yuan in 1986 to 27 billion yuan in 1988 and the processing fee for overseas firms from 1 billion to 3 billion yuan with a rise of the number of joint venture with overseas firms from 2,405 units in 1986 to 4,762 units in 1988 (*CTVEY*, 1991, p. 280).

7.4 Rural industrialization in process

Throughout 1984–88, TVEs had a great expansion. The number of TVEs doubled in 1985 and tripled in 1988. The total output value in 1988 was 649.6 billion yuan, three times more than that in 1984. TVEs mainly centered in non-agriculture industries with an agricultural share of only 2 percent in their total output value. As shown in Table 7.4, TVE fixed asset original value increased very quickly and doubled from 1985 to 1988. TVE high-speed growth, based on the massive investment in fixed assets, broke through original development mode of the "three locals" pattern[6] and started to develop cross-regions and cross-sectors.

Table 7.4 TVE development 1984–88

Year	*Enterprise number (million)*	*Staff (million persons)*	*Original value of fixed assets (billion yuan)*	*Total output value (billion yuan)*	*Industrial share in total output (%)*	*Agricultural share in total output (%)*
1984	6.1	52.1	57.5	171.0	73	3
1985	12.2	69.8	82.3	272.8	67	2
1986	15.2	79.4	121.6	354.1	68	2
1987	17.5	88.1	160.4	476.4	68	2
1988	18.9	95.5	209.9	649.6	70	2

Source: *CTVEY* 1978–87, 1989 and 2003.
Note: the fixed asset original value is the rural collective enterprise's data.

Table 7.5 The contribution of TVEs to rural economy (billion yuan)

Year	*Share in rural labor (%)*	*Share in total rural social output value (%)*	*Fund for agriculture*	*Fund for rural collective welfare*	*Fund for rural construction*
1985	19	43	0.9	2.0	6.3
1987	23	52	0.9	1.8	6.2
1988	24	58	1.2	2.5	5.7

Source: *CTVEY* 1978–87, *CSY* 1984 and 1996.
Note: the data of the funds for agriculture, rural collective welfare undertakings and construction come from the collective enterprises.

The TVE role in the rural economy rose rapidly. In 1988, the share of TVEs in rural total social output value already surpassed one half and achieved 58 percent. They had become an important prop to the rural economy. TVE development promoted rural labor flow and accelerated the shift of farmers from agriculture to non-agricultural industry. TVE share in total rural labor increased from 19 percent in 1985 to 24 percent in 1988, 5 percentage points up. At the same time, TVEs also provided funds to support agricultural production, rural welfare and other constructions. Besides, the share of rural industry in national industrial output rose quickly from 18 percent in 1985 to 26 percent in 1988. TVE share in national tax grew from 7 percent in 1985 to 13 percent in 1988. TVE development promoted national economy greatly.

Farmer life continued to improve. The per capita annual net income of rural households increased continuously from 355 yuan in 1984 to 545 yuan in 1988 with a decrease of the Engel Coefficient of rural households from 59 percent in 1984 to 54 percent in 1988, 5 percentage points down. The rural poor population living below the poverty line decreased from 128 million in 1984 to 96 million in 1988, a drop of 25 percent. However, after the bumper crop in 1984, China's agriculture entered a slow

Table 7.6 Per capita annual net income and Engel coefficient of rural households in China 1978–83

Year	*Per capita annual net income of rural households*		*Engle Coefficient of rural households*
	Value (yuan)	*Index (1978=100)*	(%)
1984	355	250	59.2
1985	398	269	57.8
1986	424	278	56.4
1987	463	292	55.8
1988	545	311	54.0

Source: *CSY* 2001.

growth period. Its growth rate in 1988 was only 3 percent. At the same time, the grain yield continued to decline and the national per capita grain decreased from 393 kilograms in 1984 to 358 kilograms in 1988, a drop of 9 percent. The share of agriculture in national GDP glided down unceasingly from 32 percent in 1984 to 26 percent in 1988, 6 percentage points down.

7.5 Policy effects

Abolishing the communes and overall control relaxation stimulated TVE expansion greatly

The great success of the rural reform centering on the HRS in 1978 finally led to the abolishment of the commune system that had existed for more than 20 years, which is not only an affirmation for the experimental HRS, but also a thorough elimination of the military, overall and direct control on farmers through compulsory restriction of grain rations and housing. Abolishing the commune symbolized that the state relaxed comprehensively its control on the countryside, which greatly promoted rural economical liberalization, enormously promoted the element of production to move to non-agricultural industry and fundamentally changed the rural economic development pattern of "grain priority" and "concentrating on one thing only."

One of the reasons for China to start its reform first from the countryside in 1978 was because rural economy had a small influence on national economy and with a small risk. So rural reform was an experiment. Similarly, developing rural industry was an experiment too. There had been intense arguments about rural industry since the reform. Because of the agricultural harvest in the reform, the argument concentrated on the relation between rural and state-owned industry. That is, whether or not developing rural industry harms the industrialization strategy centering on state-owned industry, such as the so-called "three competitions" (competition for raw materials, competition for energy and competition for market), and the "two crowding" (small industry crowding big industry and backward industry crowding advanced industry) in 1981 (*CTVEY* 1978–87, p. 1). In order to prevent rural industry from harming state-owned industry, the State Council (4 May 1981) decided to reorganize CPBOEs and strengthened its restriction on rural industry. The CPCCC sway on TVE development caused the investors and managers, especially local governments at all levels, to sway too. They did not dare to give TVEs a free hand in their development. Therefore, affirming TVEs' important significance in rural and national economy and relaxing control in 1984 enormously strengthened local government and farmers' confidence and incentives to develop rural industry. Zhang (1990, p. 181)) argued that both CPCCC No. 1 and No. 4 documents in 1984 were a "timely rain" expected for a long time by farmers and cadres at basic units and brought the "Second Spring" and "Golden Age" to TVE development. Both validity and huge economic benefits induced local governments to organize and impel rural resources to go in for rural industry, which finally led to the expansion of rural industry and the complete disintegration of traditional dual economic structure.

The TTS supported TVE rapid expansion

Although the relaxation of control raised incentives to develop rural industry greatly, the industry was unable to get enough production factors in rural areas only for its expansion. The TTS supported the big expansion significantly. Although the goal of the TTS was not to support rural industry, it enabled part of producer goods to get out of the plan and enter markets, which helped TVEs to get the necessary producer goods. Because the producer goods prices in markets were much higher than the planning ones, producers often put these producer goods, which should have been at planning prices, in the markets for more benefit. On the other hand, because of simple and nimble organization and low cost such as cheap labor and free land, TVEs had a market competition power stronger than SOEs, therefore, they could obtain more producer goods from markets. Therefore, the TTS not only raised producer's incentives and increased producer goods supply, but also enabled part of the producer goods controlled by the state to get out of the plan and go to market. All of these provided the rural industry, which was out of the plan, with conditions to expand. On the contrary, because SOEs were weak in market competition, the TTS actually decreased the production material supply for SOEs.

Two ways for TTSs to support TVEs

- Increasing producer goods for TVEs directly
  Suppose that before the TTS, the planned producer goods are Q_2 at the price P_0. After the TTS, some planned goods enter the market legally, the

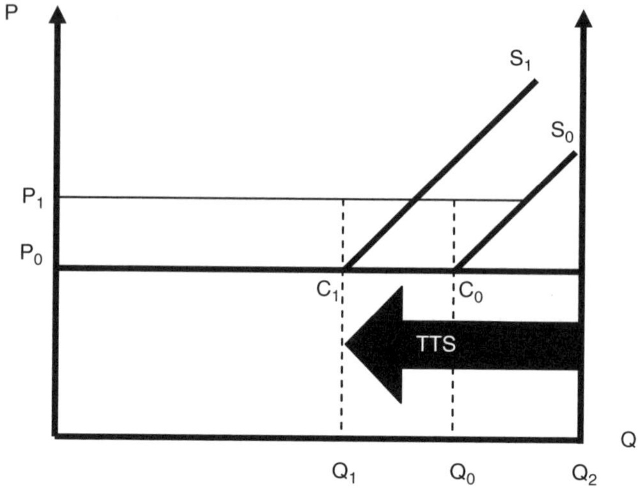

Figure 7.5 The supply of producer goods for TVEs under the "Two-Track System"

planned producer goods reduce from Q_2 to Q_0 and the price keeps invariable. The increment of the goods supply out of the plan is Q_2–Q_0. Because they are in the market, the supply curve for this part is S_0. $\Delta Q = Q_2 - Q_0$ is out of the plan and will flow to TVE.

- Increasing producer goods for TVEs indirectly
  However, because another part of the planned producer goods after the TTS also entered the market illegally for benefit, the planned producer goods further reduce to Q_1. Thus, the total change is Q_2–Q_1. The supply curve in market is S_1. Under the benefit push, there are more producer goods in the market with higher prices. As a matter of fact, the TTS provided TVEs with the goods of $\Delta Q = Q_2 - Q_1$ for its rapid expansion.

The overall control relaxation for rural industry damaged agriculture seriously

The relaxation of control made the TVE expansion depend mainly on large numbers of input into fixed assets and had a very big impact on agriculture. One was the big fund reduction in agriculture. The other was the big labor reduction in agriculture. As shown in Figure 7.6, fund reduction caused the agricultural production function curve to drop from F_a (k_2) to F_a (k_1). The agricultural labor supply reduced from L_2 to L_1 and caused the agricultural output to drop rapidly. Therefore, the TVE expansion caused agricultural output to drop from Y_2 to Y_1. Although the TVE expansion also had a minus effect on SOEs, its influence concentrated on agriculture because local governments have more power in rural areas.

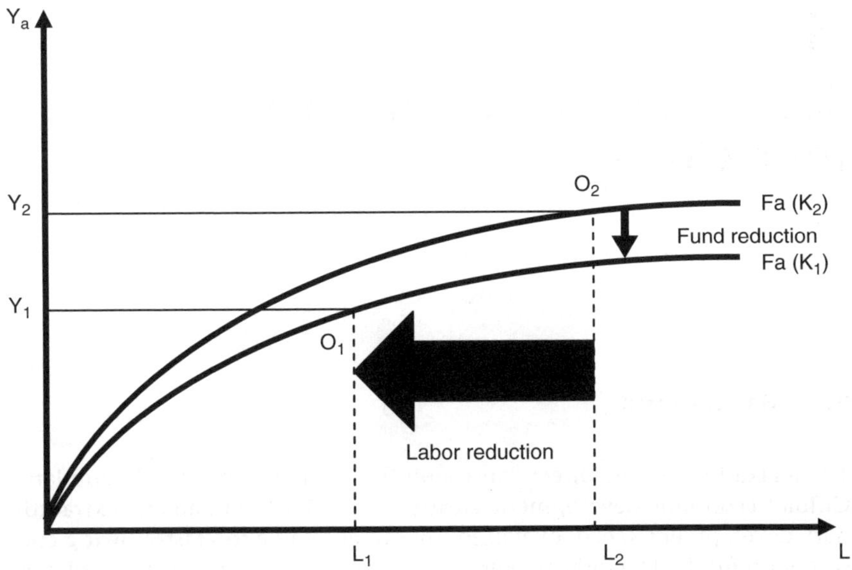

Figure 7.6 The impact of the overall control relaxation for the rural industry on agriculture

The "third-class citizen" private industry and rural dual industry structure

Although because of the HRS, private enterprises appeared naturally, they had no legal status at all. In order to survive and develop, many private enterprises had to operate with collective brands. This is called "wearing a red hat." In 1984, the ban lifting on private enterprises was the first time the CPCCC allowed private enterprise to develop since 1958. The ban lifting promoted rural private economy to develop greatly and formed the rural industry dual structure. However, private industry was still "half legal," because the CPCCC didn't give up its policy to take collective economy as the mainstay, and opposed private economy generally, and wanted finally to change private economy into cooperative economy. So in the dual structure of rural industry, the collective industry enjoyed a dominant status. Private enterprises became a "third-class citizen."

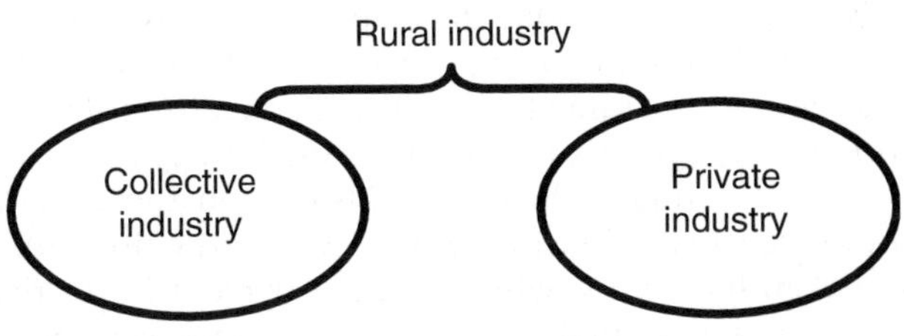

Figure 7.7 The dual structure of China's rural industry

8
Setbacks in the Emergency Braking for a Crisis

8.1 Background

The relaxation of state direct control on the economy after 1984 stimulated China's economic development greatly. In 1988, China had an "extraordinary development speed, oversized investment and a too fast-growing consumption fund." The industrial gross output value above township level grew at a rate of 17.7 percent. The total social investment in fixed assets increased from 379.2 billion yuan in 1987 to 475.4 billion yuan in 1988, an increment of 25 percent. The high-speed expansion brought serious inflation. Although in October 1988, the CPCCC decided to "govern, reorganize and reform" the over-heated economy and started to reduce the money supply, the prices still continued to rise rapidly. There were four large-scale panic purchasing rushes and the overall level of annual retail price rose by 18.5 percent in 1988. In the first quarter of 1989, the overall retail price rose by 27 percent, compared to the same period of the previous year (*Chinese Price Statistics Yearbook* 1990, p. 3 and 11). The inflation caused a rather short supply of producer goods. Many TVEs suspended their production because of lack of raw materials and energy. "In January and February 1989, electricity was unable to meet the demand. In some regions there was no electricity during daytime at all and electricity came only after 10 o'clock in the evening. Some supplied electricity four days and stopped three days each week. Self-generated electricity was also difficult because it was hard to buy oil, and even coal was seriously short" (Zhang, 1990, p. 349).

While TVEs grew rapidly, SOEs developed relatively slowly and their share in national industry unceasingly dropped from 69 percent in 1984 to 57 percent in 1988. At the same time, China's agriculture stagnated with a great reduction in both grain and cotton. In 1985 the grain yield decreased 7 percent, a record annual reduction of 28 million tons. Again in 1988 there was an overall reduction in grain, cotton and edible oil. The grain yield fell to 394 million tons, which was 3.3 percent lower than that in 1984 and the staple agricultural products had continuously paced back and forth around the 1984 level for four years. Because of the population increase, China's per capita grain in 1988 was 35 kilograms less than that in 1984, which made many regions restore the planned supply of main agricultural products, which had been already abandoned for years.

During the big expansion, collective shares in TVE numbers, employees and output value dropped significantly. From 1984 to 1988, the share of collectives in total TVE employees fell from 77 to 51 percent, a drop of 26 percentage points. In the total output value the share decreased from 86 to 67 percent, 19 percentage points down. At the same time, the big expansion also made a heavy contribution to China's rural pollution, which was becoming increasingly serious.

8.2 Policy goals

To develop agriculture with all effort

The high-speed economic expansion and rapid reform advancement under government impetus starting from 1984 led finally to a frantic investment and consumer's panic, which made the economy get out of control. The CPCCC (9 November 1989) acknowledged: "Both the CPCCC and the State Council are responsible for the difficulty in our economy. We must take lessons seriously from the problem." In 1989, the CPCCC started to comprehensively change its economic policy. The rural policy adjustment was mainly to strengthen CPCCC control on the rural economy, stop overheated development of rural non-agricultural industry and get rid of the agricultural stagnation and grain reduction. The CPCCC (9 November 1989) argued: "in recent years, our estimation for the rural situation was too optimistic and we did not correct the blind development of the industry vigorously. In the process of reforming the excessively controlled system, we neglected the necessary and suitable central control." "The proportion between industry and agriculture is seriously out of balance and the existing agriculture already cannot support the oversized industrial production." It argued that in many regions irrigation and water conservation facilities had not been maintained for a long time and were even destroyed. Massive farming lands were taken for industry use while excessive rural labors were shifted too early to non-agricultural industry with a reduction in land investment of government, collectives and farmers. "It can be said that our agricultural foundation has been in a frail and weak situation." "To realize stable agricultural development is the foundation to stabilize the economy, politics and society, which relates to national safety and is also the key to adjust the economic structure. We must raise an upsurge to attach much importance to agriculture and support and develop agriculture in the whole party and the whole country." The CPCCC made a call "to mobilize the entire party and the whole nation to concentrate strength in developing agriculture" for guaranteeing a stable growth of grain, cotton and other main agricultural products.

To limit TVEs strictly to protect both agriculture and SOEs

In order to prevent resources from excessively flowing to rural industry, which leads to an insufficient input in agriculture, the CPCCC (9 November 1989) emphasized: "under the premise to develop agriculture with great effort, we will positively develop TVEs. We must arrange rural labor between agriculture and TVEs under an overall plan." The Ministry of Agriculture, on 31 May 1990, indicated: "Agricultural development is the first priority and TVE development cannot harm agricultural development, on the contrary, TVEs must benefit and support agricultural development."

As to TVE competition with SOEs, the CPCCC emphasized once more the central role of SOEs in the national economy and gave the policy priority to SOE development. TVEs must coordinate and could not harm SOE development. "To fully display the backbone role of large and middle-scale SOEs in the national economy, we must firmly set up the concept that only by making the large and middle-scale enterprises develop well, we are able to stabilize the whole national economy, to strengthen state economic power and to gradually realize modernization. We must truly help them overcome their difficulties and develop" (CPCCC, 9 November 1989).

The CPCCC stressed again that TVEs were SOE supplements and in an assistant and necessary status. "TVEs must implement state industrial policy, positively adjust their product structure and develop steadily and healthily. We must support TVEs and small enterprises engaged in agricultural and subsidiary products processing, outward-oriented production, energy and raw materials, as well as these with a good profit. Also we must transfer or suspend those that compete with SOEs for raw materials or have serious pollution or are in loss" (the State Council, 15 March 1989). The CPCCC urged to adjust, reorganize, reform and improve TVEs in a planned and step-by-step way (CPCCC, 9 November 1989).

To limit private economy and protect the collective economy

Facing the big development of rural private economy impelling rural economy, and the economic chaos caused by private economy, the CPCCC decided to limit private economy. "Under the premise of taking public ownership as the mainstay, we will develop a diversified economy. Private economy is a beneficial and essential supplement to the socialist economy and we must utilize economic, administrative and legal measures to strengthen their management and guidance and encourage them to develop with in the scope permitted by the state, to display their active role in developing social production, to make things convenient for people's lives and employment. We must limit their negative effect on the socialist economy" (CPCCC, 9 November 1989). In other words, the CPCCC emphasized that the essential target of China's economic development was not private economy, but public economy. Private economy was only in a supplemental status and could develop only in "the scope permitted by the state." It could not develop at will. Secondly, private economy could not affect or harm state-owned and collective economy development.

To limit farmer migration and "digest rural labor surplus locally"[1]

Although after the reform the CPCCC relaxed its control on the rural population and permitted farmers to move cross-region, even into towns and cities, its basic population policy did not change and still limited farmers in rural areas not to immigrate to the city. "We have such a large agricultural population, that after agricultural development the rural surplus labor should not rush into the city, but should be digested locally" (Jiang, 19 June 1990). China wanted to digest and shift its huge rural surplus labor from agriculture to non-agriculture industry locally through developing TVEs and constructing rural small towns and cities.

To make use of international resources to promote TVE expansion

At the end of 1987, the state decided "to display the superiority of the union between industry and trade and open up a new prospect for TVE export." At the beginning of 1988, China started to implement the "large international cycle" developmental strategy in its coastal areas to vigorously develop its outward-oriented economy and to increase exportation. The strategy is to export and import with large quantity. TVEs were given an important status in this strategy. The CPCCC decided to implement a more nimble policy to display TVE superiority, to vigorously promote "processing trade" and to make the coastal regions have more progress in their outward-oriented economy (the State Council, 27 February 1988).

The CPCCC pointed out that besides urban and large and middle-scale key enterprises, "at present the most important thing is to take TVEs as an important base to promote and utilize the results of scientific researches ... and to establish outward-oriented TVEs with high-quality" (Yao,[2] 26 March

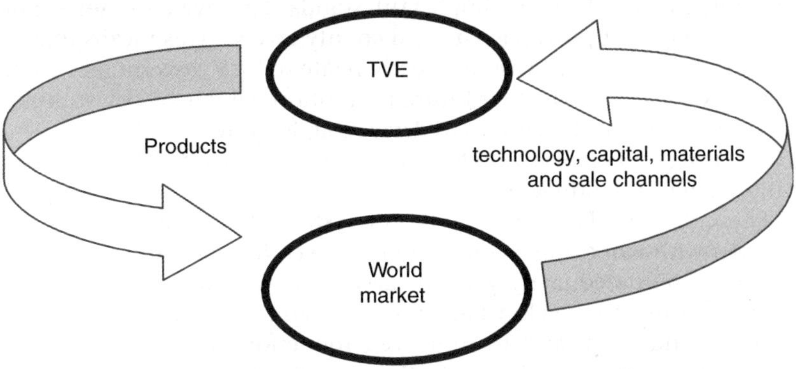

Figure 8.1 The "large international cycle" developmental strategy

1988). China wanted to promote its rural surplus labor to shift from agriculture, to stimulate its rural economy and to obtain foreign exchange through making use of international resources and markets for making up China's resources shortage.

8.3 Policy controls

To increase input in agriculture

From 1989, the CPCCC started to strengthen its agriculture. On 9 November 1989 it urged central and local party committees and governments to give agriculture an important status, and all economic works must implement the policy to take agriculture as the foundation. "Provincial governments must strengthen their leadership to agriculture, especially those governments in the provinces taking grain from other regions to meet their own needs which must plan to enhance their level of self-sufficient grain." It requested governments at prefecture and county levels to put their main energy in to agricultural development, especially in grain and cotton production. "Each sector must increase agricultural input. The share of agriculture in the capital construction investment of the central budget must increase year by year, and provinces, prefectures, cities and counties all must put their financial resources as much as possible into agricultural construction."

Methods to increase agricultural input

- Making agricultural development as an index to evaluate local government achievement
  Because local governments focused on non-agricultural industry and neglected agriculture, the CPCCC on 9 November 1989 stipulated: "whether or not the yields of grain, cotton and other main agricultural and subsidiary products are able to increase and agriculture is truly strengthened will be an important standard to evaluate government achievements at province, city and county levels." This means that agricultural development would directly relate to local government leaders' own interests such as their future promotion, which greatly stimulated local government incentives to develop agriculture.
- Increasing both central and local government agricultural investment
- Increasing agricultural labor
  "The collective labor accumulation system should be restored. Each farmer with work ability must provide the collective with some working days accumulated every year to carry on farmland water conservancy construction, to develop land resources and forestation, to construct bridges and roads and to improve production and living conditions under collective unified organization and plan" (Song,[3] 22 June 1990).
- Raising the share of TVE expenditure for supporting agriculture

The CPCCC urged "to enhance gradually the share of TVE expenditure for supporting agriculture in its profit after tax."

- Guiding farmers to increase agricultural investment
  "We must positively guide farmers to increase their investment and accumulate labor in agriculture. This is the main way to increase agricultural input."
  (CPCCC, 9 November 1989).

Throughout 1989–91, China's government investment in agriculture increased obviously, especially the government investment in agricultural capital construction. From 1988 to 1991, the share of agriculture in total government finance investment in capital construction grew by 4 percentage points. At the same time, the labor supply in primary industry also increased greatly from 322 million in 1988 to 391 million in 1991, an increment about 70 million persons (*Chinese Rural Statistic Yearbook* 1994 and *CSY* 2003)

To close, suspend, merge and transfer the TVEs[4]

The CPCCC carried on a strict reorganization of TVEs to stop the overheated expansion. Deng Xiaoping (June 1989) ordered: "we must stop the TVEs wasting electric power and raw materials and must take decisive action. Local comrades must guarantee this action with their party spirit." The CPCCC (9 November 1989) urged local governments to reorganize TVEs and to guide the TVEs with good profits to develop positively according to state industrial policy. "We must firmly make up our mind to close down, suspend, merge or transfer the TVEs with a high energy consumption, bad quality, serious pollution or those competing with large-scale enterprises for raw materials and in loss."

Methods to close, suspend, merge and transfer the TVEs

- Stipulating three directions for TVE development
  The CPCCC on 9 November 1989 stipulated:
  1) The processing of agricultural and subsidiary products and local raw materials, but not to compete with major industry for raw materials and energy.
  2) Labor-intensive, traditional handicraft and export products.
  3) Forming a complete set with and serving for major industry.
- Formulating laws and regulations
  In order to limit the TVEs, the state formulated many laws and regulations such as these in environmental protection:
  1) "Rule of Preventing and Controlling Noise Pollution of People's Republic of China," 26 September 1989.
  2) "Implementation Regulation of Preventing and Controlling Water Pollution Law of People's Republic of China," 12 July 1989.

3) "Environment Protection Law of People's Republic of China," 26 December 1989.

- Making industrial policy to determine the targets to reorganization

1) The following products to be strictly limited (except for export)

A. Automobiles, motorcycles and ordinary mechanical and electrical products with low quality outside the production units fixed by the state, such as ordinary machine tools and forging equipment.

B. Products with high electricity-consumption such as air-conditioners and vacuum cleaners.

C. High-grade products produced by domestic scarce materials such as aluminum windows and doors, aluminum and copper decoration materials of construction.

D. Products produced by backward methods, which seriously waste resources and cause environmental pollution, such as coking by native methods, making non-ferrous metal and sulfur with indigenous methods.

E. Inferior white liquor, ordinary imitation leather, ordinary man-made fur and so on.

2) The following products to cease production

A. Colored metal ore, chemistry ore, coal mines and so on without license.

B. 437 products for elimination announced by the former Ministry of Machinery (committee).

C. Textile machinery to be eliminated announced by the Ministry of Spinning and Weaving.

D. The first batch of products to be eliminated announced by the Ministry of Construction and five other ministries.
(The State Council, 15 March 1989).

3) Productions to be limited by the Ministry of Agriculture.
Besides the State Council policy, the Ministry of Agriculture also stipulated some productions to cease or be limited.

A. Small-scale spinning and weaving.

B. Small-scale papermaking

4) Establishing leading teams of government combining the TVE management departments, the industry and commerce administrative departments, banks and other relevant departments of government headed by the leading cadres of local parties or governments.
(Chen,[5] 25 July 1989)

Under the strict state reorganization, TVEs, mainly the small ones, decreased greatly. Employees also reducted. "According to the statistics at the end of June, the number of TVEs reduced was 800,000 compared to the end of last year, and 80,000 collective enterprises were closed with a drop of more than 5 million employees" (the Ministry of Agriculture, 20 October 1989). The ministry reported that in Liaoning Province 60 percent of small spinning and weaving productions had been suspended. In Sichuan province 34 percent of rural brewery outputs were cut and Jilin Province closed down or suspended 97 small enterprises out of 111 TVEs with high energy consumption.

To support the key industries centering on SOEs

The state industrial policy was not only to strictly limit and suspend some industries and products, but also to support the key industries and products centering on SOEs. "Each industry must make a classification of existing large and middle-scale SOEs ... to distribute resources according to economic return. We must guarantee their needs for energy, raw materials, transportation and funds first" (CPCCC, 9 November 1989).

Methods to support key industries centering on the SOEs

- Determining the key industries and products to support
  1) Agriculture and industry for agriculture.
  2) Light industry and spinning and weaving industries.
  3) Infrastructure facilities and fundamental industries.
  4) Machinery, electronics industries (mainly large-scale mechanical and electrical products with high added value for exportation to earn foreign exchange).
  5) High-tech industries.
  6) Products for exportation and foreign exchange with good return (the State Council, 15 March 1989).

  Because of their low technology and small scale, TVEs were unable to enjoy state support. Therefore, the state mainly supported SOEs with a bigger scale and higher technology.
- The key rural industries decided by the Ministry of Agriculture
  1) Processing industries of agricultural and subsidiary products.
  2) Energy and raw materials industries.
  3) Industry for agricultural production (small farm tools, chemical fertilizers, agricultural chemicals and so on).
  4) Exportation.
  5) Products serving for major industry, necessary for the market or in short supply, and famous or special or superior products (The Ministry of Agriculture, 31 May 1990).
- Guaranteeing first the need of SOEs, especially the large and middle-scale SOEs, for energy, raw materials, transport and funds.

  "No one may intercept and capture the funds, energy and raw materials assigned to large and middle-scale key enterprises" (CPCCC, 9 November 1989).
- Preferential funds and tax policies

  The banks must draw their funds from the limited industries and put them into the key industries, and the key industries are to enjoy a priority in bank loans. At the same time, they will also enjoy a favorable tax rate.

- Guiding foreign investment to the key industries
  The State Planning Commission formulated an industry order table for absorbing foreign capital to the key industries and restricting foreigners to invest in the limited industries.
- Supporting TVE key industries
  The Ministry of Agriculture formulated a preferential policy for TVE key industries and required relevant government departments "to support TVE key industries, to increase floating capital and loans for their technological transformation and to give them a priority in materials, power supply and transportation" (the Ministry of Agriculture, 31 May 1990).

Although the state adopted a policy to support the SOEs, the policy did not affect the decline of the SOEs. On the contrary, state policy at that time actually caused SOEs to decline suddenly. Similarly, the tightening policy also had a tremendous influence on both collective and urban and rural industries, which contained their tendency to expand excessively.

To cut TVE capital construction

In 1989, the CPCCC wanted to control excessively rapid TVE growth and to make the development speed adapt to both the state and their own capacity, and to coordinate TVE development with SOE and agricultural development. "TVE development speed must be controlled to about 20 percent; the speed of rural industry to about 15 percent" (the Ministry of Agriculture, 20 October 1989). Because TVE super-velocity expansion was mainly realized by expanding capital construction, in order to suppress the excessively quick growth, the state decided to cut TVE capital construction on a large scale. "In the reorganization or over a longer period, TVEs must focus on adjusting their industrial structure, product structure, organizational structure, carrying on technological transformations and improving their quality and management. Generally, they should not start new projects" (the Ministry of Agriculture, 28 November 1989).

Methods to reduce TVE capital construction

- Determining which industries and products to halt or limit in capital construction
  1) Every product, projects and industry in capital construction limited or stopped by the state.
  2) Products lacking raw material supply and also having excessive processing ability.
  3) Small scale, low economic return and serious pollution industries such as small steel and iron, small non-ferrous metal, small chemical, small oil, small building materials and small paper mill industries.
- Controlling new projects severely
  "We must strictly control new projects. Except enterprises for export, agricultural and sideline products processing enterprises with raw mate-

rials guaranteed, enterprises to develop energy and raw materials, enterprises to cooperate with major industry, enterprises to produce items in short supply and products for the people's daily life, no project will be allowed to start, or will be suspended in three years" (the Ministry of Agriculture, 20 October 1989),

1) Making a stricter project examination and approval system.
   "A TVE new capital construction project must get the examination and approval of the relevant government department responsible for TVE management. For a project without the examination and approval, the relevant government departments will not give it loans and the industry and commerce registration. We must determine the right of examination and approval at each level according to the level-to-level administration principle. The examination and approval for a project must be strictly based on the industrial policy and adjustment plan in order to guarantee the fixed asset newly increased to go to industries supported by the policy ... we should coordinate the examination and approval of projects with land use, bank loans and industry and commerce registration" (the Ministry of Agriculture, 31 May 1990).
2) Controlling strictly the right of new project examination and approval.
   The Ministry of Agriculture on 28 November 1989 stipulated: "any new project truly needed and with an investment over 500,000 yuan must be examined and approved by the government department responsible for TVE management at county level." No government below county level had the right to carry out the examination and approval of a new project.

- Compressing the existing projects
  The state also compressed the existing projects of TVEs. "The current primary mission is to take all powerful measures to complete the projects of 18.8 billion yuan left behind since 1988 as soon as possible. We must make up our mind to stop or suspend those projects which cannot be completed" (the Ministry of Agriculture, 28 November 1989).

Under the severe state control, both TVE capital construction projects and investment were reduced greatly. "According to the preliminary statistics in 19 provinces and cities, more than 10,000 projects were stopped or postponed with a investment cut of more than 6 billion yuan, which is equal to 26 percent of the total new increment of fixed assets in these provinces and cities in 1988. This year new projects are extremely few" (The Ministry of Agriculture, 20 October 1989). TVE annual increment of investment in fixed assets had a significant reduction from 49.5 billion yuan in 1988 to 35.8 billion yuan in 1990 (*CTVEY* 1989 and 1992).

To control commodity circulation and crack down on false and poor products

Facing economic crisis, the CPCCC decided to reorganize the economic order, especially in commodity circulation. "We must further clean up and reorganize companies, especially the companies in commodity circulation, and eliminate gradually the chaos in commodity circulation. Next year we must first have a breakthrough in the reorganization of the coal market." It requested: "We must firmly cut those middle links that practice usury, harass the market and inflate prices" (CPCCC, 9 November 1989). At the same time, the state promulgated a series of laws and regulations to crack down on false and poor products.

Methods to control commodity circulation and crack down on false and poor products

- Recovering the state monopoly of producer goods such as coal to guarantee the supply of large and middle-scale SOEs (CPCCC, 9 November 1989).
- State monopoly of chemical fertilizer, agricultural chemicals and plastic film
  The State Council on 28 September 1988 stipulated that only the agricultural producer goods companies of the Ministry of Commerce and the SMCs could be engaged in the business of chemical fertilizer, agricultural chemicals and plastic film and prohibited any person or unit from marketing these commodities. At the same time, the state also requested: "each department of planning in material or petroleum or electric power must really guarantee the supply for large and middle-scale enterprises of chemical fertilizer, agricultural chemicals and plastic film."
- Reorganizing the rural market and promoting standardized management
  1) Standardizing basic business activity (transaction behavior centering on credit and commodity quality).
  2) Standardizing market management.
  3) Standardizing servicing facilities in the market (*Chinese Agriculture Yearbook* 1990, p. 129).
- Strictly prohibiting private business of agricultural producer goods
  "We must firmly reorganize the market order ... strictly prohibit private business in the market of important producer goods. Any region, any sector and any unit must strictly implement the highest limits of prices stipulated by the state. In important consumable commodity circulation, the state-owned commerce and SMCs must grasp the wholesale link and play their main channel role in it. We must strictly prohibit private business engaged in long-distance wholesale service" (CPCCC, 9 November1989).
- Cracking down severely on non-licensed production, false products, price violations and so on
  China made many rules, laws and regulations for cracking down on non-licensed production, false products, price violations and so on. For example,
  1) "Notice about Strengthening Agricultural Chemicals Management, Severely Cracking Down the Activity to Manufacture and Sell Counterfeit and Inferior Agricultural Chemicals," the State Council, 13 January 1989.

2) "Stipulation on Illegal Price Case," the State Price Bureau, 14 March 1989.
3) "Temporary Provisions on the Investigation Procedure of Specially Significant Accidents," the State Council, 29 March 1989.
4) "Notice on Severely Punishing the Persons Responsible for Selling Spurious and Poor Commodities," the State Technology Supervision Bureau, transferred by the State Council, 27 June 1989.
5) "Stipulation on Qualification Management of Construction Enterprise," the Ministry of Construction, 28 June 1989.
6) "Notice on Severely Cracking Down Mixing Impure and False Materials in Commodities," the State Council, 3 September 1989.
7) "Implementation Regulation on Investigating the Products Without a Production Permit License," the State Technology Supervision Bureau and the Ministry of Finance, 30 September 1989.
8) "Rule on Sanitary Supervision of Cosmetics," the Ministry of Public Health, 13 November 1989.

Because the above products were made mainly by TVEs, the focus on cracking down was the TVEs, especially the small ones.

To control tax reduction and exemption strictly[6]

In 1989, the CPCCC started to strengthen tax levies on TVEs. On 9 November 1989 it requested: "we must really strengthen the tax levy, especially the levy on collective, private enterprises. We must strictly clean up each kind of preferential policy of tax reduction and exemption. Any which do not conform to state industrial policy, must be canceled. We should gradually enhance the share of state financial revenue in the national income and the share of central financial revenue in the entire financial revenue."

Methods to control tax reduction and exemption

- Controlling strictly the right of tax reduction and exemption and prohibiting local governments from reducing or exempting tax under bypass leadership

  The State Council on 3 January 1989 strictly controlled the right of tax reduction and exemption, and prohibited local governments from reducing and exempting tax under bypass leadership. "No region, department or person has the right to change national tax law, and cannot reduce and exempt tax randomly. Various tax reduction and exemption regulations made by local governments must be checked one by one strictly. Any regulation which does not conform to the tax law and made under bypass leadership, must be corrected immediately." "Any regulation made in the scope of local government but being improper should also be stopped. The tax levy must be restored immediately if a regular tax reduction or exemption becomes due." The state stipulated that all regulations of tax reduction and exemption made by local governments and tax institutions must take the form of the official document. The tax institutions have the right to refuse to carry out any tax reduction and exemption made bypass leadership and must report it promptly to the higher tax authority. "From now on, any tax reduction and exemption made under bypass leadership will be seriously punished according to the 'Temporary Provisions about Punishment on Violation of Financial Laws and Regulations' made by the State Council" (the State Council, 27 December 1988).

- Making tax institutions independent of local government control
  Before 1989, each local tax institution was under the leadership of local government at the same level. In order to guarantee tax levy and get rid of local government interference, the state made local tax institutions be independent of local governments and be controlled directly by the central government. "The national tax system implements a dual leadership of both the higher tax institution and the government at the same level and takes the tax institution vertical leadership as the mainstay. The organization establishment, cadre management, personnel organization and expenditure of local tax bureaus at prefecture, city and county should be decided directly by the tax bureaus at province, autonomous region and municipality levels" (the State Council, 27 December 1988). The provincial tax bureaus were under central government leadership directly. "The main heads of provincial tax bureaus will be appointed by the State Tax Bureau directly" (the State Council, 4 March 1989).
- Adjusting industry tax rates according to industrial policy
  In order to carry out the national industrial policy, the state made low tax rates for key industries and high tax rates for industries which were to be limited. The State Council on 27 December 1988 stressed that all the consumables and surplus goods strictly limited by the state could not enjoy any tax reduction and exemption. "We must adjust the existing tax variety and rate according to the industrial development sequence, continue to levy and readjust appropriately construction tax, and display the guiding role of difference tax rates in industrial development" (the State Council, 15 March 1989).
- Punishing strictly the evasion of tax in private enterprises
  Facing serious tax evasion in private enterprises, the state decided to take strong measures. The State Council urged to strengthen the guiding, supervising and managing of private economy. "All income earned legally must pay tax according to regulations. We must use tax and other means to adjust too-high incomes and to alleviate the unfair contradictions in distribution. We must severely punish those persons who get sudden and huge profits through evading tax and other illegal methods" (the State Council, 30 August 1989).

Although from 1989, the state started to strengthen the tax levy, the tax paid by TVEs did not increase. On the contrary, because the entire national economy deflated, the increment of TVE tax actually dropped greatly, especially in 1990 when the increment of tax the TVEs delivered was only half as much as that in 1989 (*CTVEY* 1991 and 1992).

To reduce loans and strengthen control on rural finance

The state strengthened control on rural finance. Yao Yilin on 21 March 1989 argued: "we must implement a command-planned management on bank loans for investment and strictly control the expansion of construction scale through collecting social funds. We will not extend investment loans to ordinary TVEs, private economy and the projects out of the national plan."

Methods to reduce loans and strengthen rural financial control

- Reducing bank loans for TVE greatly
  According to industrial policy, banks must pull out funds from those industries to be limited and put them into those industries which are to be supported, in order to promote a positive cycle of social funds (the State Council, 15 March 1989). The state banks cut the loans for TVEs significantly. From the second half of 1988, the ABC reduced TVE loans three times. In 1989, many local ABCs adopted a policy of "taking back only and not extending" loans to TVEs (Zhang, 1990, p. 349). At the same time, in order to control the TVE investment scale, the state banks also raised the loan interest rate of TVE capital investment. The increment of ABC loans for TVEs at the year-end dropped sharply from 5.8 billion in yuan 1988 to 1.3 billion yuan in 1989 (*China Rural Finance Statistics* 1989 and 1991).
- Limiting strictly TVE collection of social funds
  On 5 March 1989, the State Council started to strictly control the enterprises' interior fund collections. The State Tax Bureau (16 June 1989) limited TVE social fund collection. For example, non-production TVEs were forbidden to collect social funds and the funds collected must be paid back in no more than one year. The interest rate cannot be 40 percent higher than the bank interest rate of the same regular deposit. At the same time, all interest paid for the fund from staff and workers must pay tax.
- Reorganizing the finance organizations of the non-state bank system
  The CPCCC on 9 November 1989 argued that the goal of financial system reform was to strengthen centralized and unified management, strengthen the macroeconomic regulation of the Central Bank, and strictly limit currency release and overall credit scale in order to control the over-heated economy and inflation. In the countryside, the state implemented a strict reorganization of the rural finance organizations of

the non-state bank system to control fund flows for cleaning up the rural financial chaos. The main content of reorganizing is:

1) Reorganizing, cutting and firmly merging financial organizations of the non-state bank system and the trust and investment companies run by the banks.
2) Reorganizing, cutting and firmly merging collective financial organizations such as rural cooperatives foundations.
3) Banning old-style Chinese private banks.

The fund reduction made by the state, along with the price rise of raw materials and energy, had a significant influence on TVE development. Funds, especially floating funds, were extremely scarce for most TVEs. In many TVEs, the loans owed could not be repaid, because the other party also could not take funds or get loans from the bank. "From 1989, the banks stopped extending loans to TVEs in order to guarantee major industry and agriculture, which made many TVEs unable to carry out regular production" (Zhang, 1990, p. 349).

To control rural private enterprises strictly

In limiting the TVEs, the CPCCC implemented a strict control on rural private enterprise. First, it reiterated that it supported collective enterprise. "We must persist with the policy to keep the public ownership system as the mainstay and simultaneously to develop a diversified economy. Collective ownership at two levels of township and village is the main body in the rural socialist economy of public ownership." At the same time, the CPCCC emphasized: "private enterprises are the essential supplement to the socialist economy and we must encourage them to develop continually according to state policy, and to operate according to the law. Meanwhile under the voluntary and mutually beneficial premise, we should gradually guide them to develop along the direction of the shareholding system" (He,[7] 5 January 1990).

Methods to control private enterprises strictly

- Inspecting the tax payment of private enterprises comprehensively
  The state decided from the end of October 1989, to carry out a comprehensive and centralized inspection and reorganization of private enterprises. The focus was the operation and tax payment since 1988.
  1) Self-examination. All private enterprises must carry out the inspection of tax paid according to state stipulation themselves.
  2) Spot-checking for enterprises with large scale and serious problems.
  3) Encouraging self-reporting of problems.
- Punishing strictly private enterprises that do business arbitrarily out of their operation scope
  The operation scope of private enterprises was a focal point of the reorganization. Private enterprises could not do business out of their opera-

tion scope, which ratified by the government, and would be punished severely if they surpassed the scope. "Industry and commerce administrative departments at all levels must carry on a universal inspection of the operation scope of private enterprises. If an enterprise violated the stipulation, the administration must issue a warning to it or fine or confiscate the illicit income separately according to the different situations and order it to stop production for reorganization. If the violation is serious, its operation license should be revoked. We must firmly ban the enterprise which does business without a license" (the State Council, 30 August 1989).

- Prohibiting rural private enterprises from making use of state or collective licenses
  In the cleaning up and reorganizing, the state requested that the private enterprises "wearing a red hat"[8] must be corrected immediately and their licenses would be revoked if they refused to do so (the State Council, 30 August 1989).
- Requesting to keep accounts compulsorily
  The State Council on August 30, 1989 requested: "Both private enterprises and merchants with the scale stipulated must keep accounts. The administrative departments must order any one who is requested to keep accounts but does not do it, to stop business for reorganization or revoke their business license, and must severely punish anyone who constructs forged accounts."
- Prohibiting strictly business operations without license, bills or receipts
- Limiting strictly private-run mines
  In 1984, the state encouraged farmers to develop private mines, but in the government reorganization of 1989, rural mining was strictly limited, especially privately-run mining. "In the reorganization, we must positively support township and village collective enterprises, and manage and transform individual and private enterprises and crack down on and ban illegal mining" (the Ministry of Agriculture, 31 May 1990).
- Prohibiting illegal business
  The State Industrial and Commercial Administration Bureau (28 July 1989) requested a comprehensive inspection of illegal private business. "For those illegal businesses found in the inspection, we must deal with them according to the different situations including criticism, fines, confiscation, business suspension for reorganization and license revocation. Those offending criminal law must be delivered to the judicial department for punishment."

In general, although rural private enterprises were strictly limited by the CPCCC, their shares in total TVEs kept almost unchanged. For example, the share of private enterprises in the gross production value of TVEs was 33 percent in 1988 and 34 percent in 1991. The share in total employees of

TVEs was 49 percent in 1988 and 50 percent in 1991 (*CTVEY* 1991 and 1992). The policy suppressed their super-velocity expansion tendency only.

Export-orientation

Although the state implemented a compressing policy to TVEs, it vigorously supported TVE exportation. The State Council on 15 March 1989 argued that we must support TVEs in the "processing trade," which got raw materials from, and exported their products, to overseas. On 9 November 1989, the CPCCC requested that in the reorganization, TVEs must "display their superiority of labor-intensive and traditional techniques and positively develop exportation to make foreign exchange and move towards the world market."

Methods to promote exportation

- Promoting "processing trade" with great effort
  In the "large international cycle" strategy, the "processing trade" played a important role. In 1989, the State Council listed the "processing trade" as one of the key industries it wanted to support and requested "to make use of the international market, based on our characteristics of rich labor supply and few resources, and to positively develop the processing trade with overseas raw materials, samples and parts, and compensation trade as well as the exportation raised by importation" (the State Council, 15 March 1989). The "exportation raised by importation" means to import and process foreign resources, then export the products to the international market.
- Promoting the union between trade and industry and setting up the "export base of trade, industry and agriculture"
  In order to push TVE exports, the state urged to combine TVEs with those state-owned foreign trade companies that controlled China's foreign trade. The State Council on October 1987 authorized the establishment of the Export Production Bases of Trade, Industry and Agriculture (EPBTIA). The procedure to establish the EPBTIA is:
  1) The economic committees, economic and trade committees and TVE bureaus at province, city and autonomous region choose the candidate TVE and apply to the State EPBTIA Office.
  2) The experts chosen by the Office appraise the candidate enterprise of the EPBTIA.
  3) The Ministry of Agriculture and the State Economic and Trade Committee ratify the EPBTIA.
  4) The fund source of an EPBTIA:
  A. Central government funds.
  B. Local government funds.
  C. Enterprise funds. Most funds in an EPBTIA were from the enterprises.
- Allowing TVEs to participate in the bids of state projects of export bases: The state projects of export bases were usually decided by the state ministries and related commissions and generally were distributed in state-

owned enterprises. From 1988, the state decided to allow TVEs to participate in the bids of these projects and enjoy the same policy as SOEs (the Ministry of Agriculture, State Planning Commission et al., 12 July 1988). The state projects of export base mainly were of two types:

1) The capital construction projects of light industry and textile exports formed by the State Planning Commission.
2) The mechanical and electrical export bases and enterprises with expansion rights.

These bases and enterprises were decided by the State Council Mechanical and Electrical Export Office for SOEs only at first. TVEs were allowed to participate in the bids for them in 1988. By 1990, the bids obtained by TVEs were 150 projects of the mechanical and electrical export bases and enterprises with expansion rights, 106 projects of light industry and textile export capital construction and 192 projects of the EPBTIA (*CTVEY* 1991).

- Favorable loan, tax and reward policies for exports
  1) Favorable loan policies for the EPBTIA
     An EPBTIA could enjoy preferential bank loans to support its technological transformation. The loan was to be for no longer than two years and central and local finance would each pay the loan interest at no more than 5 million yuan every year. The enterprise would pay the remaining interest.
  2) Preferential reduction or exemption of custom duties and taxes for imported technology and equipment that is imperative for the TVEs.
  3) Priority of raw materials and imported parts for TVE export production.
  4) Rewarding exportation.
     Foreign trade companies will pay a reward to the TVEs providing products for export according to the amount exported (The Ministry of Agriculture, State Planning Commission et al., 12 July 1988).

Table 8.1 China's TVE outward-oriented economy 1986–90 (billion yuan, %, unit)

Year	*Fees of processing trade*	*TVE delivery value of export goods*	*TVE share in national delivery value of export goods* (%)	*Number of TVE joint ventures with foreigners*
1986	1.1	10.0	11	2405
1987	2.4	16.2	15	2996
1988	2.9	26.9	19	4762
1989	5.1	37.1	22	5915
1990	8.0	48.6	24	6987

Source: *CTVEY* 1991.

- Organizing export commodity exhibitions
  The first TVE commodity for export exhibition was held from 27 August to 5 September 1986. The second was from 23 September to 4 October 1989 in Beijing. The state support for TVE exports mainly concentrated on improving TVE technology. For example, the favorable loans provided were used for TVE technological transformations.

Export-orientating provided TVEs with new opportunities to expand, especially in the government reorganization period, when the domestic market was worn out. TVEs with their huge low-cost labor supply and rural natural resources unceasingly expanded their outward-oriented economy, which impelled not only their own development, but also the national outward-oriented economy. The share of TVEs in national exportation rose rapidly and TVEs became an important sector in China's foreign trade.

To limit farmer workers[9]

The relaxation of control and allowing farmers to enter cities to do business in 1984 stimulated farmers' movement across regions and millions of farmers rushed into cities for job opportunities, which led to the large-scale "wave of farmer workers" in spring 1989. The State Council on 5 March 1989 sent out an urgent notice and pointed out: "after the Spring Festival, the farmers in Sichuan, Henan, Hubei, Shandong, Shaanxi, Jiangsu, Anhui and other regions massively and centrally went to the northwest, northeast and Guangdong regions and caused the railroad passenger flow to rise suddenly, which has created an enormous pressure on railway transportation. Some of them have a hard life there because they cannot find a job and have to go around the streets. The huge numbers of farmers also created chaos in local society." It requested to stop farmers moving out of rural areas in order to avoid transportation pressures and a minus effect on agricultural production. The State Council on 25 February 1991 again requested to stop the blind movement of farmer workers to Guangdong immediately.

Methods to limit farmer workers

- Mobilizing and persuading farmers from going out of rural areas
  Local governments strengthened their management of farmers going out of rural areas to control the farmers going out blindly and in large numbers.
- Mobilizing the farmers already arrived at train stations to return home
- Those regions, to which farmer workers migrated, made strict regulations to prevent farmers from moving in. For example, in Guangdong province, no unit could recruit farmer workers arbitrarily, otherwise the enterprise would be punished economically and the leaders would be investigated. The farmer workers already working in Guangdong were not allowed to introduce new farmers into Guangdong and would be fired if they secretly took new farmers in.

In the economic reorganization and strict limitation of farmer migration, the farmer workers were restrained in 1989 and 1990. The labor from rural areas to city employment dropped from 1.60 in 1988 to 1.20 in 1989 and 1.18 million in 1990 (*CSY* 1990 and 1992).

8.4 Rural industrialization in process

Rural industry experienced a setback during the reorganization. From 1989, the number of TVE staff and workers dropped significantly. The number of TVEs reduced from 18.9 in 1988 to 18.5 million in 1990, a drop of 380,000 TVEs with a cut of 2.8 million staff and workers. Although TVE total output value still kept a rapid growth, its high-speed growth tendency had slowed down, from 36 percent in 1988 to 14 percent in both 1989 and 1990.

Although TVEs experienced a setback in the economic reorganization, the share of TVEs in the rural economy continued to rise. In 1991, the share achieved 59 percent. The output value of rural industry already surpassed that of agriculture and became the largest industry in the rural economy. Through 1989–91, TVE funds to support agriculture and other rural enterprises continued to increase. The fund to support agriculture increased from 1.2 billion yuan in 1988 to 7.1 billion yuan in 1989. In

Table 8.2 TVE development 1988–91 (million units, million persons, billion yuan)

Year	*Number of TVEs*	*Staff and workers*	*Original value of fixed assets*	*Total output (value-added)*
1988	18.9	95.5	209.9	174.2
1989	18.7	93.7	250.0	208.3
1990	18.7	92.7	285.7	250.4
1991	19.1	96.1	338.5	297.2

Source: *CTVEY* 2003.

Table 8.3 TVE contribution to rural economy 1988–91 (%, billion yuan)

Year	*Share in rural labor*	*Share in rural social output value*	*Funds to support agriculture*	*Funds to support rural collective warfare*	*Funds to support rural other enterprises*
1988	23.8	58.1	1.2	2.5	5.7
1989	22.9	58.0	7.1	n	9.1
1990	22.1	57.7	7.8	2.4	10.5
1991	22.3	59.2	8.7	2.9	12.2

Source: *CTVEY* 1978–87, 1990 and 1992.
Note: the data of funds to support agricultural, rural collective welfare and other enterprises are from the collective enterprises only.

Table 8.4 The structure of China's rural social output value 1988–91 (%)

Year	*Agriculture*	*Rural industry*	*Rural construction industry*	*Rural transportation*	*Rural commerce*
1988	46.8	38.1	7.1	3.5	4.5
1989	45.1	40.7	6.3	3.6	4.3
1990	46.1	40.4	5.9	3.5	4.1
1991	42.9	43.5	6.0	3.5	4.1

Source: *CTVEY* 1991, 1990, and 1992.

1991 the fund amounted to 8.7 billion yuan. Similarly, TVE funds for other rural enterprises also doubled.

The share of rural industry in national industry also unceasingly rose from 26 percent in 1988 to 28 percent in 1990. At the same time, the tax TVEs paid also continued to increase from 3.1 billion yuan in 1988 to 4.6 billion yuan in 1991. Rural industry gradually became a vital part of China's industrialization process. TVE development caused the rural economy to change greatly and changed completely the rural economic structure. China's rural economy gradually transformed into one taking TVEs, the non-agricultural industries, as the mainstay, and broke away from taking agriculture as the mainstay with 80 percent of the total population being engaged in agriculture and working only for food to eat.

Except for 1990, agriculture continued a slow growth at an annual rate of 2–3 percent. The grain production stopped gliding down and changed for the better with a slight increase in national per capita grain from 358 kg in 1988 to 378 kg in 1991. The per capita net income of rural households continued to increase from 545 yuan in 1988 to 709 yuan in 1991; however, the Engel Coefficient of rural households did not drop, instead it rose from 54 percent in 1988 to 58 percent in 1991, up 4 percentage points. The rural infrastructure was improved significantly with an increase in rural telephone subscribers from 1.1 million in 1988 to 1.74 million in 1991, 58 percent up. The rural electricity consumption changed from 712 kW in 1988 to 963 kW in 1991, 35 percent up (*CSY* 2001, p. 304).

8.5 Policy effects

Why was rural industry not stopped as it was after the GLF?

Although the crisis China faced in 1989 did not cause a big famine, as it did under the GLF, the rural industry development harmed not only agriculture, but also state-owned industry. Simultaneously, it also led to the great expansion of private industry and environmental pollution. All these factors caused the state to severely suppress rural industry. However, the

CPCCC was unable to "cut rural industry with one stroke of the knife" as it had after the GLF failure, because the reform and liberalization caused the rural economy to have a fundamental change:

- Rural economy holding an important status in China's economy
  The countryside was no longer a sector purely for supporting the city and major industry and a purely agricultural production base. It had become an important part of the national economy. Rural development and enhancement of farmers' living standards directly affected national economic development. Therefore, the state had to take rural economic development, and farmers' benefit as well as local government benefit into account.
- Rural industry became the main industry in the rural economy and the main fund source for agriculture
- Rural industry had become the main channel to shift the rural labor surplus
  Unlike the GLF, in the crisis in 1989 there was not a shortage in rural labor, but a huge rural labor surplus waiting for transferring. Employment had become one of the priority targets in rural economy development. Developing rural industry had become the main method to absorb the rural labor surplus.
- The CPCCC was unable to control the rural areas completely
  The liberalization, especially the disintegration of the people's communes, caused the CPCCC to be unable to completely control the countryside. The market played a very important role in the rural economy. The CPCCC certainly did not completely prevent local governments from developing rural industry for much higher profit.
- Rural industry had become an important tax resource for the government

Therefore, the CPCCC had have to face a difficult choice while suppressing the rural industry and was unable to take the same measures as that after the GLF. As a result, rural industry was still able to keep up rapid development.

The suppression decreased incentives to develop the TVEs greatly

The reorganization of TVEs stopped the TVE overheated expansion and contained chaos through compulsory administrative methods. That indicated that although rural industry had a rapid development after the reform and opening up, in the national economic development strategy, it still was a "second-class citizen." The state only allowed it to develop by relying its own efforts, but did not allow it to affect and impede the development of both state-owned industry and agriculture. The national developmental strategy still was based on the dual structure model. Supporting agriculture and state-owned industry and suppressing rural industry was an attempt to strengthen the original dual pattern in which the countryside dealt with agriculture only and the city with industry only.

Supporting agriculture and SOEs and suppressing TVEs and private economy decreased the incentives of both local governments and farmers to develop TVEs and made rural industry diametrically opposed to both agricultural and state-owned industry, which threw local governments, especially the grass-roots units, into great confusion over developing rural industry. The policy affected the determination and confidence of both local governments and farmers to develop rural industry. They questioned: "how long can the TVE flag last?" (Zhang, 1990, p. 333). The policy to strictly limit private economy also put private enterprises, the "third-class citizen." under a severer discrimination, which constrained private economic development significantly.

"Farmer worker-making" caused a China-style Lewis model and "recessive urban population"

Unlike after the GLF, suppressing rural industry did not cause rural labor to shift into agriculture completely; on the contrary, it made many farmers flow to the city to seek a job, which formed waves of "farmer workers." This is a special form of the Lewis development model. Obviously, the prerequisite for Lewis development is labor liberalization. Only when production factors can move freely, is it possible for farmers to shift. If farmer movement is limited, like the "farmer-making" after the GLF, it is impossible for a Lewis development model to appear. Lewis-style development was postponed about 25 years (1961–86) and took the

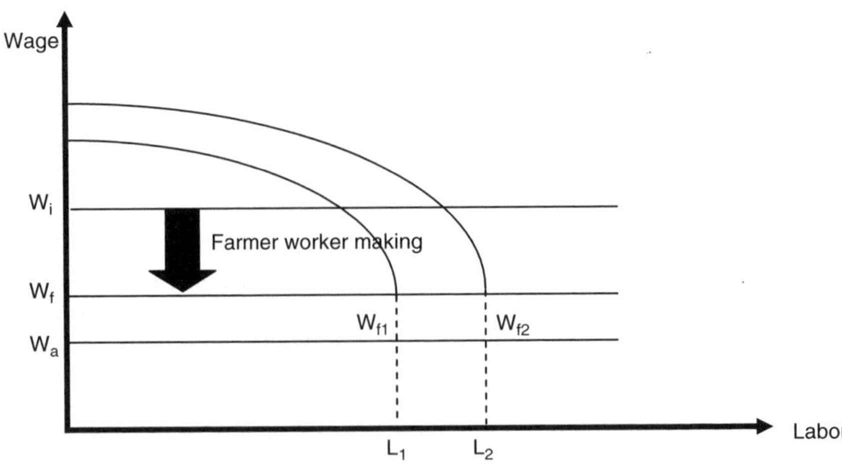

Figure 8.2 China's Lewis development under "farmer worker making" in the 1990s

Where W_i, W_f and W_a are the real wages of urban workers, farmer workers and farmers respectively

special form of "farmer workers" because the "second-class citizen" farmers had only partial freedom. They could enter the city to work and do business, but still could not migrate to the city, and could not change their status of being the rural population. They are farmers and also workers in the city. Making "farmer workers" has had a big influence on China's development.

Cutting labor costs and making farmers poor

- Cutting labor costs for urban industrial development
  In Lewis development, as long as the wages in urban industry are higher than the wages in agriculture, liberalized farmers will migrate to the city unceasingly. As shown in Figure 8.2, in China, the real wages of labor in the city (W_i) is much higher than that in agriculture (W_a). However, the real wage of a farmer worker (W_f) is much lower than that for an urban worker. That is, the state cuts the cost of the farmer worker and simultaneously keeps a lower income in the rural areas through administrative methods, which shifts cheap farmers to urban industry. Farmers gradually flow to the city and shift into non-agricultural industry; simultaneously, the urban economy expands rapidly and brings national economy a high speed growth. This is the Lewis development in China and also the industrialization process.
- Making farmers poor
  Although the emergence and rapid flourish of "farmer workers" on a large-scale promoted the opening and liberalization of the sealed and conservative countryside and enhanced farmers' incomes, it was "farmer workers" who guaranteed and promoted the rapid development of the urban economy. As shown in Figure 8.2, farmer worker-making lowers the farmer worker's wages and decreases their income. Compulsorily cutting down farmer worker costs in the city benefited city industry but sacrificed farmers' interests. Farmers failed to overcome their poverty in the high-speed economic growth.

Making "recessive urban population" and fettering market expansion and urbanization

Although "farmer workers" are registered as rural residents, they work and live in the city for most of the year. In fact, they have already become urban inhabitants. They are the "recessive urban population."

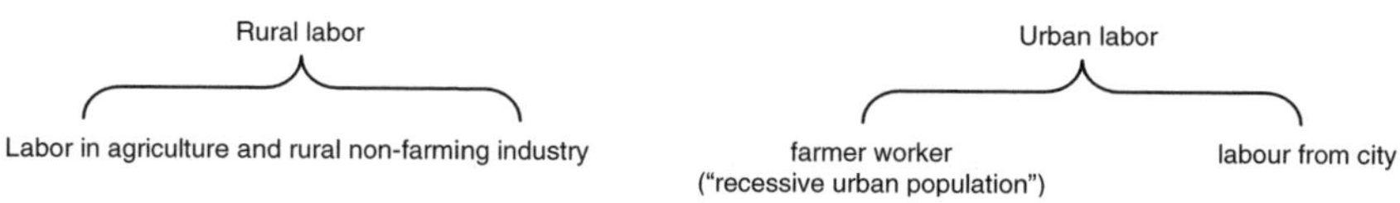

Figure 8.3 China's labor structure and farmer workers in the 1990s

Generally, industrialization advances along with population urbanization synchronously, and the industrialization process also is a process of population urbanization. However, in China, although economical development was rapid and the share of agriculture in the national economy unceasingly decreased, urban population grew slowly. The share of agriculture in China's GDP dropped from 51 percent in 1952 to 25 percent in 1989, about 26 percentage points down, however, the share of agricultural population in the national population decreased from 86 percent in 1952 to 79 percent in 1989, only seven percentage points down in 37 years. The huge rural population not only led to farmers' poverty, but also hindered China's population urbanization and restricted both domestic markets and city development, which impeded national industrialization.

Export-orientation providing TVEs with new funds, materials and markets

Export-orientation introduced TVEs into the international market, which not only provided TVEs with funds, raw materials and sales markets, but also relaxed TVE competition with SOEs. Export-orientation made TVEs get new funds not only from international markets, but also from domestic markets because of the favorable policy for export. Export-orientation promoted and continued TVE rapid expansion. In coastal areas, the TVEs for exportation drove the entire rural economic development. For instance, in Guangdong Province, most local rural enterprises in many areas were begun and impelled by the exporting enterprises.

9

New Great Leap Forward after the Collapse of the Soviet Union

9.1 Background

In 1991, China's economy had an overall recovery. Most of the main economic index approached or surpassed the average annual growth rate in the thirteen years since the reform and opening up, even that of the ten years from 1979 to 1988. The national economy entered a normal stage of growth. The annual growth rate of GDP was 7.3 percent with a rate of 14.2 percent in industry. State-owned industry had a big restoration with an annual growth rate of 8.6 percent, 5 percentage points more than that in 1989. China's exports in 1991 were 71.9 billion US dollars increasing by 15.8 percent annually with an import of 63.8 billion US dollars. In agriculture, although the gross output value grew slowly at a rate of 3.7 percent, the grain yield increased from 1989 to 1991 continuously and the national per capita grain grew from 358 kg in 1988 to 378 kg in 1991. In many areas, it was difficult for farmers to sell grain.

In 1991, one of the most influential events was the collapse of Soviet Union on 8 December 1991, which shocked the whole world greatly. The sudden collapse of the first socialist nation in the worlds, which had existed for nearly seventy years brought enormous impact not only to politics, but also to the world economy, especially to the socialist countries. The collapse is a fatal blow and comprehensive denial of the Stalin-type development pattern of central command economy, which had a decisive and profound influence on China's economic development.

9.2 Policy goals

To abandon the central planned system and launch a new Great Leap Forward

From 18 January to 21 February 1992, Deng Xiaoping made his Southern Journey Speech in Wuchang, Shenzhen, Zhuhai, Shanghai and so on and requested to speed up the reform of China's traditional central planned economic system and the transformation to the market economic system and to launch a new great leap forward. The main points of the speech were as follows:

- "Development is the hard truth":[1]
  This means that economic development is "the only way to win the trust and support of the people." If an economy develops quickly, the system is good; if develops slowly, the system is bad and people will abandon and "topple" the system. "If we are not adhering to socialism, not implementing the reform and opening policy, not developing the economy and not improving people's lives, we would find ourselves in a blind alley." Although Deng also proposed to continue with socialism, he mainly requested to abandon traditional socialist ideology, which fettered China's economic development seriously.
- Abandoning the centralized planning system and establishing the market economy system
  China had to give up the centralized planning system and establish the market economy system because the market economy system can impel the economy to develop more quickly. Market economy is not equal to capitalism. Socialism should make use of the market to develop its economy rapidly.
- Launching a new great leap forward
  China must develop its economy at a high speed. Although the government reorganization from 1989 was necessary, the high-speed economic development through 1984–88 was a leap forward different from the GLF and greatly promoted the national economy. "It seems that we must often make use of opportunity to accelerate development at some stages for several years, find and solve the problems promptly, then go ahead again."

According to Deng's speech, Jiang (12 October 1992) explicitly announced two decisions:

- To establish a socialist market economy system
  The socialist market economy system is "to make markets play a foundational role in resource distribution under the macro regulation of the socialist state and to optimize resource dispositions through economic levers and competition." "In the ownership structure, we must take public ownership including the ownership by the whole people and the collective ownership economy as the mainstay, and individual economy, private economy and foreign-funded economy as a supplement to develop a diversified economy with various ingredients jointly for a long time."
- To launch a new GLF
  The CPCCC decided to adjust "the Eighth FYP" and enhance the planned growth rate of the economy (GDP) from 6 percent to 8–9 percent. China started to launch a new round of the GLF comprehensively (CPCCC, 7 March 1993).

To relieve TVE limitation and permit TVE high-speed growth to impel the new GLF

The TVE was a key for realizing the new great leap forward because although the state had adopted various measures to limit TVEs since the reform, they had still maintained an astonishing development speed. It can be said that high-speed TVE development promoted China's high-speed growth after the reform. Deng Xiaoping highly praised TVEs and pointed out that the rapid economic development was from 1984 to 1988. In those five years, the increase of agricultural and subsidiary products, rural market expansion and rural surplus labor shift all powerfully impelled industry development. "In this way, agriculture and industry, countryside and city influence each other and impel each other. This is an extremely vivid, extremely persuasive development process. It can be said that in this period the wealth of our country had a enormous increase and the entire national economy got up a new stair" (Deng, 1992). The new GLF must inevitably depend on TVE development. In other words, without TVEs, it is impossible to make a new GLF. Therefore, in 1992 the CPCCC decided to change its TVE policy since 1989, comprehensively relieved its limitations on TVEs and permitted and impelled TVEs to develop at high speed. In 1993, in order to implement the new GLF, the state changed the original "Eighth FYP of TVEs" made in 1991 and raised almost all of the targets greatly.

At the same time, TVE importance for the national economy was enhanced further in 1992. The State Council (18 March 1992) defined TVEs as "the only way" to bring about a prosperous rural economy, increase farmer income, promote agriculture modernization and national economic development and proposed for the first time the vital significance of developing TVEs in the realization of the national industrialization. In other words, the state started to regard TVEs as one part of national industry and to bring it into the national industrialization strategy. This is a very big change. The state requested "to impel TVEs to develop continually and

Table 9.1 The target of the "Eighth FYP of TVEs" made in both 1991 and 1993 (billion yuan, hundred million persons)

	The target made in 1991		*The target made in 1993*
	by 1995	*by 2000*	*by 2000*
Total output value	1640	2640	7600
Industrial output value	1200	1930	5400
Employees	1.1	1.4	1.6

Source: *CTVEY* 1992 and 1994.
Notes: 1) The target made in 1991 is at 1990 price.
2) The target made in 1993 is at current price.

healthily and to make greater contribution to the realizing the strategic target in our nation's modernization."

To develop TVE positively for solving rural problems

There were three very difficult problems to solve in China's rural areas. The first is how can farmers become well off? The second is how to shift the rural labor surplus from agriculture to non-agricultural industry. The third is how to speed up agriculture development. Obviously it is impossible to solve the three problems through developing agriculture only. So, one of the goals for the CPCCC to permit and develop TVE vigorously was to solve the three difficult problems through TVE development. The State Council argued that it had been proved by practice that vigorous TVE development could not only solve the rural labor surplus, help agricultural production, raise farmers' living standards and cause millions of farmers to step onto a common enrichment path, but also played an important role in increasing exportation for foreign exchange and national tax revenue, realizing national industrialization, constructing rural markets and towns, reducing gradually the differences between town and country, consolidating the alliance between worker and peasant and government grass-root units and promoting the political, economic and social stability and development of our country (the State Council, 18 March 1992).

To impel TVEs in poor regions and eliminate regional unbalance

TVE development was very unbalanced regionally; the Central and West regions having approximately two-thirds of the national population held only one-third of national TVE output value. TVE unbalance had become the main reason for the economic disparity between the East and Central-West regions. Therefore, accelerating TVE development in the Central-West regions has "an extremely vital economic and political significance" in "narrowing gradually the disparity between the east and western regions, promoting the economy in national minority regions, changing poverty and backwardness, consolidating and developing unity and stability, and realizing common enrichment" (the State Council, 18 March 1992). Jiang (12 October 1992) requested that we must "develop TVEs continually with great effort, and especially support and accelerate the TVEs in the Central and West regions and national minority regions." This means that the CPCCC wanted to impel the economy in poor regions and eliminate regional disparity through vigorously developing the TVEs in the Central and West regions.

To open to the world with multi-channel and multi-level methods

The CPCCC requested to further expand the opening up to foreign countries and to establish multi-channel, multi-level and all-round opening patterns to absorb more overseas funds, resources, technology and managerial experience. Jiang (12 October 1992) urged "to expand the opening up of regions to foreign investment" such as the Pudong in Shanghai and open "more industries" such as finance, commerce, tourism and real estate to foreign investment. "We must continue to consummate the investment environment, provide more convenient conditions and fuller legal safeguards for foreign investors." At the same time, the CPCCC requested to develop the international market, promote trade multiplication, expand exportation, and simultaneously increase imports to make use of more overseas resources and advanced technology.

9.3 Policy controls

To reduce discrimination and permit TVEs to compete with SOEs

For a long time, as the representative of the "socialist economy" and "advanced modern big industry," SOEs had always enjoyed state protection, support and priority. On the contrary, TVEs were the result of "the small peasant economy" and the representative of "the backward and small industry" and was a "second-class citizen," which was not allowed to compete with SOEs. From 1992, the CPCCC started to change its discrimination over TVEs and changed the traditional ideas that to pay close attention to industry is to stress state-owned industry, and to pay close attention to rural economy is to stress agriculture, and it began to promote coordinately the development of TVEs, SOEs and agriculture. Local governments must pay close attention, under the premise to persist taking agriculture as the foundation, to TVEs' development while paying close attention to large and middle-scale SOEs (the State Council, 14 February 1993). Chen Junsheng[2] on 16 November 1992 argued: "practice has proved that it is not comprehensive to pay close attention to large and middle scale SOEs only when grasping industry and to pay close attention to agriculture only when grasping rural economy. We must realize two 'grasping two things': in industry, to grasp both large and middle-scale SOEs and TVEs; in rural areas, to grasp both agriculture and TVEs." The CPCCC (7 March 1993) urged: "All of the SOEs, collective enterprises and other-type enterprises will enter markets to compete equally, and to display the SOE's leading role through equal competition."

Methods to reduce discrimination

- Cleaning up the discrimination rules and regulations to relax the limit
  In order to guarantee and support SOE development, the central and local governments formulated many discrimination rules and regulations against TVEs. So, in order to eliminate the discrimination, the state requested government departments concerned to positively serve for TVEs and clean up, abolish or revise, if necessary, those discrimination rules and regulations which limited TVE development. Each government

department concerned must formulate "a policy to support TVE development and clean up and abolish all discrimination rules and regulations against TVEs, and announce them publicly" (the State Council, 14 February 1993).

- Bringing TVEs into line with the national industry plan
  Although TVEs experienced high-speed development for more than ten years, they were not a part of national industry, but only a part of rural economy in the state plan and were repelled out of the national industry in China's economy. In September 1993, the State Council held a national working conference of TVEs and requested local governments to bring TVEs into line with the national industry plan "to plan, manage and serve for TVEs" (*CTVEY* 1993, p. 19).

Although the state requested to reduce discrimination against TVEs, it did not take real measures to support them. In fact, what the state did is to relax its limitations to TVEs and allow them to develop. However, the relaxation stimulated TVEs greatly and led the share of rural industry in national industry to rise rapidly and surpass that of state-owned industry.

Table 9.2 The growth rates and shares of both state-owned and rural industries in national industry (%)

Year	*State-owned industry*		*TVE industry*	
	Growth rate	*Share in national industry*	*Growth rate*	*Share in national industry*
1991	8.6	56.2	44.0	32.7
1992	12.4	51.5	56.6	38.1
1993	5.7	47.0	72.0	48.7
1994	6.5	37.3	37.9	49.4
1995	8.2	34.0	58.5	55.8

Source: *CSY* 1996 and *CTVEY* 1992–6.
Note: the shares are calculated according to the data in the yearbooks. State-owned industry does not include the industry controlled by the state through share holding.

To accelerate TVE development in the central and west regions

In November 1992, in order to impel TVE development in the central-west regions, the state convened the "National Experience Exchange Conference about Accelerating TVE Development in the Central and West Regions" and requested local governments in central-west regions to concentrate their strength to develop TVEs. The State Council on 14 February 1993 made the "Resolution on Accelerating TVE Development in the Central and West Regions" and urged the promotion of TVE development there.

Methods to accelerate TVEs in the central and west regions

- Making TVE as the center of development in the central and west regions
  At the end of 1992, China officially determined accelerating TVE development in central-west regions to be a key point of national economic strategy. The State Council requested: "from now on, the development of both secondary and tertiary industries in counties of central-west regions, besides the projects developed by the state plan, must gradually shift to the primary track taking TVEs as the mainstay to enrich farmers and simultaneously the county."
  1) Bringing TVEs into line with the national economic plan and arranging important projects such as energy, transportation and resources development for them in the central-west regions.
  2) Requesting government departments to support and serve TVEs.
- Giving priority to develop TVEs in industries using local resources
  1) Agricultural products processing and so on;
  2) Natural resource development such as mining, construction materials, small power stations;
  3) Commerce, service industries, handicraft industries, construction, transportation, traveling and so on.
- Giving private TVEs a free hand
  The state urged to impel all forms of economy in the region. "We must permit and support the 'wheel' (developing way) suitable to the local level of productive force and not limit its development speed. The poor regions with weak collective economy and difficulty in developing collective enterprises may give individual, private and share-cooperation enterprises a free hand to develop. All enterprises with different ownership must enter the market and compete with each other equally" (the State Council, 14 February 1993).
- Encouraging and supporting talented persons to develop TVEs
  1) Giving local capable persons a free hand to develop TVEs.
  2) Encouraging cadres in the party and government to develop TVEs.
  3) Attracting university and college graduates.
  4) Supporting technicians, staff and workers and retirees in research institutions, universities and state-owned enterprises to serve for TVEs in their leisure time.
  5) Rewarding persons who made a prominent contribution to TVEs.
- Concentrating TVEs in existing small towns and regions with a foundation for TVEs
- Developing a market system, mainly commodity and production-factors market construction
- Multi-channel to increase investment:
  1) State special loans of 5 billion yuan for TVEs in the regions each year from 1993 to 2000, besides the normal bank loans for the TVEs.

2) Increasing credit of specialized banks and other financial organizations for the TVEs.
3) Funds from local government finance.
4) Local social funds.
A. Foundation for TVE development.
B. Establishing development funds for technological transformation and new products.
C. Raising funds by shares.

- Promoting the union of city and countryside, mainly the large and middle-scale SOEs in central-west regions through spare part production proliferation, raw material development, technical proliferation and processing to develop TVEs with local farmers jointly.
(the State Council, 14 February 1993)
- The demonstration project of cooperation between the East and West
In September 1993, the State Council officially decided to implement the "TVE demonstration project of cooperation between the East and West" aiming to combine the technology, management and funds in the eastern region with the rich raw materials, energy and labor resources in the central-west regions, to promote TVE and rural development in the central-west regions. The Ministry of Agriculture (1 February 1994) proposed the plan for the project.
1) The target of "Demonstration Project of TVE Cooperation between the East and West regions" by 2000
A. For the Central and West regions
    a. Annual output value of 6,300 billion yuan with an annual growth rate of 30 percent
    b. Annual profit and tax 350 billion yuan with an annual growth rate of 25 percent
    c. To shift 10 million rural labor surplus from agriculture
    d. To increase more than 1,000 small towns, each with a TVE output value more than 1 hundred million yuan
    e. To invest more than 180 billion yuan fund in the Central and West regions through the cooperation projects
B. For the Cooperation Demonstration Projects
    a. To realize an annual increase of output value of 100 billion yuan
    b. To realize an annual profit and tax of 15 billion yuan
    c. To shift 0.5 million rural labor surplus from agriculture
C. For the Model zones made by the Ministry of Agriculture
    a. To realize an average annual output value of more than 1 billion in each zone
    b. To realize an average annual profit and tax of more than 1 hundred million yuan for each zone
    c. To make the per capita net income of farmers attain the level in coastal regions
(The Ministry of Agriculture, 1 February 1994)

2) Method to implement the cooperation demonstration project

A. Enjoying technology project priority.
The national technical projects such as the SP projects will first support the cooperation demonstration projects. At the same time, the state planned to popularize 1,000 new technologies and new products in the TVEs of the central-west regions.

B. Organizing the cooperation between counties and cities in the east and central-west regions.

C. Training 10,000 technicians and managers for the central-west regions.

D. Fund support. Arranging 500 million yuan loans from the special loans of 10 billion yuan for TVEs in the central-west regions each year to support the demonstration projects. The projects also enjoyed a priority for the funds from central and local government finance.

E. Relaxing the requirement for the license to import and export.

(The Ministry of Agriculture, 1 February 1994)

Although under the government's vigorous impetus, the TVEs in Central and West regions had a quicker development, they didn't change their share in TVE national output. The share of the Central region in TVE national output increased from 28 percent in 1992 to 33 percent in 1995 but the share of the West region kept unchanged at 4 percent from 1992 to 1995 (*CTVEY* 1993 and 1996).

To make an overall relaxation and give rural private enterprises a free hand

In 1992, the state abolished its restriction and gave rural private enterprises a free hand again to impel TVE growth. State Council member Chen Junsheng (16 November 1992) argued that we should give private enterprises a free hand and encourage them to develop. "This 'supplement' (to the public economy) of private and foreign-funded economy is not too much, but is insufficient and needs to develop further." The State Council requested to support and give private enterprise a free hand in its development, especially in the central and west and the national minority regions (Chen Junsheng, 18 September 1993).

Methods to give rural private enterprises a free hand

- Relaxing the restrictions and encouraging farmers to set up private enterprises
- Expanding industry access for private enterprises
- Tax reduction and exemption.

Although the state mainly relaxed its restriction and permitted private enterprises to develop, the relaxation and permission played a very great

Table 9.3 TVE private enterprise development 1991–95 (billion yuan, %)

Year	*Total output value*	*Growth rate of total output value*	*The share in TVE national output value*	*The share in TVE national employees*
1991	390	28.9	33.6	50.4
1992	588	50.6	33.3	51.3
1993	1,118	90.3	35.7	53.3
1994	1,372	22.7	32.4	47.9
1995	2,720	98.2	35.9	52.3

Source: *CSY* 1996
Notes: 1) The shares are calculated on the data in *CSY* 1996.
2) The total output value was at 1990 price.

role in the rapid development of rural private enterprises. As shown in Table 9.3, private enterprises had a rapid growth in that period.

To relax control and promote TVE tertiary industry with great effort

Jiang (12 October 1992) argued that because the share of our tertiary industry in national GDP is much lower than that in developed and many developing nations, we must "accelerate tertiary industry development and raise its share in the GDP significantly." The CPCCC on 18 June 1992 made a resolution to accelerate tertiary industry with great effort. The Ministry of Agriculture (25 February 1993) also requested to promote TVE tertiary industry vigorously and positively impelled rural tertiary industry. "The TVE tertiary industry development cannot meet the needs of national economy and society development." Therefore, "to accelerate TVE tertiary industry development is a strategic measure to impel rural commodity economy to a wider range and higher level, to adjust and optimize the rural industrial structure, to accelerate the shift of rural labor surplus, to narrow the differences between city and countryside and to realize the goal of 'Moderate Prosperity'."[3]

The target TVE tertiary industry development by 2000 made in 1993

- The share of tertiary industry in TVE gross income (23.8 percent in 1990) reaching 27 percent by 1995, more than 35 percent by 2000.
- The share of tertiary industry in TVE total employees (22.8 percent in 1990) reaching 28 percent by 1995, about 40 percent by 2000.
  (The Ministry of Agriculture, 25 February 1993)

Methods to promote TVE tertiary industry

- Determining the key industries to impel
  1) The key industries in the eighth FYP
  A. Commerce, transportation, traditional services such as the catering trade.

B. Tourism, real estate, finance, consultation information, technical services and so on.

- Developing collective and private enterprises in different industries
  A. Concentrating the collective enterprises in high level, large-scale industries and projects.
  B. Concentrating private enterprises in less investment, quick profit, fluid, and dispersed industries.
- Allowing TVEs to develop tertiary industry in cities
- Allowing and encouraging industrial and construction TVEs to develop tertiary industry
- Making use of foreign funds to develop tertiary industry
- Allowing TVEs to collect funds for tertiary industry through non-state bank system channels such as bonds, joint ventures and share holding. Rural collective economic organizations were allowed to use collective lands to develop tertiary industry after government authorization. Local governments, banks and the RCCs were requested to increase their financial support or loans for TVE tertiary industry.
- Simplifying the procedure of examination and approval for the license
- Tax reduction or exemption for new enterprises or to promote technological progress, or those which have a bad efficiency but benefit society.
- Introducing and fostering talented personnel
- Implementing a contract system
  (The Ministry of Agriculture, 25 February 1993)
- Relaxing control on agricultural producer goods and changing the state monopoly on chemical fertilizers, agricultural chemicals and agricultural plastic film to allow non-government channels to be engaged in the field.
  1) Main channel for the planned producer goods.
     China Company of Agricultural Producer Goods and SMCs.

Table 9.4 TVE tertiary industry development 1991–95 (billion yuan, %)

Year	*Transportation*		*Commerce, catering trade and other services*	
	Output value	*Share in total TVE output value*	*Output value*	*Share in total TVE output value*
1991	76.7	6.6	82.6	7.1
1992	109.5	6.1	125.3	7.0
1993	197.8	6.3	248.7	7.9
1994	217.7	5.1	342.2	8.0
1995	411.7	6.0	618.5	9.0

Source: *CSY* 1996.
Note: Shares are calculated according to the data in the yearbook CSY 1996.

2) Auxiliary channel for the producer goods out of the planned goods.
A. Agriculture plant protection stations, land and fertilizer stations, agricultural technique spreading stations (or centers)
B. Production enterprises
C. Agricultural chemicals reserve
(State Council, 25 October 1992)

To improve the TVEs technologically

In order to improve TVEs technologically, the Ministry of Agriculture (25 May 1992) formulated the "Implementation Program for TVE Technology Progress Strategy." The main content of the program is:

- Technological transformations, technical introduction, new product and technology development and promotion
- Quality and standardization
- Production technology
- Management modernization
- Developing qualified personnel.

Main targets of TVE technology progress by 2000 made in 1992

- To popularize the advanced and suitable technology used by advanced countries in the 1970s and at the beginning of the 1980s in key TVEs.
- Technical equipment in main export TVEs for food, textiles, machinery and light industry approaching or achieving the world advanced level.
- To selectively develop newly emerging industry and new technology such as micro electron, information, biology and new material.
- Average labor productivity of 12,000 yuan, 52 percent higher than that in 1989 (7,900 yuan in 1992).
- Labor productivity of collective enterprises at two levels of township and village of 15,000 yuan, 54 percent higher than that in 1989 (9,700 yuan in 1992).
- The contribution of technology progress to total output value reaching 48 percent (35 percent in 1992).
- The rate of input to output reaching 1: 2.2 (1: 1.57 in 1992).
- The rate of input to both profit and tax reaching 25 percent (16 percent in 1992).
- The share of staff and workers with high school education in total employees reaching 35 percent.
- The share of technicians in total staff and workers reaching 3.5 percent (2.6 percent in 1992)
(The Ministry of Agriculture, 25 May 1992).

Methods to improve TVEs technologically

- Determining the main points for technology progress in ten main industries such as building materials, food, mining, mechanical and electrical, light industry, feed, textiles and clothing, chemistry, building, and papermaking, emphasizing application of advanced and suitable technology.
- Determining key technology progress in different regions
  1) Key technology progress in the east and coastal regions
     Concentrating on advanced technology and management and high-grade quality to enhance both economic and social efficiency and outward-oriented competitive power.
  2) Key technology progress in regions with medium level
     Focusing on a advanced and suitable technology
  3) Key technology progress in regions with low level
     Concentrating on the technology to end poverty and suitable and traditional technology to use local resources with market needs and quick effects.
- To develop qualified personnel and improve staff quality
- To accelerate the introduction and renewal of technical equipment and vigorously develop new products
- To promote the SP further
- To establish and perfect a support system for TVE technology progress
- To establish and consummate TVE interior mechanisms for technology progress
- To popularize management science to enhance management levels
- To display the superiority of the research and production unified body made by TVEs and the research institutes and positively set up enterprise groups
- To launch the mass campaign of rationalization and technological innovation
- To exchange and cooperate widely with domestic and foreign firms technologically
- To fully display the stimulating role of central and local policies and increase investment in technology progress
- To strengthen the government leadership and guarantee TVE technology progress.
  (The Ministry of Agriculture, 25 May 1992).

To relax financial control and establish a rural multi-channel financial system

In order to establish a new finance system, which can adapt to the needs of the market economy, China separated its rural finance into two parts. One is to implement the policy to support agriculture and "to guarantee that the state fund for agriculture can get into agriculture and be used effectively." The other is commercial finance. The multi-channel financial system had both policy and commercial functions (CPCCC and State Council, 5 November 1993).

Methods to establish a multi-channel financial system

- Commercializing the ABC

  Before the reform, the ABC was not only a commercial bank to seek profit, but also a bank to implement state policy. In other words, in order to carry out state policy, sometimes the ABC must operate regardless of economic return. However, it concurrently was a commercial bank and had to consider economic return, which caused the ABC to be extremely chaotic. In 1993, the state decided to set up a rural policy bank and made ABC a pure commercial bank.

  1) Relaxing the limit and increasing ABC loans for TVEs

  A. Abolishing the restriction on the loan scale of TVE fixed assets.

  B. Guaranteeing loans for special projects such as the "Trade, Industry and Agriculture" bases, the SP and the Promoting Development in Central-West Regions.

  C. Increasing the loans for TVE joint venture with SOEs.

  D. Extending deducted interest loans to the TVEs in national minority regions.

  (The Ministry of Agriculture, 5 February 1993).

  2) Focus of ABC loans for the TVE.

  A. Key industries to support.

  a. Agricultural products processing, raw and building materials industries using local resources.

  b. Industries serving agriculture and the rural economy and the tertiary industry.

  B. Key products to support.

  a. Agricultural processed products with value added.

  b. Products to earn or save foreign exchange, necessary products for the SOEs and "famous, special or superior" products with higher technology.

  c. Farm machinery and other agricultural producer goods.

  d. Labor-intensive products.

  e. Consumable products relating to people's daily life.

  C. Key enterprises to support.

  a. Corporation groups.

  b. Farmer city, industry district and economic development zones.

  c. Share-holding enterprises.

  D. Focus of ABC loans for the TVEs in different regions

  a. In the East and coastal regions, outward-oriented enterprises, foreign-funded enterprises, joint ventures with inland enterprises, labor-intensive enterprises and so on.

b. In the suburbs of large and medium cities, joint ventures by rural and urban cooperation, enterprise serving for SOEs and the member enterprises of large and middle scale enterprises.
c. In the central-west regions, enterprises using local resources.

E. Focusing on improving TVE technology.
The transformation of traditional technology, high-tech introduction, TVE R&D and rural technology market developing

- Establishing the Agricultural Development Bank of China (ADBC)
China officially established the ADBC on 30 June 1994. The ADBC is mainly responsible for agricultural policy finance.
- Relaxing control on RCCs to expand RCC rights to operate independently.
- Allowing TVEs to collect social funds
The government reorganization in 1989 implemented a severe restriction on rural social fund collection, however, in 1992, the CPCCC again allowed and encouraged farmers to gather social capital for economic development. Regardless of its promotion of the TVE in the central and west regions or acceleration of TVE tertiary industry, the CPCCC always encouraged TVEs to increase investment through gathering social funds themselves.
- Relaxing control on non-bank system financial organizations and markets such as the rural cooperative foundations, the service companies for the rural economy, the financial service departments, the financial companies, the trust and investment companies and the folk lending market. However, the state still limited these organizations to the "field of regional, non-profit and fund cooperation organization and not allowing them to do any saving and loaning business."

Under the central policy stimulation, loans from ABC and RCC for the TVEs increased greatly. At the same time, the non-bank system finance organizations developed very quickly. By 1992, there were 17.4 thousand townships

Table 9.5 Total remaining loans at year-end of ABC and RCC for TVEs (billion yuan, %)

Year	*ABC loans for TVEs*		*RCC loans for TVEs*	
	Total	*Share in ABC total loans*	*Total*	*Share in RCC total loans*
1990	4.1	6	16.1	50
1991	6.5	9	21.0	53
1992	8.4	10	38.4	60
1993	19.1	18	48.7	60
1994	16.4	21	49.2	55

Source: *China Rural Finance Statistics Yearbook*, Chinese statistics publishing house, 1991 and 1995.
Note: The shares are calculated according to the data in the yearbooks above.

(or towns), 36.7 percent of the total townships, and 112.5 thousand villages, 15.4 percent of the total villages, having rural cooperative finance organizations; most of them were rural cooperative foundations (*China's Agriculture Yearbook* 1993, p. 138). Because of the rural multi-channel financial market, TVEs got funds not only from the state bank system, but also from the non-state bank system. Wei (1993) indicated that more than 50 percent of TVE loans come from the non-state bank system (*China's Agriculture Yearbook 1993*, the editorial board of China's Agriculture Yearbook, 1993, p. 138).

However, the relaxation of control on rural finance had a very big impact on the state banks. According to the People's Bank of China's investigation, in 1992, "the annual interest rate of local fund collections was 15–25 percent, far higher than the 7.6 percent of the saving deposit interest rate in state banks" (*China's Financial Yearbook*, 1993, p. 37). The high rate led to a decrease in deposits in the state banks because people withdrew their saving and put them into enterprises for social fund collections for higher returns. In 1992, "according to the report of Jiangsu Provincial People's Bank, because of the large-scale withdrawal of bank savings deposits due to the rapid and large-scale development of social fund collections, many banks had a extremely tight fund supply. One-third of city and county sub-branches of banks had payment difficulties, and some sub-branches even went overdrawn ... Chongqing has a social fund collection of about 2 billion yuan annually, more than 80 percent of which comes from the bank savings deposits" (*China's Financial Yearbook*, 1993, p. 37). The State Council on 11 April 1993 had to stop the social fund raising. "At present, this kind of randomly raised fund has a tendency to expand further. If we don't stop it, it will not only harass the financial order, but also initiate a serious social problem."

To reform supply and marketing cooperatives

The CPCCC (27 February 1995) decided to reform the SMCs. It emphasized that SMCs were very important for rural economy. On the other hand, it proposed that SMCs must meet the urgent needs of farmers for economic, technological and information services and entering markets. Simultaneously, SMCs must also satisfy the state's requirements to strengthen their instructions and regulations on the rural economy. "If we do not change SMCs as soon as possible, they will separate from farmers, change, and wither away." Therefore, SMCs must be reformed.

The targets of SMC reform

- A true farmer's cooperative economic organization
- Strengthening CPCCC control on farmers
- Focusing on the grass-root units.

Methods to reform the SMCs

- Persisting with collective ownership
  SMC collective property cannot be distributed to individuals. SMCs cannot be changed into shareholding companies or share-cooperation enterprises.
- Persisting with the cooperative system
  Persisting with voluntary, mutual benefit, democratic management and surveillance, and guaranteeing farmer member rights.
- Adjusting the organization system:
  1) To be able to join and quit an SMC freely to attract more farmers to join the SMCs.
  2) Implementing a representative congress system and establishing a council and board of supervisors.
  3) Establishing economic and cooperative relations between SMCs at all levels.
  4) The SMC is not a government administrative organization though it may undertake government tasks.
  5) Separating the council from SMC business.
     A council is the representative and superintendent of SMC collective property rights, has the right to appoint and dismiss the main managers in charge, to examine and approve significant operations and investments, supervise and inspect the operations and management and enjoy the property returns, but it does not intervene in concrete business. The enterprises of SMCs at all levels are independent and legal enterprises with the right to operate independently and are responsible for their own profits and losses.
- Strengthening the service for agriculture
  1) Giving priority to the service for agriculture.
  2) Establishing and consummating a socialized service system for agriculture.
  3) Developing economic, trade and technical cooperation with foreign nations.
- Consummating the SMC management mechanism
  1) Non profit for members.
  2) Commercialized operations for other economic activities.
  3) Implementing contract systems at all levels in SMCs.
  4) Implementing contract systems for employees.
- Strengthening grass-root SMCs
  1) Becoming a synthesized service organization.
  2) Implementing the contract system.
  3) Non-private operation generally
  4) Centering on large market towns and merging small SMCs to expand the business scale.
  5) Taking the County Federation of SMCs as the head to enhance scale benefits.

- Strengthening surveillance and management for SMCs
- Strengthening government protection and support for SMCs in order to avoid the violation of SMC rights and benefits
- Establishing the All-China Federation of Supply and Marketing Cooperative
  The federation is the national union organization of SMCs under the leadership of the State Council. Its main duties are:
  1) Making a national developmental strategy and plan for SMCs and instructing SMC development and reform.
  2) Organizing, coordinating and managing important agricultural means of production, and agricultural and subsidiary products authorized by the government.
  3) Protecting the rights and interests of all levels of SMCs and instructing SMC operations nationally.
  4) Participating in international cooperative activity.
  (CPCCC, 27 February 1995)

To enlarge the opening of domestic markets to the world and attract more FDI

Although China implemented an opening up policy from the beginning of the reform, it made a strict restriction on foreign direct investment (FDI). In fact, before 1992 FDI in China was limited and concentrated on textiles and light industry. From 1992, China sped up its attraction of FDI. Jiang (12 October 1992) requested a more nimble policy, to consummate the investment environment and provide more convenient conditions and fuller law safeguards to expand the fields for foreign investment. At the same time, the CPCCC (18 March 1992) urged TVEs to persist developing both domestic and overseas markets, vigorously develop outward-oriented economy and positively develop exportation. "TVEs should vigorously increase exportation for foreign exchange, positively introduce foreign capital, new technology, and essential equipment to enable their outward-oriented economy to have a new breakthrough."

Methods to expand FDI

- Increasing the opening up of cities and regions to expand regional access for foreign investment
  In 1992, the State Council decided to open six port cities along rivers, thirteen inland border cities and eighteen inland provincial capital cities to foreign investors.
- Expanding industry access to foreign investors
  China expanded industry access to foreign investment in 1992, to commerce, finance, insurance and so on, which previously had been forbidden to foreign investors. In August 1992 the State Council decided to carry on the experiment to introduce foreign funds to domestic commerce and retail and determined to set up one or two cooperative or

joint venture retail enterprises with overseas firms in Beijing, Shanghai, Tianjin, Guangzhou, Dalian and Qingdao and five SEZs (Special Economic Zones) respectively.

- Preferential policies
  Foreign-funded enterprises enjoyed preferential policies such as the favorable loan policy. The state banks provided the necessary loans for these enterprises. In addition they also enjoyed tax reduction or exemption.

Methods to promote TVE exports

- Issuing export and import licenses to TVEs
  Because of the state monopoly on foreign trade, before 1992 TVEs for export had no license for foreign trade and had to import and export through the state-owned foreign trade companies. The CPCCC on 29 November 1991 decided to issue the license for foreign trade to the qualified TVEs and allow and encourage them to import and export independently and to participate in international competition.
  1) Requirement for the license of importing and exporting independently.
  a. The delivery value of export goods generally should be more than 2 million US dollars for two years continuous for mechanical and electrical enterprises.
  b. The delivery value of export goods generally should be more than 4 million US dollars for two years continuous for non-mechanical and electrical enterprises.
  2) Procedure for the license
  The department in charge of TVEs applies to both the economic and trade committee and economic committee at province or city or regional level. After passing the examination, they jointly apply to the ministry of Economics and Trade and the State Economic committee. Then the Ministry of Economics and Trade issues the license (Wang, 1993, *CTVEY* 1993, p. 275).
  The number of TVEs with the license increased from 20 in 1992 to 156 in 1993 and most of them were engaged in textiles and light industry (*CTVEY* 1994, p. 437).
- Accelerating the development of the "Trade, Industry and Agriculture" base (TIAB)
  Under state support, the bases as the key project developed rapidly. There were 546 TIAB technological transformation projects in 1990–94 with an investment of 1.37 billion yuan in which there were 0.5 billion yuan favorable loans from the state (*CTVEY* 1993 and 1998).

In 1992–3, foreign investment in China had a great expansion and China, next to USA, became the second largest host nation for FDI and the largest developing country to absorb foreign capital in the world. In order to attract foreign capital, local governments offered many favorable policies for foreign-funded enterprises such as low-price land, priority to use infrastructure and loans, and tax reduction or exemption. Foreign-funded or cooperative enterprises increased very quickly in rural areas. By 1995, there were 28 thousand foreign-funded TVEs with total accumulated foreign capital of 26.7 billion US dollars and in 1995 TVE delivered value of export goods reached 540 billion yuan with a income of 52 billion yuan from processing for overseas firms (*CTVEY* 2003). At the same time, TVE outward-oriented economy also expanded from the coastal regions to frontier regions such as that of China with Vietnam, Burma, Russia and North Korea. The constructing export bases made many large-scale TVE groups with better efficiency, higher return and more foreign exchange, which promoted TVE export. Both attraction of foreign capital and export promotion not only expanded the relation between China's rural enterprises and the world economy, but also promoted TVE investment overseas. In 1993, there were more than 450 TVE-funded enterprises overseas (*CTVEY* 1994, p. 436).

To promote the share-cooperative system

On 30 December 1992, the Ministry of Agriculture pointed out that the share-cooperative system was a new organization form created by farmers and suitable for TVE development. "We must positively promote, correctly guide, and unceasingly consummate it. We must take effective policy measures to encourage farmers vigorously to develop the 'share-cooperative system'." "All of the TVEs with a share-cooperative system belong to the new socialist collective economy and we must vigorously support them."

The differences between the share-cooperative system, the shareholding system and the cooperative system

- Different forms of cooperatives
  The shareholding system is a fund union; the cooperative system is a work union and the share-cooperative system is the union of both.
- Different ways to raise funds
  The shareholding system raises funds from the whole society primarily, the cooperative system is invested by its interior members in the system and the share-cooperative system collects funds mainly from interior members and also accepts social investment.
- Different rights of shareholders
  In the shareholding system, one share has one vote, shareholders with different shares have different votes and different rights. In the cooperative system one member has only one vote, and all shareholders are equal. Similarly in the share-cooperative system one member basically has only one vote, and also there are votes for shares. The shares in the

share-cooperative system generally include the township and village share, the enterprise share, the social legal person share, personal share and foreign capital share.

Methods to promote the share-cooperative system

- Determining the scope to implement the system:
  1) New TVEs
  2) Existing collective TVEs
  3) TVEs to unite or merge or reorganize
  4) Private TVEs
  (the Ministry of Agriculture, 30 December 1992).
- The steps for implementation
  1) Experimenting
     Choosing some TVEs as experiment sites to implement the share-cooperative system
  2) Promoting the system
  A. Propaganda and massive education of the system
  B. Clearing up and verifying property and deciding shares
  C. Formulating regulations and establishing organizations
  D. Formulating enterprises' rules
  E. Issuing "the certificate of shareholder's right" after due investigation
  F. Checking and approving by TVE administrative departments at county level
  (the Ministry of Agriculture, 24 December 1992).

Methods to change existing TVEs to the share-cooperative system

- Expanding the shares through increasing investment
  First appraising enterprise original property and keeping the stock unchanged, then expanding shares through absorbing funds from operators, staff and workers, farmers and other investors to establish the system.

Table 9.6 The collective share-cooperative TVEs (thousand units, million persons, billion yuan)

Year	*Number of the TVEs*		*Employees*		*Output value*	
	Total	*Share in total collective TVEs (%)*	*Total*	*Share in total collective TVEs (%)*	*Total*	*Share in total collective TVEs (%)*
1993	130	8.5	4.9	9.4	212.2	11.5
1994	204	12.4	8.0	13.6	483.0	15.8

Source: *CTVEY* 1994 and 1995.
Note: The collective stock cooperative TVEs are those controlled by the collectives.

- Establishing a share-cooperative enterprise by selling original property
  First making shares according to original net assets, then selling part or total of the shares to the operators, staff and workers.
- Distributing shares through quantification
  Separating shares into two parts; one is capital shares made by investment, the other is work shares made by the work of staff and workers. So the investors hold the capital shares and the staff and workers take the work shares.
- Determining the shares first, then contracting or renting the real estate to establish gradually the share-cooperative system
  (*CTVEY* 1997, p. 300).

Under the government's impetus, the stock cooperative enterprises developed rapidly in the countryside. As one of the original collective enterprise's substitution forms, it was promoted in the collective TVEs by local government vigorously.

To abandon state monopoly for the supply system and open grain market

Jiang (25 December 1992) requested that the basic reform direction of the agricultural and subsidiary products price and circulation system should be to open the price and market, and to establish the mechanism to decide the price by the market. Therefore, after abolishing the state monopoly for purchasing agricultural product systems, China started to reform its state monopoly for marketing systems and promoted the structure change and development of agricultural and subsidiary products through market competitive systems. The State Council (8 March 1993) requested local governments "to gradually open the prices of agricultural products such as grain, cotton, edible oil and others" and to implement the market system.

Methods to abandon state monopoly for the marketing system and open grain market

- Enhancing grain price in 1992
  To cause both the state fixed purchase price and state monopoly for the selling price of grain gradually to approach market price (the State Council, 6 March 1992).
  1) Enhancing the grain price of the state fixed purchase from 1st April 1992.
  2) Enhancing the grain price of state monopoly marketing from 1st April 1992.

  After the price change, China still implemented the quota supply for urban inhabitants.
- Opening the grain price and market gradually in 1993
  1) Retaining state fixed purchase grain quota but with the price decided by the market.

2) Formulating the lowest protection price and the highest selling price in order to protect both producers and consumers.
3) Retaining the quota grain supply for urban inhabitants after opening up the price.
4) Retaining the central grain subsidy for three years in order to support local grain price reform.

- Opening the purchasing and selling price and markets of edible oil comprehensively in 1993
- Allowing qualified non-state-owned enterprises to operate edible oil and grain business
  (the State Council, 15 February 1993).

9.4 Rural industrialization in process

In both 1992 and 1993, TVEs had a new Great Leap Forward with an extraordinary increase in their numbers, employees and output. The growth rate of the output value achieved an astonishing level of 56 and 75 percent respectively. In both 1994 and 1995, although growth slowed down, it still kept at a pace of 35 and 49 percent. The TVE Great Leap Forward had a tremendous influence on both rural and national industrialization. First, TVE share in total rural output value rose significantly. On the contrast, agricultural share in the rural economy dropped unceasingly from 36 in 1991 to 28 percent in 1995, about 8 percentage points down. Rural industry held a share of more than 50 percent in the rural economy and became the main pillar in China's rural economy.

Secondly, it caused rural agricultural labor to drop and promoted the shift of rural labor surplus from agriculture significantly. TVE funds for agriculture and rural public enterprises unceasingly increased from 16 billion yuan in 1991 to 22 billion yuan in 1994, which powerfully supported

Table 9.7 China's TVE development 1991–95 (million units, hundred million persons, billion yuan, %)

Year	*Enterprise number*	*Employees*	*Original value of fixed assets*	*Total output value*	*Growth rate of output value*
1991	19.1	1.0	339	1161	24
1992	20.9	1.1	454	1805	56
1993	24.5	1.2	696	3154	75
1994	18.7	1.1	887	4259	35
1995	22.0	1.3	1,284	6351	49

Source: *CTVEY* 1992, 1993, 1994, 1995 and 1996, and *China's Rural Statistical Yearbook* 1995.
Notes: 1) The output value is at 1990 price.
2) The growth rate of output value is calculated on the data in the yearbooks above.

agricultural and rural development. In the new GLF, the share of the rural population in the national population also dropped from 74 percent in 1991 to 71 percent in 1995, 3 percentage points down (*CTVEY* 1992, 1994, 1995 and 2003, *China's Agriculture Yearbook* 1993, *China's Rural Statistics Yearbook* 1995 and 1998). At the same time, the share of TVE industry in national industry also rose greatly, from 33 percent in 1991 to 56 percent in 1995, surpassing that of state-owned industry. Rural industry had already become an important part of China's industry.

Since 1992, agriculture had continued to grow at a pace of about 5 percent yearly. However, the share of primary industry in national GDP unceasingly dropped from 25 percent in 1991 to 21 percent in 1995. The growth of grain yield was slow with a per capita grain of about 378 kilograms. Per capital net income of rural households continued to increase from 709 yuan in 1991 to 1,578 yuan in 1995, more than double. Rural infrastructure developed rapidly. In 1995, rural telephone subscribers were more than four times that in 1991. Rural electric consumption also increased by 72 percent annually (CSY 2001, *China's Rural Statistics Yearbook* 1994, 1995, 1997 and 1998, and *New China 50 Years Agricultural Statistics Material, 2000*).

9.5 Policy effects

The collapse of the Soviet Union spurred both the abandonment of the planning system and the new GLF

The "South Journey Speech" driven by the collapse

From 18 January to 21 February 1992, only one month after the collapse of the Soviet Union, Deng unexpectedly made his "South Journey Speech." Although the speech does not mention the collapse of the Soviet Union, it centers on economic development and the introduction of the market mechanism and warned that a system with poor economic performance would be toppled by the people, which explicitly showed the decisive influence of the Soviet collapse. It was the collapse of the Soviet system that led to the "South Journey Speech."

Abandoning the central planned system and launching the new GLF driven by the collapse

- Spurring the CPCCC to abandon its highly centralized system
  What does the collapse mean for the highly centralized system? The collapse marks the failure of the Stalin-style traditional central planned system and is a denial of the traditional planned economy. As a unique economic system in the world, the Soviet Union's central planned system once created many "myths" of high-speed economic development and was imitated by many countries including China

because it seemed to be superior to the capitalist system. The Soviet Union also therefore became one of the two superpowers in the world. However, though it was implemented for nearly 70 years, the huge Soviet system not only did not surpass advanced countries economically, but collapsed instead. The collapse brought an extremely profound influence to the world and promoted economic liberalization comprehensively in many countries, especially the central planned economy countries. The collapse caused the CPCCC to stop pacing back and forth and make a resolution finally to abandon the central planned system.

- Spurring the CPCCC to introduce the market mechanism and launch a new GLF

  What does the collapse mean for China's economy? Although Deng in 1992 still insisted that socialism would inevitably replace capitalism, the core of his speech is that "development is the hard truth." In order to maintain national stabilization and obtain the people's support, China has to have rapid development and to improve the people's life. The advanced capitalist countries have a strong economy because they have a market mechanism. So, the CPCCC decided to introduce the market mechanism and to launch a new GLF.

Abandonment of the dual pattern led to the TVE Great Leap Forward

Enhancing the incentives of both local governments and farmers greatly

The abandonment of the dual pattern to lift the ban comprehensively on TVEs is the direct result of China's abandoning its traditional planned economic system and introducing the market mechanism after the collapse of the Soviet Union. This policy change indicated not only that the CPCCC decided to abandon the traditional industrialization dual pattern, but also that the CPCCC regarded rural industry as an important force to promote industrialization. Although this policy change merely relaxed control and lifted the ban on rural industry, and the CPCCC still persisted "taking the state-owned industry as the mainstay," lifting the compulsory ban and allowing TVEs to compete with SOEs greatly raised the confidence and incentive of local governments, farmers and other investors. Under the impetus of local governments at all levels, rural industry expanded rapidly at an unprecedented rate. Similarly, the rural private economy also had a great jump forward in both 1992 and 1993. In 1993, the growth rate of output value of TVE private enterprises achieved 90 percent.

Making a big investment increase in rural industry

Lifting the ban strengthened rural industries' financing ability greatly and caused a massive fund inflow to TVEs. In 1992 the TVE original value of

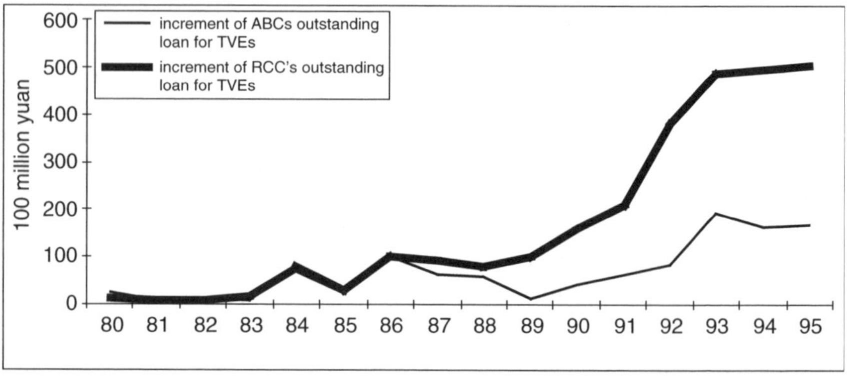

Figure 9.1 Annual increment of remaining loans at year-end of both ABCs and RCCs for TVE 1980–95

Source: *China Rural Financial Statistical Yearbook* 1991, 1995 and 1996.

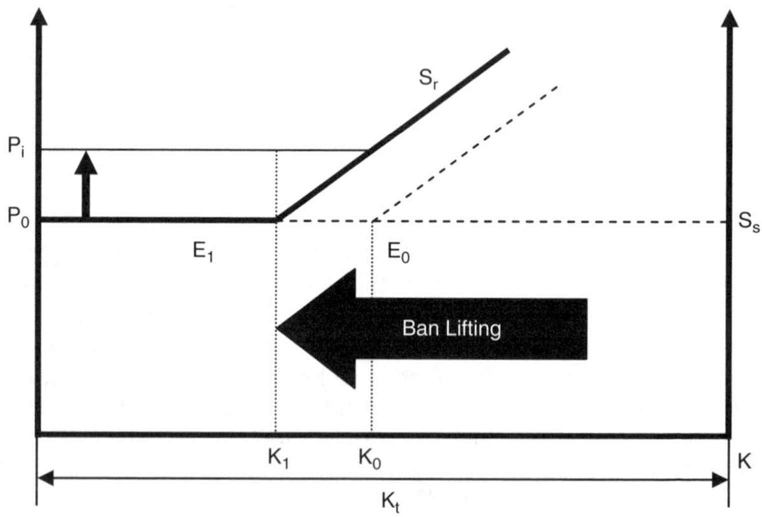

Figure 9.2 The increase of TVE fund supply under the ban lifting

fixed assets was 451.2 billion yuan, growing at a rate of 71.8 percent annually. The investment in the fixed assets of TVE collective industrial enterprises was 104.7 billion yuan with a annual growth rate of 180 percent.

- Loans of the state bank system for TVEs increased greatly
  The ban lifting made both state banks and RCCs increase their loans for TVEs significantly. As shown in Figure 9.1, in both 1992 and 1993, both ABCs and RCCs had a very big increase in their loans to TVEs.

- Social funds for TVEs increased massively
  The ban lifting enabled TVEs to obtain not only more loans from the state bank system, but also more social funds. First, the liberalization made more social funds get away from state control, even funds in SOEs, and into the market. Secondly, the ban lifting strengthened TVE financing ability because TVEs can provide investors not only with higher returns privately, but also with a legal sector in which to invest. They can attract not only social idle capital, but also bank deposits as well as SOE funds, and even technology and technicians for extra benefit, which cannot be obtained in SOEs.

As shown in Figure 9.2, supposing S_r, S_s are the capital supply curve of the market and the state bank respectively. Because the price of the capital in state banks is fixed, its supply curve is a level line. Supposing total capital is K_t and initial balance point is E_0, at which the planned capital is K_0 and the free one is K_t–K_0. When liberalization makes more capital flow to the market, it leads the planned capital to reduce from K_0 to K_1, in other words, the increment of free capital is $D=K_0-K_1$. The balance point transfers to point E_1. Because TVE competitive ability is strong in the capital market, the increase in free capital means a capital increase for TVEs. Liberalization enables TVEs to obtain more capital.

Although TVEs had a great leap forward, the rapid expansion is an extensive growth centering on expanding the production scale, which was made mainly by massive investment, especially in fixed assets. Their technology did not get improve and was still at a very low level.

10
Slowing Down in the Privatization Wave

10.1 Background

After the new great leap forward from 1992, China's economy had a soft landing in 1995. It kept a steady and quick growth at a rate of 10.5 percent, while its inflation slowed down significantly. Its added value of industry grew by 14 percent annually with an operation improvement of state-owned industry. The total investment in fixed assets with a growth rate of 11 percent dropped down further, 13 percentage points less than the previous year. There was an improvement in finance in China too. The national financial revenue increased more than the increment of disbursement in 1995 and changed the situation that the revenue had increased less than the increment of disbursement for many years. At the same time, China's trade expanded greatly and grew by 18.6 percent annually with a favorable balance of trade of 16.7 billion US dollars.

In 1995, TVEs continued to grow rapidly at a rate of 33.6 percent of output value with a share of 25.3 percent in China's GDP. TVE share in national industrial output was 44 percent, 34 percent in export and 25 percent in tax revenue. At the same time, it held a share of about 25 percent in total rural labor. TVEs played an important role not only in the rural economy but also in the national economy. In 1995, China's agriculture had a bumper crop too. Almost all main agricultural products had a good harvest with a record-high grain yield of 4.7 thousand million tons, 20.4 million tons more than that in 1990. Both edible oils and sugar surpassed the targets of the eighth FYP.

10.2 Policy goals

To keep TVEs developing rapidly, stably, healthily and continually

On 17 March 1996, China made its ninth FYP. This is a plan with high targets based on high-speed economic expansion. The main national targets of the ninth FYP by 2000 were:

- To control national population not surpass 1.3 billion persons

- To have a per capita GDP four times as much as that in 1980
- To eliminate poverty in the population basically
- To realize moderate prosperity in living standards
- To accelerate the construction of the modern enterprise system and establish initially the socialist market economy system
- To lay a better material and economic system foundation for starting the third strategic plan at the beginning of the twenty-first century (the State Development Planning Commission, 1996).

The main targets of rural economy in the ninth FYP by 2000 were:

- To have a grain yield of 5 hundred million tons
- To realize moderate prosperity of life in rural areas with a per capita net income of rural inhabitants of 1,200 yuan annually (at 1990 prices)
- To make 65 million of the impoverished rural population get out of poverty ("Rural development institute of the Chinese Social Academy and the Rural Social and Economic Investigating Team of the State Statistical Bureau," 1996).

It is clear that without high-speed economic growth, strategic targets cannot be completed. In the plan, TVEs would play an important role because of their pivotal status in the national economy. "TVEs have already become the main body of rural economy and a large prop of the national economy, and have made a great contribution to shifting the rural labor surplus, increasing farmer income and agricultural investment, consolidating and expanding the collective economy and constructing a new, socialist, wealthy, civilized and prosperous countryside." The CPCCC (11 March 1997) argued: "Developing TVEs is an important strategic decision to promote our socialist modernization for a strong nation with well-to-do people. The next fifteen years will be a crucial time for our socialist modernization, and the TVEs are shouldering a new historical heavy responsibility." It requested government departments concerned to support TVEs more vigorously for realizing the strategic targets of the ninth FYP. At the same time, the state formulated the ninth FYP for TVEs. The targets of the ninth FYP for TVEs (1996–2000) were:

- Total value added of about 3,000 billion yuan
- Annual growth rate of total value added of about 15 percent
- Industrial value added of about 2,000 billion yuan
- Delivered value of export goods of about 1,000 billion yuan
- Total employees of 160 million persons with about 30 million newly employed (the Ministry of Agriculture, 31 January 1997).

To establish the market system and transform TVE extensive growth pattern

The CPCCC indicated that the key to complete the ninth FYP was to realize two fundamental transformations. One is the transformation of the economic system from the traditional planned system to the socialist market system; the other is the transformation of the economic growth pattern from an extensive to an intensive one. That is, China wanted to introduce market mechanisms to improve and promote its economic development. Although TVEs were the forerunner in China's market economy and had formed some of the market-oriented mechanisms more nimbly than the SOEs because they were thrust out of national plans, however, this result was made under the self-sufficient small peasant economy and under the traditional planned economy system. The TVE development pattern in fact was an extensive one and depended on quantity expansion to realize its high-speed growth. Their quality, technology and management levels were very low. "If these problems cannot be solved, they will inevitably restrict TVE further development and enhancement, and then will affect the overall rural economy, the entire national economy and society." Therefore, "we must positively support and correctly guide TVEs to deepen their reform and define their property rights clearly" for optimizing operation mechanisms and raising the incentives of both investors and employees to strengthen enterprises' vitality and improve economic efficiency (CPCCC, 11 March 1997).

To eliminate TVE negative influence on the national economy

Because TVE development cannot always be consistent with state policy, the state, while impelling and supporting TVEs, also wanted to standardize TVE behavior and guide them to develop healthily. That is, through policy guidance and control, the state causes TVEs to conform to national policy, laws and regulations and eliminates TVE negative effect on the national economy in its high-speed growth. The TVEs must:

- Support agriculture and not harm agricultural development
- Make use of resources reasonably such as saving and protecting land and water
- Protect the environment
- Guarantee product quality.

To limit farmers' migration to large and medium cities

Although huge numbers of "farmer workers" entered the cities to work every year, the state had not been relaxing its limit on farmers' migration to the city, especially to the large and medium cities. In order to solve rural labor surplus employment, the CPCCC requested to develop rural small towns and cities. The CPCCC (14 November 1993) proposed to guide TVEs to concentrate suitably, fully make use of and transform existing small towns and cities, and to construct new cities. "We should gradually reform the household register system in small cities, allow farmers to enter small cities to work or do business, develop rural tertiary industry and promote the shift of rural labor surplus." "Developing small cities and towns is a great strategy to promote the development of rural economy and society, and advantageous to the relative concentration of TVEs, to the larger-scale shift of rural labor surplus, and to avoid farmers' flowing blindly to large and medium cities" (CPCCC, 14 October 1998). Even so, the CPCCC still persisted with the policy of "not allowing farmers to enter the city," and still limited the transformation of rural to urban registered residents strictly. Farmers could enter cities to work or do business, but they could only temporarily reside in the city and could not enjoy the favorable treatment and social welfare the state provided for urban registered residents.

To make use of international resources further for TVE expansion

Since China's application for restoring its membership of the General Agreement on Tariffs and Trade (GATT) in July 1986, China had been managing diligently to return the world trade system and join the World Trade Organization (WTO). Jiang (12 September 1997) argued that opening up to the outside world was a long-term and basic national policy. As he said, China must diligently expand opening up to develop an outward-oriented economy, strengthen international competition and positively, reasonably and effectively make use of foreign capital. The CPCCC wanted to make use of both domestic and overseas markets and resources to promote TVE expansion, optimize TVE economic structure and improve TVE product quality. The CPCCC (11 March 1997) requested local governments "to vigorously support rural outward-oriented economy," "to guide and encourage TVEs to positively and reasonably attract foreign capital, advanced technology and modern management."

10.3 Policy controls

To formulate the TVE law for protecting and standardizing TVEs

"In order to support and guide TVEs to develop steadily and healthily, to protect TVE legal rights and interests, to prosper the rural economy and to promote socialist modernization," the state (29 October 1996) formulated "The People's Republic of China Law of Township and Village Enterprises."

Main content of the TVE law

The law affirmed the important status of TVEs in the national economy and the validity of rural private enterprises. It indicated basic policies, cardinal principles and the primary mission for developing TVEs, established the relations of TVE property rights and management systems, protected TVE legal rights and defined the preferential policies to support TVEs and TVE behavior standards.

- TVE definition (the essential factors each TVE must have)
    1) Main investment body must be rural collective economy organization or farmer(s).
    2) Undertaking the duty to support agriculture.

3) Located in rural towns or villages. (TVE branch offices may be in the city, or the enterprise may be in the city but run by a rural collective economy organization and undertake the duty to support agriculture).

- TVE status in the national economy and its primary mission
  1) TVEs are an important prop to rural economy and important part of the national economy.
  2) TVEs' primary mission is to develop commodity production, provide social services, increase effective supplies for society, absorb rural surplus labor, enhance farmer income, support agriculture, advance agriculture and rural modernization and promote the development of the national economy and society.
- Main principles to develop TVEs
  To persist taking the rural collective economy as the mainstay and to develop a diversified economy with various ingredients.
- TVE rights and interests
  Accounting and operating independently and being responsible for their own profits and losses.; TVE property to be owned by the investor. "No organization or individual can violate the law and administrative regulations to intervene in TVE production and management, to replace the TVE manager in charge and illegally hold or use TVE property freely." "Except for the law and administrative regulations, no other institution, organization or individual may change TVEs in any way."
- Rights and interests of employees after a TVE is closed
  They will be treated according to the contract. They have the right to return to the original rural collective economy organization from which they came to work in agriculture or to seek other jobs by themselves.
- The state preferential policies to support TVEs
  The state support focuses on developing TVEs in under-developed and national minority regions. The state also encourages TVEs or other economic organizations in developed regions to support TVE development in under-developed and national minority regions.
  1) Tax preferential policy
     Tax preferential policy is tax reduction for a certain period for middle and small scale TVEs such as collective TVEs with difficulties in initial operations, those in under-developed and national minority regions or in agricultural processing industries, and those supported by state industry policy.
  2) Loan preferential policy
     The state banks and related financial organizations will give loan priority to those TVEs which qualified for tax preferential policy and the conditions for a bank loan. The TVEs that have market potential to develop and have funding difficulty for production can enjoy favorable loans from the banks.

3) Establishing a TVE Development Foundation out of the state bank system
In order to support TVEs, the state specially authorized the establishment of the TVE development foundation.
A. Allowing only governments at the level above county to set up the foundation.
B. The scope for using the funds.
The scope includes the TVEs in under-developed and national minority regions or in agricultural industry and agricultural product processing; technical transformation and development, staff training and so on.
C. Fund sources.
Government funds, a part of the tax TVEs' paid, the income from the foundation operations and the funds provided by rural collective economy organizations, TVEs and farmers voluntarily.
D. The State Council stipulating the establishment, use and management of the foundation.
4) Encouraging outward-oriented economy
Encouraging TVEs to cooperate and exchange with foreign firms both economically and technically and to construct export production bases. The qualified TVEs will be granted a license to import and export independently. The decisive rights for these favorable policies belongs to the State Council.

- Standardizing TVE behavior
  1) Supporting agriculture and rural social enterprises.
  TVEs must provide funds from the profits after tax to support agriculture and rural social enterprises.
  2) Observing state laws and regulations.
  3) Establishing a financial accounting system and recording financial activity truthfully.
  4) Paying taxes legally and banning irregular tax reductions or exemptions made by local governments.

"Ownership reform" campaign

Taking the collective economy as the mainstay and permitting private enterprise to develop before 1996

After the reform, although China lifted the ban on private economy, it still persisted with the policy "to take the public ownership system as the mainstay" in economic development. Even on 12 October 1992, Jiang still requested "to take the public ownership system including ownership by the whole people and collective as the mainstay, and the individual, private and foreign-funded economy as the supplement to develop the diversified economies with different ingredients for the long-term." In rural areas, the CPCCC had been repeatedly emphasizing "taking the collective economy as the mainstay" and "taking collective TVEs as the mainstay."

Abandoning "taking collective economy as the mainstay" and impelling privatization after 1996

However, the policy began to change after 1996. The TVE Law made in 1996 affirmed the legal status of private TVEs and started to reform the TVE collective ownership system for establishing a modern corporation system. Jiang (12 September 1997) further explained that we must comprehensively understand the meaning of a public ownership system. A public ownership economy includes not only the state and the collective economy, but also the state-owned and collective-owned ones in the mixed ownership economy. The leadership of public ownership is manifested mainly by the superiority of public property in total social property, the control of state-owned economy on national economy and the leading role in economic development. "We must adjust the layout of state economy strategically. In some regions and industries, public ownership may not hold the status of mainstay."

- Diversifying public ownership
  Jiang (12 September 1997) requested to try and make various forms of public ownership and appraised the shareholding system. He argued that the shareholding system was a form of modern corporations to collect funds "capitalism can use this and socialism can also use."
- Changing the policy for the non-public ownership economy
  The policy was changed from "the supplement part of national economy" in 1992 to "the important part of national economy" in 1997 to impel private economy to develop.
- "To respect farmers' practice, creation and choice"
  At the same time, the CPCCC urged local governments "to adopt various forms to positively support and correctly guide TVEs to deepen their reform and to define the relations of property rights unequivocally."
  (CPCCC and the State Council, 11 March 1997).

Main content of the "ownership reform" campaign

- Defining property and property rights unequivocally
- Effective transfer of property rights (establishing a transaction market of property rights)
- Final realization of property rights to occupy, use, benefit and transact the property
- Surveillance and management of property rights.

Methods to promote the "ownership reform" campaign

- Permitting and impelling by the CPCCC:
  In 1996 the TVE law affirmed the legal status of rural private enterprises. Jiang (29 May and 12 September 1997) made a call for adjusting and

optimizing the ownership structure to boldly explore diversified public ownership forms and to permit, encourage and impel the reform of the public ownership system.

- Organizing and impelling of local governments directly
  Under CPCCC impetus, local governments launched an overall TVE ownership reform. For example, in Jiangsu Province where there were strong collective TVEs. Before 1997, the provincial government still did not dare to promote positively the ownership reform of collective TVEs. In Nantong city of Jiangsu Province, from May to the end of 1996, under the leadership of local government, 6,276 collective industrial TVEs, about 90 percent of total collective TVEs in Nantong, carried on the ownership reform. However, the reform in Nantong was reprimanded by some people as "a complete capitalist restoration" and brought about a broad argument nationally (the editorial committee of Jiangsu Province local chronicle compilations, 2000, p. 473). Until Jiang Zemin's report on 12 September 1997, Jiangsu provincial government did not start to promote TVE ownership reform positively. In October 1997 after Jiang's report of September, Jiangsu provincial government immediately made an "Opinion on Further Deepening TVE Reform" to promote TVE ownership reform in Jiangsu province, which caused the privatization of collective TVEs to develop rapidly (Wu, 1999, pp. 53–4).
- Types of reform
  1) Selling out.
     TVEs with low profit or in loss generally
  2) Limited liability companies and limited liability shareholding companies
     Mainstay enterprises with good market prospects and better benefits
  3) Enterprise groups
     Taking key enterprises or leading products as a head to organize the groups
  4) Share-cooperative system
  5) Renting or contracting
  6) Uniting or merging.
     (the Ministry of Agriculture, 10 July 1998).
  7) "Second ownership reform"
     In the initial period of "public ownership reform," because it was in the category of traditional collective economy, the share-cooperative system obtained a widespread approval and was impelled positively by governments nationally. However, as the reform developed, these TVEs with the share-cooperative system having still a unequivocal ownership faced a so-called "second ownership reform" and had to be reformed again.

From the end of the 1980s, TVEs have started to carry on ownership reform. However the reform developed at a slow pace. Only after the

CPCCC lifted the ban on non-public ownership, and requested "to create multi-forms of public ownership" in 1997, did TVE ownership reform get a real progress, which led to a great expansion of private TVEs. The expansion was different from that of 1992. The rapid expansion of private enterprises in 1992 was in companies with a very quick growth of collective enterprises. However, in the ownership reform in 1997, the expansion of private enterprises was based on changing the collective enterprises into private enterprises. In other words, this is "to privatize public TVEs." "The ownership reform" finally caused the collapse of collective enterprises and a privatization wave started.

Table 10.1 The share of collective enterprises in total TVEs (%)

Year	*Enterprise number*	*Employees*	*Original value of fixed assets*	*Bank loans*	*Output value*	*Net profit*	*Tax revenue*
1995	7	47	71	85	64	46	63
1996	7	44	69	84	58	45	63
1997	6	41	65	83	49	40	56
1998	5	39	62	79	45	37	55
1999	5	34	58	72	40	32	51
2000	4	30	52	65	35	29	47
2001	3	26	47	58	31	28	42

Source: *CTVEY* 1996, 1997, 1998, 1999, 2000, 2001 and 2002.
Notes: 1) The output is the value added.
2) Bank loans are the remaining loans at year's end.

To accelerate the construction of industrial zones to concentrate rural industry

In 1996, the state started vigorously to impel TVEs to concentrate in and to construct TVE zones.[1] The Ministry of Agriculture (12 January 1996) argued: "guiding TVEs to concentrate in industrial zones and accelerating construction of the zones is a benefit to adjusting rural industrial structure, speeding up the development of rural secondary and tertiary industries, enhancing TVE scale efficiency and investment efficiency, saving land and protecting the environment, speeding up the shift of rural labor surplus, impelling the construction of rural small cities and strengthening the management and service for TVEs." "This is a strategic measure to realize the transformation of TVE growth pattern, to expand TVE scale, to improve TVE efficiency and to accelerate rural industrialization, urbanization and modernization in the period of the ninth FYP."

Methods to accelerate the construction of industrial zones

- Government planning
  1) Development principle
  A. To conform to state industrial policy and development plans, to be suitable for local condition, to take economic, social and environment benefits together into account and to emphasize private economy.
  B. To develop a resource conservation economy, raise the utilization ratio of resources, improve infrastructure efficiently and enhance the scale advantage and the industrialization of the regions where the zones are located.
  C. To combine industry zones with the construction of small cities to raise the level of urbanization.
  2) Deciding industrial structure
  The under-developed regions will develop labor-intensive and resources processing industries primarily and give a priority to the industries of agricultural and subsidiary products processing, mining and building materials. The developed regions develop technology and capital-intensive industries primarily and give priority to light industries and textiles, processing, mechanical electrical, high tech and exports with high foreign exchange income.
  3) Constructing infrastructure
  4) Social service
- Relying on self-raised funds while making the state loan subsidiary
  1) Mainly self-raised fund by farmers and enterprises. Allowing collective organizations and individuals to invest in construction and operation of the infrastructure in the zones.
  2) State loan assistance. The state will extend loans to TVE concentration development and construction of the zones.
  3) Setting up special foundations for infrastructure construction in the zones.
  The source of foundations was TVE tax revenue newly increased at a suitable rate.
- Preferential policy for land use, tax, examination and approval of projects, trade, the social security system and so on.
- Establishing national TVE model zones to guide and promote the construction of TVE zones
  (The Ministry of Agriculture, 12 January 1996). In 2002, there were 8,699 TVE zones with 1.1 million TVEs, 16.3 million employees; 2,264 billion yuan output value and 67 billion yuan tax (CTVEY 2003).

To cultivate large and medium-scale TVEs

The Ministry of Agriculture and the State Planning Committee (4 October 1996) pointed out that along with the establishment of the socialist market economy system gradually and integration of the economy with world economy, economic competition did not depend merely on quantity, more importantly, it depended on strength, technology and efficiency. Practices had proved that without scale, there would be no superiority, no competitive ability and no initiative in market competition. "To positively cultivate large and medium-scale TVEs is an urgent need for promoting TVEs further, and the inevitable choice for enhancing TVE competitive ability and improving overall quality."

The targets of cultivating large and medium-scale TVEs by the end of the ninth FYP (2000)

- 10,000 large and middle-scale TVEs (there were 4,531 TVEs by the end of 1995).
- A share of 15 percent (20 percent in the East) in total TVE fixed assets (10.8 percent in 1995).
- A share of 10 percent (15 percent in the East) in total TVE sales income (6.5 percent in 1995).
- A share of 12 percent (17 percent in the East) in total TVE profits and tax (8.1 percent in 1995).
- 10 thousand large and medium scale TVEs
- 2,000 super and large-scale TVEs (240 each year), of which 200 (40 each year) with a sale income of 1 billion yuan and a profit and tax of more than 0.1 billion yuan; 100 (20 each year) with a sale income of 3 billion yuan and a profit and tax of more than 0.3 billion yuan and 50 (10 each year) with a sale income of 5 billion yuan and a profit and tax of more than 0.5 billion yuan (the Ministry of Agriculture and State Planning Committee, 4 October 1996).

Methods to cultivate large and middle-scale TVEs

- Pushing the element of production to flow into large and middle-scale TVEs by breaking the limits made by ownership, region and industry, and organizing enterprise groups.
- Reforming the ownership system and consummating the management mechanism.
- Promoting management modernization and technology advancement
  1) Establishing a scientific and modern management system.
  2) Impelling technology advancement.
     Raising the share of technological transformation in the fixed asset and establishing institutes or centers to promote technical development and transformation.
  3) Paying great attention to the development of qualified personnel.
  4) Creating famous product brands.
- Accelerating the development of outward-oriented economy to form TVEs with strong competitive ability in international markets.

- Strengthening the mechanism for both enhancing incentive and control to cultivate entrepreneurs.
- Developing centrally in TVE industry zones.
- Raising funds through the stock market

Although under government impetus, large and medium-scale TVEs increased rapidly and played a major role in TVE development, the target of establishing super and large-scale TVEs was not achieved. By the end of 2000, there were only 111 TVEs with a business income surpassing 1 billion yuan, 14 TVEs surpassing 3 billion, 3 surpassing 5 billion, all much less than the target. By 2000, there were 100 TVEs with a profit and tax surpassing 100 million yuan, 14 surpassing 300 million and 4 surpassing 500 million yuan, also much less the target made in 1996. By 2000, there were 53 thousand large and medium-scale TVEs, each with an business income of 10 million yuan, about 24 percent in total TVE business income. Also there were 4,121 TVEs with a business income over 100 million yuan, about 10 percent in total TVE business income (*CTVEY* 2001).

Constructing the demonstration projects of the cooperation between the East and Central-West regions

In order to promote rural industrial cooperation between the central-west and east regions, both the CPCCC and the State Council (22 February 1995) decided to organize and construct the demonstration projects of the cooperation. The Ministry of Agriculture (5 July 1996) made the concrete goal for the projects.

Targets of the demonstration projects in the ninth FYP

- Constructing 200 TVE demonstration zones in the Central-West regions. By 2000, each zone must have more than 10 cooperation projects between the East and Central-West regions; these projects will have an output value of at lest 1 billion yuan, with a profit and tax surpassing 100 million yuan and newly absorbing 20,000 labor personnel. In the model zones, the per capita annual income of farmers achieves 3,000 yuan and the share of tertiary industry in total TVE income is more than 25 percent.
- Constructing 1,000 demonstrations projects.
  These projects must have a total output value of more than 100 billion yuan and with a profit and tax of more than 10 billion yuan annually.
- Promoting 1,000 new technologies and new products in the Central-West region, more than half of which must form production scale.
- Training 10,000 technicians and management staff for the Central-West regions.
- Forming 100 friendship counties and cities between the Central-West and East regions.

- Expanding the cadre exchange between the Central-West and East regions.
- Absorbing 500 thousand farmers through the demonstration projects. (the Ministry of Agriculture, 5 July 1996)

Methods to construct the demonstration projects

- Increasing investment:
  The state provided special loans of no less than 500 million yuan for the projects. The projects also enjoyed a priority in using the state special loans for the development in the Central and West regions and in local government finance. At the same time, the state managed to introduce foreign funds into the projects.
- Preferential policies
  1) Government subsidy for the demonstration projects.
  2) Tax reduction or exemption for the projects in minority, frontier and poor regions.
  3) Encouraging outward-oriented economy.
  4) Giving priority to TVEs in these projects for license of import and export.
  5) Giving priority to TVEs in these projects for the SP and technology promoted.
- Managing the projects strictly (the Ministry of Agriculture, 5 July 1996).

Implementation stages

- Starting in 1995 with propaganda and construction of a national working system for the cooperation.
- Implementing stage from 1996–1999.
- Concluding stage in 2000. Completing the remaining task in the cooperation demonstration projects and making the goal from 2000 to 2010 (the Ministry of Agriculture, 5 July 1996).

Although the state impelled cooperation between the East and Central-West regions, the effect of the cooperation is not obvious. The eastern part still holds a dominant share in TVEs with much weaker TVEs in the Central-West regions, especially in the West region, which had a share of less than 4 percent in total TVE output (*CTVEY* 2000).

To promote TVE technological progress

"In order to realize the goal of the ninth FYP and the Prospect in 2010, TVEs are undertaking more arduous tasks and urgently need to improve their own quality and level through technological progress." The state argued that only by firmly depending on technology, could TVEs develop continuously, rapidly and healthily and made "the Program of TVE Technology Progress in the Ninth FYP" (the Ministry of Agriculture, the State Planning Commission et al., 24 December 1996).

Targets of TVE technology progress in the ninth FYP

The program is the same in many fields as the similar program made by the Ministry of Agriculture in 1992, but there are some changes also.

- Higher targets for the key TVEs
  The program in 1992 aimed to make the key TVEs achieve by the end of the twentieth century the level of technologically developed countries in the 1970s or at the beginning of the 1980s. However, the goal in 1996 was changed and the key TVEs generally should by 2000 adopt advanced but suitable technology used by developed countries in the 1980s.
- Lower targets for main technical equipment in TVEs for exporting products of textiles, light industry, mechanical and electrical industries, food industries and so on
  The target by the end of 2000 of the equipment made in 1992 is to achieve or approach the world advanced level in 2000. In 1996 the target of the equipment was changed to the world advanced level in the 1990s.
- Higher contribution rate of technology progress to TVE growth
  The target of the rate made in 1992 was 48 percent for TVEs by the end of 2000. In 1996 the target of the rate was 55 percent, 7 percentage points up.
- Higher share of technicians in total TVE employees
  In 1992 the target of the share by the end of 2000 was 3.5 percent. In 1996 the target increased to 6.5 percent.

Methods to accelerate TVE technology progress

- Focus of the ninth FYP of TVE technology progress
  1) Accelerating the construction of technology innovation mechanisms to impel the transformation of technical achievements.
  2) Guiding TVEs to become the main body for the R&D of applied technology.
  3) Speeding up TVE technological transformations and new product development.
  4) Devoting much attention to training and introduction of qualified personnel.
  5) Realizing gradually management modernization.
  6) Increasing investment in technology progress.
  7) Establishing a service system for science and technology.
  8) Consummating the mechanism to drive technology progress.
  9) Strengthening government leadership to TVE technology progress (the Ministry of Agriculture, the State Planning Commission et al., 24 December 1996).

Energy saving and pollution control

In order to control increasing pollution of TVEs and save energy in their fast development, the Ministry of Agriculture (4 April 1996) made a program on

TVE energy saving and pollution control and on 5 March 1997, the State Environment Protection Bureau, and the Ministry of Agriculture jointly formulated a regulation for TVE environmental protection.

Targets of TVE energy saving and pollution control in the ninth FYP

- Waste water discharge of less than 6.5 billion tons
- Waste gas discharge of less than 3.8 (1,000 billion standard cubic meters)
- Waste residue discharge of less than 1.8 (hundred million tons)
- Total energy consumption of less than 3.2 tons (standard coal) for every value added of ten thousand yuan (the Ministry of Agriculture, 4 April 1996).

Methods to save energy and control pollution

- Determining the key industries and regions to control and the control targets
  1) There were 12 key industries to control strictly such as brick and tile making, cement, coking and casting, and the TVE industry zones.
  2) Key rivers and regions to control such as a) Huaihe River, Haihe River, Liaohe River, Tai Lake and Chaohu Lake; b) the coal and coking production zones in the contiguous areas of Shanxi, Shaanxi and Inner Mongolia, and the sulfur production zones in Yunnan, Guizhou and Sichuan.
- Determining the enterprises and the projects to close down or ban
  1) The enterprises to be closed down.
  A. The paper mills with an annual output below 5,000 tons.
  B. Tanneries with an annual output below 30,000 standard cowhide.
  C. Enterprises for dye with an annual output below 500 tons.
  D. Various small chemical industries, coking, smelting, earth kilns, agricultural chemicals made by indigenous methods, asbestos and radioactive mineral resources.
  E. Illegal importing, processing and use of overseas solid waste.
  2) The projects to ban strictly.
  Projects to establish chemical papermaking, small dying, brewing and other heavy pollution industry projects in the key national water pollution control regions such as Huaihe River, Haihe River, Liaohe River, Tai Lake, Chao Lake, and also the projects not conforming to national environment protection regulations.
- Strengthening supervision and enforcement of the laws and regulations.
- Announcing those technological designs and production equipment with heavy pollution and high energy-consumption, which need to be eliminated, and recommending advanced suitable production technology and equipment.
- Starting "Green Factory" and "Synthesis Management of Energy" campaigns.
- Constructing the technical service system for TVE environmental protection and energy conservation.

- Technical training for TVE environmental protection and energy management, and international cooperation (the Ministry of Agriculture, 4 April 1996).
- The heads of a county or township (town) must guarantee local environment quality and environmental quality become an important content to evaluate their work. By 2000, all industrial TVEs must meet the standards to discharge pollutants.
- Concentrating TVEs to construct TVE zones and forbidding setting up TVEs with serious pollution in villages, towns and inhabited areas.
- Without the approval of environmental administration, any project will be prohibited from land using, licensing, loaning and so on.
  (The State Environmental Protection Bureau, the Ministry of Agriculture et al., 5 March 1997).

Although the state formulated strict regulations to control TVE pollution, in fact it was unable to control the countryside after the disintegration of the people's communes. The regulations, which seem to be comprehensive and strict, in fact are empty and unable to restrict the desire of farmers to accelerate economic development and get rich as soon as possible. As we know, the execution of the regulations must depend upon local governments greatly, but, in order to develop local economy, many local governments not only did not implement these regulations, on the contrary, they became protectors for those TVEs destroying the environment. Along with TVE high-speed expansion, the rural environment is getting worse and worse and is bringing a serious impact to the entire national environment.

To establish a rural financial system with cooperative, commercial and policy finance

In 1996, China decided to reform its rural finance system "to establish and consummate the rural finance system taking cooperative finance as the foundation, with both commercial and policy finances" to meet "the commercial needs of industry and commerce enterprises, the needs of farmer household cooperations, the needs of agricultural development and technology progress, and the needs of state policies to guarantee agricultural and subsidiary products purchase" (the State Council, 22 August 1996). The new system aimed to restructure rural finance and eliminate the chaos of rural finance.

The targets of rural finance system reform

- Restoring the RCC cooperative nature.
- Strengthening the policy finance service.
- Displaying a fully leading role of state-owned commercial banks in rural finance.

Methods to reform and establish the new rural finance system with three functions

- Reforming the RCC management system
  1) The ABC no longer leading the RCC.
     The People's Bank of China supervises the RCC financially and manages RCC organization establishment, business direction, interest rate, risk management and so on. The federation of RCC at county level is responsible for RCC business management.
  2) Strengthening the county federation of the RCC and the county branch of the People's Bank of China
  3) Standardizing the RCC according to cooperation principles again.
  4) No RCC doing business above county level.
- Promoting further ABC commercialization and displaying further its leading role in rural finance
- Establishing rural cooperative banks (RCB)
  1) The RCB is a shareholding commercial bank.
  2) Forming the RCB by reorganizing and merging RCCs with commercialization operations. An RCB must have a real capital of 50 million yuan at least.
  3) The RCB mainly for agriculture, agricultural products processing and other rural enterprises and its loans for fixed assets must be no more than 30 percent of its total loans.
  4) The RCB locating in county or city at county level.
  5) The RCCs not joining the RCB may retain original RCC status.
- Increasing the sub-branches of the ADBC to strengthen the management of purchase funds for agricultural products
- Establishing various agriculture insurance organizations
- Cleaning up and closing down the rural cooperative foundations

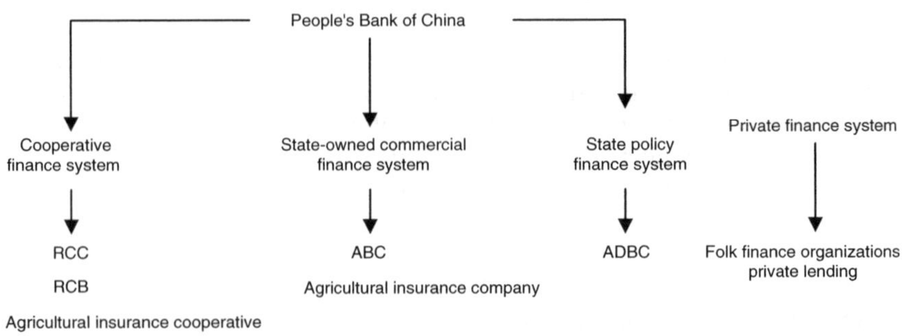

Figure 10.1 China's rural finance system under the rural finance reform in 1996

Source: "Decision on Rural Finance System Reform," the State Council, 22 August 1996.

In 1996, the state prohibited the rural cooperative foundations from dealing with deposit and loan business and the State Council (January 1999) requested to clean up, reorganize and close down rural cooperative foundations comprehensively in order to prevent financial risk and maintain the stability of rural economy and society.

- Establishing rural finance reform organizations at four levels of state, province, prefecture and county (State Council, 22 August 1996).

To develop TVE outward-oriented economy with great effort

"The state encourages TVEs to carry out economic and technical cooperation and exchange with foreign firms and to construct the commodity production bases for export to increase export and foreign exchange" (the TVE Law, 1996). This is the first time in legal form that the state positively encourages TVEs to develop an outward-oriented economy. Developing vigorously the outward-oriented economy has already become an important content for the state to promote TVE development (CPCCC and the State Council, 11 March 1997).

Methods to develop TVE outward-oriented economy

- Cultivating the dragonhead enterprises, which can bring small enterprises together to develop outward-oriented economy:
  1) Constructing enterprise groups
  "We must accelerate the progress of pushing the large and medium-scale TVEs to participate in international market competition and strive to form by the end of this century a batch of TVEs (groups) having certain

Table 10.2 The construction of the state "Trade, Industry and Agriculture Export Base"

Year	*Number of projects*	*Total investment (million yuan)*	
		Total	*State favorable loans*
1988	213	513	116
1989	72	97	40
1990	154	230	100
1991	122	252	100
1992	110	234	100
1993	78	320	100
1994	82	338	100
1995	84	543	100
1996	105	791	200
1997	114	997	200
Total	1134	4314	1156

Source: *CTVEY* 1998.
Note: Government finance pays interests of favorable loans.

influence in international markets. Some qualified large and medium-scale TVEs may also invest overseas according to the state industrial policy" (the Ministry of Agriculture and the State Planning Commission, 4 October 1996).

2) Increasing favorable loans for the construction of the TIAEB.
The state decided to increase favorable loans for the construction of the TIAEB in the ninth FYP period and from 1996, annual favorable loans doubled from 100 million to 200 million yuan (*CTVEY* 1997, p. 89).

- Expanding industries access to foreign investment to attract more foreign capital
- Raising the technical level and adjusting the product structure of exports
  1) Duty exemption for imported equipment to promote the import of advanced equipment and technology (the State Council, 29 December 1997).
  2) Providing funds mainly for TVE technological transformations for export.
  3) Supporting exports of mechanical and electrical products, chemical products, famous brand goods, high value-added products and complete sets of equipment (the Ministry of Agriculture, 17 December 1999).
- Impelling TVE outward-oriented economy in the Central-West regions
  1) Expanding local rights of foreign capital project examination and approval.
  The State Council (22 August 1996) decided to expand local rights to approve the projects with an investment from below 10 million US dollars to below 30 million US dollars in the Central-West regions.
  2) Relaxing the standard for import and export license for TVEs in the Central-West regions.
- Relaxing restriction and accelerating issue of licenses of imports and exports for TVEs
- Exempting, offsetting and returning tax for export products
  1) Exempting value-added tax made in the production and sale process of export goods of the enterprise, which produces and exports the goods.
  2) Offsetting the tax an enterprise should pay for its products sold in domestic markets with the tax the enterprise paid for its export goods, which should be exempted.
  3) Returning the tax for export products, which has been paid but should be exempted.
  4) The State Council deciding all of the rates of exempting, offsetting and returning tax for export products.
  (The Ministry of Foreign Trade and Economic Cooperation, 1998).

TVE outward-oriented economy had great progress during the ninth FYP and its products have flooded the world market. For example, its share in total world textile exports was 15 percent, and 35 percent in total Asian textile exports in 2000. It also set up 1,765 enterprises overseas with an investment of 16 billion yuan by 2000 and delivered value of export goods of 867 billion yuan. The number of joint venture with overseas firms was 26,000 with an accumulated amount of foreign capital used of 30.7 billion US dollars (*CTVEY* 2003).

To control farmer workers

The State Council (25 November 1997) argued that there were tens of millions of rural surplus labor flowing to the city on an unprecedented scale. If we could not guide them properly, it would become a problem and affect social stability. "Presently, both the city and countryside are facing great employment pressure. On one hand, the city must solve the reemployment problem; on the other hand, rural massive surplus labor is seeking new jobs. Therefore, if we do not control the flow of farmer workers, the flow is disadvantageous not only to reemployment in the city, but also to the use and development of rural labor resources, which will harm the broad masses' vital interests."

Methods to control farmer workers

- Encouraging and guiding rural surplus labor to shift locally.
  1) Increasing agriculture investment and guiding farmers to develop agriculture, forestry, stock raising and fishing.
  2) Promoting and taking TVEs as the main channel to employ rural surplus labor, especially supporting TVEs in the Central-West regions.
  3) Reducing farmer burdens and protecting farmers' legal rights and interests.
  4) Stabilizing the HRS, reforming the grain, cotton purchase and selling system and implementing a reasonable price policy.
  5) Accelerating the construction of rural small cities to attract farmer workers to return to their home village for starting an undertaking.
- Establishing the labor market and promoting farmer workers to flow reasonably and orderly.
- Organizing farmer worker transportation during the period of the Spring Festival properly.
- Implementing the target responsibility of the leader system to control the flow of farmer workers (the Ministry of Labor, the Ministry of Public Security et al., 29 October 1997).
- Strengthening rural household registration management
  1) Consummating the rural household registration management system
  A. Establishing and optimizing rural population registration, resident identification card and gate (building) brand management systems comprehensively.
  B. Establishing and consummating rural control systems for household register investigation, notification, statistics, files and so on.

2) Establishing and perfecting household register management organizations during the ninth and tenth FYPs according to one police station for each township (town).

(The Ministry of Public Security, 20 May 1997).

To reform the household register system in small towns and cities

Although in November 1993 the CPCCC proposed to reform the household register system in small towns and cities, it did not carry on this reform until 1997 "to allow rural residents having a job, already living in small towns and meeting certain conditions to apply and to be registered as non-agricultural population and a permanent resident in small towns in order to promote rural surplus labor to shift locally and orderly to small towns, to impel the overall development of both small towns and the countryside and to maintain social stability." At the same time, the CPCCC requested to control continually and strictly the growth of the population in major and medium cities, especially in Beijing, Tianjin, Shanghai and other super cities (The State Council, 10 June 1997).

Methods to reform the household register system in small towns and cities

- Experimenting first, and then promoting the experience of reform.

1) The scope of reform.
   Districts in counties or cities at county level or towns
2) Determining the towns and small cities for experiment.
   These being representative locally and with higher level of development, good financial situation and infrastructure
3) Numbers and times of the experiment

A. The numbers for the experiment
   No more than 10 experimental towns or cities for each province or autonomous region or municipality in the West region; no more than 15 experimental towns or cities for each province or autonomous region or municipality in the Central region; no more than 20 experimental towns or cities for each province, autonomous region or municipality in the East region. The local government below the provincial level has no right to determine or expand the experiment scope. The poor counties temporarily do not carry on the reform.

B. The time of the experiment
   Two years

4) Quota control
   The state controls the total quota of new permanent residents in the towns and small cities
5) Promoting the reform by stages.
6) Preventing local governments from blindly expanding their scale to avoid a rush of "entering the city" or a rush of "city making," which will need massive farming lands and weaken agriculture.

- The basic requirement for new permanent residents in small towns and cities.
  Rural residents to have a legal and stable non-agricultural occupation or a stable source of income, a legal fixed residence and to have lived for two years in small towns or cities.
  Besides the basic requirement, the state also made other conditions for the application for the new residents. The rural lands contracted by the new residents in small towns and cities will be taken back by the rural economic organizations in their home villages.
- The newcomers will enjoy the same policies as local original residents such as urban employment, grain and cooking oil supply, social security policies.
- Prohibiting local governments to charge newcomers any fees for their settling down in small towns or cities, which would increases public expenses there.
  (The Ministry of Public Security, 20 May 1997).

In the two years of the experiment, there were 382 small towns and cities carried in the experimental reform and a total of 544,031 newcomers settled in small towns and cities nationally (Sun Chunying, 2002).

10.4 Rural industrialization in process

Although from 1996, TVEs continued to develop rapidly, their growth rate of the output slowed down greatly from 21 percent in 1996 to 9 percent in 2000. The slowing down had a significant influence on both rural and national economies. First, TVE funds to support agriculture and rural society enterprises decreased unceasingly (*CTVEY* 1998 and 2001). Second, TVE employees dropped down greatly from 135 million in 1996 to 128 million in

Table 10.3 TVE development 1995–2000 (million units, million persons, billion yuan, %)

Year	*Enterprise number*	*Employees*	*Original value of fixed assets*	*Output value (value-added)*	*Growth rate of output value*	*Fund to support agriculture and rural society*
1995	22	129	1284	1460	34	25
1996	23	135	1605	1766	21	27
1997	20	131	1943	2074	17	23
1998	20	125	2157	2219	17	19
1999	21	127	2398	2488	11	19
2000	21	128	2622	2716	9	17

Source: *CTVEY* 2003.
Note: The growth rate is calculated according to the data in the yearbook CTVEY 2003.

2000, which made TVE ability for absorbing rural labor stagnant. At the same time, the share of agriculture in rural labor dropped from 72 percent in 1995 to 68 percent in 2000, 4 percentage points down while the rural share in the national population decreased by 8 percentage points from 71 percent in 1996 to 63 percent in 2000. The labor decrease in both agriculture and TVEs pushed rural labor to go out for jobs. There were more than 20 million rural laborers every year, with approximately 5–6 percent of total rural laborers not shifting to rural non-agricultural industry, but flowing to outside regions, mainly to the cities to work.

Although TVEs experienced a slowing down, their share in the national economy continued to increase. Their share of output value (value added) in national GDP rose from 26 percent in 1996 to 30 percent in 2000 with a increase of its share in national industry from 43 percent in 1996 to 48 percent in 2000, nearly a half of national industry. Rural industrialization had become an important part of China's national industrialization. However, TVE share in national tax income did not increase, instead it dropped to 16 percent in 2000, which is not corresponding to its share in national GDP (*CTVEY* 1997 and 2001, *CSY* 2001).

Table 10.4 The labor share in rural industries 1995–2000 (%)

Year	*Agriculture*	*Rural industry*	*Rural architecture*	*Rural transport, storage, post and communication services*	*Rural commerce and catering trade*	*Other*
1995	72	9	5	2	3	10
1996	71	9	5	2	3	10
1997	71	9	5	2	3	10
1998	70	8	5	2	3	10
1999	68	8	5	2	3	10
2000	68	9	6	2	4	11

Source: The shares are calculated according to the data in *Chinese Rural Statistics Yearbook* 1997, 1998, 1999, 2000 and 2001.

The agricultural growth slowed down unceasingly with an annual rate of only 2 percent in 2000. Its share in national GDP dropped from 20 percent in 1996 to 16 percent in 2000. The national per capita grain decreased from 414 kilograms in 1996 to 366 kilograms in 2000, 12 percent down. Simultaneously the per capita net income of rural households continued to increase slowly at an annual rate of about 2 percent. There was also a reduction in the national impoverished population, from 58 million in 1996 to 32 million people in 2000. The rural infrastructure such as roads and electric power had an obvious development with an increase in the number of rural telephone subscribers from 12 million in 1996 to 52 million in 2000, 324 percent up (*CSY* 2001, p. 304. The impoverished population data comes from "Monitor report of Chinese Rural poverty 2000," the rural social and economic investigation team of SSB, 2000, p. 7 and *Chinese Population Yearbook*, 2003, p. 335).

10.5 Policy effects

Why is it still difficult for TVEs to get bank loans without wearing the hat of "second-class citizens"?

The promulgation of TVE laws indicated that through nearly 20 years of reform practice, the CPCCC finally made the decision to stop its swing and hesitation on developing rural industry, thoroughly relieve its compulsory administrative control on TVEs, and take off the TVE hat of "second-class citizen." The law determined the validity of farmers to access all of rural non-agricultural industry freely, which enhanced the incentives of both local government and farmers, and promoted rural economy liberalization and industrialization enormously.

However, although, the CPCCC took off the TVE hat of "second-class citizen," the loans of the state-owned banks and financial organizations were still extended to SOEs mainly. This is not only because China's banks are basically controlled by the state and SOEs are China's industry backbone, but also because SOEs are an important tool to implement central policy. SOEs enjoy the so-called "policy loan." The "policy loan" is the favorable or priority loan extended according to state policy. Generally, there are two kinds "policy loan." One is used to subsidize the loss of an enterprise made by state policy, that is, the loans for the "policy deficit" enterprises. The other is applied to support the enterprises, which are protected or impelled by state industrial policy, that is, loans for "key industries" such as basic and high tech industries.

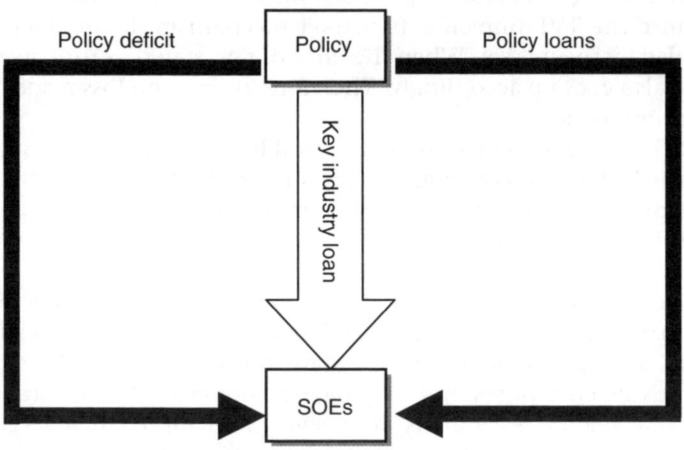

Figure 10.2 Policy deficit and policy loans in China

Why can SOEs obtain "policy loans"?

- There is the deficit made by surplus labor policy in SOEs
  Because of "the secured job" system in SOEs, especially "the lifelong employment system" for old workers, SOEs are unable to cut their surplus labor. Simultaneously, under the policy to increase social employment, SOEs sometimes had to recruit extra staff they do not need. Generally there is surplus labor in SOEs. Therefore, in market competition, the labor surplus causes SOEs to lose out, even to go to bankrupt.
- There is the deficit made by price distortion policy in SOEs
  In order to stabilize the market and suppress inflation, the state often makes some price policies which distort market prices. The price distortion leads some SOEs in to deficit. For instance, in the electric power industry, although the price of raw materials such as coal rises unceasingly, the price of electricity produced by state-owned power plants is unable to go up in order to carry out the policy to stabilize the market. So many state-owned power plants suffer heavy losses.
- Many SOEs are engaged in basic and high tech industries supported by the industry policy

Why can TVEs still not obtain "policy loans" without wearing the hat of "second-class citizens"?

- There is no deficit made by labor surplus policy in TVEs:
  Because the TVE has a contract employment system, it has no labor surplus basically. Simultaneously, the employees in a TVE still hold a piece of land. If a TVE gets in to deficit, they are able to cultivate the land again, which creates no unemployment and also no instability. Thus, the TVE has no policy deficit made by a labor surplus.
- There is no deficit made by price distortion policy in TVEs:
  Because the TVE implements market mechanism, its product price is decided by the market. When the price of raw materials rises, its product price also goes up accordingly. Therefore, there is no loss made by price distortion policy.
- Most TVEs are not engaged in basic and high tech industries supported or impelled by industry policy. They are mainly medium and small-scale enterprises with low technology engaged in labor-intensive and daily consumable industry.
- Poor credit and no state guarantee
  It is very difficult for an enterprise to obtain a loan without good credit or a strong guarantee in China. SOEs are able to get loans because they have a strong guarantee from the state, however, most TVEs, especially the private enterprises, not only have a poor credit but also cannot get the state guarantee for loans. So it is very difficult for them to get loans from banks. So, TVE share in total national bank loans was very low, about 6 percent in 2000.

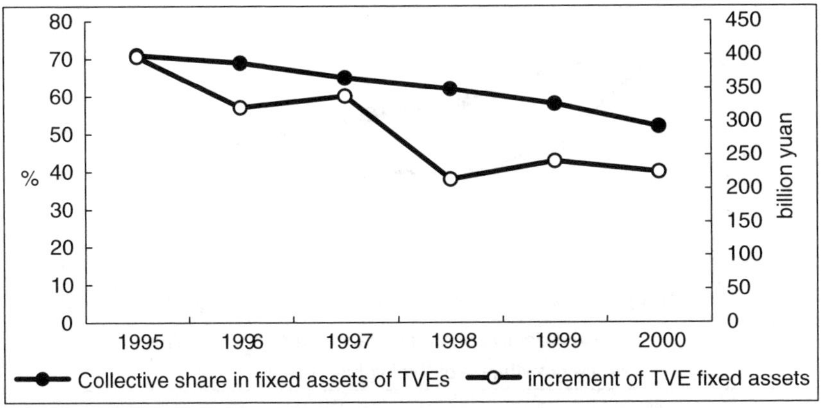

Figure 10.3 The collective share and increment of investment in total TVE fixed assets 1995–2000
Source: *CTVEY* 1996, 1997, 1998, 1999, 2000 and 2001.
Note: The increment of investment in TVE fixed assets =TVE original value of the fixed asset in current year –TVE original value of fixed asset in previous year.

Great deceleration under the collapse of collective enterprises

The great drop of investments in TVE fixed assets in the collapse

The collapse separated TVEs from local governments and made TVEs lose the ability to collect funds through local government administrative means, which could mobilize and organize massive funds, especially in a short time. On the other hand, because unlike local government, private enterprises pay more attention to economic efficiency, blind investment regardless of efficiency will be reduced significantly. As shown in Figure 10.3, as the share of collective enterprises in total TVE fixed assets is reduced, the annual investment in TVE fixed assets was decreased correspondingly, which indicates that the investment in TVE fixed assets have a close correlation with the collective enterprises. That is, during the period when the collective enterprises held a large share, the huge investment in TVE fixed assets mainly came from the collective enterprises through local government organization and mobilization. Similarly, the collapse led to a reduction of both TVE numbers and employees. The number of TVEs reduced from 23 million in 1996 to 21 million in 2000 with a reduction of employees from 135 million in 1996 to 128 million people in 2000 (*CTVEY* 2003).

The great deceleration of TVE growth in the collapse

As shown in Figure 10.4, along with the decrease of the collective share in total TVE output, the growth rate of TVE output dropped significantly. This reflected the close relation between collective share and TVE growth rate. The collective was the main strength to drive extraordinary TVE growth.

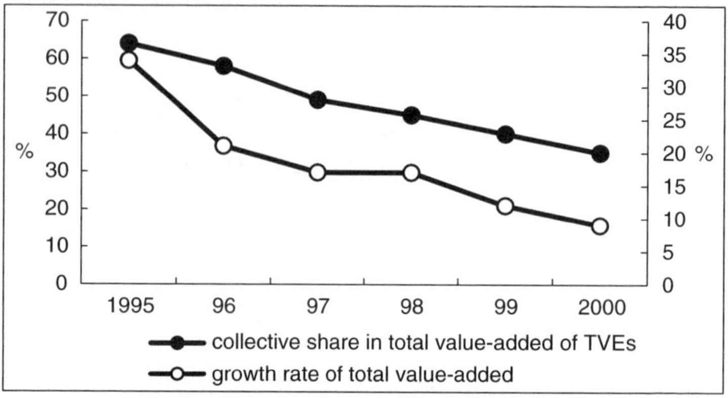

Figure 10.4 Collective share in total TVE output and the growth rate of TVE output (value added)
Source: *CTVEY* 2003.

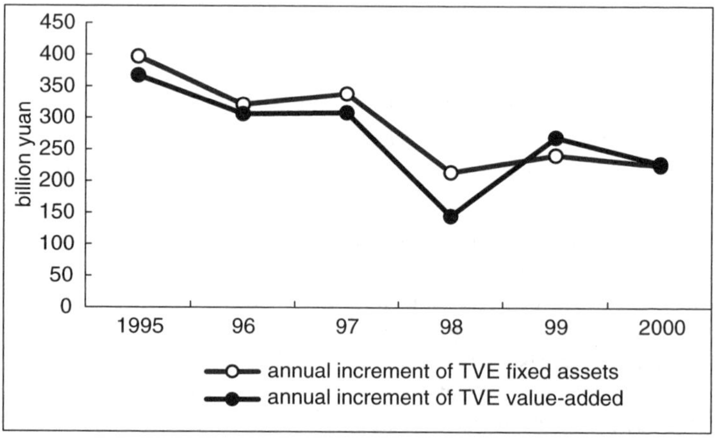

Figure 10.5 The annual increments of both TVE output and original value of fixed assets
Source: *CTVEY* 2003.
Note: The increment of TVE value-added = TVE value-added in current year –TVE value-added in previous year.

Also as shown in Figure 10.5, the increment of TVE value-added not only has a close correlation with TVE increment of fixed assets, but also has almost the same value as the increment of fixed assets. This reflected the vital role of investment in fixed assets in TVE rapid growth. However, along with the collapse of collective TVEs, the reduction of fixed asset investment

Table 10.5 TVE economic efficiency and labor productivity 1995–2001

Year	*TVEs at loss (ten thousand units)*		*Share of TVEs at loss in total TVEs (%)*	*Labor productivity (ten thousand yuan)*	*Annual increment of net profit (billion yuan)*
	Total	*Collective*			
1995	98	8	4.5	1.1	96
1996	197	9	8.4	1.3	64
1997	41	9	2.0	1.7	47
1998	128	7	6.74	1.8	28
1999	211	6	10.2	2.0	75
2000	72	5	3.5	2.1	49
2001	48	4	2.3	2.3	12

Source: CTVEY 1996, 1997, 1998, 1999, 2000, 2001, 2002 and 2003.
Notes: 1) The data from 1997 is based on the new statistic standard.
2) Annual increment of net profit = the net profit in current year–the net profit in previous year.
3) The labor productivity=total value-added / total employees.

Table 10.6 The characteristics of both the Southern Jiangsu and Wenzhou models in the 1980s

	Southern Jiangsu model	*Wenzhou model*
Main system of ownership	Collective	Private
Main investor	Local government and collective organization	Farmer
Manager	Appointed by local government or collective organization	Farmer
Financing and land using	Local government or collective organization with cheap land	Farmer with some government support and land rented
Enjoying favorable policy	More	Less
Main products	Industrial products	For every day use
Funds for agriculture and community	More	Less

Source: China's rural society and economy evolution 1949–89, Chen Jiyuan, Chen Jiaji and Yang Xun, eds, Shanxi economic publishing house, 1993.

caused the growth of TVE output to go down correspondingly. That is, the government's withdrawal from TVE investment of fixed assets led to the slowing down of TVEs.

The efficiency improvement in the collapse

Although TVEs experienced a slowing down during the privatization, their economic efficiency improved gradually, with a growing labor productivity and the dropping of enterprises with loss, especially those collective enterprises with significant loss.

Case study: A comparison between the "Southern Jiangsu" and "Wenzhou" models

Main differences between the two models

After the rural reform, in the middle of the 1980s, both the "Southern Jiangsu Model" and "Wenzhou Model" appeared in China's rural industry. They represent different development patterns of China's rural industry. The main difference between them is their ownership system.

- Southern Jiangsu model
  Southern Jiangsu refers to Suzhou, Wuxi and Changzhou cities in the south part of Jiangsu province, which has 12 counties and cities. Southern Jiangsu is a rich region in the south of the Yangtze River delta. The Southern Jiangsu model was the pattern to develop TVEs there in the 1980s.
- Wenzhou model
  Wenzhou is a city in the west part of Zhejiang province. It is also a developed commercial region historically. The Wenzhou model was the pattern to develop TVEs there in the 1980s.
- The characteristics of two models in the 1980s
  As shown in Table 10.6, the two models have different characteristics.

No. 1 model of "Southern Jiangsu" under "Taking the Collective Economy as the Mainstay"

The TVEs in southern Jiangsu started early and developed very quickly. In the 1980s, the TVEs of Jiangsu province had been No. 1 in TVE output value, fixed assets, profit and so on nationally. In 1985 its share in TVE total output value was 8.9 percent. Because the "Southern Jiangsu" model was "taking collective economy as the mainstay," it became the national model of TVE development encouraged by the CPCCC vigorously. Unlike the "Southern Jiangsu" model, the TVEs in Wenzhou developed quite late. In 1984, after the No. 4 document of the CPCCC, a delegation of the Zhejiang provincial government visited Jiangsu to study the Southern Jiangsu model for developing TVEs. They realized that in the past TVEs lacked government support; after all, because the influence of "left" thought was not eliminated thoroughly and people worried about the competition of TVEs with SOEs for raw materials and would weaken SOEs, so TVE development was limited. However Jiangsu government relaxed the restrictions on TVEs and allowed them to compete with SOEs. This was an important experience that TVEs in Jiangsu could develop quickly (Zhang, 1990, 165). However, under the push of the Zhejiang provincial government, although collective TVEs had a rapid development, the "Wenzhou model" of private ownership primarily appeared, which is different from the "Southern Jiangsu model." Because it is private ownership primarily, a representative of capitalism, the "Wenzhou model" experienced restriction, suppression and even condemnation. But, because it suited the regions with a weak collective economy where collective TVEs were unable to develop, the "Wenzhou model" became one of the models to develop TVEs though there was heated argument about it.

No. 1 model of "Wenzhou" under "Ownership Reform"

However, along with the development of China's reforming public ownership system the "Southern Jiangsu model" was abandoned and the "Wenzhou model" started to obtain government approval and promotion. It expanded from Zhejiang to the whole country. In the rural industry privatization wave, it dominated TVE ownership reform and started to surpass TVEs in Jiangsu in output value, fixed assets, profit and so on to become the new No. 1 in China's rural industry. On the contrary, TVE development in Southern Jiangsu was slow and the collective TVEs became the target of "ownership reform." Under the impact of reforming the public ownership system in 1997, the collective TVEs in southern Jiangsu started to slide down rapidly. As shown in Table 10.7, it was precisely in 1997 that TVEs in Jiangsu started to fall behind TVEs in Zhejiang. It may be said that it was the CPCCC policy change that caused collective TVEs in southern Jiangsu to disintegrate so fast. It is a satire that TVEs in southern Jiangsu in turn started to study the "Wenzhou model" to develop private TVEs in the ownership reform. In other words, the "Southern Jiangsu model" transformed into the "Wenzhou model." In 2001, the non-collective TVEs already held a dominant position in southern Jiangsu with the same share of non-public TVEs in total TVEs as that in Zhejiang. Entering the twenty-first century, the "Southern Jiangsu model" of twenty years came to an end.

Table 10.7 Collective share in the TVEs in both Jiangsu and Zhejiang provinces 1987–2001 (billion yuan, %)

Year	*Total output*		*Share in employees*		*Share in total output value*		*Share in total fixed assets*	
	Jiangsu	*Zhejiang*	*Jiangsu*	*Zhejiang*	*Jiangsu*	*Zhejiang*	*Jiangsu*	*Zhejiang*
1987	81	45	79	75	89	84	92	90
1990	145	77	75	71	86	78	95	87
1995	889	748	72	48	89	49	94	70
1997	827	899	60	49	72	48	83	74
1999	1051	1155	48	39	60	39	76	64
2000	1139	1341	35	34	46	36	64	58
2001	1290	1546	26	31	35	33	52	52

Source: *CTVEY* 1978–87, 1991, 1996, 1998, 2000, 2001, and 2002.

Notes: 1) The data from 1997 is based on the new statistic standard.

2) Collective share is calculated according to the data in the yearbooks CTVEY 1978–87, 1991, 1996, 1998, 2000, 2001, 2002.

11
New Century Shifting in the Campaign to Increase Farmer Income

11.1 Background

Entering the twenty-first century, China continued to maintain a fast growth and its per capita GDP surpassed 1,000 US dollars. In 2003, China's GDP grew at an annual rate of 9 percent, the highest one in the world. Similarly, TVEs expanded rapidly and output (value added) was about 3,660 billion yuan with an annual growth rate of 13 percent in 2003. However, under the high-speed growth, the so-called "three rural issues"[1] about the development of rural areas, farmers and agriculture in China were becoming increasingly serious. First is the slow agricultural development with a grain reduction. In 2003, China's grain-sown area decreased and the grain output was 431 million tons, a cut of about 5.8 percent annually. The annual growth rate of agriculture (value-added) was 2.5 percent, far behind the rate of 12.5 percent of its industry (SSB, 26 February 2004).

Secondly, the farmer income increase was very slow. Since 1997, the slow increase of farmer income had continued for seven years at an annual rate of around 2–4 percent, much lower than the urban one. In 2000 the rural per capita net income was only 1,066 yuan (at the price in 1990) (SSB, 2000, 2001, 2002 and 2003), merely 88.8 percent of the target of 1,200 yuan planned (Li, 2003). Lastly, the countryside was still a very poor region. By 2000, there were three unfulfilled targets for realizing rural moderate prosperity in the ninth FYP, which are the per capita net income of rural households, the per capita protein quantity taken daily and the share of rural counties qualifying for the basic medical care standard in total counties. At the same time, the reduction of the rural impoverished population slowed down. One of the targets of the ninth FYP is to eliminate the numbers of rural population living below the poverty line by 2000. However, the target was not realized. There were still 30 million below the poverty line at the end of 2000, about 3 percent of the total rural population. During the eighth FYP, China reduced the numbers of more than 6 million of its rural impoverished population each year, however, in 2001 and 2002, only 2 million of the impoverished population were reduced yearly. In 2003 the rural population living below the poverty line was 29 million (annual per capita net income lower than 637 yuan), which was not a reduction, but an increase of 800,000 people compared to 28.2 million people in 2002 (*People's Daily*, 17 July 2004). Also, TVE ability to absorb labor surplus began to stagnate. One of the targets of the TVE ninth FYP is to employ 160 million staff and workers by 2000. However, the TVE failed to complete the target. Its total employees were below 130 million persons in 2000, even less than its employees of 135 million persons in 1996.

11.2 Policy goals

To reduce farmer poverty and construct rural moderate prosperity in all respects

The tenth FYP (passed on 15 March 2001) aims to attain the target of GDP of about 12,500 billion yuan with per capita GDP of 9,400 yuan (at the price in 2000) at an average annual growth rate of about 7 percent by 2005. Its rural targets are:

- To attain a growth rate of 5 percent in annual per capita net income of rural households
- To shift 40 million agricultural laborers to non-agricultural industry
- To reduce the numbers of people living below the poverty line.

The CPCCC (8 November 2002) proposed the grand goal "to construct comprehensively the society of moderate prosperity in all respects, and basically realize industrialization." Because of the tough "three rural issues," the CPCCC wanted to realize its goal through focusing on "three rural issues." The CPCCC (January 2004) indicated that to realize rural moderate prosperity in all respects is "the key of the keys of our entire party's work." Only by solving the "three rural issues," could China realize the goal to construct a society of moderate prosperity in all respects (CPCCC, January 2004). Simultaneously, at the Scaling Up Poverty Reduction: A Global Learning Process Conference in Shanghai, 25–27 May 2004, China announced to strive vigorously to solve the food and shelter problem of its impoverished population by 2010 (*People's Daily*, 17 July 2004).

To abandon both "countryside supporting the city" and "keeping farmers in the countryside" to support the countryside with great effort

The CPCCC decided to abandon "countryside supporting the city" and request industry and city to support the countryside in order to solve the tough "three rural issues." It (January 2004) made a call for policy change "to increase rural and agricultural investment of government finance continually, and strengthen capital construction of agriculture to solve the 'three rural issues'." "We must adjust further the structures of both national income distribution and government expenditure ... to encourage and guide various social capital to go to agriculture and the countryside." This changed away from the old policy to take rural products and resources for industry and urban development and provide the countryside with little.

At the same time, the CPCCC started to abandon "keeping farmers in the countryside" and lift the ban on farmer immigration. It indicated that the shifting of rural labor surplus to non-agricultural industry and the city was the inevitable trend of both industrialization and modernization. In January 2004 it requested to "promote the household register system reform in large and medium cities and relax restriction on the employment and settlement of farmers in the city while guiding more farmers to enter small cities and towns." It indicated that the policy of "preventing farmers from entering the city," which had been implemented for almost half a century, was coming to an end in China.

To promote TVEs for increasing rural employment

The CPCCC wanted to increase rural employment, and to enhance agricultural synthesis productivity through promoting TVE development. It (January 2004) argued: "developing TVE is an important way to make full use of rural resources and elements of production to develop rural economy comprehensively and expand rural interior employment." "We must focus on agricultural products processing industries, service industries and labor-intensive industries." It was a strategic change to request TVEs to center on labor-intensive industries because for a long time the state had been striving to transform TVEs from labor-intensive to technology or capital-intensive industries. Focusing on labor-intensive industries aimed mainly to expand rural employment. "Because the medium and small-scale enterprises in rural areas are able to increase farmer employment, we should allow them to exist and develop as long as they meet the requirements of production safety and environmental protection and use resources in a reasonable way." The targets of the tenth FYP of TVEs (2000–05) are to reach:

- Total value added of 4,300 billion yuan with an annual average growth rate of about 10 percent.
- Total industrial value added of 2,800 billion yuan with an annual average rate of about 8 percent.
- Total delivered value of export goods of 1,270 billion yuan.
- Increasing by 10 million to attain 137 million employees.
- An industry structure of 1 percent for primary industry, 74 percent for second industry and 25 percent for tertiary industry.
  (The Ministry of Agriculture, 20 August 2000).

To strengthen TVE international competition power and resist the impact of the WTO

China's accession to the WTO on 11 December 2001 brought TVEs both new development opportunities and also a stern challenge. The CPCCC (January 2002) argued that the accession to the WTO would damage agriculture heavily, which would have a significant influence on not only rural development but also national development and requested to enhance the competitive power of the agricultural products. The state strived to strengthen TVE competition power to reduce the impact of the accession to the WTO through adjusting industry structure, expanding enterprise scale, improving technology, making use of more foreign capital and resources and investing overseas. Wen Jiabao (March 2004) urged to increase the imports of key raw materials, technology and equipment, and also to implement the "going out" strategy to encourage enterprises to invest overseas.

11.3 Policy controls

The "increasing farmer incomes" campaign

In order to solve rural problems, the CPCCC launched the "increasing farmer incomes" campaign. In January 2004, the CPCCC pointed out that the slow growth of farmer income had continued for many years and the income of many farmers in agriculture had stagnated, even dropped, which caused the income disparity between urban and rural inhabitants unceasingly to expand. "The long slow growth of farmer income affects not only farmer living improvements, but also the grain production and agricultural products supply; it restricts not only rural economic development, but also the entire national economic growth; it relates not only to rural society progress, but also to the realization of the moderately prosperous society in all respects; it is not only an important economic problem, but also an important political problem." The CPCCC requested: "to adjust the agriculture structure, and increase the employment of farmers ... to strive vigorously to reverse the tendency of the unceasing expansion of income disparity between urban and rural inhabitants as soon as possible." It decided "to take the increase of farmer income as an important standard to evaluate local government achievements."

Methods to increase farmer incomes

- "Giving more and taking less"
  1) Giving more
  A. Increasing investment of government finance in agricultural and rural development.
  Establishing and optimizing a mechanism to increase government financial support for agricultural and rural development and to encour-

age and guide social capital to go to agriculture and the countryside through diversified economic levers such as tax reduction and subsidy.

B. Putting most of new increments of expenses for education, health and culture into the countryside.

C. Stabilizing and enhancing the share of agricultural and rural areas in the state investment in fixed assets to increase input in agriculture and rural infrastructure construction.

D. Establishing "Three Subsidies."

The direct subsidy for farmers in grain production, the subsidy for improved agricultural variety and the subsidy for agricultural machines and tools purchase.

E. Increasing the share of agriculture in national bonds.

(CPCCC, January 2004)

2) Taking less

A. Cutting agricultural tax and agricultural special product tax.

China is the only nation in the world to levy agricultural tax from farmers. The total tax rate was about 8.4 percent. The CPCCC (January 2004) requested "to gradually reduce the agricultural tax rate and simultaneously cut the agricultural special product tax except for tobacco leaf tax" and decided to cut the agricultural tax in five years. On 5 March 2005, Wen Jiabao announced that in 2006 China would completely exempt the agricultural tax two years ahead of time.

B. Cutting and merging town and township governments to reduce expenditure.

The CPCCC (January 2004) urged "to further simplify township and town governments and their personnel on government finance to adjust the township and town system positively and to merge villages if possible" for reducing rural government expense.

C. Abolishing random collection of fees and funds in rural areas by local governments.

- Encouraging farmers to egress or enter the city for working

The CPCCC (January 2004) instructed to improve the employment environment of farmers entering the city and to guarantee the legal rights of the farmers in the city. "Local governments must clean up and cancel the discrimination stipulations and unreasonable charges for farmers who enter the city for a job and simplify the related procedures for farmer to cross regions and enter the city for working. The farmer workers having a job in the city have already become an important part of industrial workers and have created wealth and tax for the city." The CPCCC urged to pay wages of farmer workers promptly, to improve their work conditions, to solve their children's education issues and safeguard their legal rights and interests. The methods to encourage farmers to work in the city are:

1) Improving further the management and service aiming to promote farmers to work in the city.

A. Canceling the discrimination stipulations and limitations for farmers to work in the city and relaxing the requirements for farmers to work and settle down in the city.
B. Promoting and improving local government service to organize farmers to work in the city.
C. Optimizing the labor market and reorganizing the labor market in order to establish an integrated labor market for both urban and rural areas.

2) Safeguarding the legal rights and interests of farmer workers in the city.
3) Strengthening professional training for farmers.
   The CPCCC (January 2004) instructed to strengthen professional training for rural labor. "This is an important foundational work to enhance farmer professional ability for jobs and to strengthen the industry competitive ability of our country ... All levels of government finance must arrange special funds for farmer professional training. Local governments must provide subsidy and aid for farmers doing training." It requested "to make farmer workers benefit directly." The state (22 March 2004) decided to implement the "sunlight program of rural labor training."

Under the state push, the farmer workers in China increased greatly and reached approximately 100 million people, an increase of 5 million people annually. About 47.8 percent of the increment of farmer incomes in China came from working outside in 2003 (Chen,[2] 9 February 2004).

"Farmer reducing" campaign

Although the tenth FYP proposed that "the promotion of urbanization in our country has been maturing gradually and we must instantaneously implement the urbanization strategy," China didn't lift its ban on farmer immigration to the city. In 2004 the CPCCC decided "to promote the household register system reform in large and medium cities and relax the condition required for farmers to work and settle down in the city" (CPCCC, January 2004).

Methods to reduce farmers

- Abolishing officially the "Temporary Regulation of Managing Urban Registered Permanent Residence" made by the Ministry of Public Security on 16 July 1951, which is the main regulation to prevent farmers from immigrating to the city and had existed for 53 years (the Ministry of Public Security, 3 September 2004).
- Promoting household register reform in small cities and towns to lift the restriction on farmer registered permanent residence in small cities and towns.
  The reform started from 2001 officially after a two-year experiment from 1997. On 30 March 2001, the State Council decided to reform its population policy and lift the restriction on farmer immigration to small cities and towns.

1) Implementation scope of the reform
   Urban districts of cities at county level, towns with county government stations and other towns
2) Methods to reform the household register control system in small cities and towns

A. Abolishing the quota control and introducing the living condition control. China strictly controls its population movement from countryside to city by the quota, which is made directly by the State Planning Commission and occupies 2/1000 of the local urban population annually. That is, the share of annual local people immigrating from rural to urban areas in the local urban population every year is no more than 2/1000. Now China uses the living condition to control population immigration. As long as a person has a legal and fixed residence, stable job or income, any one is able to settle down in a small city or town.
B. Unifying different registered residence cards such as urban temporary registered cards into the common urban registered residence card.

- Recognizing farmer workers working in the city as urban industrial workers
  Although working in the city, farmer workers were defined as agricultural population. The CPCCC (January 2004) argued: "rural labor entering and working in the city has already become a part of industrial workers" and classified the farmer workers as non-agriculture population.
- "Cutting the county to establish the district" campaign to expand the city
  From the beginning of the twenty-first century, large and medium cities in China started to cut the administrative counties belonging to them and change these counties into their own administrative districts, which expanded the scale of these cities greatly. For example, both Beijing's Pinggu and Huairou Counties were changed into Beijing's districts separately on 17 and 18 April 2002, which made Beijing increased by two districts (*Beijing Evening News*, 18 April 2002). The campaign changed a number of the rural population in the counties into non-agricultural ones.
- Canceling the agricultural population registration
  From 2001, China started to reform its population registration system and many provinces such as Jiangsu, Fujian and Hunan are unifying the agricultural and non-agricultural population registration into one unified population registration, in which there is only common population and no classification of both agricultural and non-agricultural population at all. Immigration depends on a stabilized job and living conditions only, that is, farmers are able to immigrate into city as long as they have a stabilized job and living conditions. Farmers settled down in the city will enjoy urban welfare as the urban residents do.
- Canceling the restriction of registered residence cards on collage graduates
  The state requested provincial capitals and the cities below provincial capital level to cancel the restriction and allow college graduates to enter and allow them to get employment crossing province and city (Beijing Youths, 22 November 2002).

To support the "dragon head enterprise" (DHE)[3]

The CPCCC (January 2004) made a call for supporting the DHE. In 2005, it requested "to strengthen continually the support for agricultural industrialized DHEs in various forms of ownership and to encourage them to cooperate in various forms relating economic interest to bring along the development of both production bases and farmers."

Methods to support the DHE

- Establishing special funds of local government finance for agriculture industrialization and increasing the investment in DHEs.
- The technological transformation loans of DHEs conforming to certain conditions enjoying deducted interest by government finance.
- Providing DHEs with government subsidy for their training, marketing services for farmers, R&D, base construction, pollution control and so on.
- Perfecting a tax policy for value added of agricultural products processing.
- Eliminating discrimination of ownership and making non-public ownership DHEs enjoy favorable government aid, tax and finance policies.
- Supporting DHEs to export, and to bring along national agricultural product exportation.
- Extending loans of the ADBC to those DHEs qualifying under certain conditions and primarily in production, circulation or processing of grain, cotton and oil.
- Improving the credit service of state-owned commercial banks and solving the problem of DHEs lacking purchase funds.
- Improving the service of collective economy organizations to help DHEs cooperate with farmers.
  (CPCCC, January 2004 and January 2005)

To reform and create a new rural financial system

The CPCCC (January 2004) urged the reform and creation of a new rural finance system. "We must establish a rural financial system to serve the rural community according to rural and farmer real needs, according to benefiting both the increase of farmer and rural enterprise loans and improvement of rural finance service."

Methods to reform and create a new rural financial system

- Defining the duty of the financial organizations in a county serving for agriculture, farmer and rural development.
- Expanding the fluctuation scope of interest rates of rural loans.
- Consummating further the related policy about rural postal saving.
- Reforming RCCs to alleviate the outflow of rural funds.
- Creating new financial products and service patterns of commercial banks such as the ABC to expand credit fund channels for supporting agricultural development.

- Expanding the financial services of policy banks such as ADBC for agriculture and rural development.
- Promoting the experience of the experiments in RCC reform nationally.
- Expanding the small loan service for farmer households.
- Encouraging the establishment of financial organizations of multi-ownership serving directly for agriculture, farmer and rural development through attracting social and foreign capital.
- Encouraging various credit guarantee organizations made by the government to develop the guarantee service suitable to rural characteristics, to set up agricultural guarantee organizations if possible, and existing commercial guarantee organizations to develop rural guarantee service.
- Accelerating the construction of the policy agricultural insurance system.
  (CPCCC, January 2004)

To promote agricultural products processing industries and resist the impact of the WTO

China's access to the WTO will bring its rural industry both opportunity and challenge. The Ministry of Agriculture (20 June 2002) pointed out: "after joining the WTO, our agricultural development faces greater challenges and the competition in agricultural product markets will become more intense." The State Council (6 November 2002) pointed out that because the level of domestic agricultural products processing was very low, developing the agricultural products processing industry not only had an extremely vital significance for realizing agricultural industrialization and promoting the strategic adjustment of agriculture and rural economy structure, but also enabled to promote agricultural product exports and benefited strengthening the international competition power of our agriculture. "From now on, we must vigorously develop the agricultural products processing industry, closely centering on the strategic adjustment of agricultural and rural economy structure." The CPCCC (January 2004) instructed "to strengthen the support and service for newly established medium and small-scale enterprises of agricultural and sideline products processing."

Methods to promote agricultural products processing industries

- Making programs.
  1) "Regional Layout Plan of Superior Agricultural Products (2003–7)," the Ministry of Agriculture, 20 January 2003.
  2) "Acting Program of Agricultural Products Processing Industry Development." the Ministry of Agriculture, 29 July 2002.
  3) "Science and Technology Program of Promoting Competitive Power of Superior Agricultural Products," the Ministry of Agriculture, 27 January 2003.

4) "National Program of Main Agricultural Products Processing Industry Development," the Ministry of Agriculture, 20 June 2002.

- Defining the key products processing for development.
  1) The deep processing of important agricultural products such as grain, cotton and edible oils; meat, milk, aquatic products and vegetables.
  2) The traditional processing of sugar, tea, silk, hemp, leather and so on.
  3) The special processing of wild resources and agricultural products with characteristics.
- Focusing on the construction of thirty-five material production bases to produce eleven kinds of superior agricultural products for resisting import impact and expanding export.
  1) Constructing the thirty-five bases of eleven products in two stages.
  A. Implementing five programs of high oil soybean, special-purpose wheat and corn, cotton and milk in 2003–2005.
  B. Implementing six programs of high quality rape, citrus fruits, sugar cane, apples, beef and mutton and aquatic products in 2005–07. (The Ministry of Agriculture, 27 January 2003).
  2) The state focusing on model counties.
  3) The Ministry of Agriculture responsible for national implementation with thirty-five leading teams at province level for each production base.
- Establishing a new mechanism of production and management to encourage agricultural products processing enterprises to cooperate stably with farmers through directional investment, directional service and directional purchase.
- Supporting DHEs.
- Promoting technology advancement and innovation.
- Improving quality and safety systems referring to international standards.
- Strengthening and supporting the profession associations of agricultural products processing industries, intermediary organizations of specialized technical services and so on.
- State preferential policies.
  1) Increasing state investment.
  2) Financial support such as priority commercial loans of commercial banks and the priority of financing through stock markets.
  3) Preferential tax policies such as 3–5 years exemption of income tax for key enterprises in agricultural products processing industries.
  4) Other necessary measures such as power and land supplies.
- Expanding agricultural product exportation. The state (18 October 2004) argued: "practice has proved that expansion of agricultural product exportation is an important way to increase farmer employment,

promote the increase of farmer income and the structure adjustment of agriculture, and enhance agricultural competitive power." The goal of agricultural product exportation was:

1) 30 billion US dollars or more in the next 4–5 years.
2) 40 billion US dollars or more by 2013 with a great improvement in both quality and health safety.

To promote TVE outward-oriented economy

The Ministry of Agriculture and the Ministry of Foreign Trade and Economic Cooperation (22 January 2002) jointly indicated that at present TVE outward-oriented economy had already become an important part and growing point of China's foreign economic and trade strategy and after the accession to the WTO, the dependence of both national economy and TVEs on the world economy would be further strengthened. "Further promoting TVE outward-oriented economy has a vital significance for expanding its exportation, impelling TVEs to invest overseas, improving the quality of foreign capital used by TVEs and promoting TVE industry and product structure adjustment to strengthen its market competition power."

Methods to promote TVE outward-oriented economy

- Striving for bank loans such as loans from various commercial banks and China import-export banks, favorable loans for processing and trade enterprises beyond the border and "international market development funds for medium and small-scale enterprises."
- Accelerating the establishment of TVE development funds to support TVEs with orders and payment ability mainly.
- Organizing TVEs to apply for export projects of mechanical and electrical products and to accelerate the product structure adjustment of exports to support and cultivate mechanical and electrical products with famous brands for export.
- Depending on technology progress to expand TVE exports.
- Encouraging TVEs to set up enterprises overseas.
- Expanding the absorption of foreign capital, and cooperation with foreign firms.
- Strengthening services for TVE outward-oriented economy.

To expand industry access and vigorously develop rural non-public economy

In order to promote TVE development, the CPCCC (January 2004) requested: "to vigorously develop the rural private and other non-public ownership economy." The Ministry of Agriculture (26 July 2004) urged to further emancipate the mind, to speed up ownership reform, to unceasingly promote the system innovation and to impel TVE development by the new system and mechanism.

Methods to develop the rural non-public ownership economy

- Expanding access to industry.
  "To allow rural private enterprises to access any infrastructures, public utilities and other industries which are not banned by the laws and regulations."
- Policies supporting rural private enterprises in tax, financing, resources use and qualified personnel.
- Tax and registration exemption for rural legal small traders and peddlers, except those restricted by stipulations (CPCCC, January 2004).
- Accelerating ownership reform of collective TVEs to guide them into shareholding, share-cooperatives, partnership, individual or private enterprises.
- Impelling and supporting the outward-oriented economy.
  Private enterprises were able to enjoy state policies to support trade and joint ventures with foreign firms such as the fund for medium and small-scale enterprises to develop international markets, the export credit guarantee fund for supporting development, favorable loans for processing projects beyond the border and so on.

To concentrate TVEs in small cities and towns and vigorously develop small cities and towns

The tenth FYP proposed: "to develop small cities and towns with emphasis" and "it is an important way to promote urbanization in our country." The CPCCC (January 2004) requested: "to prosper the small city economy." "The construction of small cities and towns must combine with the expansion of county economy, TVE development, promotion of agriculture industrialization and immigration to guide more farmers to enter small cities and towns and gradually form the mechanism of industrial development, population concentration and market expansion for strengthening the ability of small cities and towns to absorb rural population and bring along rural development." It instructed that the state fixed asset investment must continue to support small city and town construction.

Targets of concentrating TVEs in small cities and towns

By 2005, 40 percent of TVEs should concentrate in small cities or towns in the eastern region, 30 percent in the central region and 25 percent in the western region. By 2015, the TVE concentrating share should be more than 60 percent, and 70 percent of TVE business income should be from the TVEs in small cities or towns (the Ministry of Agriculture, the Ministry of Construction and the Ministry of National Territory Resources, 28 August 2001).

Methods to concentrate TVEs in small cities and towns

- Strengthening infrastructure construction.

- Establishing a multi-investment mechanism of governments, collectives and individuals to abstract the entire social fund for the construction of small cities and towns.
- Preferential policies in firm registration, tax, credit, market financing and so on for TVEs in small cities and towns.
- Except for a few enterprises not suitable for small cities or towns, in principle, new TVEs must be set up in small cities or towns. At the same time the TVEs dispersing in rural areas should be gradually concentrated in small cities or towns.
- Cultivating pillar industries and products with characteristics in each small city and town.
  1) Developing mainly labor and resources-intensive industries in underdeveloped areas.
  2) Promoting mainly technology and capital-intensive industries and simultaneously developing labor-intensive industries in developed areas.
  3) Accelerating the development of large scale, technological, outward-oriented and agricultural industrialized TVEs.
  4) Giving priority to TVE tertiary industry.
- Guaranteeing the land necessary for TVEs in small cities and towns under the premise to protect farming lands.
- Encouraging the set up of TVEs cross-region and to move TVEs to small cities and towns in different regions.
- Constructing TVE gardens.

To promote TVE technical innovation

The state has been aiming to improve TVEs technically. The Ministry of Agriculture (19 January 2000) indicated that although since the reform, TVE economic scale had expanded rapidly, the majority of TVEs lacked technicians, technical development organizations, advanced technical equipment and products with high technology, all of which were a main restriction on TVE development. It argued that TVEs must vigorously advance technical innovation in order to maintain their vigor and competitive ability. The tenth FYP proposed: "to support and guide TVEs to promote their own structure adjustment, technology progress and system innovation for TVE reasonable concentration and healthy development."

The targets of TVE technology innovation (2000–5)

- All large-scale TVEs and some medium and small-scale TVEs should establish their own technical development organizations.
- Raising the share of technicians in total employees of collective TVEs from 6.7 percent in 1998 to more than 10 percent.
- Raising the share of high-tech industry in total TVE sale income from 4 percent in 1998 to about 15 percent.

- Establishing 300 TVE science and technology gardens (zones) nationally
- Rewarding and promoting 100 achievements from TVE technology innovations yearly.
- Raising the contribution of technical progress to collective TVE output growth from 40 percent in 1998 to about 45 percent.

Methods to promote technical innovation

- Formulating plans
  1) "The Tenth FYP Summary of TVE Technical Progress," the Ministry of Agriculture, 30 July 2001.
  2) "The Tenth FYP of TVE Education and Training," the Ministry of Agriculture, 11 April 2001.
  3) "The Tenth FYP of TVE Quality Promotion," the Ministry of Agriculture, 20 July 2001.
- Establishing TVE scientific and technical gardens (zones) and creating key TVEs with famous brands.
- Establishing and optimizing technical innovation systems and mechanisms by taking the enterprise as the main body to unite social intermediary service organizations, research institutions, universities and so on.
- Absorbing technicians from university and technical institutes, and training staff.
- Increasing the investment in technical innovation and encouraging TVEs to invest in their own technical innovation.
- Developing applied high and new technology
  1) Focusing on technological transformation of traditional industry and high-tech application.
  2) Focusing on key TVEs.
     By 2005, the Ministry of Agriculture would pay special attention to the technological transformations of 100 large and middle-scale TVEs, 100 high-tech TVEs, 100 agricultural industrialized DHEs and 100 large TVEs for export.
- Promoting vigorously 100 technical achievements and patents in TVEs each year.
- Strengthening TVE management and quality control, especially setting up an account in private enterprises.
- Establishing and improving technical standards, working standards and management standards systems and encouraging TVEs to use international standards.
- Raising the incentives of technical personnel and employees by various policies and measures.

To deepen the grain circulation system reform

The State (6 June 2004) decided to comprehensively open the grain purchase market in 2004 and advance the grain circulation system reform positively.

The overall targets of the reform

Under the state macro regulation and control, these were to open the grain purchase and sale market and form a multi-channel system taking state-owned grain enterprises as the main channel in order to establish a grain circulation system conforming to China's condition, and to guarantee national grain security.

Methods to deepen the reform of the grain circulation system

- Lifting state control on the purchase and price of grain and allowing non-state owned enterprises to be engaged in the grain market to perfect the grain market system.
    1) Making the lowest purchase price of grain only when the grain supply and demand has a tremendous change in order to guarantee market supply and protect farmer interests.
    2) Establishing a nationally unified, open, competitive and orderly grain market system, abolishing the grain transportation license system and strictly prohibiting various regional blockades for grain.
- Subsiding farmers directly in grain production nationally from 2004.
- Accelerating the reform of state-owned grain enterprises to make them responsible for their own profits and losses, operate independently and strengthen their market competition ability.
- Reforming the supply method of the grain purchase fund.
  The ADBC must guarantee the credit fund for the state grain reserve and government grain regulation. Commercial banks also must support grain production and marketing.
- Strengthening grain market management and maintaining its normal circulation order.
- Strengthening and improving grain macro regulation and control to guarantee national grain security.
    1) Implementing a strict farming land protection system according to state laws and regulations.
    2) Consummating the vertical management system of central grain reserves and establishing local grain reserves for 3–6 months.
    3) Consummating the grain responsibility system of provincial governors and investigating the leadership responsibility of local governments if there is a grain problem leading to a turbulence of the market or society.

To enhance TVE credit

The Ministry of Agriculture (8 October 2002) proposed to strengthen TVE credit management and improve the TVE credit environment and gradually realize scientific, systematic, standard and informative credit management of TVEs in order to raise TVE credit and eliminate their dishonest activity.

Targets of enhancing TVE credit

By 2010, to gradually establish the TVE basic credit system, credit information collection and appraisal system, credit guarantee system and credit service and supervising system. In eastern regions, key industries and large and middle-scale TVEs should set up their own basic credit system in five years.

Methods to strengthen TVE credit management

- Establishing basic credit systems such as credit management, finance and accounting management, quality control, good faith and law-abiding mechanisms.
- Cultivating a good credit image.
- Strengthening interior credit management.
- Strengthening the credit service system.
- Promoting advanced methods of credit management and initiating a campaign to construct good faith and law-abiding TVEs.
- Establishing a TVE credit information collection and appraisal system.
- Establishing a TVE credit guarantee system.
- Establishing a TVE inquiry system of credit information.

To lighten the TVE burden

The state (18 March 2002) formulated a regulation to severely limit and prohibit random charges, fines and government various allocations to TVEs such as funds, labor and resource provisions.

Methods to lighten TVE burdens

- Establishing special agencies at all levels of governments to lighten TVE burdens.
- Controlling the items and standards to charge TVEs administratively. Local governments below provincial level have no right to decide these items and standards, some of which must be decided by the State Council directly.
- Limiting strictly the fines, government fund collections and foundations, and economical inspections to TVEs.
- Implementing strictly state law, regulations and preferential policies for TVEs.
- Charging no extra fees for registration, operation certificate and license.
- Prohibiting the charges to TVE through examination, consultation, appraisal and so on.
- Forbidding any behavior that increases TVE burdens using administrative powers or monopoly status such as the request for financial support and donations.
- Establishing a leadership responsibility system. The main leaders at all levels of governments to be responsible for local TVE burdens.
- Punishing severely any departments and individuals making TVE burdens heavier.

Concluding Remarks

Characteristics, miracle, dilemma and ending of China's rural industrialization

Under central government control, China created rural industrialization with China's characteristics and the rural industrialization experienced a winding course full of miracles and dramatic development processes. The process can be divided into two stages. One stage developed under central control in a highly centralized system, the other was under central control in the transition to liberalization.

Characteristics, miracle and dilemma under central control in the highly centralized system

China's characteristics (1949–78)

- The people's commune
- Great Leap Forward of rural industry (1958–60)
- "Farmer making"
- "Grain priority"
- "Countryside supporting the city"
- "Taking SOEs as the mainstay"
- "Taking the collective economy as the mainstay"
- "State monopoly for purchase and supply"

The miracle

- Rural industry's great leap forward (1958–60).
- Large-scale capital construction projects of farmland and water conservation systems made mainly by farmers' hand labor with no machine at all.

The dilemma

- National serious economic crisis and big famine with a large number of farmers' deaths after the GLF

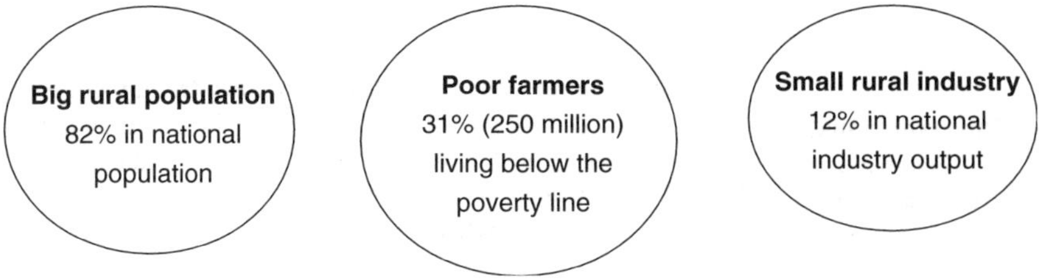

Figure C.1 China-style rural industrialization and dilemma in 1978 (national per capita GDP: 379 yuan (220 US dollars))

Source: *CSY* 1984, 1996 and 2003, *CTVEY*, 1978–87 and "China's Agricultural Transformation and Development," Liu Ruofeng, 1997 p. 424.

Note: The exchange rate of US dollar to PMB in 1978 is 1 US dollars = 1.72 RMB (CSY 1996, p. 580).

- Huge number of poor farmers and poor countryside
- Slow growth of agriculture.
  China's per capita grain was 319 kilograms in 1978, merely 13 kilograms more than that of twenty years previously (1957), and lower than that (323 kilograms) 42 year ago (1936), when China had its maximum grain yield before 1949.[1]

Characteristics, miracle and dilemma under central control in the liberalization

To abandon "China's characteristics" (1979–2000)

- Abolishing the people's commune system to introduce the HRS
- Abolishing "grain priority" to allow rural industry to develop
- Abolishing "taking SOEs as the mainstay" to allow TVEs to compete with SOEs
- Abolishing "taking collective economy as the mainstay" to impel TVE privatization
- Abolishing the SMPS to open agricultural product markets.

To create new "China's characteristics"

- Dual industry pattern to separate urban and rural industries
- "Leaving the land but keeping in the countryside"
- "Farmer worker making"
- Constructing small towns and cities.

The miracle

A huge and fast growing rural industry driving both the rural and national economy and the emerging of a large number of rural small towns and cities.

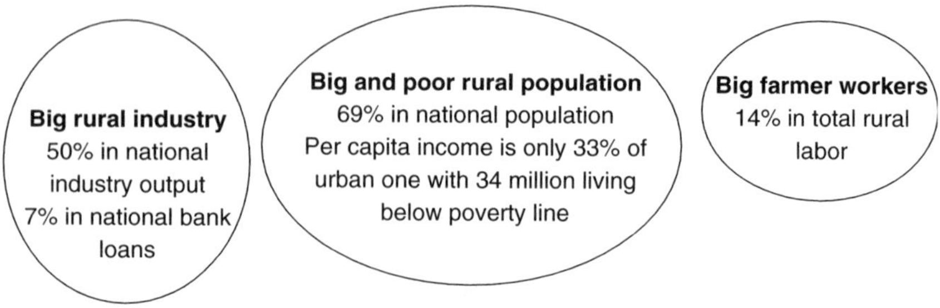

Figure C.2 China-style rural industrialization, miracle and dilemma in 1999 (national per capita GDP: 6551 yuan (791 US dollars))
Source: *CSY* 2001, *CTVEY* 1999, 2000 and 2001. "The National Rural Social and Economic Typical Cases Survey Data Assembly 1986–99, CPCC Policy Research Office, the Rural Fixed Observing Office of the Ministry of Agriculture, Chinese agriculture publishing house, 2001, pp. 482 and 484.
Note: the average exchange rate of US dollars to RMB is from *CSY* 2001, p. 586.

The dilemma

Huge numbers of poor farmers and poor countryside with stagnant agriculture under high-speed growth of GDP.

The ending and dilemma of rural industrialization under central control in the twenty-first century

To abandon "China's characteristics"

- Abolishing "keeping farmers in the countryside" to reduce farmers.
- Abolishing the "countryside supporting the city" and "agriculture supporting industry" to increase rural investment and farmer income, and cut agricultural tax.

The ending of China's miracle

To abandon "keeping farmers in the countryside," "countryside supporting the city, agriculture supporting industry" and to implement "farmer-reducing" means to abandon the strategy to construct rural moderate prosperity in all respects and realize rural industrialization through developing rural industry, relying on rural inhabitants' own efforts and shifting rural labor surplus locally. The policies, especially those to abandon "keeping farmers in the countryside" and to implement "farmer reducing" may fundamentally change rural industrialization because it will cause a liberalization of population movement, which is able to accelerate the urbanization of China's population greatly. The farmer reducing will change the nature of rural enterprises, which are owned by farmers. Original rural enterprises may be changed and owned by urbanites. Therefore, a rural enterprise may not be a "farmer enterprise," but becomes an ordinary enterprise. The rural industry will mix with urban industry and form a unified national industry. At the same time, as farmer entry into the city progresses rapidly, rural markets will wither and the urban economy will expand significantly. Finally, the engine to drive economic development will move from the countryside to the city, which is precisely the industrialization pattern many countries including western countries have taken. Rural industrialization with China's characteristics will vanish, and China's industrialization pattern of dual industries will come to an end. To replace them, a unified national industry and industrialization will appear.

Dilemma

China's rural industrialization strategy had great success in both the 1980s and 1990s and became a miracle. However, in the twenty-first century, it is coming to a deadlock.

- The stagnating ability of the rural industry to absorb rural labor surplus.
  Since the late 1990s, TVE employees have decreased which shows that depending only on TVEs will not solve China's rural labor surplus completely.
- The limited ability of man-made rural small towns and cities for the urbanization of the rural population.
  "Small town and city making" not only needs massive funds, but is also unable to effectively concentrate TVEs and reduce numbers of farmers to solve rural employment. While wasting massive resources and making pollution, some of them are facing disintegration. For example, the Sun Geng town of Jiyang County, Jinan city, Shandong Province was an agricultural town in the 1980s. In 1992, under local government push, it established an industrial development zone and had an extraordinary development, which made it a strong town countywide and a model for TVE concentration development nationally. But after 1997, it faced a serious crisis because its enterprises withdrew from the zone unceasingly, its capital construction projects were cancelled and employment decreased significantly (Wang, 2002).

In the twenty-first century, along with further relaxation of central control and further melting of China's economy under the WTO frame into the world economy, the rural industry miracle created with China's characteristics will vanish gradually under CPCCC control. China's rural industrialization under the control, from establishment and development to its end, has experienced a large historical cycle. Similarly, CPCCC control on rural industry and economy, from establishing control with China's characteristics to abandoning the control and from constructing the system to discriminate against farmers to abandoning the discrimination system, also experienced a large cycle.

Although China reformed her highly centralized economic system to enable the economy to obtain partial liberalization and the military withdrew from economic management, the CPCCC still controls the key fields of the economy, specially the financial domain. The basic characteristics of the "general (military) economy" system did not vanish completely and China is still impelling its economic development under CPCCC control and through initiating "campaigns" with high targets and at high speed. On the other hand, economic liberalization caused economic development to gradually get out of CPCCC control. "The military campaign" policy with high targets is unable to control the partially liberalized economy efficiently and has caused great confusion. China has "to cross the river by groping the stone" and "to treat the head when the head aches, and to treat the foot when the foot hurts." After promoting industrialization by the "military campaign" for more than fifty years, China still faces the tough problem of solving the poverty of farmers dominating its population. The most difficult task is how to realize the urbanization of hundreds of millions of farmers while maintaining fast development and protecting the environment in the half-centralized and half-liberalized economy in the twenty-first century.

Notes

Introduction

1. In order to avoid confusion this study uses day, month and year to indicate the time of reference, if necessary.
2. Chen Yun was one of the vice premiers of the State Council and head of the Central Financial and Economic Committee in 1951.
3. Cheng Shiqing was a general, an army commander of the People's Liberation Army and the head of the Jiangxi provincial revolutionary committee during the Great Cultural Revolution.
4. The dual structure pattern is that the countryside deals with agriculture only and the city deals with industry only.

1 Shifting in the Land Reform Campaign

1. "Industry leading agriculture, the city leading the countryside" means that agriculture supports and serves for industrial development; and the countryside supports and serves for urban development.
2. China was divided into five large regions. They are the Northeast, East, Central South, Southwest, and Northwest regions
3. This is the report made by Liu Shaoqi at the second plenary session of the first political consultative congress.
4. A unit of length (1 Chi =1/3 meter).

2 Sprouting in the Cooperative Campaign

1. "The general line for the transition period" was made at the Central Political Bureau Conference of the CPCCC on 15 June 1953 and was put into the Constitution of the People' Republic of China in September 1954.
2. The rural socialist transformation includes the socialist transformation of both agriculture and rural handicraft industries and commerce. The rural socialist transformation means to change private small-scale production in agriculture, handicrafts and commerce into collective large-scale production.
3. Zhu De was one of the vice chairmen of the Central People's Government of China in 1953.
4. The CPCCC requested SMCs to support HPCs in its "Instruction to authorize the report made by the party team of the Fiscal and Finance Committee of North China," 12 April 1954. Authorizing a report means to approve the report and request other sectors to follow it nationally.

3 Great Leap Forward in the People's Communization Campaign

1. Bo Yibo was the vice premier of the State Council and head of the National Economic Planning Committee in 1958.

2. The Beidaihe Conference was the Extending Central Political Bureau Conference of the CPCCC and was held from 17 to 30 August 1958 at Beidaihe, Hebei province.
3. The speech was made at the Zhengzhou Conference from 27 February to 5 March 1959.
4. "Pulling down the white flag and hoisting the red flag" is to deprive a cadre who resisted or hindered the campaign of authority or other rights, and to appoint a new cadre who supported the campaign.
5. "Small, indigenous and mass" referrers to small plants such as small backyard furnaces, "indigenous methods" and the "mass campaign."
6. "The indigenous method" is to produce on a small scale with few funds, simple tools and equipment and local technology. Production using "indigenous methods" is easy to set up in a short time.
7. Egalitarianism is to merge cooperatives with different conditions and development levels to form a commune, and then hand over all properties to the commune, no matter if a cooperative is rich or poor. At the same time, the personally owned properties such as private plots, domestic animals, and fruit trees were also all turned over to the commune, which led to a serious egalitarianism between original cooperatives and between the commune members. The "free transition" is that government and communes freely use land, materials, labor and even private houses and furniture of the production brigades, production teams or farmers in various campaigns.
8. See, for example, Chang, Gene Hsin and Guanzhong James Wen, "Communal Dining and the Chinese Famine of 1958–1961," *Economic Development and Cultural Change*, Vol. 46, no. 1, 1997.

4 Great Leap Backward in the Panic Famine

1. The "five winds" refer to the "communism wind, exaggeration wind, commandism wind, cadre privilege wind and managing production by wrong orders wind." The communism wind refers to egalitarianism and free transition.
2. "Grain priority" means to produce grain with most of the resources from rural areas.
3. Li Fuchun was one of the vice primers of the State Council and the head of the State Planning Committee in 1961.
4. A basic accounting unit is the unit that carries out independent accounting, is responsible for its own profits and losses, and organizes production and distributes income with a unified standard. As a basic accounting unit, it has more rights to use production resources directly. Arguments about the basic accounting unit had been continuing since the establishing of the communes in 1958. The focus was at which level the basic accounting unit should be put, the commune, the production brigade or the production team.
5. To transfer the urban population to the countryside is to immigrate part of urban population to the countryside and make them become farmers.

5 Recovery in the Campaign to Accelerate the Mechanization of Agriculture

1. "Depending on the weather" means to depend upon climate and other natural conditions. "Depending on the state" means to develop agriculture mainly on state investment and aid.

2. "Strengthening the collective economy" is not merely to keep its "absolute superiority" in rural economy, it is also to expand the basic accounting unit, raise the public ownership level and transit to ownership by the whole people gradually.
3. "Poor transition" is to expand the scale of the basic accounting unit and raise the public ownership level from the production team to the production brigade or commune when farmers are quite poor and the economical level is very low.
4. "Cutting off the capitalist tail" is to limit and prohibit private activity, such as reducing the size of private plots, restricting private sideline production and closing rural fairs.
5. "Loving the nation" includes two things. One is to complete the state grain procurement plan on time, even under a serious natural disaster. The other is the "grain priority" to produce more grain, to offer more grain to the state to support national industrialization. For example, farmers in Dazhai ate coarse food grain such as corn themselves, but offered flour and rice to the state. "Loving the collective" is to persist with the people's commune system, and to consolidate and expand the collective economy.
6. "Five-Small industries" (FSI) are the small steel and iron, machinery, chemical fertilizer, coal and cement industries. Originally the FSI referred to county-owned industry.
7. Speculation is to carry out commercial trade secretly for benefit without government permission.
8. The "educated youths going to the mountain and countryside" (EYGMC) is to mobilize urban junior middle school, high school and university graduates (including some cadres) to migrate from the city to the countryside and become farmers.
9. Ye Jianying was the vice chairman of the CPCCC in 1973.

6 Rise under the Household Responsibility System

1. The household responsibility system (HRS) includes many forms such as the individual farmer, and also several farmers contracting together.
2. At that time, levying only industry and commerce tax for SOEs; but for the collective enterprises there were both industry and commerce tax and income tax.
3. The "eating by dividing cooking stoves" system is to make governments at various levels responsible for their own financial revenue and expenditure.
4. The number of RCCs deals with independent accounting organizations only.

7 Great Expansion in the Disintegration of the People's Commune System

1. "To leave the land but keep in the countryside" is to make farmers get out of agriculture but still remain in the countryside.
2. Separating rural government from the commune is to cut the administrative function of the people's commune and establish local government and economic organization respectively. In the new system, local governments no longer directly manage economic activity and the economic organizations also no longer have the administrative function. In fact, this is to abolish the commune system.
3. The rural cooperative foundation was established by rural collective economic organizations and farmers according to voluntary and mutual benefit principles. It is a community fund cooperative organization aiming to serve for farmers,

agricultural production and rural collective economy. The fund sources for the foundation mainly are: the member payment for shares, their own accumulated capital and supporting funds from the government.
4. Zhao Zhiyang was the premier of the State Council in 1984.
5. In the TTS, there are two different prices for one product at the same time and same place. These are the planning price and the market price out of planning.
6. "Three locals" are local materials, local processing and local selling. That is to produce by local materials, to process locally and to sell the products locally.

8 Setbacks in the Emergency Braking for a Crisis

1. "Digest rural labor surplus locally" is to solve the rural labor surplus in rural areas.
2. Yao Yilin was the Standing Member of the Political Bureau of the CPCCC, vice premier of the State Council and the Minister of the State Planning Committee in 1988.
3. Song Ping was the Standing Member of the Political Bureau of the CPCCC in 1990.
4. Transferring a TVE is to change its products into other products to meet the regulations.
5. Chen Yaobang was the vice minister of the Ministry of Agriculture in charge of TVE development in China in 1989.
6. During TVE expansion, the state not only implemented a preferential tax policy for TVEs, but also local governments made various policies to reduce and even exempt TVE tax, which led to a great confusion in tax collection.
7. He Kang was the Minister of Agriculture in 1990.
8. In order to enjoy government favorable policies or raise funds, many private enterprises registered as a branch of a state-owned or collective enterprise by offering some of the profit to the state-owned or collective enterprise. However, they in fact were private enterprises. This is the so-called "wearing a red hat" enterprise.
9. "Farmer workers" are farmers going to the city to look for a job. Farmer workers are still registered as agricultural population and have a family and contracting land to plant in their rural hometowns. Usually they work in the city or other regions most of the year and return home at year's end for the New Year festival. These are the so-called "migratory birds." Farmer workers are part-time workers with a low wage and cannot enjoy the welfare that regular urban workers enjoy such as urban housing, medical care and education. They are engaged mainly in simple, hard and dirty physical work such as construction work and so on.

9 New Great Leap Forward after the Collapse of the Soviet Union

1. This means that economic development, rather than political ideals, decides everything including the choices for the social system.
2. Chen Junsheng was one of the standing members of the State Council in 1992 in charge of TVE development in the State Council.
3. The main standard of "Moderate Prosperity" is a per capita GDP of 800 US dollars.

10 Slowing Down in the Privatization Wave

1. TVE zones were made by governments to concentrate TVEs.

11 New Century Shifting in the Campaign to Increase Farmer Incomes

1. "Three rural issues" are the problems about the slow development of agriculture, poor farmers, and poor rural areas.
2. Chen Xiwen, Assistant Director of the Office of the Central Finance and Economy Leading Team.
3. "Dragon head enterprise" (DHE) is a key enterprise, which has competitive products and is able to bring other enterprises and farmers together to form a production or development chain centering on these products.

Concluding Remarks

1. The highest grain yield before 1949 was 150 million tons in 1936 (*CSY* 1983, p. 185) with a population of 465 million people (*China Historical Population Data and the Relevant Studies*, Yang Zihui, China Reform Publishing House, 1996, p. 1288).

Bibliography

Statistical works

China Supply and Marketing Cooperative Chronicle and Development Survey 1949–85, China's Supply and Marketing Cooperative Historical Data Collection Editorial Office (Beijing: China Financial and Economic Press, 1988)

China Trade and Price Statistical Data 1952–83, the trade and price statistics department of the State Statistical Bureau (Beijing: Chinese statistics publishing house, 1984)

China's Finance Yearbook 1993, the Chinese Finance Society (Beijing: Chinese finance yearbook editorial department, 1993)

China's Industry Development, Statistical Data 1949–84 (Beijing: Chinese statistics publishing house, 1985)

China's Labor and Wages Statistical Data 1949–85, the social statistical department of the State Statistical Bureau (Beijing: Chinese statistics publishing house, 1987)

China's Price Statistics Yearbook 1990, the urban social and economic investigation team of the State Statistical Bureau (Beijing: Chinese statistics publishing house, 1990)

China's Rural Finance Statistics 1979–89, 1991, 1995 and 1996, the Agricultural Bank of China (Beijing: Chinese statistics publishing house, 1989, 1991, 1995 and 1996)

China's Statistical Yearbook (various years), the State Statistical Bureau (Beijing: Chinese statistics publishing house)

China's Township and Village Enterprise Yearbook (various years), the editorial committee of China's Township and Village Enterprise Yearbook (Beijing: agricultural publishing house)

Complete Statistics of China's Rural Economy 1949–86, the planning department of the Ministry of Agriculture, People's Republic of China (Beijing: agricultural publishing house, 1989)

New China Fifty Years Agricultural Statistics Material, the rural social and economic investigation team of SSB (Beijing: Chinese statistics publishing house, 2000).

New China Fifty Years Government Finance Statistics, Lou Jiwei, ed. (Beijing: Economic science publishing house, 2000)

New China Fifty Years Statistical Data Assembly, the national economic synthesis statistics department of SSB (Beijing: Chinese statistics publishing house, 1999)

The People's Republic of China National Economy and Society Development Statistical Bulletin, (various years), The State Statistical Bureau

Central documents cited

Bo Yibo, "Report on national economic planning for 1958 (draft)," 3 February 1958, *Review on Some Major Policy-Making and Events* (Beijing: The central party school publishing house, 1993).

Central Fiscal and Finance Committee (in time order):

"Decision on dividing business fields of industrial and handicraft products between state-owned commerce and SMCs," 5 December 1953.

"Decision on preliminary division of urban and rural commerce for state-owned commerce and SMCs," 24 July 1954, *ILCSFN*, No. 5.

Cheng Zihua, "Working report of temporary council of all-China federation of cooperative union," 20 July 1954, *ILCSFN*, No. 5.
Chen Junsheng (in time order):
"Speech at the national conference of exchanging experience of accelerating TVE development in the Central and West regions," 16 November 1992, *CTVEY* 1993.
"Speech at the national TVE working conference," 18 September 1993, *CTVEY* 1994.
Chen Yaobang, "Speech at the national symposium of the directors of TVE management Bureau," 25 July 1989, *CTVEY* 1990.
Chen Yun (in time order):
"Unifying financial and economic work," 3 March 1950, *ILCSFN*, No. 1.
"Present economic situation and measures to adjust industry, commerce and tax," 15 June 1950, *ILCSFN*, No. 1.
"Financial and economic policies since the war to resist US aggression and aid Korea," 15 November 1950, *ILCSFN*, No. 1.
"Main points for financial and economic work in 1951," 4 April 1951, ILCSFN, No. 2.
"On grain plan purchase and plan supply," 10 October 1953, *ILCSFN*, No. 4.
"Solving the difficulty for private industrial production," 31 December 1954, *ILCSFN*, No. 5.
"To mobilize urban population to countryside," 31 May 1961, *ILCSFN*, No. 14.
"Adjusting Public and Private Relations and Tax," 6 June 1950, *ILCSFN*, No. 1.
"Adjusting National Economy to Develop the Economy Proportionally," at the Central Political Bureau Conference of the CPCCC, 21 March 1979, *Important Central Literature Since the Third Plenum of the Eleventh CPCCC, CPCCC Instruction Committee for Party Consolidation* (Beijing, People's publishing house, 1983).
Chinese People Politics Consultation Committee, "Chinese People Politics Consultation Common Program," 29 September 1949.
CPCCC (in time order):
"The outline of China's Land Law," 10 October 1947.
"The Instruction about policy for handicraft industry," 12 June 1950, *ILCSFN*, No. 1.
"Resolution on the agricultural production cooperation (Draft)," 1951, *ILCSFN*, No. 2.
"Instruction to organize and establish supplying and marketing cooperatives in newly liberalized regions," 11 May 1951, *ILCSFN*, No. 2.
"Instruction on adjusting commerce," 12 November 1952, *ILCSFN*, No. 3.
"To pay much attention to handicraft industry," 31 March 1953, *ILCSFN*, No. 4.
"Resolution on implementation of grain planned purchase and supply," 16 October 1953.
"Decision on national planned purchase of edible oils," 15 November 1953, *ILCSFN*, No. 4.
"Resolution on developing agricultural producer cooperatives," 16 December 1953, *ILCSFN*, No. 4.
"Instruction to authorize 'the report on striving for activating Basic-level market and promoting exchange of goods between city and countryside' made by the party team of the Fiscal and Finance Committee of North China," 12 April 1954, *ILCSFN*, No. 5.
"Instruction to authorize 'the report of the second national rural work conference' made by the rural working department of the CPCCC," 3 June 1954, *ILCSFN*, No. 5.

"Instruction for 'the report of the third national handicraft production cooperative conference'," 22 June 1954, *ILCSFN*, No. 5.
"Instruction on further strengthening market leadership, transforming private trade and improving rural purchase and sale," 12 April 1955, *ILCSFN*, No. 7.
"The national program for agricultural development 1956–67 (Draft)," 23 January 1956, *ILCSFN*, No. 9.
"Resolution on the political report of the eighth national congress of CPC," 27 September 1956, *ILCSFN*, No. 9.
"National Program for Agricultural Development 1956–1967 (Revision Draft)," 25 October 1957.
"Opinion about developing local industry," 23 March 1958, *ILCSFN*, No. 11.
"Authorizing 'the report of Jiangsu provincial committee of CPC about the non state-owned agricultural middle school'," 8 April 1958, *ILCSFN*, No. 11.
"Decision on both the plan in 1959 and the second FYP," 28 August 1958, *ILCSFN*, No. 11.
"Instruction on water conservation work," 29 August 1958, *ILCSFN*, No. 11.
"Resolution on establishing people's commune in countryside," 29 August 1958.
"The central political bureau enlarged meeting news release," 31 August 1958, Xinhua News Agency.
"The instruction on the general socialism and communism education movement in the countryside in this winter and next spring," August 1958, *ILCSFN*, No. 11.
"Decision on militiaman," August 1958, *ILCSFN*, No. 11.
"Notice on 'the report on the question about doing in a big way for people's commune industry' made by the party committee team of the Ministry of Light Industry," 7 December 1958, *ILCSFN*, No. 11.
"Resolution on national economic planning in 1959," 10 December 1958, *ILCSFN*, No. 11.
"Resolution on some problems of the people's commune," 10 December 1958, *ILCSFN*, No. 11.
"Urgent instruction on verifying urban population and food supply," 16 June 1961, *ILCSFN*, No. 14.
"Instruction on stopping rural labor movement," 4 February 1959, *ILCSFN*, No. 12.
"Some stipulations on management system of the people's commune," February 1959.
"The decision about strengthening rural people's commune credit management," 1 April 1959.
"Instruction on 'the report on rural eliminating illiteracy, spare-time education and future work policy and duty' made by the CPC team of the Ministry of Education," 2 April 1960, *ILCSFN*, No. 13.
"Instruction to mobilize the entire party to develop agriculture and grain with great effort," 10 August 1960.
"On guaranteeing the realization of grain transportation plan," 15 August 1960.
"Authorizing 'the report on measures of cutting the capital construction scale to guarantee production' made by the State Planning Committee and the State Construction Committee," 19 August 1960.
"On clearing up labor firmly and seriously to strengthen the agricultural front," 20 August 1960.
"On lowering the standard of the grain ration in both city and countryside," 7 September 1960.
"On the work to guarantee grain supply for this winter and next spring," 16 October 1960.

"The emergent letter about the current policy issues of rural people's commune," 3 November 1960.
"The emergent instruction to launch immediately a campaign to collect and make substitutes for food at large scale," 14 November 1960.
"Notice on acting immediately to transport grain," 17 November 1960.
"Authorizing 'the report on enhancing grain purchase price' made by the grain price team of CPCCC," 15 January 1961.
"Authorizing 'the report of arranging the production of daily industrial products emergently' made by the party team of the Ministry of Light Industry," 7 January 1961.
"Stipulation on several policy issues of current agricultural products purchase," 15 January 1961.
"Some temporary stipulations of reorganizing the management system," 20 January 1961.
"Summary of the discussion on rural rectification and reorganization of communes and certain policy issues," 20 January 1961.
"The letter on discussion of 'the working regulations of the rural people's commune (revised draft)' for all of party members," 22 March 1961.
"Authorizing 'the report on adjusting rural labor force and simplifying and transferring staff and workers to countryside' made by the five-person team of CPCCC," 9 April 1961.
"The rural people's commune working regulations (revised draft)," 15 June 1961.
"The annotation on the rural people's commune working regulations (revised draft)," 15 June 1961.
"The stipulations on the ownership of both urban and rural handcraft industry and related policy issues (trial implementation draft)," 19 June 1961.
"Stipulations on correcting firmly equalitarianism and indiscriminate transfer, of resources and returning property thoroughly," 19 June 1961.
"The nine measures to reduce urban population and cut urban grain sale," 16 June 1961.
"Authorizing 'the report on adjusting agricultural tax burden' made by the CPC team of the Ministry of Finance," 23 June 1961.
"Notice on some issues for simplifying staff and workers," 28 June 1961.
"The instruction on rural basic accounting unit for the party committees at province, city and autonomous region level," 7 October 1961.
"Instruction on 'the suggestion of simplifying the staff of state organizations, parties and people's organizations to countryside' of the five-person team of CPCCC for the simplifying," 22 February 1962.
"The working regulations of the rural people's commune (the second revised draft)," 27 September 1962.
"Authorizing 'the stipulations on several issues of rural credit cooperatives' made by the People's Bank of China," 9 November 1962.
"Instruction about opposing embezzlement, stealing and speculation," 5 February 1970.
"The bulletin of the second plenary session of the ninth CPCCC," 6 September 1970.
"Decision on some issues concerning the acceleration of agricultural development," December 1978 and passed on 28 September 1979.
"Notice on several issues of further consummating agricultural production responsibility system," 27 September 1980.
"Summary of the national rural working conference," 1 January 1982.

"On some issues about current rural economic policy," 2 January 1983.
"Notice on rural work in 1984," 1 January 1984.
"Decision on economic system reform," 20 October 1984.
"Decision on further governing, reorganizing and deepening the reform," 9 November 1989.
"Decision on further strengthening agricultural and rural work," 29 November 1991.
"Suggestion on adjusting some targets in the eighth FYP," 7 March 1993.
"Decision on some issues in establishing socialist market economy system," 14 November 1993.
"Decision on some important issues in agricultural and rural work," 14 October 1998.

CPCCC and the State Council (in time order):
"Several decisions on releasing industrial enterprise," 11 April 1958, *ILCSFN*, No. 11.
"Decision on improving rural management system of finance and commerce to adapt people's communalization," 20 December 1958, *ILCSFN*, No. 11.
"Instruction on organizing rural fair trade," 23 September 1959.
"Decision on further simplifying staff and workers and reducing urban population," 27 May 1962, *ILCSFN*, No. 15.
"Instructions about some issues of current urban work," 6 October 1962.
"Decision on developing rural sideline production," 22 November 1962.
"Notice on separating rural government from economic organization and establishing township government," 12 October 1983.
"Notice on 'the report of creating new prospect of commune and brigade-run enterprise' made by the Ministry of Agriculture," 1 March 1984.
"Ten policies on further stimulating rural economy," 1 January 1985.
"Decision on accelerating the development of tertiary industry," 18 June 1992.
"Some policy measures on current agricultural and rural economic development," 5 November 1993.
"Decision on deepening SMC reform," 27 February 1995.
"Notice on authorizing 'the report of the opinion on TVE current development and its reform and development in future' made by the Ministry of Agriculture," 11 March 1997.
"Opinion about some policies to promote increase of farmer income," January 2004.
"Opinion on some policies to strengthen further rural work and enhance agricultural comprehensive production ability," 30 January 2005.

CPCCC Literature Laboratory (in time order):
The important central literature collection since the 13th national congress of CPC (Beijing: People's publishing house, 1991).
The important central literature collection since the 14th national congress of CPC (Beijing: People's publishing house, 1996).

CPC committee of Gansu province, "The fourth report about implementing CPCCC urgent Instruction letter," 25 November 1960, *ILCSFN*, No. 13.

CPC leading team of All-China Federation of Cooperative Union, "Report of the third national handicraft production cooperative conference," 6 January 1954.

CPC teams of both the state planning committee and the Ministry of Labor, "The report on current labor arrangement and employee wage," 11 September 1960, *ILCSFN*, No. 13.

Deng Xiaoping, "Southern Journey Speech in Wuchang, Shenzhen, Zhuhai, Shanghai and so on, 18 January–21 February, 1992" (Beijing: the people's publishing house, 1992).

He Kang (in time order):
"Speech at the national working conference of TVE export for foreign exchange," 14 December 1987.
"To implement earnestly the spirit of the fifth plenum of the thirteenth congress of CPC and to guide positively rural enterprise health development," 5 January 1990.
Hu Yaobang, "Creating comprehensively a new prospect of constructing socialist modernization," 1 September 1982.
Jiang Zemin (in time order):
"Speech at the symposium on rural work," 19 June 1990.
"The political report of the fourteenth congress of CPC," 12 October 1992.
"Speech at the agricultural and rural work conference of six provinces from 24–25 December 1992 in Wuhan," *CTVES* 1993.
"Speech at CPCCC School," 29 May 1997.
"The political report at the fifteenth congress of CPC," 12 September 1997.
"The political report at the sixteenth congress of CPC," 8 November 2002.
Li Fuchun, "the Opinion on the national economic plan in 1961," 14 January 1961.
Li Xiannian (in time order):
"Strengthening the leadership to commerce and transformation of private business," April 1955, *ILCSFN*, No. 5.
"Opinion on regaining rural basic finance organizations," 22 June 1959.
Liu Shaoqi (in time order):
"Work report at the second plenary session of the first political consultative congress," 14 June 1950, *ILCSFN*, No. 1.
"National industrialization and enhancement of people's living level," 1950, *ILCSFN*, No. 1, 1992.
"On how to transit China gradually to socialism," 20 October 1952, *ILCSFN*, No. 3.
"On the problems of handicraft producers' cooperatives," 8 December 1953, *ILCSFN*, No. 4.
"The report at the second Conference of the eighth CPC congress," 5 May 1958, *ILCSFN*, No. 11.
Mao Zedong (in time order)
"Comment on the policy for national bourgeoisie, private industry and commerce," April 1950, *ILCSFN*, No. 1.
"Youth league's work needing to consider youth's characteristics," 30 June 1953, *Selected works of Mao Zedong*, vol. 5 (Beijing: People's publishing house, 1977).
"On problems of agriculture cooperativization," 31 July 1955, *People's Daily*, 17 October 1955.
"Preface of China's rural socialist high tide," 27 December 1955, *China's rural socialist high tide* (Beijing, People' publishing house, 1956).
"To accelerate the handicraft industry socialist transformation," 5 March 1956, *Selected works of Mao Zedong*, vol. 5 (Beijing: People's publishing house, 1977).
"Speech at CPC national propaganda working conference," 12 March 1957.
"The conversation with Chinese students in Moscow," November 1957, *New China Economic Development History*, Cong Shuhai, Zhang Hen (Shanghai: the Shanghai finance and economy university press, 1999).
"Introducing a Cooperative," 15 April 1958, *ILCSFN*, No. 11.
"Comment on 'lowly intelligently, noble stupidest'," May 1958, *ILCSFN*, No. 11.
"Speech at central military committee Enlarged Conference," 21 June 1958, *ILCSFN*, No. 11.

"Speech at 15th Supreme State Conference," 8 September 1958, *China's rural society and economy evolution 1949–89*, Chen Jiyuan, Chen Jiaji and Yang Xun, eds (Taiyuan: Shanxi economic publishing house, 1993).
"Speech at Zhengzhou Conference," 27 February–5 March 1959, *ILCSFN*, No. 12.
"Instruction on the report of five-person team of CPCCC for grain problem," 15 November 1960.
People's Daily (in time order):
"To strive for a complete stability of price," editorial, 11 June 1950.
"To struggle for the lofty goal of socialist industrialization," editorial, 1 October 1953.
"Developing heavy industry is the center link for realizing national socialist industrialization," editorial, 3 March 1954.
"To develop credit cooperatives positively," editorial, 7 December 1954.
"The New Year's Editorial," 1 January 1958.
"Striving for Top Speed," editorial, 21 June 1958.
"Using both indigenous and foreign methods is the shortcut to accelerate iron and steel industry," 8 August 1958.
"To act immediately to attain the great mission of doubling steel output," 1 September 1958.
"To promote the common dining hall," editorial, 25 October 1958.
"Uniting and relying on the masses to strive for world peace and new victory of domestic socialist construction," editorial, 1 January 1961.
"Editor commentary," 22 December 1968.
"Fifth edition," 17 July 2004.
Rural Finance Administrative Bureau of the People's Bank of China, "The work report of credit cooperation in recent years," 1953, *PRCERMC, financial volume 1949–52*.
Song Ping, "Strengthening rural work and deepening rural reform," 22 June 1990, *Important Central Literature Since the Thirteenth Plenum of the Eleventh CPCCC*, Central Literature Research Office of CPCCC (Beijing, People's publishing house, 1992).
The Agriculture Bank of China (in time order):
"Notice on stopping the fund raising with high interest of commune, production brigade-owned enterprises," September 1979.
"The trial method of the Agriculture Bank of China to extend loans to rural commune and production brigade-run enterprises," 10 November 1979.
"Notice on loan interest rate for commune and production brigade-run enterprises and joint venture enterprises by state and communes," 19 May 1980.
"Notification on rural free lending," May 1984.
"Notice on several policy issues for current TVE loans," 26 October 1984.
"Temporal implementing method of rural industry loans," 9 December 1985.
"Opinion on strengthening further TVE credit work," 5 February 1993.
The Central People's Government, Land Reform Law of People's Republic of China, 28 June 1950, *ILCSFN*, No. 1.
The Chinese People's Liberation Army Representative in People's Bank of China, "Notice on implementing the summary of the symposium of the 'struggle, critique and reform in RCC'," 7 January 1970.
The investigation team of TVE environmental pollution and the Ministry of Farming, Forestry, Animal Husbandry and Fishery, "Investigation report of TVE environmental pollution," 1985.

The Ministry of Agriculture (in time order)
"Report on Opening up New Prospects of Commune and Production Brigade-Owned Enterprises," 26 December 1983, authorized by CPCCC, 1 March 1984.
"The Report of the TVE situation and the opinion on governing and reorganizing TVEs," 20 October 1989.
"Notice on excavating fund potential to alleviate fund difficulty," 28 November 1989.
"Some opinions on TVE adjustment," 31 May 1990.
"The summary of China's TVE ten-year program and the eighth FYP," 1991.
"Implementation program for TVE technology progress strategy," 25 May 1992.
"Notice on promoting and consummating TVE stock-cooperative system," 24 December 1992.
"Main points to deepen TVE reform," 30 December 1992.
"Opinion on developing TVE tertiary industry vigorously," 25 February 1993.
The demonstration project of TVE cooperation between the East and Central-West Regions," 1 February 1994.
"The report of the opinion on TVE current development and its reform and development in future," 31 January 1997.
"Notice on related issues in deepening TVE reform," 10 July 1998.
"Some opinions on guiding TVEs to concentrate to develop and accelerating the construction of TVE zones," 12 January 1996.
"The program of TVE environmental protection and energy saving in the ninth FYP," 4 April 1996.
"The program outline of TVE cooperation between the east and central-west regions in the ninth FYP," 5 July 1996.
"Opinion about accelerating TVE structure adjustment," 17 December 1999.
"Opinion about vigorously promoting TVE technology innovation," 19 January 2000.
"The tenth FYP of TVE development," 20 August 2000.
"The plan of the tenth FYP of TVE education and training," 11 April 2001.
"TVE quality promotion during the tenth FYP," 20 July 2001.
"The outline of the tenth FYP of TVE technical progress," 30 July 2001.
"National program of main agricultural product processing industry development," 20 June 2002.
"Acting program of agricultural products processing industry development," 29 July 2002.
"Opinion about strengthening TVE credit management," 8 October 2002.
"Region layout plan of superior agricultural products 2003–2007," 20 January 2003.
"Science and technology program of enhancing competitive power of superior agricultural products," 27 January 2003.
"Opinion about deepening ownership reform to further promoting TVE system innovation," 26 July 2004.

The Ministry of Agriculture and the Ministry of Foreign Trade and Economic Cooperation, "Opinion about further promoting TVE outward-oriented economy," 22 January 2002.

The Ministry of Agriculture and the State Planning Committee, "Opinion about promoting the development of large and medium-scale TVEs," 4 October 1996.

The Ministry of Agriculture, the Ministry of Construction and the Ministry of National Territory Resources, "Notice to promote TVE development to concentrative in small cities and towns," 28 August 2001.
The Ministry of Agriculture, the Ministry of Finance, the Ministry of Labor and Social Security, the Ministry of Education, the Ministry of Science and Technology and the Ministry of Construction, "Notice about the sunlight program of organization and implementation of rural labor training for shifting," 22 March 2004.
The Ministry of Agriculture, the State Economy and Trade Committee, the State Development Planning Committee, the Ministry of Finance, the State Audit Office and the State Council Office for Correcting Abnormal Activities.
"Notice on governing illegal charges, fund-raising, economic punishment and so on for TVEs," 7 June 2000.
"The method to supervise and manage the TVE burden," 18 March 2002.
The Ministry of Agriculture, the State Planning Committee, the Ministry of Foreign Economy and Trade, the Ministry of Finance, the State Tax Bureau, People's Bank of China, Agriculture Bank of China, "Stipulation on some policies to promote TVE export for foreign exchange," 12 July 1988.
The Ministry of Agriculture, the State Planning Committee, the State Economy and Trade Committee, the State Education Committee, the State Science and Technology Committee, "The outline of the ninth Five-Year Plan of TVE science and technology progress," 24 December 1996.
The Ministry of Commerce, "Notice on implementing earnestly the decision of the state monopoly of agricultural producer goods with strict discipline," 22 December 1988.
The Ministry of Commerce, the Ministry of Finance, the Ministry of Agriculture, the People's Bank of China, the State Bureau of Tax, the State Bureau of Quality Testing and the National Supervisory Committee, "Instructional opinion about expanding agricultural product exportation," 18 October 2004.
The Ministry of Construction, "Stipulation on qualification management of construction enterprise," 28 June 1989.
The Ministry of Finance:
"Notice on several concrete issues for implementing 'the additional stipulation about adjusting industry and commerce tax burden of rural commune and brigade-run enterprises of the State Council,'' No. 127, 1982, *CTVEY*, 1978–87.
"Stipulation about adjusting industry and commerce income tax rate of rural communes and brigade-run enterprises and SMC basic units," 3 September 1983.
"Notice about further reducing industry and commerce income tax of TVEs," 25 March 1984.
The Ministry of Finance and the Ministry of Foreign Economy and Trade, "The trial method to manage the fund for medium and small-scale enterprises to develop the international market," October 2000.
The Ministry of Light Industry, "Summary of the symposium handicraft industry production," 6 April 1950, *PRCERMC, industry volume 1949–52*.
The Ministry of Public Health, "Regulation on sanitary supervision of cosmetics," 13 November 1989.
The Ministry of Public Security:
"The People's Republic of China Household Registration Regulation," 9 January 1958.
"Opinion on consummating rural household register management system," 20 May 1997.
"No. 76 Order," 3 September 2004.

The National People's Congress (in time order)
"The constitution of the People's Republic of China," 20 September 1954.
"The People's Republic of China Sino-Foreign Joint Venture Enterprise Law," July 1979.
"The constitution of the People's Republic of China," 4 December 1982.
"The Environment Protection Law of the People's Republic of China," 26 December 1989.
"People's Republic of China Law of Medium and Small Enterprise Promotion," 29 June 2002.

The party team of the Ministry of Water Resources and Electricity, "Work report about current water conservation," 25 November 1961, *ILCSFN*, No. 14.

The People's Bank of China (in time order)
"The record of first session of national rural finance conference," May 1951, *PRCERMC, financial volume 1949–52*.
"The rural credit cooperative regulation (draft)," May 1951, *PRCERMC, financial volume 1949–52*.
"Decision about rural finance organization of first national rural finance conference," May 1951, *PRCERMC, financial volume 1949–52*.
"The preliminary opinion on supporting communes and brigades to realize mechanization of agriculture gradually," 9 January 1970.

The Propaganda Department of CPCCC, "The Study and propaganda compendium for the transition period," December 1953, *ILCSFN*, No. 4.

The Rural Department of CPCCC, "Report on national situation and question in establishing agricultural producers' cooperative," 12 February 1954.

The Rural Finance Administrative Bureau of PBC, "Report of credit cooperation work for several years," 1953, *PRCERMC, financial volume 1944–52*.

The Rural Finance Bureau of The Ministry of Finance, "Report about several issues of rural credit cooperatives," 11 May 1974.

The rural social and economic investigation team of the State Statistical Bureau, "Monitor Report of China Rural Poverty 2000," Chinese Population Yearbook 2003, the Institute of Population and Labor Economy of Chinese Academy of Social Sciences.

The State Council (in time order):
"Decision on uniting national state-owned trade," 10 March 1950, *PRCERMC, commerce volume 1949–52*.
"Decision on edible oils planned purchase," 15 November 1953.
"Order on implementation of grain planned purchases and supply and tentative method to manage the rural grain market," 19 November 1953, *ILCSFN*, No. 4, 1993.
"Order on cotton plan purchase," 9 September 1954, *ILCSFN*, No. 5.
"Decision on national planned purchase of cotton," 9 September 1954.
"Tentative method for state monopoly for rural grain purchase and supply," 25 August 1955.
"Tentative method for city and town grain rationing," 25 August 1955.
"The temporary method of urban fixed quota grain supply," 5 August 1958.
"The Stipulations on several issues in credit departments of the people's communes and the floating capital issues in state-owned enterprises," 20 December 1958.
"Report of the agriculture conference for the northern regions," 11 December 1970.

"Report on accelerating the realization of the mechanization of agriculture," 3 December 1971.
"Notice about restoring the Agricultural Bank of China," February 1979.
"The stipulations on some issues about developing commune and brigade-owned enterprises (trial implementation draft)," 3 July 1979.
"Outline of the report of national grain conference," 1980, *New China economic development history*, Cong Shuhai and Zhang Hen (Shanghai: Shanghai financial and economic university publishing house, 1999).
"Temporary stipulations on implementing the government finance management system of 'dividing revenue from expenditure and contracting at each level'," February 1980.
"Authorizing 'the report on rural lending' made by the Agriculture Bank of China," May 1981.
"Decision on dredging commodity circulation channels between city and countryside and promoting industrial products to the countryside," June 1982.
"Several policy stipulations on urban individual non-agriculture economy," 13 April 1983.
"Implementation regulation for Sino-Foreign Joint Venture Enterprise Law of People's Republic of China," 20 September 1983.
"Stipulation on some issues of trafficking agricultural and subsidiary products by cooperative commerce organizations and individuals," 25 February 1984.
"Stipulation on some issues about organizing and developing agricultural and subsidiary product processing locally," 25 February 1984.
"Some stipulations on rural individual industry and commerce," 27 February 1984.
"Some stipulations on individual farmer or several farmers purchasing vehicles, ships and tractors for transport business," 27 February 1984.
"Instruction on 'the report on further promoting rural circulation of commodity' made by the State System Reform Committee, the Ministry of Commerce and the Ministry of Farming, Animal Husbandry and Fishery," 19 July 1984.
"Stipulations about strengthening the environment management of village, town and street enterprises," 27 September 1984.
"Authorizing 'the report on reforming RCC management system' made by the ABC," October 1984.
"Notice on farmers to settle down in small towns," 13 October 1984.
"Implementation regulation for Sino-Foreign Joint Venture Enterprise Law of People's Republic of China (revised)," 15 January 1986.
"Stipulations about encouraging foreign investment," 11 October 1986.
"Authorizing 'the report on constructing the export bases uniting trade, industry and agriculture' made by the State Economic Committee, the Ministry of Foreign Economy and Trade and the Ministry of Agriculture," October 1987.
"Authorizing 'the overall plan of deepening economic system reform in 1988' made by the State System Reform Committee," 27 February 1988.
"Decision on state monopoly of chemical fertilizer, agricultural chemicals and plastic film," 28 September 1988.
"Decision on reorganization of tax revenue order and strengthening tax management," 27 December 1988.
"Authorizing 'the notice of opinion on cleaning up, reorganizing and strictly controlling tax reduction and exemption' made by the State Tax Bureau," 3 January 1989.

"Notice about strengthening agricultural chemicals management, severely cracking down the activity to manufacture and sale counterfeit and inferior agricultural chemicals," 13 January 1989.
"Authorizing 'the notice of main points on economic system reform in 1989' made by the State System Reform Committee," 4 March 1989.
"Notice on strengthening enterprise interior bond management," 5 March 1989.
"To control strictly the going-out of farmer workers blindly," 5 March 1989.
"Decision on main points of current industrial policy," 15 March 1989.
"Temporary regulations on the investigation procedure of specially serious accidents," 29 March 1989.
"Implementation regulation of The Preventing and Controlling Water Pollution Law of People's Republic of China," 12 July 1989.
"Authorizing 'the notice of the opinion on punishing severely the persons responsible for selling spurious and poor commodities' made by the State Technology Supervision Bureau," 27 June 1989.
"Decision on vigorously strengthening tax levy in urban and rural individual and private enterprise," 30 August 1989.
"Notice on severely cracking down mixing impure and false materials in Commodity," 3 September 1989.
"Regulation of preventing and controlling ambient noise pollution of People's Republic of China," 26 September 1989.
"Notice on stopping the blind flow of farmer workers to Guangdong," 25 February 1991.
"Decision on enhancing the selling price of the state monopoly of grain," 6 March 1992.
"Notice of authorizing 'the report on promoting TVEs to develop continuously and healthily' made by the Ministry of Agriculture," 18 March 1992.
"Notice on chemical fertilizer, agricultural chemicals, agricultural film marketing and management," 25 October 1992.
"Decision on accelerating TVE development in the central and west regions," 14 February 1993.
"Notice on accelerating grain circulation system reform," 15 February 1993.
"Notice on 'the main points of economic system reform in 1993' made by the State System Reform Committee," 8 March 1993.
"Notice on firmly stopping raising funds randomly and strengthening bond issuing management," 11 April 1993.
"Notice on authorizing 'the plan of the demonstration projects of TVE cooperation between the east and central-west regions' made by the Ministry of Agriculture," 22 February 1995.
"Decision on rural financial system reform," 22 August 1996.
"Notice about expanding project examination and approval rights of inland provinces, autonomous regions, single planning cities and the related departments of the State Council to absorb foreign direct investment," 22 August 1996.
"Notice authorizing 'the opinion on the plan to reform the household register management system of small cities and towns in the experiment units and on consummating the rural household register management system' made by the Ministry of Public Security," 10 June 1997.
"Notice on authorizing 'the opinion about organizing further farmer workers to flow orderly' made by the Ministry of Labor, the State Economy and Trade Committee, the Ministry of Public Security, the Ministry of Civil Administration, the Ministry

of Railways, the Ministry of Transportation and the Ministry of Agriculture," 25 November 1997.
"Notice about further improving work environment of farmers to work in city," 27 December 2004.
"Authorizing 'the Opinion about promoting the household register control system reform in small cities and towns' made by the Ministry of Public Security," 30 March 2001.
"Opinion about promoting agricultural products processing industry," 6 November 2002.
"Opinion about deepening further grain circulation system reform," 6 June 2004.
The State Environment Protection Bureau, the Ministry of Agriculture, the State Planning Committee and the State Economy and Trade Committee, "Regulation of TVE environmental protection," 5 March 1997.
The State Industrial and Commercial Administration Bureau, "Notice on strengthening the management of merchants and private enterprises," 28 July 1989.
The State Office of Spark Program, "Working report for 1988," April 1989.
The State Planning Committee (in time order):
"The first Five-Year Plan 1953–57," 30 July 1955.
"The sixth Five-Year Plan 1980–85," 10 December 1982.
"The ninth Five-Year Plan of national economic and social development and the outline of the prospect goals in 2010 of People's Republic of China," 17 March 1996.
"The tenth Five-Year Plan summary of national economy and social development of People's Republic of China," 15 March 2001.
The State Price Bureau, "Stipulation on trying illegal price case," 14 March 1989.
The State Tax Bureau, "Stipulation on finance issues about interior fund collection and the shareholding system of collective enterprises," 16 June 1989.
The State Technology Supervision Bureau and the Ministry of Finance, "Implementation regulation on investigating the products without production license," 30 September 1989.
Wen Jiabao (in time order):
"The government working report at the second plenum of the tenth national people's congress," 5 March 2004.
"The government working report at the third plenum of the tenth national people's congress," 5 March 2005.
Yao Yilin (in time order):
"Report on the plan of national economic and social development in 1988 (Draft)," 26 March 1988.
"Report on the plan of national economic and social development in 1989 (Draft)," 21 March 1989.
Zhao ziyang, "Government work report," 15 May 1984.
Zha Ya Mountain Satellite People's Commune, "The general regulations of Zha Ya Mountain Satellite People's Commune in Suining County, Henan province (draft)," 7 August 1958, *ILCSFN*, No. 11.
Zhou Enlai (in time order):
"Current finance and economics situation and several relations in new Chinese economy," 22–3 December 1949, *ILCSFN*, No. 1.
"Report at the second national people's congress," 3 April 1961.
"Government working report at the first session of the third national people's congress, 21–2 December 1964.

Zhou Enlai, Ye Jianying, et al, "Speeches at national EYGMC working conference and the CPC Committee Member Enlarged Meeting of the General Logistics Department of Chinese People's Liberation Army," 6 August 1973.

Zhu De, "To organize handicraftsmen and make them take the socialist road," 4 December 1953, *ILCSFN*, No. 4.

Books, articles and newspapers cited

Beijing Evening News, 18 April 2002.

Beijing Youth, 22 November 2002.

Chang, Gene Hsin and Guanzhong James Wen, "Communal Dining and the Chinese Famine of 1958–61," *Economic Development and Cultural Change*, Vol. 46, No. 1.

Chen Jiyuan, Chen Jiaji and Yang Xun, eds, *China's rural society and economy evolution 1949–89* (Taiyuan: Shanxi economic publishing house, 1993).

Chen Xiwen, "Speech at the press conference of the News Office of the State Council," *China Youth*, 9 February 2004.

Cong Shuhai and Zhang Heng, eds, *New China Economic Development History 1949–98* (Shanghai: Shanghai Finance and Economy University Press 1999).

Farmer Daily, "The first township of China's rural reform," 4 November 1998.

Gui Shiyong, et al., *China's planning system reform* (Beijing: Chinese finance economical publishing house, 1994).

He Baoshan, Gu Jirui and Yan Yinglong, *China's technology transfer and technology progress* (Beijing: The economic management publishing house, 1996).

Hu Biliang and Zheng Hongliang, *China's TVE and village development* (Taiyuan: Shanxi economic publishing house, 1996).

Jhonson, D. G., "The Gains and Problems of Reform in China's Agriculture and Rural Areas," *Economic Research*, No. 1, 1997.

Landes, David S, "Why are we so rich and they so poor?," *American Economic Review*, Vol. 80, No. 2, 1990.

Lewis, W. Arthur, "Economic Development with Unlimited Supplies of Labor," *The Manchester School* (22), May 1954.

Li Bingkun, "Several issues about comprehensively accelerating rural moderate prosperity construction," *Management World*, No. 7, 2003.

Liu Ruofeng, *China's agriculture transformation and development* (Beijing: Chinese statistics publishing house, 1997).

Liu Suinian and Wu Qungan, *China's Concise History of Socialist Economy* (Haerbing: Heilongjang Peoplel's Publishing House, 1985).

Lu Jianxiang, "Rural credit cooperative for 40 years," *Economic Cooperatives in China*, Qin Liufang and Lu Longwen, eds (Beijing: Chinese literature and history publishing house, 1994).

Ma Hong and Sun Shangqing, *China's economy and forecast 1995–96 (economic white paper)* (Beijing: Chinese development publishing house, 1996).

Ma Hong and Sun Shangqing, eds, *On China's economic structure* (Beijing: People's Publishing House, 1981).

Nakagane Katuji, *On China's Economic Development* (Tokyo: University of Tokyo press, 1992).

Qiu Gongfu, Chi Xiaoxian and Shi Jianwei, "China's supply and marketing cooperatives for 40 years," *Economic Cooperatives in China*, Qin Liufang and Lu Longwen, eds (Beijing: China literature and history press, 1994).

Sun Chunying, "Demolishing the threshold, 2002," the internal report of the Ministry of Public Security, 2002.
The editorial committee of the "China's electrical history," *Contemporary China's electrical industry* (Beijing: Contemporary China publishing house, 1994).
The editorial committee of the "Chinese Foreign Economy and Trade White Paper" of The Ministry of Foreign Trade and Economic Cooperation of People's Republic of China, *Chinese foreign economy and trade white paper 1998* (Beijing: the economic science publishing house, 1998).
The editorial team of the "People's Commune Leaping Lorward," "Persisting self-reliance to accelerate the realization of the mechanization of agriculture, the investigation of Xu Hang people's commune, Jiading County, Shanghai," *People's commune leaping forward* (Shanghai: Shanghai people's publishing house, 1974).
The Jiangsu provincial local chronicle editorial committee, *The TVE in Jiangsu province* (Nanjing: Fangzhi publishing house, 2000).
The Rural Development Institute of Chinese Academy of Social Sciences and the rural social and economic investigating team of the State Statistical Bureau, *Report of China's rural economic development in 1995 and an analysis on the development in 1996* (Beijing: Chinese social science publishing House, 1996).
Wang Defu, "The initial success of TVE self-import and export," *CTVEY* 1993.
Wang Haibo, *The people's republic of China industry economic history* (Taiyuan: Shanxi economic publishing house, 1998).
Wang Ruipu, ed., *China's economic system reform literature assembly* (Beijing: People's Liberation Army publishing house, 1995).
Wang Sihua, "On handcraft production," December, 1954, *PRCERMC, industry volume 1953–57.*
Wang Yuhua, "Land system innovation of TVE concentration and small town and city development," *Management World*, No. 3, 2002.
Wei Nongmin, "Establishing the rural finance market," *China's Agriculture Yearbook 1993*, the editorial board of Chinese Agriculture Yearbook (Beijing: the agricultural publishing house, 1993).
Wen Tiejun, *Research on China's rural basic economic system* (Beijing: China economic publishing house, 2000).
Wu Qun, ed., *Jiangsu rural industry for 50 years* (Nanjing: Jiangsu people's publishing house, 1999).
Wu Si and Liu Jiangbo, "The factual record of Dazhai evolution: 1979–87," *Farmer Daily*, 30 September 1987.
Xu Tangling, *China rural finance epitome of history* (Beijing: China Finance Publishing House, 1996).
Xu Xiaobo, Deng Yingtao, et al, *China Rural Finance Transformation and Development* (Beijing: Contemporary China publishing house, 1994).
Yang Zihui, *China's historical population data and relevant studies* (Beijing: China reform publishing house, 1996).
Yao Jinguan, Ji Lianggang, et al., *China's agricultural product circulation and price system* (Beijing: China price press, 1995).
Zhang Zhuoyuan, "China's price reform," *China's path 1978–94*, the expert team of China Reform and Development Report (Beijing: Chinese finance economic publishing house, 1995).
Zhang Yi, The *hard course of China's TVE* (Beijing: the law publishing house, 1990).

Index